Psychosis
And
Sexual
Identity

SUNY Series Intersections: Philosophy and
Critical Theory
Rodolphe Gasché and Mark C. Taylor, Editors

Psychosis
And
Sexual
Identity

Toward a Post-Analytic View of
The Schreber Case

Edited by

David B. Allison
Prado de Oliveira
Mark S. Roberts
Allen S. Weiss

State University of New York Press

Published by
State University of New York Press, Albany

For information, address State University of New York Press,
State University Plaza, Albany, N.Y., 12246

Library of Congress Cataloging-in-Publication Data

Psychosis and sexual identity.

   (SUNY series in intersections. Philosophy and critical theory)
   Includes index.
   1. Schreber, Daniel Paul, 1842-1911—Mental health.
2. Paranoia—Case studies. 3. Identity (Psychology)—Case
studies. 4. Sex (Psychology)—Case studies. 5. Psychosexual
disorders—Case studies. I. Allison, David B. II. Series:
Intersections. Philosophy and critical theory. [DNLM:
1. Schreber, Daniel Paul, 1842-1911. 2. Bipolar Disorder—case
studies. 3. Identification (Psychology)—case studies.
4. Psychoanalytic Theory—case studies. 5. Transsexualism—case
studies. WM 40 P9742]
RC520.P78 1988   616.89'09   87-10077
ISBN 0-88706-616-X
ISBN 0-88706-617-8 (pbk.)

10 9 8 7 6 5 4 3 2 1

True!—nervous—very, very dreadfully nervous I had been and am; but why *will* you say that I am mad?

—Edgar Allan Poe

"The Tell-Tale Heart"

At first, people spoke only in poetry, and learned to reason only long afterwards.

—J-J. Rousseau

Essai sur l'origine des langues

Contents

Acknowledgments

"Schreber's Other" by Antonio Quinet: translated by A. Sampson. Used by permission of the author.

"Writing and Madness: Schreber als Schreiber" by Octave Mannoni: translated by Jeffrey Gaines, Prado de Oliveira, and Matilda Sitbon. First published as "L'Autre scène: Schreber als Schreiber" in *Clefs pour l'imaginaire* (Paris: Seuil, 1973). Used by permission of the author.

"Figures of Delusion" by Jean-François Rabain: translated by Allen S. Weiss and Chantal Khan Malek. First published as "Démembrement de la figure" in *Confrontations,* No. 4, Autumn, 1980 and "Lectures du 'cas Schreber' " in *Revue Française de Psychanalyse,* 1980. Used by permission of the author.

"On President Schreber's Transsexual Delusion" by Janine Chasseguet-Smirgel: translated by John Moore. First published as "A Propos du délire transsexuel du président Schreber" in *Revue Française de Psychanalyse* (5–6), 1975. Used by permission of the author.

"Schreber, Ladies and Gentlemen," by Prado de Oliveira: translated by David B. Allison and Mark S. Roberts. First published as "Schreber, Mesdames et Messieurs" in *Revue Française de Psychanalyse* Vol. 46, No. 1, 1982. Used by permission of the author.

"Paranoiac Fantasies: Sexual Difference, Homosexuality, Law of the Father" by Micheline Enriquez: translated by Yifat Hachamovitch and Beátrice Loeffel.

First published as "Fantasmes paranoïaques: différence des sexes, homosexualité, loi du père" in *Topique,* 1974. Used by permission of the author.

"Vertiginous Sexuality: Schreber's Commerce with God" by Jean-François Lyotard: translated by David B. Allison and Mark S. Roberts. First published as two parts, "Le nom, l'intensité" and "Faites usage de moi," of *Economie libidinale* (Paris: Minuit, 1974). Used by permission of the publisher.

"The Pathogenesis of Creation or the Liberation of Women" by Octave Mannoni: translated by Hélène Volat-Shapiro. First published as "La Pathogenèse de la création (ou la libération des femmes)" in *Fictions freudiennes* (Paris: Editions du Seuil, 1978). Used by permission of the author.

"The Institution of Rot" by Michel de Certeau. Originally published in *Heterologies* (Minneapolis: University of Minnesota Press, 1986. Used by permission of the publisher.

All other articles were written expressly for this volume, and are used by permission of the authors.

The New Schreber Texts were translated by Christine Granger.

The editors wish to acknowledge their sincere appreciation to Carola Sautter and Marilyn Semerad of SUNY Press for the care, concern and professional expertise they contributed to make the present volume possible.

Introduction

I. Daniel Paul Schreber

"'T he month of November, 1895, marks an important time in the history of my life and in particular in my own ideas of the possible shaping of my future. I remember the period distinctly; it coincided with a number of beautiful autumn days when there was a heavy morning mist on the Elbe. During that time the signs of a transformation into a woman became so marked on my body, that I could no longer ignore the imminent goal at which the whole of my development was aiming. In the immediately preceding nights my male sexual organ might have actually have been retracted had I not resolutely set my will against it, still following the sense of my manly honor; so near completion was the miracle. Soul-voluptuousness had become so strong that I myself received the impression of a female body, first on my arms and hands, later on my legs, bosom, buttocks and other parts of my body. I will discuss details . . ."[1]

"The second point to be discussed . . . is the tendency, innate in the Order of the World, to _unman_ a human being who has entered into permanent contact with rays. This is connected on the one hand with the nature of God's nerves, through which blessedness . . . is felt, if not exclusively as, at least accompanied by a greatly increased feeling of voluptuousness; on the other hand it is connected with the basic plan on which the Order of the World seems to rest, that in the case of world catastrophe which necessitate the destruction of mankind on any star, whether intentionally or otherwise, the human race can be removed. When on some star moral decay ("voluptuous excesses") or perhaps nervousness has seized the whole of mankind to such an extent that the forecourts of heaven . . . could not be expected to be adequately replenished by their excessively blackened nerves, or there was reason to fear a dangerous increase of attraction on God's nerves, then the destruction of the human race on that star could occur either spontaneously (through annihilating epidemics, etc.) or, being decided on by God, be put into effect by means of earthquakes, deluges, etc. Perhaps God was also able to withdraw partially or totally the warmth of the sun from a star doomed to perish . . ."[2]

When the author of the above indicated that his *Memoirs of My Nervous Illness* was written to inform persons in his "circle of acquaintances" of his "religious conceptions," he could not have known that this circle would extend to such figures as Bleuler, Jung, Freud, Lacan, Canetti, Deleuze, and Lyotard. Indeed, Daniel Paul Schreber (see Fig. 1) is by far the most famous mental patient ever, and the account of his "nervous illness" still remains one of the most widely read and translated of its kind.

But what do we know about the person of this Schreber? He was a lawyer, a judge, the president of the Saxon Supreme Court, a candidate for the Reichstag—an enormously successful bourgeois in every respect. He was also a solid family man, a good provider, a loving husband, a devoted son, even a poet of sorts. His greatest fame, however, is undoubtedly due to the publication and subsequent effect of the aforementioned *Memoirs,* which chronicled his descent into a hellish world far removed from the one in which he had garnered such success and honor—a world populated by three millimeter men, miraculous rays, and talking birds: a world where he was at last to become God's wife.

Schreber's descent began in 1884, when he entered the nerve clinic of Professor Paul Emil Flechsig (see Fig. 1A) (a neurologist, who some now contend contributed to Schreber's decline), and left six months later, apparently cured of severe hypochondria. Following his discharge from the university clinic, he resumed his judicial duties and was named Senatspräsident of the Saxon Court of Appeals in October, 1893. Shortly after, he was readmitted to Flechsig's clinic for a period of seven months, after which time he was transferred to the Sonnenstein asylum (see Fig. 2) and placed under the care of Dr. G. Weber for nine years. In the early part of his stay at the asylum, he suffered from acute hallucinations, which took the form of apocalyptic visions, both of his own and the world's utter destruction. He recovered sufficiently to complete his *Memoirs* in 1901 (published in 1903 and soon after almost completely suppressed by the Schreber family), and to help draft the appeal which led to his release in 1902. After leaving Sonnenstein he lived a life of quiet retirement until 1907, when he relapsed and was admitted to the mental hospital at Leipzig-Dösen (see Fig. 3), where he died in a state of physical deterioration and total madness in 1911.

II. Background of the Case

Freud's Analysis

Freud's reading of the *Memoirs,* "Psycho-Analytic Notes Upon an Autobiographical Account of a Case of Paranoia" (*Dementia Paranoides*)"[3] (1911), was to become the *locus classicus* of the general psychoanalytic theory of paranoia and psychosis. He was so impressed by the work that he concluded Schreber himself should have been appointed head of a hospital psychiatric unit, and that knowledge of what Schreber called the "basic language" (*Grundsprache*) was essential for all psychoanalysts. But while Freud was immediately struck by the great range of intelligence and the literary imagination shown by the work, his analysis remained basically schematic; indeed, he even went so far as to excuse himself for the paucity of psychoanalytic explanation. As with his earlier work on neurosis, Freud once again found that what transpired was a version of the Oedipus complex, which in this particular case was solved in a negative way. Schreber held a feminine position toward his father (see Fig. 4), a position which years later became the object of the transference toward his first doctor, Flechsig, and afterwards to the ultimate father figure—God. Schreber's intense resistance to this transference gave rise to a defensive position which ultimately evolved into a delusion of persecution. The persecution was principally characterized by Schreber's castration fantasies, which took the form of his desire to be transformed into a woman. Unable to resolve the conflict between the object of erotic fantasy and the object of persecution, due to its humiliating aspect, Schreber replaces his former doctor, Flechsig, with the divine figure of God. Henceforth Schreber could willingly submit himself to satisfying God's voluptuous demands, not only finding personal satisfaction, but also inscribing himself within the cosmic order of things, the so-called "Order of the World." A transformation of sexuality would now allow him to give rise to generations of new souls. This procreation fantasy would satisfy the megalomaniacal aspect of his delusion, which would in turn unburden him of any humiliation involved in passive homosexual submission. Thus, according to Freud's reading, paranoia must be understood as the repression of a homosexual wish, which here took the form of a castration complex. Ultimately the delusions of sexual persecution become converted into religious delusions of grandeur, wherein Schreber would save the world and become God's wife.

The Anglo-American School

What we shall call the Anglo-American School (not only because of the language in which they wrote but, even more so, because of the authors' distinctive concerns) can be divided into three major groups. (1) Those who are especially interested in the Schreber case and wish to confirm Freud's reading. (2) Those who, though particularly interested in Schreber, diverge from Freud's analysis. (3) Those who, whatever their position with regard to Freud, are above all interested in paranoia, and see in Schreber nothing but one possibility among others to shore up their own theories. In short, the "orthodox," the "dissidents," and the "others."

The "orthodox" members are first and foremost Maurits Katan and William G. Niederland, between whom certain differences of opinion existed until 1975, the year in which Katan, just prior to his death, posed questions essential to the continuation of the debate. Niederland's *The Schreber Case,* while partially summing up the debate, did so in a somewhat unsatisfactory way due to the omission of several essential articles. The essence of their disagreement bears on the mode of the psychoanalytic construct, which serves to explain certain aspects of Schreber's delusion. Their agreement bears upon the notion that only theoretical constructs can explain the case and that Freud's analysis is essentially correct.

Katan studied the delusion of the end of the world, the hallucination of the little men, and then returned to the mechanisms at the origin of hallucinations. Afterwards he studied the entire pre-psychotic phase, the construction and the failure of the after-world in Schreber's writings, finally concluding with the question of the relations between the memories of childhood, delusion and hallucination.[4]

Niederland devoted his analyses to the beginning of Schreber's two illnesses, and to linguistic explanations for certain elements of his delusion. While for Katan, following up one of Freud's notes, the relation between the little men and spermatozoa seemed a matter of so to speak natural kinship, Niederland referred back to the German words which designate them (*Flüchtig hingemachte Männer*) so as to deduce their fecal nature and their relation to soul murder. Likewise, if for Freud and Katan the passage from father to Flechsig to God seemed obvious, given the importance of these characters in Schreber's life, Niederland played upon *Gott*lob in the name of Schreber's father and *Theo*dor in the name of his doctor, both signifying *God,* to arrive at the linguistic nature of the transfer. But when he resumed his studies on Schreber, Niederland entirely abandoned this path. His concern with the miraculated world of Schreber's childhood, and the relation between the Schrebers, father and son, did little more than point to his true interest—namely, the centrality of Schreber's father and the truth within the son's delusions. He then went on to discover new facts and memorable events concerning the case, and again contributed to the establishment of a core of truth concerning the delusion by a study of the personality and work of Flechsig, Schreber's doctor.

For Katan, there was very definitely a truth in delusion, but of a fantasmatic kind, such that the past must be entirely reconstructed only from those elements directly furnished by the *Memoirs.* In this way he arrived at a marvelous description of the power plays that occurred within the Schreber family during the childhood of the psychotic-to-be. Katan's references to Schreber no longer bear upon a few lines, but rather involve whole chapters. Entire chapters and paragraphs of the *Memoirs* are referred back to paragraphs and chapters of books written by Schreber's father. Moreover, both Niederland and Katan cite Freud as one uses prepositions in a sentence. While their interpretation and the structure of the whole are the same, there remain differences in details. The construction thereby achieved tends to be more misleading, since it claims to be an explanatory and exhaustive view. As for like-minded writers such as Numberg (who comments on Katan), Baumeyer (who presents Schreber's psychiatric file), and Kitay (who comments on Niederland), what is of principal concern are the details, which are also discussed by Katan and Niederland—details such as the role of onanism, the meaning of the little men, the soul murder or the sexual bodily assaults on Schreber, whether real or imagined.[5]

The "dissidents" are primarily interested in Schreber himself. To them, Freud's ideas seem quite questionable, at least insofar as they concern explanations of the most archaic, or most specifically psychotic, aspects of the "case." Thus Macalpine and Hunter, for example, accept Freud's theories on the neurotic aspects of Schreber, but criticize him for having in no way explained the hypochondriacal elements at the origin of the psychosis and throughout its development.[6] Moreover, they criticize Freud for failing to disclose Schreber's central fantasy of parthenogenesis, where hypochondria and the incapacity to establish a clear differentiation between the sexes plays a major role. All of the elements described in the *Memoirs* are related back to the one central fantasy, Schreber's concern for procreation. The tendentious movement of this construction of delusion complies with norms other than those proposed by Katan and Niederland. It no longer consists in practically rewriting the *Memoirs,* but rather in reordering the elements of the *Memoirs* in a manner radically different from that of Freud.

Fairbairn and White were not so concerned to give an exhaustive explanation of the whole.[7] Fairbairn recognized that Macalpine and Hunter successfully interpreted the hypochondriacal aspects of Schreber's illness, and also affirmed that the real paranoiac element of the illness had already been properly interpreted by Freud. He simply proposed to clear up an enigma left by Freud: why was the appointment to Senatspräsident the deciding factor in unleashing Schreber's psychosis? Fairbairn's response was quite simple: because of the importance it had in reactivating his fantasies of the primal scene. To furnish proof for this he offered a quotation drawn from Schreber. For the rest, Fairbairn was content to postulate a theory which should have resounded to this day, had not so many factors arisen to stifle it: if Schreber's mother never appears in the *Memoirs,* this is certainly not because of her lack of importance. On the contrary, it is due to her centrality. It was left to White to develop this theory, with supporting quotations from numerous authors. All of the principal themes of the *Memoirs,* such as the eternal life of the souls, soul murder, the linking of the nerves, and unmanning are explained by Schreber's relations with his mother and by the maternal role played by his father. The father's role prevented his son from acquiring any autonomy whatsoever vis-à-vis the maternal influence. Somewhat later, in 1963, White applied these ideas to the whole of Schreber's life, from childhood right up to his death.

The question formulated by Katan in 1975 still remains largely unanswered. It could be summarized as follows: All that has been said about Schreber may very well be true, but what remains incomprehensible is why he could not simply remember all of this—and perhaps suffer from it—rather than becoming psychotic. A tentative response may be found in the work of Morton Schatzman, who attempted to apply the theories of the Palo Alto School to the Schreber "case."[8] He surmised that Schreber had been incessantly subjected to paradoxical demands, which besieged his personal and social life at every level. Thus a psychic apparatus capable of recalling entire segments of his experience—notably the most intimate ones, those which would contribute to the formation of this very apparatus—was unable to develop. Schreber was only capable of remembering what he had read, and of that just what he had read after childhood. He could therefore be an excellent lawyer and scholar, yet could only recall his religious upbringing through his delusions, and, unless he reproduced them, his most intimate personal experiences remained inaccessible.

Carr and Nydes are the principle exponents of the group we are here calling the "others."[9] They are interested in paranoia in general, and in the evolution of the theories about it derived from Freud. For them, Schreber is but one case among others, and Freud's ideas, taken beyond those theories which he applies to the explanation of this case, only interest them as starting points. They insist upon the role of aggression, of masochism, and upon the fantasy of patricide, as well as upon defense mechanisms other than projection, such as denial, identification with the aggressor, and the turning back upon the subject. No single theory regarding the Schreber case seems to interest them; nor do they seem to think that Freud's theories are unique or monolithic.

III. *Toward a Post-Analytic View of the Case*

What tends to lessen the hold and centrality of both Freud's and the Anglo-American School's readings of the case is a relatively recent trend which focuses on much the same subject-matter as these earlier readings but which deals with it through markedly different approaches and perspectives. These new perspectives tend to incorporate dimensions of interpretation which, rather than reinforcing the historical, theoretical and etiological aspects of the case, invoke some of its more oblique possibilities. Hence much recent work on the case—post-analytic interpretations—leans toward the kinds of considerations that were simply not available to Freud and the Anglo-American School or which they deemed marginal. These recent concerns may be summed up as follows: (1) An increased emphasis on the symbolic or metaphorical role played by the father.

(2) An attempt to explain the origin of psychosis in terms of a theory of linguistic structure. (3) A renewed interest in the theoretical foundations of psychosis and sexual identity, especially in their relation to contemporary deconstructivist and feminist theory and to fields collateral to psychoanalysis. (4) A marked use of the Schreber case and, especially, the *Memoirs,* as a *means* by which to explore a variety of issues in the arts, sciences and humanities.

Lacan

To a large extent, the origin of the first and second of these newer perspectives can be traced back to the work of Jacques Lacan. Lacan initiated his study of the Schreber case in the first two terms of the seminar held in 1955–56, and its results were originally published in an article, "On a Question Preliminary to any possible Treatment of Psychosis," which appeared in *La Psychanalyse* (1958). The essay contains some rather harsh criticisms of traditional approaches to the case, and these polemics have been viewed in some circles as both a subtle appropriation of the ideas of Niederland, Katan, Macalpine and Hunter, etc. and an attempt to "rewrite" Freud's theory of psychosis. In any event, Lacan was surely the first to approach the case from the perspective of the father's symbolic role, and it is precisely in taking this role as the starting point that he is able to undertake an explanation of Schreber's psychosis. For the symbolic father is a very significant factor in normal development, and it is in contrast to this that Lacan explains the psychotic process.[10]

As is the case with his earlier notion of the "mirror stage," Lacan sees the role of the symbolic father as essentially metaphoric in nature, and even goes so far as to create the formula "paternal metaphor," to describe this process of development. Now metaphor, for Lacan, always involves some form of substitution of one signifier for another while the original signifier continues to carry a powerful meaning for the subject. The paternal metaphor conforms to this pattern, since when the subject reaches the oedipal stage, the symbolic father (the "Law" or "Name-of-the-Father") intervenes in the mother-child relation as a replacement for the child's desire for the mother.[11]

This is the case with normal development. In Schreber's case, however, Lacan proposes that something went amiss. For some reason the Name-of-the-Father (the metaphoric substitute for Schreber's desire for his mother) is rendered inadequate, seriously affecting his affirmation of the father's sexual identity, so necessary for successfully overcoming the oedipal conflict. It is the inadequacy of the signifier that causes the "default" of this fundamental affirmation. This default is termed "foreclosure" by Lacan, which is his translation of Freud's term *Verwerfung.* The ultimate effect of this foreclosure is the creation of a "hole" in the symbolic order, in the field of the signifier, which in turn creates a "hole" in the Other.

According to Lacan, it is precisely this basic default in the metaphoric aspect of the symbolic father that makes it possible to conceptualize Schreber's psychosis, which is exactly what he does in the abovementioned article. In brief, Lacan proposed that in Schreber's case the foreclosed signifier Name-of-the-Father returns to the "Real" in the form of fantasies, that is, the foreclosed signifier colludes with imaginary material—hallucinations, for example—to fill the gap in the symbolic order. The rather extraordinary delusional system that Schreber concocted was thus, in Lacan's view, an unconscious attempt to metaphorically substitute material for the imaginary castration which never took place during Schreber's oedipal phase. Incapable of becoming the "phallus" that his mother lacked, Schreber simply deluded himself into believing that he was the woman that men lacked. Hence the central fantasy of Schreber's entire illness: "It really must be rather pleasant to be a woman succumbing to intercourse."

Besides having dramatically conceptualized Schreber's psychosis, Lacan was also the first to take him seriously as a literary figure, due mainly to the remarkable richness of his imagination, as expressed in the *Memoirs*. In fact, Lacan even went so far as to suggest that Schreber was a true disciple of the Enlightenment—perhaps its last avatar—and that his rigorous and highly formalized style was reminiscent of certain traditional philosophical systems. Lacan even compared Schreber to literary figures of no less stature than St. John of the Cross, Gérard de Nerval and Marcel Proust. But, in the end, he was unwilling to grant Schreber true literary stature—terming the *Memoirs* a mad account of madness—only because his book lacked a successful poetic quality; it was therefore incapable of effectively transporting us to another world.

Lacan's ideas on the literary dimension of Schreber's work, as well as those on the relation between psychosis and sexual identity, were of course subsequently emended, refined, and sometimes rejected by a variety of thinkers both within and outside of his orbit. Even so, his work on the case must be considered the point at which Schreber studies radically departed from the "schematic" psychoanalytic account presented by Freud and the largely Freudian accounts of the Anglo-American School. Many of these authors, including Freud himself, acknowledged the remarkable possibilities presented by the case in general, and the *Memoirs* in particular, but few pursued these avenues to their conclusion. Freud, for example, extolled the literary merits of the text, and Niederland saw considerable potential in it for linguistic analysis. Neither, however, fully exploited these aspects—perhaps because they were not really interested in extending their analyses beyond strictly psychoanalytic concerns. Lacan on the other hand, though always seriously interested in psychoanalytic theory, provided a far more extensive basis for interpreting the case by introducing forms of phenomenological, structural and even literary analysis into its investigation. Thus the seminar of 1955–56 and the subsequently reworked accounts of it that appeared in 1958 and 1966 clearly constitute a move towards what we are calling a post-analytic view of the case, a view which eventually not only opened the case to conceptual modifications but also brought it within the ambit of a number of other disciplines.

Psychosis and Sexual Identity

It is precisely with the expanded means provided by Lacan's reading of the case that a new generation of theorists has begun to elaborate the now broader concepts of psychosis and sexual identity, drawing less upon the traditional psychoanalytic motifs of etiological and developmental concerns than on the resources of the linguistic, semiotic, philosophical and critical domains. The new dimension afforded by this expanded field of discourse serves as the occasion for the present volume of essays. Understandably, some of these texts attempt to reconsider the questions of psychosis and sexual identity in ways which both modify and amplify Freud's initial analysis, while remaining decidedly non-Lacanian. In each case, however, the analyses try to broaden and extend the nature of the categories and concepts through which these very issues are made significant. This extension of the categories by which the case may be understood at the same time admits the possibility of quite different approaches towards psychosis and sexual identity.

In following our proposed shift in the analysis of the case, we have opened the first part of the volume with two texts which underscore the fundamental importance of the symbolic and semiotic registers, so that the notion of delusion and psychosis can be understood in the broader context of the post-analytic orientation. In William Richardson's "Lacan and the Problem of Psychosis," the essential aspects of the 1955–56 seminar are discussed, with particular attention given to the relation between the constitution of psychosis and the foreclosure of certain parts of the symbolic order. Richardson pays particular attention to the most unique aspects of Schreber's delusional system, and relates these formations to certain metaphoric and metonymic oppositions which govern the chain of signifiers forming the unconscious. In the second article, Antonio Quinet ("Schreber's Other"), working through the socially symbolic domain of the unconscious, tries to articulate the distinctively psychotic formations brought about by the ego-defining concept of the Other. Quinet, closely following Lacan, argues that if the Name-of-the-Father is excluded from the signifying chain, psychotic behavior will be marked by the emergence of an archaic super-ego, one which commands the subject absolutely. Hence Schreber's virtual enslavement to Flechsig, to his God, and to the Divine "rays."

What remains peculiarly problematic about the Schreber case is not only its fundamental significance for classical psychoanalytic theory, in that psychosis is there fixed in etiological fashion with the repression of the subject's homosexual tendencies—characterized, in large part, by the emergence of a paranoiac delusional system—but also the fact that Freud based his analysis exclusively on the written testimony, the text of the *Memoirs,* without having met its author.[12] It is precisely those questions which have to do with the relation between the subject as subject and the subject as author, the literary status of the *Memoirs,* and the relation of the author to his madness, as well as the complex issues of transference, that concern Octave Mannoni, in his "Writing and Madness: Schreber als Schreiber." Here Mannoni postulates that Schreber was divided between two positions, that of the subject and that of the author, a division seemingly valid for everyone. As author, Schreber was in no way a madman, since his book is in many respects extraordinarily objective. But, if he is considered mad, it is paradoxically because the insistence with which he describes what is for him objective, opens a rift that allows us to pass from the scene of writing (where the author reigns) to the scene of the subject (where, in Schreber's case, the unconscious and delusion reign). Here, Mannoni compares Schreber to Cervantes, when he describes an insane Don Quixote, someone who keeps the two scenes, the two positions, distinct, letting neither one nor the other dominate. Mannoni accordingly concludes that Schreber's book both redefines and enlarges the realm of literature, the very concept of literature.

Similarly, literature—and particularly, rhetoric—are the principal subjects of Jean-François Rabain's contribution, "Figures of Delusion." Rabain is concerned to explain why Schreber chose to use certain tropes more frequently than others in the *Memoirs,* and why such a choice reflects the peculiar formation of the delusional framework of his psychosis. According to Rabain, the rhetorical figure which appears most often in the *Memoirs* is the oxymoron or the apposition of two antonyms. The reason for this, Rabain argues, is that Schreber has, within his delusional system, stressed the conflictual relationship between God and himself: that is, a memorable battle with God for the highest of all stakes, the future salvation of mankind. Hence the antonymic trope. The author also provides an analysis of the rhetorical elements of the "basic language," relating this analysis to theories of the sign expressed by Saussure, Benveniste and Baudrillard.

Expanding the literary and linguistic concerns of both Mannoni and Rabain, Allen S. Weiss ("The Other as Muse: On the Ontology and Aesthetics of Narcissim") explores the narcissistic components of ontological and aesthetic expression. In doing so, he reveals the portion of psychic alterity inherent in the construction of the ego, specifically its hyperbolic form in Schreber's paranoiac discourse. This paranoiac expression is typified by the fantasies of overbearing alterity, and is most recognizable in megalomaniacal and persecutory delusions. According to Weiss, these formations, which show themselves in despotic power, domination and psychotic discourse, are inherent in the very structure of language formation, of primal expressions (the *fort/da* of Freud's study or the echolalia of Antonin Artaud), and are thus not only the rantings of "madmen and poets" but necessary components of personality formation in general.

Michel de Certeau ("The Institution of Rot") engages the problematic of theology and mysticism in Schreber's discourse, delineating the contradictory relations between the aspiration to divine sublimity and the ultimate degradations of corruption and decay. It is between these limits that a radical otherness appears as the core of Schreber's psychosis.

Part two of the present volume contains a series of analyses, which are concerned with questions of sexual identity and difference insofar as these issues are poignantly raised by the Schreber case. The opening article, Micheline Enriquez' "Paranoiac Fantasies: Sexual Difference, Homosexuality, Law of the Father," sets these two issues in sharp relief. Ostensibly, the work is an attempt to formulate hypotheses and reflections about feminine paranoia, but its scope is far broader, encompassing questions concerning the role of the primal scene in fantasy formation, the similarities and differences between the constitutive elements of masculine and feminine paranoiac fantasies, and the symbolic role of the father in the formation of sexual identity and difference, among others. Enriquez proposes to clarify the above questions by comparing and contrasting two remarkable 'paranoiac' accounts: Schreber's *Memoirs* and Valerie Solanas's radical feminist tract, *The SCUM Manifesto*. The author finds a "fantasmatic constellation" common to both texts, and she postulates that the fantasies contained in this constellation maintain a relation with originary fantasies, which allow them to produce the *graftings of sense* so necessary for the more or less successful emergence of subjectivity, and also the emergence of Law, in the Lacanian sense of the term.

Investigating Schreber's desire to become a woman, Alphonso Lingis ("The Din of the Celestial Birds or Why I Crave to Become a Woman") discusses the comparative aspects of the male and female nervous system as well as its expressive capacities. He argues that sensibility is not primarily in the service of judgment, but rather, serves as the entropic, discontinuous creative principle of existence—where joy and voluptuousness is life itself. Given a pure eroticization of existence in a joyous cosmology, such an orientation—at least for Lingis— would certainly entail a reexamination of traditional philosophical views concerning the relations between sensation and understanding.

Utilizing his notion of the "tensor," Jean-François Lyotard ("Vertiginous Sexuality: Schreber's Commerce with God") stresses that Schreber's multiple attributes (just like the multiple identities Schreber gave to "Flechsig") are not merely predicates of a name, but are rather the manifestations of a "vertiginous" state of anal eroticism, wherein multiple libidinal impulses are arranged by instinctual formation. This multiplicity of identities and attributes is a sign of the libido's "stupidity," of its very anonymity—far beyond anyone's comprehension. Within this libidinal flux, where Schreber becomes God's whore, we find in Schreber's desire to become a woman the very strength of powerlessness: a liquification of all blockages of the libidinal flow, an incorporation of the "heads of power" into the libidinal band.

Janine Chasseguet-Smirgel ("On President Schreber's Transsexual Delusion") raises the question of transsexuality in Schreber's delusional transformation into a woman and his/her sexual relations with God. If in the masculine "cult of the caricatured virility" there was tremendous feelings of shame, insult and dishonor with respect to feminine identification—feelings that are expressed most forcefully in paranoia—such contempt always hides a determinate fear, envy, and uncertainty regarding the maternal powers which are denied. The denied femininity returns in delusional form—where the only point at which it is truly "pleasant to be a woman succumbing to intercourse" is at the height of psychosis, at the height of identification with the woman in the primal scene. Chasseguet-Smirgel examines this question both in terms of Schreber's own sexuality and in terms of those who quite literally live such a reversal: transsexuals.

In somewhat similar fashion, Prado de Oliveira ("Schreber, Ladies and Gentlemen") investigates the modes of homosexuality to be found in paranoia, and shows how they frequently occur in inverted form. Following homosexual projection, narcissistic identification is called upon to explain the desire for transformation into the other sex. The first stage of this problematic is largely traced out in two of Freud's well-known cases, that of the "wasp-waisted" woman whose case ran counter to psychoanalytic theory, and that of Emma, both of whose delusional states were triggered by their seeing a pair of men who were supposedly persecuting them. In each case, Freud labors to point out that a homosexual relation denied in the self becomes projected onto others. But, in Schreber's case, the situation is markedly different: he desires to become a woman—in fact, his own mother—by an identification which serves as the very inversion of masculine homosexuality.

In an extraordinary epistolary fantasy, "The Pathogenesis of Creation or the Liberation of Women," Octave Mannoni imagines Schreber's personal estimations of the ironies of his situation and the madness of his various doctors, and especially, the shortcomings of Freud's own readings of the Schreber case. However, this is but one among a variety of themes which are cleverly interwoven in the piece. Another prominent—perhaps, dominant—interest of Mannoni's is the way in which creative impulses evolve from certain sexual identifications, and, subsequently, how so-called perverse or "psychotic" identifications often lead to the most sublime and novel expressions in the arts and sciences alike.

The volume closes with entirely new material—a series of recently discovered texts published here for the first time in English. These new texts form a distinct break in style and content with the *Memoirs,* one which should eventually provoke a reevaluation of certain important features of the case.

Two texts of particular interest are "Poem for His Mother's Ninetieth Birthday" and "Poem for the Fiftieth Birthday of His Wife." In the former—the only first-hand biographical text on his mother—Schreber himself provides a remarkably lucid account of the heretofore unknown dimension of her childhood, her relationships within both the Haase and Schreber families, and his own deep respect and affection for her. In the latter text, we find another clear and poignant reflection on a largely unknown area of Schreber's personal life: his marriage to Sabine Behr. Here, there are several references to their home life, to Schreber's personal suffering, and to their newly adopted child.

In conclusion, we should note that our intention has been throughout to provide new perspectives on the Schreber case, heretofore largely unavailable to an English-speaking audience. We have tried to accommodate a variety of recent approaches to the case and to articulate them through what we deem the foundational axes established by the case, namely, psychosis and sexual identity. But, even with the discovery of the new Schreber texts and the recent approaches to the case, an entire set of problems for the understanding of delusion, identity, psychic reality and its interpretation, remains. This person, upon whose *Memoirs* modern psychoanalysis founded its several theories of psychosis, yet whom Freud never met, who articulated the specific characteristics of delusional systems while at the same time producing a poetic work of the first order, this person, who received the Iron Cross from Bismarck for helping to integrate the German legal code, yet who was incarcerated for nearly a quarter of his life, still remains more paradoxical and enigmatic than ever. Perhaps Schreber himself summed it up best when he wrote, "Whatever people may think of my 'delusions,' they will sooner or later have to acknowledge that they are not dealing with a lunatic in the ordinary sense."[13]

Notes

1.   Daniel Paul Schreber, *Memoirs of My Nervous Illness* (London: Wm. Dawson and Sons, 1955); translated by Ida Macalpine and Richard A. Hunter, pp. 147–148. Republished by Harvard University Press, 1988, with a new introduction by Samuel Weber. Pagination retained.

2.   *Ibid.,* pp. 72–73.

3.   Sigmund Freud, *Standard Edition,* V. 12, pp. 1–82, 1958.

4.   See Maurits Katan, "Childhood Memories as Contents of Schizophrenic Hallucinations and Delusions," *Psychoanalytic Study of the Child,* vol. 30, 1975, pp. 357–374.

5. See Franz Baumeyer's "New Insights into the Life and Psychosis of Schreber," *International Journal of Psychoanalysis*, 33, 1952, and P. M. Kitay, "A Reinterpretation of the Schreber Case," *International Journal of Psychoanalysis*, 44, 1953, pp. 191–194.

6. See Ida Macalpine and R. A. Hunter, "The Schreber Case," *Psychoanalytic Quarterly*, Vol. 22, 1963, pp. 328–371.

7. R. D. Fairbairn, "Considerations Arising Out of the Schreber Case," *British Journal of Medical Psychology*, Vol. 19, 1956, pp. 113–127; Robert B. White, "The Mother-Conflict in Schreber's Psychosis," *International Journal of Psychoanalysis*, 42, 1961, pp. 55–73.

8. See Morton Schatzman, *Soul Murder: Persecution in the Family* (Middlesex: Penguin Books, 1976).

9. See J. Nydes, "Schreber, Parricide and the Paranoid Mechanism," *International Journal of Psychoanalysis*, 44, 1963, pp. 208–212, and Arthur C. Carr, "Observations on Paranoia and Their Relationship to the Schreber Case," in *The Schreber Case* (New York: Quadrangle, 1974).

10. See John P. Muller and William J. Richardson, *Lacan and Language: A Reader's Guide to Ecrits* (New York: International Universities Press, 1982), p. 213.

11. *Loc. Cit.*

12. Freud was familiar with Flechsig's "therapeutic" use of castration on some of his patients (doubtless, Schreber was, too), but Freud neither met with nor discussed the case with Flechsig or Weber, the principal physicians in the case. During the period in which Freud was in possession of the *Memoirs*, prior to his 1911 article (the *Memoirs* was given to him by Jung, in 1905), Freud made no attempt to visit Schreber in the Leipzig-Dösen Asylum, or, even before his final hospitalization, at home. Since Freud himself was denied access to the teaching hospitals in Vienna, where he might otherwise have attended psychotic patients, his failure (or, perhaps, reluctance) to meet Schreber himself remains curiously problematic. Freud nonetheless responded to this issue at the beginning of his introduction to the case: "Since paranoaics cannot be compelled to overcome their internal resistances, and since in any case they only say what they choose to say, it follows that this is precisely a disorder for which a written report or a printed case history can take the place of personal acquaintance with the patient. For this reason I think it is legitimate to base analytic interpretations upon the case history of a patient suffering from paranoia . . . whom I have never seen, but who has written his own case history and brought it before the public in print."

13. Schreber, *Op. Cit.*, p. 214.

Editors' Notes

I n matters of translation and usage, we have tried to make all terminology as consistent as possible with Macalpine and Hunter's English translation of Daniel Paul Schreber, *Memoirs of My Nervous Illness* (London: Wm. Dawson & Sons, Ltd., 1955). We have found their Translators' Notes particularly helpful, due to their careful discussions of Schreber's often idiosyncratic usage. One such example—which might easily be misunderstood and lead to striking oversimplification—is the translation of *Entmannung* as "Unmanning," rather than as "Castration" or the like—for which, appropriate terms exist in German. We have also gratefully (and frequently) deferred to Hinsie and Cambell's *Psychiatric Dictionary*, Fourth Ed., (New York: Oxford University Press, 1970) and to Laplanche and Pontalis' *Vocabulaire de la psychanalyse* (Paris: Presses Universitaires de France, 1973). For its accuracy and wealth of historical data, we are most indebted to Han Israëls' *Schreber: Father and Son* (Madison, Conn.: International Universities Press, 1987).

The reader will note that certain of the contributing authors have stressed somewhat unusual forms of composition and have employed syntactical and stylistic devices they deemed crucial to their mode of approach. So far as possible, we have accommodated their wishes. Some, for example, rely on the epistolary form, others on a rather freely developed discursivity, still others have tended to use interrogative or case history approaches.

Part I
Psychosis

William J. Richardson

1. Lacan and the Problem of Psychosis

January 23, 1982 was a bad night in Boston. Only three days after an Air Florida Boeing 737 had careened into the traffic-jammed Fourteenth Street bridge in Washington, D.C., leaving 78 persons to disappear in the chill water of the Potomac—most of them still strapped to their seats, a World Airways DC 10, Flight 30 from Newark, touched down in the fog on an icy runway at Logan Airport and skidded into Boston Harbor, where the cockpit section tore away from the fuselage, leaving the latter perched on the edge of land like a fish with its head cut off. When the panic had passed, all injuries appeared minor, and happily no one was killed—or so, at least, it seemed.

But the family of sixty-nine-year-old Walter Metcalf and his forty-year-old son, Leo, refused to accept this claim, alleging that their father and brother must have been on the plane and had not been accounted for. World Airways promptly denied the fact. Audrey Metcalf (the daughter) persisted. The two had been on a Peoples' Express flight from Florida that had aborted in Newark, leaving some of its passengers to take the connecting flight on World Airways 30 to Boston. Eventually, airline officials conceded that Flight 30 had indeed taken on some extra transfer passengers in an emergency rescheduling in Newark, and that some of these names had not been recorded on the printout passenger list. Finally, after three days, in response to the importunity of the Metcalf family, officials confirmed the fact that the two had indeed been on Flight 30, had been sitting in the forward section of the fuselage and must have been washed out to sea when the cockpit section broke off. Sometime later Walter Metcalf's attache case washed ashore at the southern end of the harbor. Neither body was ever recovered.

The event was tragic and we should not trivialize it by taking it lightly. If I refer to it in approaching the question as to how Jacques Lacan conceives psychosis, it is because this bizarre twist of events suggests a way of gaining a first access to what he understands to be the core of psychotic process, namely, the "foreclosure" (*foreclusion, Verwerfung*) of a signifier. Our task is to try to understand this esoteric language of "foreclosure."

I say the incident gives us a first access. Here the names of two men disappear from the official record of their presence as if from the Book of Life, leaving an absence (a hole) in the symbolic system that records such things. The two names—signifiers of two human subjects—are not simply "repressed" (*refoulé, verdrängt*) from the passenger list, that is, somehow inscribed there, but for some reason disregarded, overlooked or forgotten, as if they had simply been misfiled. The names do not appear on the list at all, they are excluded from it. Those signifiers are rejected, repudiated, forgotten by the system as a whole, that is, 'foreclosed'. And yet, if those names as signifiers are excluded from the symbolic system of the World Airways passenger list, they have not disappeared completely. They remain somewhere, somehow as 'real' and return to plague the airline through the importunities of the family that, initially at least, appear to be groundless, fantastic or imaginary. Such for Lacan is the paradigm for a psychotic episode.

This will appear far-fetched, perhaps, not least because we are using a terminology ("Symbolic," "Imaginary" and "Real") that, though not unfamiliar to philosophers, has a meaning idiosyncratic to Lacan and as such no history at all in psychoanalytic theory prior to him. I shall first try to sketch the fundamental significance that he gives the terms and then examine in more detail how he sees their relevance for an understanding of the structure of psychosis.

The term 'Symbolic' taken as a noun and understood to mean symbolic order or system—Lacan takes from Lévi-Strauss, who used it to describe the ultimate pattern of relationships that governs all human intercourse, such as kinship systems, cultural mores, mythological themes, etc. The word "Symbolic" was congenial to Lacan for it implied a relationship to language: from its earliest origins, a symbol has always been a sign (something present) that represents something other than itself (something absent), and it is the essential nature of language to render present what is absent (or, at least, to permit an absence) through words, that is, to be symbolic. Such a term was appropriate for Lacan, since his fundamental thesis has always been that the unconscious discovered by Freud is "structured like a language." By this he means that Freud's epoch-making discovery consisted in an insight into the way that language works. In trying to articulate that insight in a scientifically respectable way, however, Freud's only model was the paradigm of nineteenth century physics, whereas in our day we have another scientific model-a specifically human one—that of the science of linguistics. Following the example of Lévi-Strauss who had taken the methodology of structural linguistics as a model for his structural anthropology, Lacan uses the same paradigm in re-interpreting Freud's notion of the unconscious. "Isn't it striking," he writes, "that Lévi-Strauss, in suggesting the implication of the structures of language with that part of the social laws that regulate marriage ties and kinship, is already conquering the very terrain in which Freud situates the unconscious?"[1]

How Lacan develops his case in detail need not detain us now. Suffice to say that from Saussure he takes the fundamental distinction between language (as system) and speech (as act), as well as the crucial distinction, within the classical notion of language as a system of signs, between the signifying component of the sign (speech sound) and signified component (mental image). From Jakobson he takes the notion that signifiers are arranged along one or another of two axes: one an axis of "combination," according to which they are strung together like words in a sentence, the other an axis of "selection," where signifiers are related to each other by reason of similarity or mutual exclusion so that one must be chosen in place of another and remain related to the one it replaces. Jakobson himself suggests that the axis of combination is the basis for what rhetoricians call metonomy, while the axis of selection is the basis of what they call metaphor. Be that as it may, Lacan takes the suggestion after his own fashion and proceeds to argue that what Freud, in the unconscious process of dream-formation, calls displacement is plotted along the axis of combination and therefore is essentially a process of metonomy; what Freud calls condensation is plotted along the axis of selection and is therefore essentially the phenomenon of "metaphor." If unconscious signifiers are polarized this way, they follow patterns that are determined by laws of language. This gives us some idea of Lacan's meaning when he says that the unconscious is "structured like a language."

Now these laws are not simply abstract skeletons. The signifiers that they polarize come out of the entire history of the race. Every child is born into a welter of signifiers that represent cultural history, ethnic background, ancestral heritage, social milieu and family context until the subject that the structure comes into the world and begins to take over his or her own life. A human infant is bathed in the signifiers (i.e., language) of his past like an embryo in amniotic fluid, and all of this forms part of the symbolic element in which he lives and moves and breathes. Or it may be thought of as a data bank that he inherits, a system in which he is inserted—somewhat the way a World Airways passenger is placed by the computer upon a list which in turn is part of a much larger system. At any rate, this system is a firm and constant principle of action that Lacan calls a law—eventually *the* Law, the "Law of *the* Father," where the Father is thought of as the Dead Father in Freud's myth of origins or simply the Name-of-the-Father, source of all law. This law functions inexorably, though often unpredictably, like a vast cosmic computer that retains a limitless number of unprogrammed options. And this massive system that penetrates every human individual is completely other than what consciousness reveals to him: Lacan calls it simply the Other, understanding it to be the Unconscious.

A second register Lacan calls the imaginary, meaning by that the domain of images, of the sensible representations that mark all our experience. But Lacan's use of the word is quite special, and to understand it properly we should recall how for him the experience of images begins. In comparison with animals, the human infant is born prematurely, a chaotic bundle of disordered impulses. But sometime between the ages of 6 and 18 months he experiences himself as a whole through a reflection of himself as a unity, whether this unity be his own image in a mirror or simply the mothering person herself who thus serves as a model of the wholeness that the child is to become. It is this reflected image that Lacan, capitalizing on an early ambiguity in Freud, calls the ego. The ego, then, is this alien image of the subject-to-be, the model of his unity and the citadel of defense. This conception of the ego is of course in sharp divergence from the later, more familiar, conception of an agency of adaptation between the id, superego, and reality. For the moment, though, let us focus on the nature of the image as image.

The main thing for Lacan is that an image has a dual polarity, one pole being the reflecting surface, the other being the reflected surface, and even though there may be physical distance between these two surfaces, there is an unmediated reciprocity between them. The consequences of this conception are multiple. You can see immediately that we must distinguish between the body as organism and the body as image (i.e., imaginary) It is the former that interests the scientist but the latter the psychoanalyst. Note, too, that the self-image as ego is that with which the inchoate subject first identifies himself. All other identifications are subsequent to the accretions upon this fundamental identification with his own reflection as ego. The same unmediated reciprocity will characterize all images, all identifications and all fantasies that constitute or accompany future psychic experience. As for the infant's relation to its mother in these early months, that, too, will be on the level of images, and in this sense, imaginary. The imaginary is the realm of all fantasy, all representations, even representations of words (when the time comes). If we dramatize for our purposes the situation of World Airways in January of 1982, we may presume that a convinced company spokesperson, insisting on the absence of the missing men's names from the printout passenger list, would dismiss the family importunities as the hysterical fantasies of a distraught daughter, that is, as purely imaginary. At any rate, the intimate, bipolar reciprocity of this image-world will be disrupted only when a third dimension is opened up, that introduces a certain distance between perceiver and perceived by reason of which things become present in their absence through the medium of language.

The third component of Lacan's triad is the Real. For Lacan, the Real is not reality. Reality, for Lacan, is the world of ordinary experience—the world of tables and chairs, the world of too-heavy-hammers that is already organized through images and the symbolic structures of language. The real is precisely not reality but rather the raw, unstructured experience of what-is, the not yet symbolized or imaged, what as such cannot be symbolized, hence the 'impossible'—impossible, that is, to inscribe in any symbolic system or to represent in any imaginary way. For example, the Real is excruciating pain, or the undiagnosed symptom, or Nagasaki under the mushroom cloud, in short, catastrophe of any kind. In the tragedy of that January evening, the Real is the ludicrous obscenity of the broken aircraft with two unrecorded passengers swept out into the swirling blackness of Boston Harbor.

If this is how the Symbolic, Imaginary and Real are differentiated, how are they related? They are absolutely linked. The Symbolic never functions without the consort of the Imaginary, the Imaginary never without orientation toward eventual symbolization—neither without conjunction of the Real that their task is to bring to representation. So closely are they intertwined that Lacan speaks of them as a knot—composed of three circles so intertwined that if one is broken the whole knot falls apart.

If it is the task of the Symbolic and the Imaginary to make the Real understandable by connecting it with images how are we to understand the passage from that initial experience to involvement in the symbolic order? As we saw, the first relationship between mother and child is a dyadic one, completely on the imaginary level. But when the infant begins to talk, the dyadic tie with the mother ruptures and he starts to relate to her by means of language. Freud describes this transition in a famous anecdote stressed by Lacan again and again. In Freud's account:

> This good little boy . . . had an occasional disturbing habit of taking any small objects he could get hold of and throwing them away from him into a corner, under the bed, and so on, so that hunting for his toys and picking them up was often quite a business. As he did this he gave vent to a loud, long-drawn-out 'o-o-o-o', accompanied by an expression of interest and satisfaction. His mother and the writer of the present account agreed in thinking that this was not a mere interjection but represented the German word '*fort*' ('gone'). I eventually realized that it was a game, and that the only use he made of any of his toys was to play 'gone' with them. One day I made an observation which confirmed my view. The child had a wooden reel with a piece of string tied round it. It never occurred to him to pull it along the floor behind him, for instance, and play at its being a carriage. What he did was to hold the reel by the string and very skillfully throw it over the edge of the curtained cot, so that it disappeared into it, at the same time uttering the expressive 'o-o-o-o'. He then pulled the reel out of the cot again by the string and hailed its reappearance with a joyful '*da*' ('here'). This, then, was the complete game—disappearance and return.[2]

The sense of this passage for Lacan is that the child, by modulating the phonemes "o-o-o-o" and "da" in this game of disappearance and return, strove to make the mother present in her absence. For the child, it is the inchoation of the spoken word; for Lacan, the paradigm of all speech. In other words, the infant is "born into language," initiated into the symbolic order.

Now Lacan tells us that the moment when "the child is born into language is also that in which 'desire becomes human' ".[3] The sense is that in the rupture of the dyadic bond with the mother there results an absence, a loss—the child is in "want" of the fullness of being that he has lost in separation from her. Lacan describes this as a "want-to-be" (*manque à être*), and this is what he means by desire. At this point there emerges the desire to restore the lost fullness of the union with the mother, which means, in Hegelian fashion, to become the desired of the mother, to fulfill her own want. But what the mother is in want of, is the phallus, where the phallus is not the male sexual organ but simply a symbol of her desire. He wants to be All for the mother and the mother All for him and thus restore the ruptured dyad, that is, he wants to be the phallus for her. But now this is impossible, for henceforth the relationship between them must be mediated by the law of language (the symbolic order), the Law which is the Law of the Father, since the name of the "no" of the Father (*le nom-(non)-du Père*) are the source of all law. The infant cannot be the mother's phallus, then, and this is an irreparable loss for him. This loss Lacan calls "castration." And so the Oedipal situation evolves. If all goes well, the infant must accept its inevitable castration (imaginary, to be sure), submit to the Law of the Father and be content to relate to the mother through the metonymic discourse of what Lacan calls the "dialectic of desire."

All this may seem terribly abstruse, but let me take one more preparatory step before discussing foreclosure and the problem of psychosis more concretely. Lacan situates what Freud calls primal repression in this insertion of the infant into the symbolic order. This is here a purely hypothetical term. The word repression itself is familiar enough. In Freud's words: "the essence of repression lies simply in turning something away, and keeping it at a distance, from consciousness"[4] as when an unconscious sexual urge is rejected and its energy converted into a bodily symptom in hysteria. But this supposes an unconscious already constituted and somehow operative. Hence, Freud hypothesizes that the unconscious itself must be constituted by a kind of repression on a more fundamental level that he therefore designates as primary. Primary repression, then, is the theoretical term to designate the first modality of the unconscious in the nascent subject. For Lacan, it is identical with the insertion of the young subject into the symbolic order and submission to the Law of the Father.

But what has all this to do with psychosis? Lacan addressed the problem directly in a weekly seminar during the year 1955–56, the full text of which has just recently been published and is available in English only in a truncated version that he entitles, "On a question preliminary to any possible treatment of psychosis."[5] What is the question? Basically it was the same as Freud's: What is there about psychosis that distinguishes it in basic structure from neurosis? In the briefest terms his answer is this: in the psychotic, primal repression—the institution of the unconscious—has somehow failed, whether in whole or in part. This failure goes by the name of foreclosure. What is foreclosure? It is essentially a gap or fissure in the signifying system, like the omission itself of the names of the Metcalfs from the signifying system of a passenger list. But, according to Lacan, what is foreclosed from the Symbolic returns to the Real in guise of fantasies, that is, the foreclosed signifier colludes with imaginary material to give some kind of edge, or border, to this gap in the form, say, of hallucinations or delusions. In the seminar, Lacan reinterprets Freud's landmark analysis of the *Memoirs* of President Schreber, perhaps the most discussed case in psychoanalytic history.[6] I shall try to summarize the argument.

[margin note: GAP]

Daniel Paul Schreber (1842–1911) was the son of an illustrious father, Daniel Gottlob Moritz Schreber, whose conception of pedagogy earned him a permanent place in the history of nineteenth century educational theory. Trained as a lawyer and functioning as a local judge, he had his first bout with madness at the age of 42 after failing in his candidacy for membership in the Reichstag. He suffered from "severe hypochondria" and was admitted to a clinic in Leipzig, where for eight months he was under the care of Dr. Paul Emil Flechsig. After discharge he managed to remain functional for eight years. At the age of 51, there was trouble again, just six months after he had been elected Presiding Judge of the Court of Appeals in Dresden. Despite his professional success, he was severely disappointed when it became clear that his wife was incapable of bearing a child. At any rate, in October, 1893 he suffered a severe anxiety attack, attempted suicide and soon was readmitted to Flechsig's clinic. After eight months he was transferred to the clinic at Sonnenstein, where he remained legally committed for almost nine years. Finally he contested the legal commitment and helped draft the case that argued successfully for his discharge, or at least for a change of status to a "voluntary" commitment. On the strength of this he soon discharged himself, even though far from well. The *Memoirs* were written during that nine year commitment and trace the course of his illness.

The *Memoirs* were not planned as a book but were composed from jottings so as to be able to give his wife and others "at least an approximate idea of my religious conceptions so that they have some understanding of the necessity which forces me to various oddities of behavior even if they do not fully understand these apparent oddities."[7] The oddities included the habit of wearing cheap jewelry, ribbons, or other feminine ornaments for several hours a day, and attacks of compulsive bellowing if the ritual that these accoutrements were supposed to accompany was impeded.

A more detailed account of the phenomenon comes from the report of the attending physician:

> The patient's delusion system amounts to this: he is called to redeem the world and to bring back mankind to the lost state of Blessedness. He maintains he has been given this task by direct divine inspiration, similar to that taught by the prophets; he maintains that nerves in a state of excitation, as his have been for a long time, have the property of attracting God, but it is a question of things which are either not at all expressible in human language or only with great difficulty, because he maintains they lie outside all human experience and have only been revealed to him. The most essential part of his mission of redemption is that it is necessary for him first of all to be transformed into a woman. Not, however, that he wishes to be transformed into a woman, it is much more a "must" according to the Order of the World, which he simply cannot escape, even though he would personally very much prefer to remain in his honourable manly position in life. But the beyond was not to be gained again for himself and the whole of mankind other than by his future transformation into a woman by way of divine miracle in the course of years or decades. He maintains that he is the exclusive object of divine miracles, and with it the most remarkable human being that ever lived on earth. For years at every hour and every minute he experiences these miracles in his body, has them confirmed also by voices that speak to him. He maintains that in the earlier years of his illness he suffered destruction of individual organs of his body, of a kind that would have brought death to every other human being, that he lived for a long time without a stomach, without intestines, bladder, almost without lungs, with smashed ribs, torn gullet, that he had at times eaten part of his own larynx with his food, etc.; but divine miracles ("rays") had always restored the destroyed organs, and therefore, as long as he remained a man, he was absolutely immortal. These threatening phenomena have long ago disappeared, and in their place his "femaleness" has come to the fore; it is a question of evolutionary process which in all probability will take decades if not centuries for its completion and the end of which is unlikely to be witnessed by any human being now alive. He has the feeling that already masses of 'female nerves' have been transferred into his body, from which through immediate fertilization with God new human beings would come forth. Only then would he be able to die a natural death and have gained for himself as for all other human beings the state of Blessedness. In the meantime not only the sun but also the trees and birds, which he thinks are something like "remains of previous human souls transformed by miracles," speak to him in human tones and everywhere around him miracles are enacted.[8]

If this delusion of becoming the saviour of the world by being transformed into a woman is the climax of the illness, the early stages of it are marked by an angry excoriation of Dr. Flechsig, his first therapist and the one who treated him successfully eight years earlier for hypochondria. In a word, Flechsig was guilty of "soul murder."[9] Freud makes much of this hostility to Flechsig as a persecutory figure. Delusions of persecution, Freud's experience tells him, may be explained by the fact that "the person to whom the delusion ascribes so much power and influence, in whose hands all the threads of the conspiracy converge, is, if he is definitely named, either identical with someone who played an equally important part in the patient's emotional life before his illness, or is easily recognizable as substitute for him."[10] The person who is now feared as persecutor was once loved and honored, and the delusion of persecution serves the purpose of justifying the change in emotional attitude. But what accounts for this change of attitude toward Flechsig? Freud postulates that there was an outburst of homosexual libido with Flechsig as its object and that Schreber's struggle against this libidinal impulse produced the conflict which gave rise to the symptoms. Freud argues the case brilliantly, and the thesis that there is a strong homosexual component in paranoia has become classical.

Lacan does not deny, of course, the appearance of homosexuality of which Freud makes such an issue, but he claims that it is not so much a determinant of the psychosis as a symptom of it. What determines the psychosis, rather, is the "hole dug in the field of the signifier,"[11] that is, some rent in the network of the signifying system, and this by reason of the way in which the Oedipal complex came to pass in Schreber. It is impossible to follow Lacan in detail, but I take him to be saying in substance this:

To begin with there was a distortion on the imaginary level insofar as the infantile desire to be the desired (i.e., phallus) of the mother was never resolved, and, therefore, imaginary castration never achieved. Lacan finds confirmation for this in the fact that the psychosis erupted when the patient had taken refuge in the mother's apartment and was seized by an anxiety attack and the suicidal raptus.[12] Presumably, then, "the divination of the unconscious very soon warned the subject that, incapable as he is of being the phallus that the mother lacks, he is left with the solution of being the woman that men lack"[13] and so the delusion of feminization develops. In any case, this would explain the much discussed fantasy that belonged to the incubation period of the second illness, namely, that "it would be beautiful being a woman submitting to copulation."[14]

Secondly, submission to the Law of the Father never took place, primal repression was never complete. This is what is meant by the "hole dug in the field of the signifier" and the very essence of "foreclosure." The crux of the matter here is that we are not talking about an absence or a failure in the actual father but a deficiency in the paternal function, hence a gap in the symbolic network, that is, in the Law that goes by the Name-of-the-Father. Given the intimate reciprocity between Symbolic and Imaginary, this hole in the signifying system finds a correlate in the imaginary order. Lacan speaks of "the induction effects of the signifier bearing on the imaginary order" meaning, I think, something like the phenomenon in electromagnetism by which one body can call forth similar properties in another body without direct contact. Thus, all at once there "opened up for (Schreber) in the field of the imaginary the gap in it that corresponded to the defect of the symbolic metaphor, the gap that could only be resolved in the accomplishment of the *Entmannung* (unmanning). At first an object of horror for the subject, it was then accepted as a reasonable compromise (*Vernünftig*)[15], consequently as an irrevocable choice (Schreber, note to p. 179–SIII), and led to a future motive of redemption for the entire world."[16] At any rate, "it is around this hole, in which the support of the signifying chain is lacking in the subject . . . that the whole struggle in which the subject reconstructed itself took place"[17] setting off "the cascade of reshapings of the signifier from which the increasing disaster of the imaginary proceeds, to the point where the signifier is signified and stabilized in the delusional metaphor."[18]

But what precipitates all this? From all that we know, up to the age of fifty-one, except for the brief bout with hypochondria at forty-two, Schreber led a relatively normal, certainly successful, life. What threw him into the skid? If I understand him correctly, Lacan would say that the fissure existed all along (like a hairline fracture) and splits open when the Name-of-the-Father is called into symbolic opposition to the subject. But how is this possible? Lacan puts the question himself: "How can the Name-of-the-Father be called by the subject to the only place in which it could have reached him and in which it has never been seen? Simply by (encounter with) some factual father, not necessarily the subject's own father, but with *A* father."[19] By "A father" I understand any social use of the Name-of-the-Father. In Schreber's case, this took place in the encounter with Flechsig who "attained a place to which the subject was unable to call him before."[20] But Flechsig in the flesh is unable to fill such a hole and is regarded with contempt ("kleiner Flechsig": "little Flechsig," the voices shout). In stressing Flechsig's relationship to the paternal function, Lacan refers with approval to Niederland's researches which draw attention to Flechsig's fantasized genealogy, "constructed with the names of Schreber's real ancestors, Gottfried, Gottlieb, Fürchegott, and, above all, Daniel, which is handed down from father to son and of which he gives the meaning in Hebrew, to show in their convergence on the name of God (*Gott*) an important symbolic chain by which the function of the father can be manifested as delusion."[21] How the figure of Flechsig and that of the factual father blend into the fantasy of God for whom Schreber becomes the redemptive spouse—all this adds up to a kind of homosexuality, no doubt, but for Lacan properly speaking only a "delusional" one.[22]

*   *   *

In all this the main thing for understanding Lacan's theory of psychosis is the notion of the "foreclosure" of the signifying chain. "It is in an accident in (the register of the symbolic) and in what takes place in it, namely, the foreclosure of the Name-of-the-Father in the place of the Other that I designate the defect that gives psychosis its essential condition, and the structure that separates it from neurosis."[23] No doubt, there is much to question about all this. Let me close by putting as simply as possible the questions that I feel are most urgent but must obviously be left to another occasion:

1. Is it true that Freud's conception of the unconscious (baseline of the entire discussion) is, as Lacan claims, that it be "structured like a language?" Is Lacan's conception, then, of the ego, desire, primal repression—for that matter, his entire triadic distinction between Symbolic, Imaginary and Real—warranted?
2. Is the hypothesis about foreclosure as the structural basis for psychosis, worked out so painstakingly for the Schreber case, applicable to other clinical cases such as fill our hospital beds every day?
3. Given the notion of foreclosure as the determinant factor in psychosis, is any treatment of it possible? What is the hope for cure?

Notes

1.   Jacques Lacan, *Ecrits: A Selection,* trans. by A. Sheridan (New York: Norton, 1977), p. 73.

2.   Sigmund Freud, *Beyond the Pleasure Principle, Standard Edition,* 18:7–64 (London: Hogarth Press, 1955) pp. 14–15.

3.   Lacan, *Op. Cit.,* p. 103.

4.   Sigmund Freud, "Repression," *Standard Edition,* 14:141– 158, (London: Hogarth Press, 1957), p. 147.

5.   Lacan, *Op. Cit.,* p. 179.

6.   See Sigmund Freud, Psycho-Analytic Notes on an Autobiographical Account of a Case of Paranoia (Dementia Paranoides), *Standard Edition,* 12:9–82, (London: Hogarth, 1958).

7.   Daniel Paul Schreber, *Memoirs of My Nervous Illness,* trans. by I. Macalpine and R. A. Hunter (London: Dawson and Sons, 1955), p. 1. (Republished by Harvard University Press, 1988, with a new introduction by Samuel Weber. Pagination retained).

8.   *ibid.,* pp. 386–388.

9.   *ibid.,* pp. 22 ff.

10.   Freud, Psychoanalytic Notes. . . , p. 41.

11.   Lacan, *op. cit.,* p. 205.

12.   *ibid.,* p. 207.

13.   *Loc. cit.*

14.   *ibid.,* p. 207.

15.   Schreber, *op. cit.,* p. 177.

16.   Lacan, *op. cit.,* p. 206.

17. *ibid.*, p. 205.
18. *ibid.*, p. 217.
19. *Loc. cit.*
20. *ibid.*, p. 207.
21. *ibid.*, p. 219.
22. *Loc. cit.*
23. *ibid.*, p. 215.

Antonio Quinet

2. Schreber's Other

I n psychosis, the very structure of the unconscious is laid bare and the subject's Other appears unveiled, consistent and absolute. Such was the case of
Schreber's Other: his God was fashioned out of language and extreme ecstasy
(jouissance.)[1] But before embarking on this subject, let us consider the status of
the Other with regard to the Oedipus complex as described in the work of
Jacques Lacan.

The Name-of-the-Father in the Locus of the Other

According to Lacan, the inclusion of the signifier "Name-of-the-Father," in
the locus of the Other is what assures the subject's entry into the symbolic order
and inaugurates the signifying chain in the unconscious. For every subject the
Other is a precondition, i.e., it is the store-house of signifiers, and is already
there from the beginning, before the advent of the subject as such. But, for the
individual to be able to take possession of the signifiers, to use them to give
utterance to words of truth, he must necessarily be put to the test of the Oedipus
complex.

Lacan sums up Freud's Oedipus in his formula of the paternal metaphor, in
which the Desire-of-the-Mother with which the child has identified himself as
an object, is substituted for the Name-of-the-Father. What is involved here is the
symbolization of the mother's absence/presence as represented by the game of
Fort-Da described by Freud in *Beyond the Pleasure Principle*. The result is the
inclusion of the Name-of-the-Father in the Other and the subsequent access to

phallic signification, which thus allows the subject to bestow meaning on his signifiers and to his or her place as man or woman in the division of sexes.

$$\frac{\text{Name-of-the-Father}}{\text{Desire-of-the-Mother}} \bullet \frac{\text{Desire-of-the-Mother}}{\text{Signified to the Subject}} \; - \; \text{Name-of-the-Father} \left(\frac{A}{\text{Phallus}} \right)$$

A loss of 'jouissance' is concomitant with the operation of the paternal metaphor. The 'jouissance' in question, that of the Other, whose place is occupied by the mother, is from there on forever lost. The inclusion of the Name-of-the-Father in the Other bars the subject's access to the Other's 'jouissance;' in other words, the subject may no longer be an object of the Other's 'jouissance.' 'Jouissance' is from then onwards correlated with an object signified by the phallus and becomes sexual pleasure properly speaking.

The Imperative of Jouissance

In a purely logical phase, before the operation of the paternal metaphor, that is, in the primal relation, the child is completely subjugated to the maternal Other. He is identified with the object of the mother's desire, the phallus, and because of this is dominated by the law of her caprice. The Other takes him as her object of jouissance. One may see in this Other, with whom the child is initially confronted, the figure of the father in the primal horde described by Freud in *Totem and Taboo,* the dominant male who possesses all the females, thereby imposing sexual abstinence on all the other male members of the horde. In this myth, the primal father is the sole free man and he loves no-one but himself. A ruthless and violent male, his narcissism is absolute: "a paramount and dangerous personality, toward whom only a passive-masochistic attitude is possible, to whom one's will has to be surrendered."[2]

For Freud, this attitude belongs to the archaic inheritance of the individual and manifests itself in the child's behavior toward his parents, and especially in the image he constructs of his father. If we take into account Freud's distinction between the ego-ideal and the super-ego, the latter is the heir to this primal father. The super-ego is the incarnation of the father's commandments, a father entirely bent on his own pleasure, and identified by the child as the licentious (*jouisseur*) father not subject to castration.

For Lacan, "the super-ego is indeed a kind of law, but it is a law without a dialectic and it may be recognized in the categorical imperative and its pernicious neutrality."[3] Thus, the super-ego legitimizes nothing, but simply imposes rules. Better still, the super-ego inflects its commandments because it is a vocal agency; it is the voice of conscience. The super-ego's senseless law is at the same time the destruction of the law itself, because it deprives the law of its normative meaning.

As Freud himself identifies the father of the primal horde with the super-ego, we may allow ourselves to superimpose the super-ego's demented law on the supreme jouissance of the primal father, who prohibits sexual relations to all other males. The primal father kept jouissance all for himself. In *Totem and Taboo,* Freud stresses the importance of the murder of the father to clear the other males' way to sexual intercourse with the females. This corresponds to the second phase of the Oedipus complex: the father must be killed in order for him to come into being as a signifier and thus fulfill his function as Name-of-the-Father. With his death, the father takes with him the key to supreme jouissance. The advent of the Name-of-the-Father as signifier of the Other is the consequence of this death which allows the boy to keep his penis and to cathect it as an object of phallic meaning, thereby acceding to jouissance. As phallic jouissance it is qualitatively different from that of the unbarred Other. After the murder of the father, the jouissance of the Other is irreparably lost, and the subject has no access to it. It is barred to him through the mere fact of the presence of the Name-of-the-Father, signifier of the primal murder. If the licentious father is the super-ego, then, according to Lacan, what he commands has its origins in the call to "pure jouissance, that is to say, in non-castration."[4] It thus gives utterance to the insatiable demand: "enjoy; come! (jouis!)" The super-ego would respond, then, to the all-powerful, uncastrated Other, who imposes the law of its caprice. It is also identified with the archaic figure of the mother: the Absolute Other who dictates to her child her own blind laws and her unmediated desire. The super-ego is, therefore, the unbarred Other, the position in which the mother is placed by her child. The super-ego is Other minus the inscription of castration; the Other without the Name-of-the-Father. Lacan calls attention to the fact that observation of young children shows us the appearance of the super-ego "at such a precocious stage that it would seem to be contemporaneous, if not previous to the appearance of the ego."[5]

For anyone who has undergone the Oedipal ordeal, i.e., the neurotic, the Other is barred by the fact of containing the signifier of castration. The neurotic's Other is inconsistent and only manifests itself through the formations of the unconscious—dreams, slips of the tongue, jokes—discovered by Freud. This is what Lacan has formulated by stating that the unconscious is the discourse of the Other. In neurosis, the questions posed by the subject with regard to existence and sex are often cut off from him through repression, though other mechanisms may also be at work.

The Other is the locus of the word, bearer of the signifier of symbolic law—the Name-of-the-Father—that bars the mother's 'jouissance' and impedes her taking her child as her own object. The neurotic's Other is emptied of 'jouissance' by the operation of the paternal metaphor. Symbolic castration has as its consequence a loss of 'jouissance,' and for the neurotic his only pleasure is phallic 'jouissance,' correlated to an object, the cause of desire.

Psychosis

Lacan has highlighted the fundamental disturbance in psychosis: the foreclosure of the Name-of-the-Father in the locus of the Other. In other words, the Name-of-the-Father is missing and this corresponds to a gap in the psychotic's symbolic order. Thus the psychotic phenomenon consists in an emergence into reality of an appeal for signification to which the subject can give no reply because it has never been part of his structure in the first place.

In his article "Neurosis and Psychosis," Freud shows that in the genesis of delusions, "the delusion is found applied like a patch over the place where originally a rent had appeared in the ego's relation to the external world."[6] The gap in the symbolic order, postulated by Lacan, thus corresponds to this rent in the reality of the psychotic subject and is filled in by delusion.

The consequence of psychotic foreclosing of the Name-of-the-Father is that the chain of signifiers at the unconscious level will also be affected. The psychotic has no words of his own to give utterance to his discourse. The stream of signifiers run rampant and, disregarding the subject himself, begins to talk to itself. Symbolic law exercises its effects upon the subject and makes him speak in a tongue which he does not know. Delusion objectifies the subject in a language without a dialectic, and a language which is constantly imposed. ". . . The subject, one might say, is spoken rather than speaking: here we recognize the symbols of the unconscious in petrified forms."[7] Nevertheless, the subject neither assumes them nor recognizes them. He is no more than a witness to his unconscious. In psychosis, the Other, in its function as bearer of the law, is excluded and the subject is confronted with the absolute Other unmarked by symbolic castration.

The absolute Other is rather the bearer of the commandments of an absurd law, one without dialectic, and which legitimates nothing. The other which has not been barred by the signifier is the archaic super-ego; it commands the subject "to be this and not to be that."

The psychotic subject is the object of the Other, and is thus at the mercy of its omnipotence and its demands. The psychotic only perceives the Other in its relation to the signifier and is therefore under the sway of a completely meaningless discourse. If the Other happens to occupy the place of someone who sustains one of the subject's imaginary identifications, this person is then perceived with fear, aggression and rivalry. The previously idealized person becomes an observer of the subject, orders him about and subjugates him to his will. The personified super-ego thus persecutes the subject. How is it possible to take this subject's relation to the omnipotent Other, and to link it to the relation with his progenitor?

Even if it proves impossible for the subject to identify the symbolic order and the father, an identification with the image of the father still remains possible.

While this kind of identification lacks a dialectic, it does allow the subject to perceive his father on an imaginary level, because the image of his father functions for him as a model, as a "specular alienation."[8] This image of his father then provides the subject with the substance for forming an ego-ideal, albeit an incomplete one, since it both lacks symbolic function, and dresses up the super-ego always on the verge of appearing in its nakedness. Nevertheless, for Lacan, the father most required for the understanding of psychosis is not so much the real father, medium for the subject's imaginary identification, as the father which serves as the metaphor of the paternal function, a function which, properly speaking, is absent.

The foreclosure of the Name-of-the-Father calls into question the subject's entire set of signifiers, and this is what provokes the characteristic disturbance of language in the psychoses.

The signifier and the signified appear radically separated. Signifiers no longer necessarily refer to a specific signified. Words may have enormous meaning, which is precisely what gives delusional intuitions their revelatory character. This kind of signification gives meaning to all of the subject's life phenomena and he constructs his own world around it. Words may come back in a kind of *ritornello,* as empty repetitive formulae. There may also be interruptions of the chain of signifiers which appear in verbal hallucinations as snatches of empty phrases. These phenomena may crop up in the psychotic's speech as phrases suddenly broken off—manifestation of the broken chain of signifiers. Speech disturbances, whether spoken or heard, are the manifestation par excellence of the foreclosure of the Name-of-the-Father. The fact that the Other speaks to the subject from outside of him gives verbal hallucination its central position in psychosis.

Schreber's Way

The construction of Schreber's Other, his God, goes hand in hand with the formation of the delusional metaphor of becoming God's wife, which substitutes for the foreclosure of the Name-of-the-Father. Schreber constructs his delusional order, his divine erotomania, around this delusional metaphor: God's wife. Once built, this delusion allows him in reality to follow the path of fatherhood which was denied him at the symbolic level due to the lack of the signifier of paternity. His delusion reveals that characteristic trait of psychotic productions highlighted by Lacan: what is foreclosed in the symbolic returns in the real.

". . . and the Word was God"

For Schreber, apart from human language, there is also the *nerve language* to which the healthy human being is oblivious. But Schreber is aware of it because his nerves are sensitive to God's nerves, to the divine rays. The nature of divine rays is that they *must* speak. God speaks the so-called "basic language," "a vigorous but somewhat antiquated German, which is especially characterized by its great wealth of euphemisms."[9] Thus Schreber's private language sets up a special relationship between the signifier and signified, which denotes the disturbance of the symbolic order. The unconscious is outside him, the source of the "basic language" is God, the Other.

Nevertheless, after subjugating God, Flechsig had the power to enjoy the rays and this made him deserve the title "leader *(Fürer)* of rays." Following Flechsig's example, all the souls that appeared to Schreber during the period of imaginary cataclysm, his catatonic phase, spoke to him as voices. They were bearers of categorical formulations, super-ego commandments which expressed rules of conduct: "Do not think about certain parts of your body"; "Not at the first demand"; "A job started must be finished."[10]

Behind all this is God, veiled but present as the source of the signifiers. If the souls have vocal characteristics, it is because of their relation to Him. According to Schreber, God was the agency for which "the individual souls appeared to act, so to speak, as out-posts."[11] God is language for Schreber.

God dwelt above the "forecourts of heaven" (souls who integrated into higher entities aware only of being part of God) and above the anterior realms, and these appeared in mid-March 1894. In July 1894, these disappear and the anterior realms of God, identified with God himself, appear under the form of *Ariman* ("lower God") and *Ormuzd* ("upper God"). At this date, according to Lacan, Schreber has a "metaphorical intuition."[12] God appears to him *in vivo* and Senatpräsident Schreber hears His voice, ". . . it sounded in a mighty bass: 'wretch' ". And this time "it was not a soft whisper—as the talk of the voices always was before and after that time."[13] It was an authentic word, "an expression quite common in the basic language to denote a human being destined to be destroyed by God and to feel God's power and wrath."[14] The absolute Other makes his appearance carrying a signifier that Schreber can signify. "Yet everything that was spoken was genuine"[15] and for that reason Schreber felt no fear or alarm. Despite the insults contained in some of the *words,* Schreber tells us that the effect on his nerves was beneficial.[16] On the following day, Ormuzd appeared to him as the sun "surrounded by a silver sea of rays which covered a 6th or 8th part of the sky"[17] and which spoke to him also. From then on, Schreber identified the sun with God.[18] These phenomena lasted a few days and after they were over, "the talk of the voices also turned again into a low whisper."[19]

Thus, here we have a signifier that has given proof of its existence in the real as capable of engendering effects of signification. Nevertheless, at this time it was still not possible for a delusional order to be established. But the discourse of the unconscious was there. This period was marked, however, by a change of "policy" of the rays toward Schreber. His situation with regard to "unmanning" became more radical: he could not consent to it because it would entail sexual abuse and at the same time it had been agreed that he must be "retain[ed] on the masculine side . . . in order to destroy [his] reason or to make [him] demented."[20] Schreber, already most seriously concerned for his manliness, now began to fear for his reason. At this point, the "writing-down system" by the rays began. All his thoughts were written down and as soon as an idea recurred which he had previously had, he would hear; "We have already got that."[21] We find here again that characteristic of the super-ego as "observer," which in Lacan's words "sees all, hears all, writes it all down."[22] The Other is always watching him.

As soon as Schreber perceived that his relation to the divine rays had become indissoluble long ago,[23] he began to worry about the consequences of an eventual withdrawal of God to extricate himself from his (Schreber's) body; he realized that he was literally plugged into the Other.

Another important change was that the voices whose words, when proceeding from the basic language, had been full of meaning, were reduced to "a kind of neutral nonsense."[24] The nature of the voices' revelation gave place to an empty discourse made up of repetitions and refrains. The disturbance of signification which had already begun, was to be manifested abundantly following the capital turning-point in the story of his life—the moment when Schreber decided to accept his unmanning. In November 1895, Schreber was fifty-three years old, the age his father was at the time of his death. (Daniel Gottlob Moritz Schreber died November 10, 1861, at the age of fifty-three).

From the moment of its encounter with the signifier of the dead father, the entire signifying apparatus was brought into play along with the phenomena of separate deployment, dissociation, fragmentation and mobilization of the signifier. Next, the reconstruction of the world was brought about with the elaboration of significations bearing on the delusional metaphor which occupied the place of the foreclosed Name-of-the-Father, thus placing the delusion in a stable position. We may affirm that upon reaching the age his father had when he died, and in the same month of his father's death, something of a symbolic nature was allowed to appear, a new signifier capable of bringing in a radically new law, where none had been before. To be transformed into God's wife, to have sexual intercourse with Him and to give birth, in imitation of the immaculate virgin, to a new race of men, was what allowed Schreber to carry out the process of becoming a father, albeit a delusional one.

After this encounter with the signifier, the voices emanating from God turned into a kind of verbiage full of "nonsensical phrases" whose content may be resumed as "neutral nonsense." They ceased to be abusive and insulting, and became forms of the "not-thinking-of-anything-thought."[25] One of the phrases pronounced by the voices shows this utter emptiness of meaning: "All nonsense cancels itself out."[26] In spite of their lacking meaning, Schreber heard them ceaselessly. The permanent and indissoluble nature of the connection of God's nerves to his body obliged him to receive speech constantly. If God withdrew, taking along with Him the annoying chatter of the voices, the bellowing-miracle would take place. He immediately felt the sensation of the pain like a sudden pulling inside of his head combined with the tearing off of part of the bony substance of his skull.[27] Under the sway of the divine influence, Schreber was forced to emit bellowing noises, as if he were obliged to follow this course in order to maintain the presence of the signifier. His bellowing was a meaningless noise. Next he heard cries of help in which the meaning was implicit. Everytime God withdrew, Schreber had to go through the dissociation of language. When the Other abandoned him, forsook him, a veritable decomposition of the signifier occurred.

The birds created by a miracle (remnants of the forecourts of heaven), following the apparition of the Sun-God, now arrived on the scene and gradually acquired a more prominent place in Schreber's delusion. These miraculously produced birds busied themselves reeling off phrases drummed into them. But they did not have the least understanding of what they said, they reeled off phrases without knowing the sense of the words, governed only by the principle of homophony, as indicated by the similarity in sound of the words: Santiago/Carthago, Chinesenthum/Jesum Christum, etc.[28] Here it can be observed that the unconscious takes more pains with the signifier than with the signified, thereby highlighting the psychotic's foreign relationship to language. This external relationship was clearly manifest in Schreber's own words: "My nerves are influenced by the rays to vibrate corresponding to human words; their voice therefore is not subject to my own will but is due to an influence on me from without."[29] "If neurotics inhabit language, psychotics are inhabited by, are possessed by language."[30]

The system of not-finishing-a-sentence made its appearance, its vibrations, in his nerves of thoughts' debris, conjunctions or adverbs "which my nerves have to supplement to make up the sense."[31] The original meaning of these incomplete phrases had been omitted and so when he heard: "lacking now is . . ." he completed the phrase with: "only the leading idea," which meant: "we, the rays, have no thoughts."[32] This system of not-finishing-a-sentence reveals where the chain of signifiers is broken off—precisely at the point where the complement which would confer a meaning is lacking. Subsequently, during the evolving course of his delusion, other incoherent words continued to make their appearance: "why, because, I be it," but Schreber no longer bothered to find their complementary meaning.[33]

Responsible for all these phenomena was God, the Other, the keeper of the treasure-house of signifiers, who subjugated Schreber to the law of His senseless word. "It is God himself who causes the nonsensical questioning," says Schreber.[34]

Little by little, as his delusion evolved, Schreber's relation to God shifted from language to eroticism. "This is connected," says Schreber, "to the increased soul-voluptuousness of my body and . . . to the great shortage of speech-material at the disposal of the rays."[35] His hallucinations lost their importance until finally he was unable to discern words in them. The God of language receded into the background and the God of *jouissance* irrupted in the real. "There where speech is absent, there is to be found the Eros of the psychotic, there where he finds his supreme love."[36]

God is Jouissance

The obvious eroticization in the phantasmagoria of psychotic delusions is a theme already present in Freud's writings: psychotics "love their delusions as they love themselves."[37]

According to Schreber, female nerves had started entering his body from the very beginning of the delusion, thus announcing that the process of unmanning had started. Schreber was destined to be feminized. We must remark that it is not a question of castration *(Kastration)* but of unmanning *(Entmannung),* the term used in the basic language to designate the transformation into a woman. These sensations of voluptuousness, perceived by Schreber's nerves, allowed him to attract the divine rays. The fact that these nerves were at the same time language and sexuality shows the attachment of the signifier to eroticism.

Schreber decided to accept the unmanning as a sacrifice so that impregnation by the divine rays might bring about a new race of men. This was the consequence that the "Order of the World imperiously demanded."[38] Before this date, the feeling of soul-voluptuousness was not always of the same intensity. But after November 1895, and after more than a year of uninterrupted contact with the rays (starting at the moment of seeing God face to face), the voluptuousness became so intense that the rays "started to like entering my body."[39]

If Schreber managed to accept this position of being God's wife, this was because it allowed him to become the signifier of the phallus and thereby to be the object of the Other's jouissance.

Schreber was convinced that his body bore the marks of his transformation into a woman due to the influx of divine rays. The female characteristics appeared with a certain regularity that corresponded to God's withdrawal and return into Schreber's body. When God drew near, his bosom swelled, and when God withdrew, it receded. As soon as he reconciled himself to the process of unmanning, God paid him visits to avail himself of his body. When alone with God, he stood in front of a mirror with the upper part of his body naked, except for a few feminine adornments; a certain transsexual practice and jouissance appeared to spring up. As "everything feminine attracts God's nerves",[40] Schreber "strives to give the divine rays the impression of a woman in the height of sexual delight."[41]

Schreber added that for him the moral limits of voluptuousness, valid for all other people, no longer existed. On the contrary, it became his duty to cultivate voluptuousness. The very term became a synonym for blessedness which is a state "of uninterrupted enjoyment, combined with the contemplation of God."[42]

Nevertheless, the cultivation of voluptuousness, which it was his duty to develop, does not imply sexual intercourse with men or women. Schreber clarifies this: "I have to imagine myself as a man and woman in one person having intercourse with myself, or somehow have to achieve with myself a certain sexual excitement . . . which has nothing whatever to do with any idea of masturbation or anything like it."[43] Dr. Weber described Schreber's sexual activities in the following terms: ". . . in the patient's behavior, in the clean shaving of the face (Schreber had shaved off his moustache to heighten the illusion of having a feminine appearance), in his pleasure in feminine toilet articles, in small feminine occupations, in the tendency to undress more or less and to look at himself in the mirror, to decorate himself with gay ribbons and bows, etc., in the feminine way, the pathological direction of his fantasy is manifested continually."[44] Schreber is compelled to adopt this sort of behavior: "God wishes it".[45] "God demands constant enjoyment;" "It is my duty to provide Him with it".[46] Schreber's God is the incarnation of the unbarred Other's imperative, absolute jouissance. The commandment of the super-ego is fulfilled: "Jouis!" According to Lacan, the "foreclusion of the Name-of-the-Father is correlative to the inclusion of 'jouissance' in the locus of the Other."[47] Schreber's reply to the imperative of 'jouissance' is: "So be it."

Soul voluptuousness was not, however, always present, because God did not always come. So Schreber was obliged to practice adopting the female role, to rest his gaze on female beings, in order to attract the God who commanded him to "excite [himself] sexually."[48] As soon as there was a pause in his intellectual activities, he had to devote himself to cultivating his voluptuousness because if not, the bellowing-miracle would occur. With regard to this coming and going of God, to the 'jouissance' provoked by his presence and the painful sundering caused by his absence, we may conjecture that Schreber was giving expression to the presence and absence of the Mother, which he had been unable to symbolize due to the lack of the Name-of-the-Father.

From the moment that he accepted his unmanning, Schreber lived in the expectation of his transformation into a woman. But by 1900, when he wrote the *Memoirs,* he still had not undergone the sex change, and no longer believed that it would occur some day. On the contrary, he believed "that to the end of his days there will be strong indications of femaleness, but that he shall die as a man."[49] His unmanning was seen as the compensation (palm of victory) for all that he had suffered in his "martyrdom." This is why he had the impression that some great and magnificent satisfaction was in store for him: "If it be true that the continuation of all creation on our earth rests entirely on the very special relations into which God entered with me, the reward could only be something very extraordinary,"[50] to wit, his unmanning. Because of his identification with the phallus, Schreber drew all the meaning of the world into himself; the entire world made signs to him, all creation depended on him: "since God entered into nerve-contact with me exclusively, I became in a way for God the only human being, or simply the human being around whom everything turns, to whom everything that happens must be related."[51] He was thus obliged to relate himself to everything that he heard spoken and to everything written in the newspapers.

We presume that, by taking onto himself his father's death, Schreber suffered the effects of induction by the signifier. The consequence was the establishment of a delusional order. The elaboration of the delusional metaphor—to be God's wife and give birth to a lineage—allowed him to follow, in the reality of his delusion, the grand path of paternity. This solution, his mission as Redeemer, in Freud's words, that he foresaw from the beginning of his illness, was unfeasible until his encounter with the signifier. The delusional metaphor, standing for the Name-of-the-Father, brought on the stabilization of his delusion. He reconstructed the world, and his relation to reality and to his fellow-men became possible. The people around him were no longer only images; they fully recovered their intensity: "I have known for a long time now that people I see before me are not 'fleeting-improvised-men' but real human beings, and that I have to conduct myself towards them as a reasonable human being usually does in his dealings with other human beings."[52] The delusional metaphor permitted him to confer meaning to his words and thus he was able to write the *Memoirs* and to appeal to the court to obtain his release from the asylum and to recover the management of his properties. He found his bearings in reality so well that he won his case.

The Other of jouissance makes his appearance as God, forcing Schreber into jouissance, with the undeniable pleasure he described. God loomed up through the intermediary of the licentious Father of the primal horde, an image of the super-ego that enveloped Schreber in His desire. From that moment on, he was plunged into absolute jouissance. This living and omnipotent God, absolute Other, this partner in words and in jouissance became for Schreber *the* Presence. As God is the only Other that counts, we may say that they formed a couple, a couple that mimed the mother-child couple in the phase of primitive identification (when the child is identified with the mother's phallus and is subjugated to the senseless law of this omnipotent Other). Schreber's God, identified with the sun, was a whore[53] who clearly showed that the Other belongs to the female sex. This position is, structurally speaking, untenable, which is why Schreber was compelled to contemplate another solution. In Lacan's words,

Schreber, "incapable as he is of being the phallus that the mother lacks, he is left with the solution of being the woman that men lack."[54] But this homosexual solution is unfeasible, as the voices recalling his virility show. Therefore, the only solution was to be God's wife and thus to mend the flaw that, in Schreber's words, "arose because the Order of the World itself was out of joint."[55]

Notes

1.   *Jouissance* is rendered in French, following the suggestion of John P. Muller and William J. Richardson in *Lacan and Language: A Reader's Guide to Ecrits.* (New York: International Universities Press, 1982); this is because *jouissance* implies pleasure and extreme ecstasy, joy and sexual release, as well as the enjoyment of the rights of property in the legal sense, a range of meanings which no English word covers. (Translator's note.)

2.   Freud. *Group Psychology and the Analysis of the Ego. SE.*

3.   Jacques Lacan. *Les Psychoses: Le Seminaire, livre III.* (Paris: Seuil, 1981), p. 312.

4.   Lacan. "D'un discours qui ne serait pas du semblant." (Unpublished seminar, 1970–1971; lesson of June 16, 1971).

5.   Lacan. "Fonctions de la psychanalyse en criminologie." *Ecrits.* (Paris: Seuil, 1966), p. 136.

6.   Freud. "Neurosis and Psychosis." *SE,* 19.

7.   Lacan. "Function and Field of Language in Psychoanalysis." *Ecrits.* (London: Tavistock, 1977), p. 68.

8.   Lacan. *Les Psychoses. . . ,* op. cit., p. 230.

9.   Daniel Paul Schreber. *Memoirs of My Nervous Illness.* (London: Dawson and Sons, 1955), p. 50.

10.   *Ibid.,* p. 141.

11.   *Ibid.,* p. 72.

12.   Lacan. *Les Psychoses. . . ,* op. cit., p. 123.

13.   Schreber, op. cit., p. 124.

14.   *Ibid.,* p. 124.

15.   *Ibid.,* p. 124.

16.   *Ibid.,* p. 125.

17.   *Ibid.,* p. 126.

18.   Freud finds the source of this comparison in mythology, and believes the sun to be a father figure.

19.   Schreber, *op. cit.,* p. 126.

20.   *Ibid.,* p. 120.

21. *Ibid.*, p. 122.
22. Lacan, *Les Psychoses.* . . , *op. cit.*, p. 312.
23. Schreber, op. cit., p. 128.
24. *Ibid.*, p. 151.
25. *Ibid.*, p. 151.
26. *Ibid.*, p. 151.
27. *Ibid.*, p. 164.
28. *Ibid.*, p. 169.
29. *Ibid.*, p. 172.
30. Lacan, *op. cit.*, p. 284.
31. Schreber, *op. cit.*, p. 172.
32. *Ibid.*, p. 173.
33. *Ibid.*, p. 174.
34. *Ibid.*, p. 198.
35. *Ibid.*, p. 175.
36. Lacan, *op. cit.*, p. 289.
37. Freud. *The Origins of Psychoanalysis. SE*, 1.
38. Schreber, *op. cit.*, p. 148.
39. *Ibid.*, p. 150.
40. *Ibid.*, p. 206.
41. *Ibid.*, p. 208.
42. *Ibid.*, p. 51.
43. *Ibid.*, p. 208.
44. *Ibid.*, p. 275.
45. *Ibid.*, p. 209 (in French in the German original.)
46. *Ibid.*, p. 209.
47. Jacques-Alain Miller. Seminar of May 19, 1982, Collège de la Formation Permanante du Champ Freudian.
48. Schreber, op. cit., p. 210.
49. *Ibid.*, p. 212.
50. *Ibid.*, p. 215.
51. *Ibid.*, p. 197.
52. *Ibid.*, p. 288.
53. *Ibid.*, p. 77.
54. Lacan. "On a Question Preliminary to Any Possible Treatment of Psychosis." *Ecrits, op. cit.*, p. 207.
55. Schreber, *op. cit.*, p. 184.

Octave Mannoni

3. Writing and Madness: *Schreber als Schreiber* (Schreber as Writer)

> . . . the only theater of our mind,
> prototype for all the rest . . .
>
> —*Mallarmé*

We cannot dispense with Schreber's *Memoirs*[1] by invoking the fact that it was undoubtedly written by a madman. Indeed, while this would not be the only book to find itself in this situation, what most mars the *Memoirs* is not so much its delusional content (this exists elsewhere in literature) as the element of reason it contains. It was written with a view towards explanation and justification, an intention we might well find questionable. But the author is careful to inform us that he intends to furnish others with all the clarifications necessary to spare them, as far as possible, too much shock or indignation at his behavior. Schreber thus grants his family, friends, and unknown readers something resembling what Rimbaud (quite wisely) refused his mother when, upon the publication of *A Season in Hell,* she demanded clarification. Had he followed Rimbaud's example, would Schreber, madman that he was, have been capable of leaving us an account of the many seasons in the hells of his psychosis, such that he might place himself (if even on the lowest rung) in that quite accommodating domain of literature? Probably not, but the question strikes us as interesting because we do not really know why it seems to call for a negative response.

In any case, what excludes Schreber from the domain of literature is not his subject-matter, fantastic as it may be. Nor can he be said to lack talent. And yet, though he tried, with the greatest sincerity, courage and regard for his readers, to give us an account of his case and of those unexpected events beyond his comprehension, his efforts resulted in his work being appropriated by the psychiatrists charged to submit reports. Dr. Weber, whom the judges from the *Landesgericht* in Dresden assigned the task of explaining Schreber's insanity, made no secret of the fact that the reading of the *Memoirs* manuscript had

43

greatly facilitated his work. It is therefore not surprising that these *Memoirs* were quick to find a place in psychiatric libraries; and if they ran the risk of figuring only as a clinical document, this is perhaps simply a reflection on the patient/psychiatrist relationship. For, after all (as Freud let it be known), this very text, with but a few modifications, could very well have been a remarkable account written by a doctor.

Thus if it is not entirely proper to speak of Schreber as one speaks of other writers, this is not due to the simple fact that he was insane and deluded. So many great writers—Cervantes, Flaubert, Gogol, Sartre, among others—wrote or tried to write, or dreamed of writing an account of a mad existence, or the *Memoirs of a Madman,* that one wonders why someone like Schreber would not have been credited with having realized some unhoped-for exploit. Perhaps it is simply that he had so such ambition; that he was in no way a writer, and that this had nothing to do with the fact that he was mad. On the other hand, it may be that madness had something to do with the fact that Schreber turned, even slightly and despite himself, toward literature. In any case, he wrote.

Around the time that Defoe had published *Robinson Crusoe,* a sailor in a London tavern was dictating the account of his own adventures as a castaway. He had spent fifteen years on an island that, although not deserted, was still unexplored—among savage peoples of whom no one in Europe had even the slightest inkling. His name was Robert Drury, and, once published, the account of his adventures had a fair measure of success with a curious public. But the account left a good deal of skeptics among those readers who attributed it to Defoe, and who only regarded it as a work of the imagination. (By way of compensation, many readers had taken the adventures of Robinson Crusoe as true). By the nineteenth century it would be discovered that, by way of his citing tribal names, customs and geographical data, Drury had told the truth—down to the last detail. This truthfulness, of course, would scarcely increase the literary interest of his work. On the contrary. Still, if we could have believed that Defoe was its author, that he had imitated the crude style of an illiterate sailor, invented an island and a people of strange customs, then the book, exactly as it is, might well have occupied a place—albeit a minor one—in the heart of what we call literature. All the same, this thought is a bit discomforting when scrutinized too closely. I do not want to take a poetic metaphor that would have us compare insanity to an unexplored island too literally, much less an island described to us (uniquely and unverifiably) by a few unfortunate castaways. I simply want to claim that the memoirs of madmen constitute a literary genre, like the accounts of voyages, and that the reasons for which Schreber's *Denkwürdigkeiten* are not accepted as literature—better reasons than those which exclude Drury's account—would make valuable subjects for analysis. They would allow us to sketch in a part of the ill-defined frontier that delimits literature properly speaking. For it is not possible to maintain, against all likelihood, that on this issue the frontier is the same one as separates reason from madness.

We must therefore reject a simplistic and destructive interpretation, one which would nullify everything Schreber wrote by invoking the incontestable fact of his mental illness. Such a procedure, though (as extreme as it may be), would be but a particular case of those interpretations which allow the reader, or critic, to resist any reading of the text. It would be to resist Baudelaire by counting the number of times he uses the conjunction "as"; to resist Joyce by comparing his text to the *Odyssey,* or Kafka, by referring back to the *Torah.*

We have already seen how the castaway Drury's *Journal*[2] met with a fate similar to that of the *Memoirs.* It has left the domain of works of the imagination, and is of interest only to a very few specialists of Sakalava tribal history. The account given by the paranoiac Schreber, which has never been taken for a "work of the imagination"—although it *appears* that nothing could be more imaginary—has, since its appearance in 1903, been of extreme interest to psychiatrists and, following Freud's article in 1911, to psychoanalysts. The document has served as an exemplary case and its delusional content has provided the basis for a number of attempts at formulating a theory of paranoiac psychoses. It is not my goal to add to these efforts, and I would like to avoid, so far as Schreber himself will permit it, taking on a psychiatric viewpoint. This is not so easy, because someone like Schreber quite naturally turns every reader, however ignorant they may be in these matters, into a psychiatrist.

The poem in the form of a puzzle that allows us to define the name of the author of the *Fifteen Joys of Marriage* is of no interest in itself. But since no one has of yet been able to find the right word, that is, the right name, it continues to interest the interpreters it defies. Does the same thing happen with Schreber's book, and is its only value that it poses the problem of paranoia? This does not seem to be the case, for in some way it must be acknowledge as having some intrinsic value. "This is something," says Lacan,

> as coherent as many philosophical systems, where we at once see a gentleman on the edge, given over to an excited dream-like trance *(bovarysme),* which he takes as the key to the universe. I do not think that Schreber's text is of any less value, and this also occurred to Freud at the moment he finished his own study: that basically Schreber had written some things that were remarkably striking. 'It resembles what I myself have written,' said Freud.[3]

At the very end of his article on Schreber, Freud even goes so far as to feel obliged to defend his own priority!

> . . . these and many other details of Schreber's delusional formation sound almost like endopsychic perceptions of the processes whose existence I have assumed in these pages as the basis of our explanation of paranoia. I can nevertheless call a friend and fellow-specialist[5] to witness that I had developed my theory of paranoia before I came to be acquainted with the contents of Schreber's book. It remains for the future to decide whether there is more delusion in my theory than I should like

to admit, or whether there is more truth in Schreber's delusion than other people are as yet prepared to believe. Though the question is no longer formulated in this fashion, we might well admit—although confusedly, when considering what actually occurs in analysis—that there is indeed a subtle link between the delusion of knowledge and the knowledge of delusion.[4]

We will see that it is not so easy to define Schreber's relation to the spoken word *(parole);* this is the very crux of the problem he poses. Yet it is clear that his relation to writing is very different: in writing and in publishing his book, he transforms the problem in a decisive way. In substituting and super-imposing the subject's relation with his insanity for the author's relation with his book, he benefits, as all authors commonly do, from a new standpoint. The benefit is, that when Schreber (and this would not be the same for a deviant) reasonably reports (almost as if he were someone else, i.e., "objectively") the kind of discourse in which he figures as the subject, he gets lost in that discourse—and thereby loses himself as subject. Objectively, then, Schreber's relation to his book is no longer delusional. He assumes his responsibilities as author, and clearly sees the risk (which Dr. Weber assures us was very real) of being sued by Flechsig for defamation of character, and willingly makes the editorial cuts he is advised to make. These cuts are of course a real loss for us; they probably contain some of the book's most important points. Yet this is not a reason to believe that his book was censored against his will. On the other hand, it is not surprising (although Weber is scandalized by it) that Schreber insists on publishing a work that will quite probably diminish him in the eyes of some, but also vindicate him by rectifying misinformed views about him. This would be done not by his describing himself in a more favorable light, but by presenting himself as the author of an important work.

However, he only assumes this work at the cost of repudiating parts of that material he recorded as an author and yet rejects as a subject—material he declares both shocking and absurd. For example, the foul terms that figure in the text (like *shit* and *fuck*), which he only records out of honesty, cannot really be his. Everyone who knows him is aware that this sort of vulgarity is completely foreign to his nature, and that he has always expressed himself with the utmost decorum. Rather, "the Voices" utter these absurdities and obscenities. In this regard our author is not so different from many others (deviants aside). If a contemporary novelist does not apologize for relating narratives or characters of which he himself does not approve and does not use assorted footnotes, as Stendahl, Baudelaire, and others did (or note in the middle of the page as Moliere did: "It is a scoundrel who is speaking," without at all fooling critics, who would respond: "Scoundrel yourself!"), this is because it has become a literary convention and is no longer necessary. In any case, there is no doubt that, in making himself a writer, Schreber—without altering his mental state— found a proven method for making this state a little more liveable. Between the time he howled violently at the sun in the corridors of Sonnenstein and otherwise raged like a madman (disturbing the other patients) all in order to quiet the "Nerves," and the moment he recounts it in writing, there is quite likely what could be called a space of "therapeutic time," as well as the distance between the illness and its memory. But this is not quite exact, since he assured us himself, in what he wrote for the court after having finished his book, that he was still subject to these involuntary fits of screaming. Even if we note his improved condition, there is yet another more important distance to consider, that between the authorial position and the subject, the immediate and unprotected position of speech.

Prior to having read Schreber, Freud was interested in the obsessional neurotic's discourse. Here such alienation is far less apparent because it is more subtle or, rather, better hidden. Like Schreber, "Rat Man" heard words that he could not recognize as his own, and which, in certain cases, he sought to impute to supernatural powers, for example, to the "Evil Spirit." Freud did not hesitate to categorize this form of speech as "delusional," even if the obsessional neurotic's delusions cannot be confused with those of the psychotic. Before hearing his "hallucinatory" words, Schreber had experiences quite similar to those of the obsessional neurotic. One morning, while still half asleep, the idea suddenly came to him that it would be rather pleasant "to be a woman succumbing to intercourse." This thought, which was obviously central to his madness, and which seemingly was already latent in his earlier hypochondria, was one that he could not, once fully awake, recognize as his own. He rejected it with great indignation as completely inconsistent with his patent virility. But he could not forget it and in self-defense he would hypothesize, like "Rat Man," that, since he himself could not think such things, it must be that some external (read: "super-natural") force was at work to "implant the idea in him." This "delusional" interpretation—in the same sense that "Rat Man's" obsessions were delusional—solved nothing. Rather, it confirmed the fantasy itself by showing us Schreber being impregnated by an external idea. It is true that we do not know the precise date of this hypothesis, whether it followed the emergence of the idea, or constituted itself in the course of his madness—or even at the moment when Schreber was writing. What is certain, though, is that the entire evolution of a ten-year madness consisted in a laborious effort to accept that this idea—being a woman submitting to intercourse and bearing new beings—could conform to a "world order."[6] That is to say, that Schreber could *subscribe* to it, yet without being able to recognize it as his own.

The obsessional neurotic, who falls prey to similar torments, makes use of certain protective means, particularly "secondary defenses." It is only when certain haunting ideas pierce these defenses that he takes shelter in the "Evil Spirit" hypothesis. The rest of the time, his ideas come to him in the form of a "dialect" which he is incapable of interpreting without the help of an analyst. It might be said that Schreber tried a similar defense by forging a "basic language" through which "the Voices" could express themselves. This, however, met with little success since this basic language, unlike the obsessional dialect, posed no problem for him. It is Schreber himself, if we recall, who interprets it for us, or rather he would interpret it, if there actually were intelligible discourses in a basic language, which, as we will see, is doubtful. He states that "at other times" he heard long discourses in a particularly solemn and noble style, and that today he only hears what would be their shabby, deteriorated residue. We know how suspect such remembrances are—especially in paranoiacs. In any case, the basic language could not provide the protection that the "dialect" gives to the obsessional neurotic. Schreber's only recourse was to become indignant, to protest vehemently in the name of his reason and dignity, to fight with all his resources including the howling which screened out "the Voices." It would be rash to conclude from this that his situation was theoretically less complex than that of the obsessional neurotic; that the Voices would directly reveal his unconscious, as if it were strikingly revealed when it occurred to him that it would be rather pleasant to be a woman. The context of the Voices involves a complex elaboration that I do not propose to try and work out here.

When, at one point during the analysis of Rat Man, Freud encountered the difficulty of trying to make him appropriate his own speech, he took recourse, as we know, to the notion of "lèse-majesté." He evoked, and even subtly invoked, the Austrian law used to punish this crime. According to this law, treasonable utterances are in themselves criminal and punishable as such, no matter what the feelings or intentions of the speaker might be, even if he merely criticizes or denounces them. Thus the obsessional neurotic was forced to abandon the indirect style which sheltered him—"I cannot rid myself of the thought that . . ." or "I would really like to know where this thought comes from that is so foreign to me . . ."—for there is a domain where such defenses are useless. This is the domain of the *sacred,* as he well knows. Sacrilegious speech is already guilty, and he who utters it finds no safety in conscious innocence. Thus sacred speech creates difficulties for the obsessional neurotic. If we have here, as I believe, a possible point of departure for an analysis of the sacred, it is Freud who first drew our attention to it, but only in passing. Since then it has barely been touched upon. Less surprising, Schreber is obliged to blame God himself, and he assumes the heroic task of demonstrating to God that the speech ("Nerve-language": *Nervensprache*) they (the "they" referring mainly to Flechsig, according to Schreber) wanted to impose on him, is unacceptable. A language which claims to bear the absolute and final truth is unacceptable for someone who is alive and in full possession of his intellectual powers. I will return to these issues. I would for the moment simply like to show that this absolute speech, which is to some extent like that of the hypnotist, this textual speech of faith (but not of belief) must indeed exist somewhere, as if in the prehistory or sub-soil of all language, and that we avoid using it in normal states (when we are "alive," as Schreber says). And that sacred and sacrilegious speech are actually one, as everything else shows us, right down to the muttering of curses.[7]

It is in this general context that we must try to understand the existence of a basic language, which, moreover, is far more postulated than actually present in Schreber's writings. It is the language through which the sacred word is uttered, that is, supposedly sacred, since Schreber contests this status.

There is no bond between Schreber's speech and his ego other than that by which he can subscribe to his own discourse; and this holds true whether he is rational or mad, or whether the speech is in the basic language or the vernacular. Schreber tells us, for example, that there arises in him continually, or at least when he is not distracted, a low murmuring that "means nothing", and in which he has no interest, but cannot always avoid. Moreover, he gives us no idea as to what it might be saying. Purely aggravating, it has nothing at all to do with the discourse of "the Voices." Birds also speak to him in much the same way, uttering ridiculous things that can only be despised. But "the Voices" that allegedly express themselves in a basic language, that oppress him, criticize him, threaten him, and which, in the name of tranquility and honor, he might fight unceasingly, they, too, say nothing. They *take the words out of his mouth,* like characters in the margins of a manuscript which a playwright is in the process of writing; they open the quotation marks, or even function as the QUOTE and UNQUOTE in a telegram, and Schreber makes no secret of the fact that he provides the text that they dissimulate and imply and that he feels he can rightly attribute to them. And he cites this text as pronounced in a basic language, but not by the Voices, who have said nothing of the kind! At the same time, we understand one aspect—perhaps the essential aspect—of his drama: whatever the Voices are, they do not want to listen; they are absurd and sacred, and, in the final analysis, he can only oppose them with blasphemous denials. We can understand these denials not only as a refusal of castration, but also and above all as a desperate effort to preserve his status as subject.

Schreber creates a very interesting literary effect when, without appearing to lie, he succeeds in giving us the impression that his book resounds with lesser and greater voices; for, in fact, it contains almost nothing of the kind. We only find about a dozen words of the basic language and a few empty statements like "Now I Shall" in the *Memoirs.* Once the Voices have, by way of such "cues," invited or authorized Schreber to speak the basic language, he can fill in what is missing, taking care to explain that the Voices have abstained. The "indirect style" of the obsessional neurotic comes strongly into play here; but the psychiatrists' explanation concerning its role, given that we have passed here beyond the range of obsessional speech to hallucination, seems to me far from definitive.

The discourse that the author of the *Memoirs* presents as his own is, naturally, the commentary on the alienated or sacred discourse. We can guess how this all began: he heard himself saying, in his inner voice that is not hallucinatory and to which, he tells us, it is better to pay no attention, that "it would be rather pleasant to be a woman . . .", and he immediately disowned it, yet without being able to forget it. How this statement became a sacred scandal which compelled him to construct a new cosmogony, a new theology, which would accommodate the new Schreber, and to become mother of a new human race, is the question to which all theories try to respond. But this is not the question I ask myself in wanting to see Schreber as a writer.

*   *   *

What interests me at this moment is this Daniel Paul Schreber who—like Jean-Jacques Rousseau, another paranoiac—presents himself with an open book in hand, and tells us: read and judge me. But Schreber the professional jurist (he was not called Daniel for nothing) knows that we can only obtain a verdict if we have judges and a case to present to them. In this regard, and in this regard only, is he less mad than Rousseau? He requests that a tribunal (in this case the *Landesgericht* of Dresden) nullify the decision that deprived him of his rights and had him institutionalized as a lunatic.

It should be noted here that he does not demand his release on the grounds that he is cured. And yet he is well aware of the fact that his condition has changed significantly. If he were still in the apocalyptic state of 1893, he certainly would not have been in any condition to either edit his *Memoirs* or prepare any kind of case for his release. At that time he spent his days, and sometimes his nights, in a padded cell—and this appears to have continued for three-and-a-half years. It was at times necessary to force-feed him, and he lapsed from an hysterically agitated state into a hallucinatory stupor. But his intellectual capacities, even though he was incapable of using them, remained intact, and he soon understood that he had to pull himself together in any way he could—a veritable Robinson Crusoe of insanity. For example, he carried with him a tin box in which, among other useful items, he kept a celestial chart that he studied during the day, so that at night he might know the time by consulting the stars (when they allowed him to open the wooden shutters of his cell). He assures us that he was able to tell the time with great accuracy in this way, and we have no reason to doubt him. (This, by the way, is another point that he, coincidentally, has in common with Rousseau, who could not be without his candle). Eventually he was able to take notes on scraps of paper that he kept in his tin box, and then to keep a journal of sorts. These documents are unfortunately lost, and this is probably due to the fact that, in editing his memoirs, he less used them than he reinterpreted them. In some passages of his memoirs he lets us see firsthand, so to speak, how reinterpretations came to him during the editing itself.

It seems that the idea of editing the memoirs came to him around the same time (ca. 1900) as that of addressing himself to the judges. When he officially petitioned for his release, the *Memoirs* became a part of the process. Dr. Weber took it upon himself to present them to the tribunal. In his eyes, they were a clinical document, annexed to his medical report. In the defendant's eyes, it was a justificatory piece, an aid to his appeal.

The tribunal *(Landesgericht)* was not the court *(Oberlandesgericht)* to which he had been named president, just before falling ill. The latter was something like a Supreme Court of the kingdom (Saxony), and we can believe that the judges of the more modest *Landesgericht* must have paid more attention to a prestigious and fallen colleague than to an ordinary defendant. That is clear, but it is also clear that they granted him no favors. What they did do for him—and this is considerable—was to insist on drafting a landmark judgment in which they placed, not for Schreber's personal benefit but in the cause of justice, the full rigor of juridical thought and a respect for the strictest legality. This was not Daniel's glib judgment in the Susanna affair. It was, in all respects, an invocation of the basic principles which guarantee individual rights. As an expert witness, Dr. Weber, director of the asylum at Sonnenstein, described in his report the psychiatric aspects of his patient's illness, while of course respecting the tribunal's competence, since only they could make the final decision. But it was Weber's duty to foresee the problems that his patient's release might entail. He noted that Schreber intended to publish his *Memoirs* (adding that, fortunately, no publisher was interested in them) and that it would certainly harm him if he succeeded, and that he might even attract lawsuits as a result. Moreover, he stated that Schreber, by his own admission, was subject to involuntary fits of howling that his neighbors could not tolerate. Finally, his wife could not put up with his insanity either, and thus his release would be the ruin of his marriage.

Schreber, for his part, did not minimize his *Nervous Illness* and all the inconveniences it would bring upon himself and those who would have to live with him. But he did distinguish it from his *religious convictions,* that is, his delusions. He knew perfectly well, he said, that because others did not suffer or benefit from the same nervous illness, they could not enter into contact with the *Nerves* of supernatural powers. And he had no intention whatsoever of trying to convince them of this, as he knew that would be impossible. He did not insist on the fact (which the judges could evidently see in the *Memoirs*) that only Professor Flechsig, who had access to the same supernatural powers due to his knowledge of neurology, could, if he really wanted to, testify to the truth of his convictions. And, finally, in a sentence which resounded with both the last residue of his insanity and his new-found wisdom, he stated: "I am like Jesus Christ, my kingdom is not of this world." In effect, far from renouncing his transformation into the mother of a new human race, he had postponed it for a number of centuries.

The actual publication of his *Memoirs* had no real ill-effect on him. As evidence, Schreber pointed to the fact that Dr. Weber paid him much more consideration after having read his manuscript.

Weber contested this. If he was giving Schreber more consideration, it was because his state had improved. That is beyond doubt, but we still have the impression that Schreber was being truthful. Besides, it is a badly posed question (it is too "medical") to wonder to what extent Schreber would have to be cured to be capable of writing, and to what extent writing has medical value. Schreber was perhaps justified, as were many—and maybe *all*—writers, including Dante, in securing something from his *Memoirs* that would certainly be different from, yet equivalent to, the *"onore"* (honor) that *"Lo bello stile"* (The good pen) grants. And this honor, this valorization, is certainly not without some "therapeutic" value. Weber would have been satisfied if his patient, who claimed that his kingdom was not of this world, had recognized that his was the world of hallucinations. It seemed as if this would be an easy final step to take. But Schreber, who had read Kraepelin with understandable interest, did not see in himself what Kraepelin described under the category of hallucinations, and was not disposed to have himself recognized as sane by admitting he was mad, according to Kraepelin. In the meantime, the court was demanding report after report from Weber, until he was talked out. In the final report, he firmly maintained his former position, but threw in a few encouraging words: after all, there are a good number of paranoiacs loose in this world. In addition, the patient had been released a number of times on his own recognizance and the asylum had received no complaints, at least not yet.

The court, after the usual consideration of facts, expert testimony, and appeals, as if passing judgment on the facts before addressing juridical questions, stated explicitly: "There is no doubt in the eyes of this court that the defendant is insane." (We know this from Schreber's scrupulous recording of this judgment in the appendix to his *Memoirs*). But this was quickly followed by the statement that a well-founded medical diagnosis is not in itself sufficient justification for the judicial decision to commit someone. The additional allegations were no more valid. A man could not be committed in order to protect him from libel suits. If his fits of howling upset his neighbors, this was a case of disturbing the peace that concerned the police. If his release might compromise his marital situation, his internment compromised it even more. There is an essay entitled "In What Circumstances Can a Person Considered Insane be Detained in an Asylum Against His Declared Will?" in Schreber's *Memoirs*. He apologizes for the lack of references: there were no law books in the asylum library. But the essay was perfectly well done and the judges could not but have been inspired by it.

Schreber was thus freed. He stayed at the asylum for a few months, so as to better prepare for his release. After his release, he lived a relatively normal life, up until 1907, when he had to be hospitalized again. He died four years later. His *Memoirs* quickly became impossible to find; the Schreber family bought all of them up to keep them out of circulation. After the remarkable judgment of 1902, the reader can appreciate the way in which the law, or at least the practices and attitudes of society in the face of these kinds of questions, have evolved. The exigencies of civil organization ultimately outdistanced those of the law.

Weber plays only a walk-on part among the *dramatis personae* of this tragedy. Professor Flechsig holds a more central place. In 1884, he treated Schreber for the first time at his psychiatric clinic at the University of Leipzig. At that time, Schreber complained of insomnia and was admitted as a hypochondriac. Hypochondria is undoubtedly a kind of insanity, but the alienated language is not there, and the patient obviously does not converse with his own organs. He has recourse to a third person, the doctor, that is, to a *dragoman* or official interpreter who understands the language of organs. In this regard his behavior does not differ from that of the ordinary medical patient, but the doctor will eventually realize that he is not one and will orient the treatment elsewhere. This was the case with Dr. S., who first tried to treat Schreber with bromides and finally brought him to see Flechsig. Schreber stayed with Flechsig for a little more than six months and left cured, satisfied and grateful. The professor had made an excellent impression on his patient, and Schreber's wife, who had regained her husband, was exceedingly grateful. And yet Schreber puts an entry in his book (the date of which we will ignore, since it is quite possibly a retrospective interpretation) stating that Flechsig did not seem to realize that he was dealing with someone of "high intelligence, uncommon perception, and with extremely acute powers of observation," a patient who was nobody's fool. His recovery would have been quicker had his true merit been realized. This remark is perhaps an effect of his extraordinary perception . . . but its effect is destroyed by the example he gives: The professor should have allowed him to operate, at least occasionally, the scale on which he weighed himself, a scale that was, by the way, of a special kind which he did not know how to operate. Here was a conflict of prestige, authority and knowledge. It is possible that Schreber only discovered this retrospectively—we do not know. In any case, the eminent jurist, respected by his peers, esteemed by his superiors, was up against an equally eminent neurologist, whose scientific competence was matched by a very sensitive administrative competence where his clinic was concerned. Running parallel to the above conflict was the one that always exists between a hypochondriac and his doctor. Could anyone have predicted that Schreber would encounter Flechsig again once he could boast of some new advantage? This was precisely what occurred ten years later when Schreber was named president of the Supreme Court. The fact that Schreber's father was a doctor certainly weighed heavily in this adventure. But it is primarily the fact that Flechsig was a neurologist that explains the form taken by the madness when, so to speak, hypochondria spread itself across the sky in the shape of the "Nerve-language" *(Nervensprache)*. We understand, upon reading it, that this language was at first the one in which he communicated with Flechsig's soul, even though—surprisingly, for Schreber—Flechsig was still alive (Schreber's father was deceased at the time). Soon enough, God would replace Flechsig. But this God is incapable of understanding the living, as his science pertains only to cadavers: Schreber did not need too much of that "uncommon penetration" to see that Flechsig's neurology, founded on autopsies, could not do much to help him with his particular problems. Indeed, although Flechsig remained a neurologist, he had, before becoming director of the clinic, taken a leave of absence to "learn psychiatry." At the clinic, he continued for the most part with his neurological research, which resulted in some important discoveries. If Freud does not explicitly state the connection between Flechsig's specialty and the content of Schreber's delusions, this is not because it escaped him, but rather because Flechsig was still alive in 1911 (He died in 1929). Of course, it was not Flechsig who rendered Schreber psychotic. But he gave him a theme for his delusions.

The promotion granted Schreber (it was the kind of promotion that one did not solicit) overwhelmed and surprised him. Such a nomination was unusual; it made him one of the highest judges in the kingdom and the superior of eminent magistrates who were for the most part older than he. There is general agreement that a relationship exists between his promotion and the relapse that immediately followed it. Schreber, naturally, saw the relapse as a result of overwork. It is more likely a question of the subtle means by which certain individuals "fail in the face of success." But even more subtly, we might wonder if, in a roundabout way, this success did not reawaken the status conflict with Flechsig; and, in the background, with his father the doctor.

In any case, when he returned to Flechsig in November of 1893, he was again suffering from insomnia. The same confrontation repeated itself. Flechsig exhibited a "remarkable elegance" by which Schreber was "profoundly affected." He made much of the great progress neurology had made, and pronounced himself quite capable, by means of new drugs (far superior to those the patient had benefited from ten years earlier) of inducing a "prolific" sleep in the patient (we are, obviously, unsure whether the term "prolific" is actually Flechsig's). What is certain is that if Schreber wanted to boast of his new promotion, Flechsig would have been the perfect person to go to, since advance in neurology had been no less extraordinary, at least in Flechsig's eyes. However, in these same eyes the promotion of his patient was not to be considered, since it did not modify the neurological problem of insomnia. This insomnia soon worsened, despite the new drugs.

The importance that must be attached to this confrontation (a confrontation that Flechsig, even if he had been less abrupt and dogmatic than is reputed, might not have avoided with a patient like Schreber) is not an empty supposition, and Schreber himself indicates this in a humorous, or in any case amusing, passage. He assures us that ". . . it was highly amusing to observe how both souls—Flechsig's and (as he calls it) von W's . . . mutually repelled one another, because of the professional arrogance of the one and the pride of nobility of the other." We learn later that von W. would take Schreber's side, and we have read before that the Schrebers "belonged to the highest nobility of heaven."

From his first days at the clinic, Schreber entered the acute phase of his "illness," with which we are the least familiar. It was truly apocalyptic: he witnessed the destruction of the world, the end of humanity that left nothing but fleeting images. He was personally tormented by "miracles:" he would lose his vital organs, such as his lungs and stomach; involuntary movements jerked his knee caps, closed his eyelids, kept him from eating, from relieving himself. The divine powers tormented him, certain that they could convince him to admit defeat, that is, make him recognize his own madness. They sought to hand him over, transformed into a woman, to the sexual abuses of Dr. Flechsig and his staff—all of this being ridiculous and contrary to "the Order of the World." Later on, our hero would endeavor to defend himself unfalteringly, howling the voices to silence, raging at the sun that paled in front of him. To feed himself he took his meals while playing the piano in a frenzied manner, and relieved himself in the same way, using a tub in place of a stool. He mentions a certain characteristic hallucination: Flechsig's soul was stuck in his belly, in the form of an indigestible ball, and he succeeded in vomiting it up. He thus presented a striking image of an hypochondriacal hallucination of pregnancy and paranoiac persecution, an hallucination that we can recognize even in hysteria. It seems that the body was the domain of his hallucination, where the traditional use of the term "hallucination," usually related to speech, is more questionable. This remark of course does not preclude our recognizing this hallucination in terms of the body being nothing but the *silent* effect of the signifier.

When Schreber finally realized that his transformation into a woman could conform to a world order, he adorned himself with feminine baubles so as to complacently observe the imaginary progress of this transformation in the mirror. As any good jurist would, he recorded the slight expense involved in the purchase of these cheap baubles with which he amused himself. For even if it was not illegal to partake privately in these innocent amusements, he could still be accused of extravagant spending, leading to financial ruin, which would have been grounds for institutionalization. In the end he reassured everyone, as we have seen, by postponing the culmination of this transformation: this inevitable transformation would take place only across centuries, and even in another world. If we strip these significant givens of their anecdotal content, a general direction for the source of his relief can be described briefly. The announcement made to Schreber in half-sleep concerning his future procreations had revolted him. Still, he had to accept it, while maintaining that he was not responsible for it. In another sense, he renounced it so as to live like everyone else, while retaining the idea that this would have to occur, in one way or another. We will see that these attempts to compromise are doubtless significant. It would be fascinating to imagine him there, in front of the mirror, like an actor making himself up before going on stage *(scène)* to play his role. It seems that this would be his route to salvation. But however close he seemed to being saved, he could not break through. For while this scenario *(scène)* is open to us, it was not to him.

*   *   *

It is tempting to try and explain the diversity and contradictions by viewing them as symptoms of a *split* personality. It is a medical concept (anatomical in origin) that if we succeed in inscribing the entire set of delusional symptoms within one zone, we would be left with another zone, free of these symptoms, which could be qualified as "sane." Yet we can only speak in this way under one condition: that we close our ears to what Schreber keeps telling us. He keeps telling us that it is we who are blocked by a barrier we cannot break, and that he is otherwise disposed to take the greatest care in dealing with us, since it is in the best interests of the "nervously ill" not to contradict the all-too healthy. We should not overlook what these remarks might teach us. If we are shocked at times that Schreber evidences so much logic and good sense (e.g., before his judges), it is because we do not pay attention to the obvious fact that this same good sense and logic are even found in the letter to professor Flechsig, which is itself perfectly mad. They are found everywhere, at every point in his madness, always avoiding what he calls silliness or absurdity, even in the Voices of divine origin. If we tend to see things otherwise, it is because when faced with psychotic thought *per se,* we generally have recourse to our neurotic defenses; we tend to translate it as obsessional thought, and treat the obsessional delusion as a secondary defense by which the psychotic person conserves his "reason" by isolating it. Thus we risk seeing a division in him that is really our own; but, in fact, he knows and says that it is ours. Schreber's other world is not located in the same place as that of "Rat Man," although the constitution of a separate *topos* might well be the goal of his efforts and compromises. If Freud linked religious practices to obsessional neurosis, this concerns the psychology of zealots *(dévots);* the same association does not apply to those theological intuitions or revelations which come to the prophets. Schreber obviously functions as a prophet. The prophecies of his revelation perhaps remain unrealized, but there is no other light to contradict the revelation.

When he tries to explain this in his book, he informs us of his ignorance at the same time that he boasts of his knowledge. "A really satisfactory solution would only be possible if one had such a complete insight into the nature of God which not even I have obtained, who have certainly gained deeper insight than all other human beings, because human capacity is limited." Nonetheless, he ventures a hypothesis which refers back to his conflict with Flechsig; all evil stems from the fact that God wrongly considers nerve-language, which is only made of vibrations, to be the actual language of human beings. In fact, this only holds true for the dead, or the sleeping. Thus Schreber devotes all his mad efforts to proving that he himself is alive and in full possession of his intellectual faculties.

The project of writing a book is precisely one of these efforts, and the book itself will constitute proof against God and Flechsig. Besides, he says, look at the effect the manuscript already had on Weber! But things are not quite that simple; for, as we have seen, he wants to prove that these "religious convictions" are true, but also that they are nothing to get upset about. He reminds one of the timid believer who affirms that Jesus died on the cross for his salvation, but who thinks it unreasonable to torture himself over this old story. At least that is the position toward which he seems to be heading, if he could—for recovery is there for him, and yet out of reach. It is the theological solution of the other world, Baudelaire's solution in terms of the absolute "truth" of poetry.[8] This is what normal people do when they keep their dreams and fantasies separate. But it is the opposite of Weber's solution (and Flechsig's) because what they call Schreber's "hallucinations" can only be phenomena of this world, for example, "neurological" or even "psychological" data. This must be the case if one adopts a scientific viewpoint of reality, which is implied as soon as one classifies Schreber as mentally ill. He certainly was ill, and he himself insisted on this viewpoint, but how? His attitude had a certain "scientific" content, without which it would have passed for mystical, poetic, or literary. But *Nervensprache* is the language of Flechsig's science! If Schreber tries hard, and not without some success, to show that the world is uninhabitable for a living person "in possession of all his intellectual capacities" (let us say, for the sane)—if the last word on reality can be articulated in *Nervensprache*—then the question for us becomes: what condemns Schreber to imprisonment in precisely this type of discourse? He revolts against the *Nervensprache,* but his protestations themselves are couched in a sort of *Nervensprache.* He lacks another language, perhaps that of imagination.

A philosopher might be shocked that Freud gave no place to the imagination in his "psychic apparatus." But what is disconcerting for classical psychology is that hallucination, related to desire, has a place at all in this apparatus. Imagination enters in only as hallucinations judged by virtue of the "reality principle;" for if the reality principle condemns hallucinatory productions, they are still not entirely cancelled. The reality principle must permit them, under certain circumstances—on condition that they be denied. It quarantines them, as it does with dreams, to "another scene" *(scène),* to use an expression that Freud borrows from the "sublime simplicity" of "old Fechner." One would search in vain, however, for this place within the psychic apparatus, it is outside the domain of the *Nervensprache,* and it is no longer part of the real world. It is as if an external world, a different space were to open up, comparable to that of a theatrical stage, a playground, or the surface of the literary work—all this in the end consisting of a certain use of language and the denial implicit in it. One could just as well say that the function of this other place was to escape the reality principle, rather than to conform to it. We might also suggest that asylums, like the one where Schreber was kept, are like "prosthetic" substitutes for this other place, when it is lacking, in that asylums materially and actually isolate what cannot be denied.

Freud tells us that the pleasure principle (the primary process) "demands" this *concession* or reserve (in the territorial sense) so that a certain indispensable amount of pleasure may be obtained. Thus in a short article (five pages) dated 1924 on the "loss of reality," Freud explains neurotic defenses by the fact that fantasy "attaches itself to one part of reality and gives it a special importance and a secret meaning that—not always correctly—we label symbolic." To this fantasy solution, he opposes the situation of the psychotic who has "lost reality." This obviously does not mean that the psychotic has lost contact with the objects of the material world or that he throws himself against trees or tries to pass through walls like "knights errant" driven by enchantresses. What gets lost is whatever agency *(instance)* may be capable of critiquing the originally given hallucination (which in Schreber's case is the *Nervensprache* itself), of constituting it elsewhere in fantasy, where it can freely be without being. This would amount to freeing itself as pure speech and making us both the fool who can say anything and the king for whom the words of his fool are of no "consequence." In this way, the king's fool is no fool, nor is the king. A simplistic theory that would reduce the *topoi* to only the material and the "psychic" reality, whatever the nature of the latter might be, would lead straight to an interpretation of "health" as pure adaptation. A third "place" must be created *symbolically,* in the Freudian sense of the word. Only language, carrier of negation and carried by negation, can supply that. The requirement of scientific positivity cannot be opposed to this chain of reasoning. Freud noted the relation between paranoia and rational systems, but we do not thereby obtain a *theory* of paranoia. The question to which such a theory would have to respond is the following: how is it that a subject like Schreber cannot free himself from a literal, absolute, sacred, and positively free discourse? When faced with this discourse, he cannot keep a distance that would accommodate fantasy instead of the fantastic.

That is not what I am looking for: I am interested in Schreber's discourse insofar as it takes the form of a book offered, as all books are, to whomever wants to read it. A reader can find far more imagination in this book than in others. It is understood that the reader may in fact dispose of defenses that Schreber himself lacked. But things are not so simple. Schreber does succeed in dislodging us from this position and he compels our appeal to a system of cruder defenses, from more banal to radical ones: from "This is simply not true" to "he's crazy."

To oppose imagination to reality—like Defoe to Drury—does not get us far. This opposition scarcely alters our position as readers. Schreber, the madman, unsettles it in a way that would be interesting to elucidate, if it is true that he ends up turning us into psychiatrists despite ourselves. But this transformation is not so unique: it is present in certain critical attitudes that aim to interpreting non-delusional literary works, and not just in the name of psychiatry and psychoanalysis. Besides, with regard to Schreber, the question must not be simplified: he was not closed to literature of the "imagination." He accurately cites literary works that he was able to read just as we would; it is only in a certain domain connected with his madness that his attitude is different. In this domain, where he argues with "the soul of Professor Flechsig" and with the *Nervensprache,* there is no more room for fantasy. Indeed, it is quite difficult for us, his readers, to state why the *fantastic* could not compensate for fantasy.

The writers of picaresque novels (like Defoe, but like Drury, too!) transported us to another place in the real world, or another time in history; and thus set up the other stage *(scène)* by naively realistic means that can move in just the opposite direction of what we call realism in literature. Cervantes, in wandering with Don Quixote across Spain, is more successful in revealing to us the nature of the other stage and the role of fantasy in literary creation: an enterprise of clarification and purification. This might have only given us a narrative of picaresque adventures, but by introducing insanity itself, Cervantes redoubled in an extraordinary way the interest of the reader in this other place. We might even wonder if he did not thus discover something essential and obscure in the nature of the literary work, even when insanity is not named. And while musing on Don Quixote, we can well imagine that if Schreber's book evicts us from our position as readers, adventures similar to his written by a "writer" would quickly put us back there.

It is not enough that the writer be the competent and lucid director *(machiniste)* of this other stage. The latter is reserved for the play of the pleasure principle and for that of the primary process, and this play is the same whether it applies to the spoken word (which inclines it toward poetry) or to fantasy (which favors fiction). The writer, however, cannot use the relationship between what he says and reality (as Schreber did—wrongly, but how could he have not!) as a criterion, even if it is purely scientific. That is the position that Flechsig holds, and in speaking of others, not of himself.

Notes

1. Daniel Paul Schreber, *Memoirs of My Nervous Illness* (London: Wm. Dawson & Sons, 1955).

2. Robert Drury, *Madagascar or Robert Drury's Journal During Fifteen Years on That Island* (1729).

3. Jacques Lacan, *Seminaire de Sainte-Anne,* December 7, 1955.

4. Sigmund Freud, "Psychoanalytic Notes Upon an Autobiographical Account of Paranoia *(Dementia Paranoïdes),*" in *Collected papers,* Volume 3 (New York: Basic Books, 1959) pp. 465–466.

5. Might this be Ferenczi or Fliess?

6. As I do not feel compelled to follow a chronological order, I will give dates so that the reader can follow along:

In December 1884, Daniel Paul Schreber (42), then presiding judge of a *Landesgericht,* enters the clinic of Professor Flechsig, in Leipzig. He is diagnosed at this time as having hypochondria.

In June, 1885, he is released cured and satisfied.

In October, 1893, he takes the position of Senatspräsident of the Saxon Supreme Court.

In a half-sleep, the idea comes to him that "it would be rather pleasant to be a woman submitting to intercourse." He suffers from a new episode of insomnia (hypochondria).

In November, 1893, he is readmitted to Professor Flechsig's clinic as a hypochondriac. He falls into a state of extreme anxiety and of "hallucinatory stupor," becoming delusional.

In June, 1894, he is transferred and officially admitted to the Sonnenstein Asylum (Dr. Weber) near Dresden.

In July, 1902, he is freed by the lower court of Dresden. He leaves the hospital in December. He publishes his *Memoirs* in 1903. In November, 1907, he is hospitalized again. He dies in 1911.

7. We might say that in the progress of each individual (as perhaps in that of humanity) *sacred speech* disintegrates in stages, first in the faith of myth, then in the myth of fiction.

8. "Poetry is what is most *real.* It is what is only completely *true* in another world." One could not better choose the adjectives underlined here.

Jean-François Rabain

4. Figures of Delusion

Dismembering the Figure

"In what part of the body does language originate?" asks Bernard Noël, in a text devoted to Hans Bellmer.[1] Isn't this also the essential question of psychoanalysis with regard to dreams, language and art works?

To oppose the surface of the visible world—body or drawing, dream or painting—to language, which is the very depth of the world, would only have descriptive value, similar to that of Freud's opposition of the manifest dream content and the latent thoughts in the *Traumgedanke*. The analyst is particularly interested in transformations, in the work upon forms which, from body to speech and from word to image, contain precise conceptual references. The model of the dream, of the *Traumarbeit*, of the dreamwork, remain for the analyst the paradigm for these processes of transposition: condensation, displacement and especially the dreams' peculiar aptitude for figuration. The *Rücksicht auf Darstellbarkeit* is a constraint upon the form which—within the dream's regradient trajectory wherein words are transformed into images and discourse into figures—organizes the skillful disorder of permutations where both the body and art are always present.

"Like dreams, the body can capriciously displace the center of gravity of its images,"[2] answers the painter to the poet who questions him. If for Freud the dream is a rebus, for Hans Bellmer the body is an anagram. "The body is comparable to a sentence which demands to be disarticulated so that its true contents can be recomposed through an endless series of anagrams." For Bellmer, in effect, *Leib* (the body) is reversed like a glove and becomes *Beil* (hatchet). Thus the language of the body is a sort of palindrome, sodomizing the verb, abolishing right and left, interior and exterior. The dream too ignores negation and does not admit contraries. Thus works can be broken into pieces, like the doll ("Poupée") of Bellmer's "Variations sur le montage d'une mineure articulée," and like the oneiric processes where the formal and topographic regression of the dream diverts its scattered members in search of new sonorous articulations. These members are linked to other verbal bodies by assonances, like in poetry, to create new meaningful units.

Bellmer's *Anagrammes*, the *Hexertexte*, Unica Zürn's "sorceress' writings," as well as their pictorial counterparts, the engraved work and the *Vexierbild*, and also the hidden images of anamorphosis, all invite us to infinitely recompose the disorder induced by the play of primary instinctual processes within the intellectual order.

Freud also postulates a language of the body, a vigorous, primitive language rooted in corporeal and sexual significance, thus invoking a "concrete" origin of language. He describes this language in terms of dream symbolism, in the natural monumental, or cultural figurations of the maternal body, and in his fascination with archaic languages and primal non-contradictory enunciations, as mythical as those of K. Abel and Daniel Paul Schreber.

Lacan wrote that, "Words are captured incorporeal images." Aren't these images in effect the first figures? Besides, doesn't the figural ability, the *Rücksicht*, cross the intermediary stage of rhetoric before the dream's regression and the transformation into images, before the transposition of words into their definitive visual form?

Isn't figural language—the language of the body and gestures—first of all figures of style, tropes, which Nietzsche understood as "the essence of language?" Hence, in the dream of the Wagnerian opera in the *Traumdeutung,* isn't the aristocrat who is seen by the dreamer on top of a tower placed in such a high place only because he is already a very "highly placed" person? Here Freud concurs with Rousseau in the *Essai sur l'origine des langues:*

> As the passions were the first topics about which people spoke, the first expressions were tropes. Figural language was first born, while the proper meaning was the last. At first, people spoke only in poetry, and learned to reason only long afterwards.

Freud insists upon this initial figural work which preceeds the definitive visual formation. "The abstract and bland expression of the dream thoughts must leave place for a pictoral expression." Thus the dreamwork first acts upon words, before translating them into images, even if for Freud the essence of the dream is the transposition of the verbal story into dream thoughts—"thoughts formulated in words"—within a specifically pictorial figuration. The dream is first of all pictographic writing, a *Bilderschrift,* organized like a rebus. In this familiar form it is only an ideogram which brings us back to the double organization—phonetic and figurative—of writing.

For Freud the rebus is not simply analogical of the passage from a hidden text to a manifest one. Rather, it offers a precise example of the possible variations of a new verbal partition of the sonorous structure. Thus the work of dream on the homophony and assonance of words is the same as that of poetic invention and wit. The dreamer who is embraced by his uncle in an automobile interprets it as "Auto-eroticism." In the course of an analysis conducted in French, one of Freud's patients declares, "Vous me trompez!" as Freud appears in a dream in the form of an elephant. Doesn't the interest of these humorous passages lie in the symbolic enrichment of language caused by the oneiric regression, where figural language, the language of figures, is equally discovered?

Schreber himself made God speak in tropes. The basic language was composed of euphemisms which, in the *Memoirs,* are less a form of attenuation to avoid the unpronounceable taboo word than a play of antonyms ("recompense" for "punishment," "impious" for "saint," etc.). Schreber describes the oxymoron with the same care as Fontanier when he evokes his relation with God. As the creative principle, God is placed in contradiction with himself in wishing to destroy Schreber's corporeal and spiritual integrity, so that in the struggle between God and Schreber, God was on Schreber's side. This expresses "the rhetorical figure of the oxymoron," characterized by the relationship between two antonyms (e.g., chiaroscuro). Besides, didn't Schreber, "in consumating coitus with himself," desire precisely the sexual, androgynous figure of the oxymoron?

The work of the figure is here, like in dreams, in the service of censorship. Schreber uses the language of tropes so as to repress resexualized instinctual representations. Euphemism, antithesis, allusion and antiphrasis in the basic language all serve to hide the psychical processes of denial and repression. Euphemism—like *blasphemy* which extends its semic efficacy by mutilating the unpronounceable name of God—is equally a system to diminish the effects of the taboo expression. Like negation, it is also an *Aufhebung* of repression. Schreber uses euphemism to counter-cathect the formidable aggression which he feels vis-à-vis his parental imagos.

On the other hand, the oxymoron evokes even more so the regression of the dream towards primary processes and non-contradiction, since it implies the annihilation of a meaning at the very core of the figure. The oxymoron evokes the amalgamating processes of projective psychotic identification, more than it entails an ordering of negation. Besides, the basic language is essentially free from all contradictory inferences, since it is characterized by its Saxon roots untainted by any foreign tongue.

With regard to the syntax peculiar to paranoia (I love him, I don't love him, I hate him), we know that, not only does it express the denial rendered by the second negative formula, but that it also stresses the affirmation of hatred. This occurs in a movement where we can read the failure of the repression and the psychotic break, evident in paranoia by the projection and the turning back upon oneself of the "he hates me."

The Schreberian rhetoric of the *Grundsprache* seems therefore to organize the contradiction at the very heart of language by utilizing tropes to maintain the separation between words and things. This is different from the schizophrenic process, and thus is part of the process of symbolization which allows President Schreber to find a temporary respite from his madness and to write his famous *Memoirs*. But this rhetoric also provides a system for the doubling and redoubling of antithesis, antiphrasis or oxymorons, where the reversibility of the primary processes operates unaware of negation. If the oxymoron can bring about the annihilation of a meaning at the very core of the figure, if God is on Schreber's side, if the homophonic poem (Santiago/Carthago) empties the signifier of its value as a sign, then the word is brought to the point of hesitation between sense and non-sense, simultaneous with a semiotic enrichment.

The Rhetoric of the Basic Language

The function of the euphemism in the *Grundsprache,* at the very core of Schreber's madness, seems to surpass the simple notion of attenuation, conceived as an effort to master the destructive impulses toward certain objects. Certainly, in one respect, the basic language seems to organize the contradiction at the very heart of language, and thus participates in the processes of symbolization which permit the delusions to progress and find an outlet in the writing of the *Memoirs*. But, in another respect, the basic language—with its play of stylistic figures and tropes ranging from euphemism to antithesis to oxymoron—represents a syntax of paranoia where the libidinal processes are held within the play of language according to a specific rhetoric where annulment by doubling translates the reversibility of this process.

We know how Schreber defined the basic or ground language, a term which in French ("langue fondamentale") as in German evokes a double connotation of primalness and anality.

Souls learn the basic language, spoken by God, in the course of a process of purification which allows access to beatitude and fusion with God. This language is an ancient form of German, "elegant and simple," characterized by its Saxon roots, free from any Latin influence. Such purity of origin, such a myth of non-contamination by a foreign tongue, evokes the non-contradiction of primitive language, an idea dear to Freud. The expressions in the basic language were communicated to Schreber by voices and remained unknown to him, although they did bear scientific and medical connotations, referring to both

Flechsig and Daniel Gottlob Moritz Schreber. All of the expressions in quotation marks (of which there are about 250) in the *Memoirs* are in the basic language. We know that Freud, in his correspondence with Jung, wrote that he wanted to make serious use of the term 'basic language,' since he thought it was, "the very language and enunciation of madness."

Schreber specifies that this language is characterized by, "its great richness of euphemisms." We know that the euphemism is characterized by its function of attenuation (for example, "disappeared" for "dead," or "beatitude" for "orgasm.") But it is interesting to note that Schreber gives as examples of euphemisms words with opposite meanings, words which are thus rather antonyms (for example, "recompense" for "punishment," "impious" for "saint", and "examined souls" for "unexamined souls").

Schreber also has recourse to another type of trope, the oxymoron, when he tries to define his relationship with God (n. 35 *Memoirs*). In effect, God as the creative principle is placed in contradiction with Schreber insofar as he wishes to destroy his corporeal and spiritual integrity. Thus in the struggle between God and Schreber, God is himself on Schreber's side (expressed by "the figure of rhetoric that is the oxymoron.") The oxymoron is defined by the relationship between the two antonyms, and it is similar to an antithesis, which is the reconcilation of two antonyms (for example: "Why do I feel cold when I'm burning with desire?"). And we should also note that Schreber's belief that he was both man and woman, effecting coitus with himself, involves precisely the sexualized figure of the androgyne as an oxymoron.

Emile Benveniste, in his chapter on euphemism in *Problems in General Linguistics,* underscores that there exists "something singular and paradoxical" in the etymology of the very term "euphemism," which is traced to a doubly contradictory meaning: "to avoid words of ill omen" and, conversely, "to pronounce words of good omen."

Thus at the very heart of the notions of "speaking euphemistically" and "euphemism," we find the process which organizes and elaborates contradiction. Euphemism is a system whereby a dangerous expression may be attenuated; it is related to the psychic activity of repression which consists in substituting a word for the taboo word which must be avoided. In this respect, euphemism, like blasphemy, produces an attenuation of its semic efficacy by softening, mutilating or replacing the unspeakable name of God ("goodness gracious" for "good God," or "Judas Priest" for "Jesus Christ"). In *Totem and Taboo* Freud, citing Wundt, already described this process of euphemy in relation to archaic mythological forms. He noted, a propos the fear of contact with taboo objects, that "the primitive concordance which goes as far as the fusion of the sacred and impure," is a concordance much later separated into veneration and execration. "We observe in mythology an anterior phase which is surpassed and repressed by a posterior phase, yet which remains in an obliterated and diminished form." It is thus a euphemism, "such that objects of veneration are transformed into objects of execration."

Thus, each time the archaic looms up, we find once again the ambivalence regarding the taboo, the *pharmakon,* which Freud, following Abel, called the antithetical sense of primal words. But this ambivalence is not reversibility or annulation by doubling, and obsessional organization is not that of the oneiric processes which evade negation. Where then must we situate the basic language in this respect?

The syntax of the basic language—its organization into precise figures, euphemisms, antitheses, allusions and antiphrases—in effect dissimulates the psychic processes of negation, denial and transformation into the contrary. Thus the figures of Schreber's style describe what relates to the psychic processes of repression, denial, projection, transformation, projective identification and reversibility. In fact, in his text on "negation," Freud reminds us that, "An intellectual function can be born from the play of primary libidinal tendencies." The *verneinung,* by organizing the relations of Eros/assimilation and destruction/rejection, not only doesn't allow the patient cited in the abovementioned article to reject the idea that his problems stemmed from his mother, and thereby at least partially alleviate the repression, but it also blocks his access to the entirety of language. And by this, one assumes that Freud means, not just figures and tropes, if indeed all of language is constituted by repression.

"Doesn't one write to erase?" asks Bernard Noël, and doesn't language represent what is already no longer there?

On each page
a page is missing,
confined perhaps
under the words.

"Treize cases du JE"

Regarding paranoia, we should indicate that Freud's famous formulation (I love him, I don't love him, I hate him) does not merely express the denial rendered by the second formula. It also expresses the passage from affirmation to hatred, the passage where we can doubtlessly read the psychotic rupture initiated by the destructive drive separated from Eros. This rupture is specified in paranoia by the projection and turning back upon oneself of the "he hates me."

Some writers, such as Katan, have insisted on the fact that the role of euphemism for Schreber is to attenuate the extreme aggressivity vis-à-vis the father, which would be demonstrated by the obsolete and emphatic aspect of certain propositions in the basic language, such as when he defines God as "the High

Guardian of all that is and that will be," or as "Eternal Majesty," etc. Adding to this extreme deference, counter-cathecting this hostility, certain elements of the *Memoirs* contradict Schreber's claim that there is no punishment, no hell, in the afterworld. In point of fact, devils, auxiliaries, Satans and *Grundteufel* (such as Judas Iscariot) all appear during the process of purification or purgation of souls. Because of their color and their repugnant odor, these devils have obvious anal connotations. During this purification process the souls learn a pure language free from all contradictory influence.

Does this then bear solely on a process of dissimulation tied to the organization of repression in relation to denial, with the linguistic factor being decisive in this process, as Benveniste, following Freud, claims? It is commonly known that it was the failure of repression which thrust Schreber into his delusion, and what is manifest in the basic language is the language of persecution, the language of God which for Schreber resonates like an inverted hallucinatory double. "God's mass of nerves has nothing other to serenade than those of my thoughts falsified into their contrary," wrote Schreber.

The Schreberian rhetoric organizes a partition within language (that of God/ that of man) which corresponds to his fantastic anatomy, as well as to the anterior and posterior realms of God. This will lead Freud to claim that paranoia splits while hysteria condenses. The homophonic poem (Santiago/Carthago) corresponds to this mirror structure. But Schreber, regardless of what he says to the bird-souls, does not fall into the trap of homophony like a patient mentioned by Letarte who threw himself under the subway train at the "Vagin" (actually, "Vavin") Station, or like the patient who arrived at the hospital with his legs slashed by a razor, screaming, "Au diable l'avarice" ("to hell with avarice," "to hell with varicose."). These examples of schizophrenic patients underscore the power of words, where things are still bound to signs.

The euphemisms of the basic language allow the separation of words from things, and thus permit one to be silent about the unbearable. In this regard, Benveniste calls attention to the curious euphemistic origin of the French word, "tuer" (to kill), which originally signified to appease, to protect the fire *(ignem tutare)*. Isn't Schreber led to devise a basic language to struggle against the invasion of primary processes, to protect himself from the "fire" of the overpowering libidinal impulses that were destroying his reason? Isn't the basic language, in fact, like Schreber's bellowing or Artaud's glossolalia, equivalent to the irruption in language of what Kristeva calls the semiotic, which is "heterogeneous to meaning and signification," and which is opposed to the symbolic aspect of language and syntax.

Yet doesn't the play of opposites in the basic language imply a play of reversibility which evokes certain dream processes as well as those which Freud believed to have found in the structure of primitive languages? Benveniste certainly corrected Abel's error which Freud had repeated: there is no language, primitive as it may be, which does not organize contradiction by opposing distinctive unities. Schreber's basic language also obeys this function. As we have seen, euphemism is a process of dissimulation, tied to the repression of the impulses, causing a play of words beneath words. The basic language questions the value of the sign, its annulment, and its function of reversibility by allowing the free play of ambivalence and the transformation into the contrary.

When Saussure defined the law of binaries in the poetic function, he only established a linguistics of recurrence or of expressive redundancy, as Baudrillard notes.[3] But poetic language, as in the basic language, is not only repetition, not only accumulation like, "pour qui sont ces serpents qui sifflent sur vos têtes," but also, "the cancellation of terms two by two, an extermination by redoubling." As Saussure writes, "Vowels always couple quite exactly, and must always have a remainder of zero." ("Numero deus pari gaudet;" "God rejoices in even numbers," writes Schreber).

The basic language does not only indicate a repetitive process where the contrary would be the back of the front; rather, it suggests a process of annulment by doubling, by antigram, antithesis and antonym. As in poetry, it suggests not only the repetition of an identity, but also its destruction.

The basic language utilizes the distance between words and things to construct contradiction, while its euphemisms represent the veiled incantation of the forbidden, unpronounceable word—like the name of God, which is hidden and dispersed in the hypograms of Latin verse, and which is to be reconstituted by the reader. But above all the basic language plays upon a double reversibility. First, there is a reversibility of reading analogous to that of a palindrome, sodomizing the word, to be read indifferently from right or left. Then there is the absolute contradiction embedded in the very core of the word as in the oxymoron (e.g., "chiaroscuro"), which carries the annihilation of meaning to the interior of its figure. As Schreber says, "all nonsense is abolished."

The pure language, the basic language, is reflected within the mirages of its doubling; the signifier is reflected in its homophonic double; and the signified in its contradictory meaning. There would be nothing more for Schreber the writer to do than construct palindromes or anagrams: reversibility or dispersion. If the word returns to its opposite, if, like in dreams, there is no longer the possibility of distinctions, if God is really on Schreber's side, then doesn't the basic language express Daniel Paul's secret intention of destroying everything, including the value of the sign? Euphemism becomes blasphemy, exterminating the name of God.

Yet the basic language remains the language of a double, that of "a shadow which never stops asking if it is its absence or its contrary." The inversion of the message heard by Schreber in his hallucinations vividly evokes Lacan's formula which stresses that the subject receives his own message, though in inverted form, from the Other. "Psychosis is that exclusion of the Other which returns in the form of verbal hallucinations, hallucinations expressing the relation of the interior echo where the subject is in relation to his own discourse." (Seminar 1955–1956) Thus the basic language only restores to the Schreberian subject its split totality, revealing to us its style as the play of figures. Isn't this what gives the *Memoirs* their quality as a written work, which is to compel that 'other' within us to speak? Isn't writing or hallucinating for Schreber a means of living his own double, a means of making his hidden part, the other sex, speak?

Notes

1. Special issue of *Obliques,* "Hans Bellmer."
2. *Ibid.,* "Notes sur la Jointure à Boule."
3. Jean Baudrillard, *L'échange symbolique et la Mort* (Paris, Gallimard, 1976).

Allen S. Weiss

5. The Other as Muse: On the Ontology and Aesthetics of Narcissism

> They will set a house on fire, and it were but to roast their eggs.
>
> —*Francis Bacon*

I s freedom, as Daniel Paul Schreber insists in his *Memoirs of My Nervous Illness*, ultimately "freedom to think about nothing"? Or does the very order of the universe depend upon a "forced play of thought," thoughts which are always imposed from without? It would seem as if this compulsion to think—a libidinal necessity before being a semiological activity—is what binds the individual to communal systems of signification and exchange. Thought: what breaks the libidinal circuit of autoeroticism. Thinking of nothing: what breaks the hermeneutic circle of culturally imposed meaning. Signification is determined within this dialectic of the thought and unthought, where perhaps madness—the eruption of unthought thoughts, of the unconscious—is the only path to a truly universal rationality. In offering his *Memoirs* to the world, Daniel Paul Schreber presents a religious epiphany, a heretical apocalypse, where the theological drama of his paranoia is symbolically played out on his own body, through the greatest torments and the greatest joys. His paranoia, resulting in those "miracles" whereby his words, deeds and bodily functions were completely controlled by God, is precisely what allows him the most intimate, erotic contact with God. But it also engenders that megalomania which transforms him into a martyr, God's whore, and which allows him the offense of suggesting that "such a relation as that which I have with the divine rays would permit one to believe oneself capable of shitting on the entire world." It is precisely between this narcissistic scatology and this universalizing eschatology—between this body and these words—that we might situate our own predicament, our own humanity.

In the year 213 B.C. the Emperor of China, Shih Huang Ti, ordered "the burning of the books:" the destruction of all books dealing with history. This attempt to destroy the past was balanced by an equally grandiose attempt to protect the present: Shih Huang Ti was also the Emperor who completed the construction of the Great Wall.[1] He called himself The First Emperor, ordained that history begin with him, and claimed that he was God. This megalomaniacal attempt to control space and time and others, to create one's self and one's world, was effected to the least detail: Shih Huang Ti claimed that during his reign all things would bear their proper names. His passion was universalized as cosmos and logos, in the extreme world-historical manifestation of narcissism.[2] This is the ultimate limit of *ressentiment,* what Nietzsche has shown to be wrath and contempt against the irreversibility of time.

Jorge Luis Borges surmises that the Emperor Shih Huang Ti might have undertaken these two immense tasks, the burning of the books and the completion of the Great Wall, as a reaction against the immensity and uselessness of the past, and against the futility of worshipping the past. Perhaps, according to Borges, the Emperor thought: "Men love the past and neither I nor my executioners can do anything against that love, but some day there will be a man who feels as I do and he will efface my memory and be my shadow and my mirror and not know it." This supposition is a simulacrum of the manner in which our Shih Huang Ti was the shadow of that legendary first Emperor whose name he took, who presumedly invented writing and the compass, and whose name undoubtedly perished many times in the vast conflagration of the burning of the books. Borges was indeed correct in his assumption: among the earliest known Chinese statues are twelve bronze colossi which were erected by Shih Huang Ti—these statues were subsequently melted down by a Han ruler in order to make small coins. And yet, just as in the First Emperor's lifetime the attempt to obliterate the past by the burning of the books was counterbalanced by the attempt to preserve the present with the completion of the Great Wall, so too at a later date was the attempt to destroy the memory of the works of Shih Huang Ti by melting down the statues to make filthy lucre counterbalanced by the continuation of another act in his memory: we are told that for centuries people befouled his grave. Yet, even in the light of the immensity and perhaps greatness of his works, we should not reproach those who befouled his grave, since we should note what Freud wrote, in a letter to Karl Abraham, about excrement: "After all, these are productions just as well as thoughts and desires." We should not forget that the immediateness of expression, while dissimulated by the objectivity of the world-historical, is also its source.

In the beginning was the word.

—*The Divine Logos*

All nonsense is abolished.

—*Daniel Paul Schreber*

We are reminded, by Elias Canetti, that formerly in China,

> . . . when the emperor laughs the mandarins in attendance laugh too; when he stops laughing, they stop. When he is sad their faces fall. One would think that their faces were on springs which the emperor could touch and set in motion at his pleasure.
> This taking the king as model is universal. Sometimes it results only in admiration and veneration: nothing he does is unimportant or meaningless. But sometimes it goes further than this and people regard his every movement and utterance as a command: for him to sneeze means "Sneeze!"; for him to fall off his horse means "Fall off your horses!" He is so full of the force of command that everything he does must be an expression of it. Abandoning words, commands become actions again; in this case actions compelling imitation.[3]

We find that this imperative function of language obtains not only at the extreme limits of political power, where oedipal memory is instilled in language as proscription and imitation, just as it is instilled in the flesh as the pain of punishment. Such an imperative language operates at the very origins of speech, where for the infant the earliest "language" is not constative, but expressive and performative. The initial interjection of the cry, the scream, marks the epiphany of subjectivity within a world of pain, but soon serves as an imperative, a command. Babble as imitation marks the differentiation inherent in language, and constitutes the entry into systems. And the repetitions of echolalia mark the epiphany of intersubjectivity, the entry into ethics and the social. Yet these repetitions of echolalia do not repeat presence, but give it a foundation. Different places, different bodies, different words are a function of the loss of the mother, of her becoming invisible, and of the consequent attempts at a magical conjuring of her presence, an attempt at recovery. And yet this magic, this desire made word, this summons, is already ambivalent in its emotional force: it expresses the pain and anger of the loss, as well as the desire for the pleasure of presence. Thus the instauration of the world through the word, the differentiation of the self and the other, is marked by the differentiation of thanatos and eros. Such a world, soon to be ordered and categorized within the domain of Oedipus, is founded upon *ressentiment*. *Ressentiment* entails the entry into temporality; temporality is the separation of the invisible (mother) from the visible (self); and language supports the invisible, which prolongs my world into transcendence.

Yet the infant does not create itself, nor its world. Its language is already the language of the other, and it is impelled to speak, to repeat. Thus not only is the unconscious, still to be formed, "the discourse of the Other;" consciousness too is founded upon the repetition of the other's speech. The world that the infant "creates" is a world already created, and recreated, by (by) it; that self which the child discovers is a self which is, ". . . the advent of difference on the ground of resemblance . . ."[4] The paradigms of such echolalia are a function of power, of the parents' omnipotence, an omnipotence which is projected upon the infant and introjected as its own megalomania. The narcissism of the infant is the projected narcissism of the parents, and is thus already a function of oedipalization. (It should be noted, though, that, ironically, the parents are discovered to be omnipotent, because of their lack of omnipresence.)

We see this clearly in the infantile game of *fort/da*, as analyzed by Freud in *Beyond the Pleasure Principle*. The infant represents the mother's disappearance by making a spool disappear, accompanied by the enunciation "o-o-o-o" (*fort:* gone); then her reappearance is represented by making the spool reappear, accompanied by the enunciation *"da"* (here or there.) We find that the mimetic here serves two functions, and expresses the emotional ambivalence of these events. The reappearance (*"da"* is obviously pleasurable because it entails the return of the desired object, the mother. But the disappearance (*"fort"*) is also pleasurable, not only because it is a passive condition for her return, but even more so because it is an active response to her absence, because it is the infant's interpretation of her disappearance as one of its own acts, as a function of its own power, its own omnipotence, its casting off of the mother. It is the infant's attempt to create its origin by changing its own past. (Thus the mother is symbolically murdered before the oedipal murder of the father.) These acts simultaneously signify love and *ressentiment;* there is a victory and a loss; as Julia Kristeva explains, the entry into syntax is a victory over the mother as distancing, and yet this is a partial victory, since all naming is but a never completed replacement of the archaic mother.[5] If, as Kristeva claims, space causes laughter, it must be added that time causes anguish. Thus the infantile imperative is equally supplication.

The functions of echolalia, of mimesis, are twofold: there is the continuation of the performance function of language as a cry of distress, a call for aid; and there is the constative function within which the world is inaugurated as a scene of passion and action. Echolalia is productive and reproductive, an egocentric enunciation which simultaneously breaks out of narcissism, since this imitation is based upon the identification with, and the need for, the parents.

Fort/da; o-o-o-o/a: the separation of linguistic differences supports the foundation of theory as *pragma*. Theory is the confrontation of spectacle with invisibility and loss, with time. The paradigms of thought, as both Freud and Merleau-Ponty teach us, are both possession and dispossession, in an eternal confusion of reversibility. The desire to know is a sublimation of the desire to grasp. The separations of self/other, self/world, inside/outside, are maintained and refined within language, and the subtleties of theory are always a function of power.

Childhood innocence is the parents' fantasy serving as a dissimulation of their own primal guilt. Innocence is not at the beginning: it is created as a screen to dissimulate the terror of the primal *ressentiment*. The "o-o-o-o/a" of the infant is as full of malice as it is of love. We find one such phantasm of innocence in Dadaist art. Consider the following stanza from the score of Kurt Schwitters' phonetic poem, the *Ursonate* (1924– 1925):

```
Oooooooooooooooooooooooooooooooo
Bee bee bee bee bee . . . . . . . . . . .
Oooooooooooooooooooooooooooooooo
Zee zee zee zee zee . . . . . . . . . .
Oooooooooooooooooooooooooooooooo
Rinnzekete . . . bee . . . bee . . .
Oooooooooooooooooooooooooooooooo
änn ze . . . . . . änn ze . . . . . .
Oooooooooooooooooooooooooooooooo

Aaaaaaaaaaaaaaaaaaaaaaaaaaaaaaaaaaa
Bee bee bee bee bee . . . . . . . . .
Aaaaaaaaaaaaaaaaaaaaaaaaaaaaaaaaaaa
Zee zee zee zee zee . . . . . . . . .
Aaaaaaaaaaaaaaaaaaaaaaaaaaaaaaaaaaa
Rinnzekete . . . bee . . . bee . . .
Aaaaaaaaaaaaaaaaaaaaaaaaaaaaaaaaaaa
Enn ze . . . . . . enn ze . . . . . .
Aaaaaaaaaaaaaaaaaaaaaaaaaaaaaaaaaaa

Oooooooooooooooooooooooooooooooo
Bee bee bee bee bee . . . . . . . .
Oooooooooooooooooooooooooooooooo
Zee zee zee zee zee . . . . . . . . .
Oooooooooooooooooooooooooooooooo
Rinnzekete . . . bee . . . bee . . .
Oooooooooooooooooooooooooooooooo
änn ze . . . . . . änn ze . . . . . .
Oooooooooooooooooooooooooooooooo
```

The primal opposition a/o (*fort/da*) is amplified and repeated amidst numerous glossalia and echolalia in this *Ursonate,* this primal sonata. While the seriousness, the tragedy, of the infantile enunciation and symbolic act is dissimulated by the parents under its labelling as "play," conversely the playfulness of Schwitters' poem is dissimulated by culture under the guise of serious "art." Yet, despite superficial structural similarities of the two works (the infant's *fort/da* and Schwitters' *Ursonate*), their significance is diametrically opposed. For the infant, the signification of the *fort/da* inaugurates re-presentation, where ultimately tropes and *typos* dissimulate *topos (corpus.)* Conversely, for Schwitters in his *Ursonate* and in all of *Merz,* we find an anti-representational, iconoclastic art which forces upon the spectator the recognition of the very materiality, the body, of the artwork. And it may be noted that in this stanza of the *Ursonate* the syllable which most directly approximates a word is *Rinn,* the German word for gutter *(Rinne.)* This is emblematic of Schwitters' entire oeuvre, *Merz,* since for Schwitters the gutter was the *topos* of discovery and creation.[6]

In Chapter XVI of his *Memoirs,* Daniel Paul Schreber also recounts an incident of glossolalia, where the very scatological materiality of his body becomes the symbolic element through which the miraculous, destructive powers of the other—the Divinity—is manifest. "W-a-a-a-r-r-u-m sch-ei-ei-ei-s-e-e-n Sie d-e-e-e-e-n-n n-i-i-i-i-icht?" "Why don't you shit?" The tormenting voices insist, over and over again. Since all of Schreber's physical and mental processes—defecation as well as speech—are controlled by "divine miracles," his diarrhea is no less significant than his loghorrea: both aim at the destruction of his rationality. Schreber's strategy to battle these malevolent symptoms proceeds through sheer repetition: he attempts to silence the voices that torment him, as well as his compulsion to speak, by reciting poems consigned to memory; and he tries to control the terrible pains of the need to defecate by simply giving in to that need—which (perhaps hyperbolically stated) results in a state of extreme "soul-voluptuousness." He fights a repetition imposed from "without" with a repetition imposed from "within." Hyperbolic paranoia is conquered by ironic reversals and repetitions; counterfeit thinking is used to battle ideas. Schreber invents a sophistic theology to evoke, and struggle with, the torments caused by an overbearing system of guilt and repression. He reinvents heresy to purify his soul, as a means of catharsis, as a means of mitigating the power of the discourse of others.

If others are divergences of my speech, it is only because I have already been constituted as divergences of theirs. We can think and communicate only because, as Merleau-Ponty claims, the universal is unthought, because ideality "has a future in me . . . with the others, and finally, having become writing, has a future in every possible reader . . ."[7] And yet this future of my speech is a discourse of power, since its origin is a past founded upon *ressentiment,* a *ressentiment* against the invisible, against the inauguration of the world as loss. Our euphemisms for this loss are transcendence, essence, ideality. Yet these terms dissimulate the dual functions of rhetoric (even the rhetoric of the monoremes *fort* and *da* which inaugurate a world.) For the infant, as well as within the Socratic tradition, genuine *logos* is *dialogos,* with the discovery of a unique, monolithic truth as its goal. Conversely, but simultaneously, for the infant as well as within the Sophistic tradition, genuine *logos* is also *dialogos,* yet within a pluralism which maintains power and influence as its goal. Thus rhetoric is simultaneously constative and performative, reproductive and productive, And this is always true of self and other, where the only source of truth is divergence, difference, between discourses.

> I cannot be caught in immanence.
>
> —*Paul Klee*

> If he never know himself.
>
> —*Ovid*

> Our identity is always a case
>
> —*Melanie Klein*

     The drama of *fort/da* with the spool was paralleled by another: "Baby/o-o-o-o." Having discovered a mirror that did not quite reach the ground, the infant found that by crouching he could make himself disappear. His ultimate ontological possibility, that of invisibility, is no different than that of his mother, and he can now begin to work, or play, upon himself the transcendence which will make of him a subject.

     As is usually the case with mirror phenomena, we find a paradox: here, it leads to the ontical/ontological difference which is the foundation of subjectivity and the world. Merleau-Ponty's analysis of this mirror phenomenon is exemplary in its explanation of the manner in which the self is always a self through confusion and narcissism:

> The flesh is a *mirror phenomenon* and the mirror is an extension of my relation with my body. Mirror = realization of a *Bild* of the thing, and I-my shadow relation = realization of a (verbal) *Wesen:* extraction of the essence of the thing, of the pellicle of Being or of its "Appearance"—To touch oneself, to see oneself, is to obtain such a specular extract of oneself. I.e. fission of appearance and Being—a fission that already takes place in the touch (duality of the touching and the touched) and which, with the mirror (Narcissus) is only a more profound adhesion to Self. The visual *projection* of the world in me to be understood not as intra-objective things-my body relation. But as a shadow-body relation, a community of verbal *Wesen* and hence finally a "resemblance" phenomenon, transcendence.[8]

To touch oneself and to see oneself is precisely the auto-erotic activity of the infant, an activity which engenders no impossibility, no paradox, but pleasure. If anything, it is the manifestation of the desire for totalization, for the self-sufficiency of primary narcissism. The "enigma of the body" commences with the loss of the illusory self-sufficiency: that is, with the simultaneous advent of the other through dispossession, and the advent of the self through a new mode of possession, possession at a distance through vision, in the mirror. And this is intensified through the mirroring phenomenon of mimesis of the other, with its circular plays of actions/reactions.

Symbolic activity is the appropriation of the invisible within language. And yet, although the origin of the invisible was the loss of a body (the mother's), this symbolic system is not divorced from the body. The ego as Freud explains, is "a bodily ego: it is not merely a surface entity, but is itself the projection of a surface."[9] The body thus serves as visible archetype, according to which the ego is "an extension of the surface-differentiation" between ego and id, self and other, self and world. The narcissistic structure of appearance obtains from the fact that the ego is based upon object libido invested in the body: the worldhood-of-the-world is always projected upon the body, even though normally the relation between *corpus* and *topos* is dissimulated within the very linguistic structures which made possible the eruption of the self in the world. Appearance is a simulacrum of origins, origins always lacking (a lack as origin). These origins are transcendent within the visible (within the future of our words as *telos*). Appearance is the perpetual dissimulation of the body as *archē* by language. The hermeneutic circle is always a narcissistic circle.

Because the ego has its origin in the loss of the other (a loss which is simultaneous with its very constitution) there can never be a cohesion of the self with itself, even at the extreme limits of narcissism. This is evident at the mirror stage, in which the narcissistic reflection is precisely the lack of cohesion with the self. The mirror stage, according to Lacan, is ". . . the transformation that takes place in the subject when he assumes an image."[10] This transformation is the production of the primal form of the "I," the "Ideal-I," which is a fictionalized origin disparate with the real "I," and a source of later identifications. If the subject is the discordance between the real "I" and the ideal "I," and the history of the subject is the attempt at reconciliation, it must be noted that this is a futile task, since the reconciliation can only be effected within language. Thus for Schreber, the discordance between the real "I" and the ideal "I"—between the human and the divine—is a discordance articulated by the very signs of corporeal transformation into a woman, into the whore of God. These signs, the prelude to an impossible martyrdom, reveal precisely the attempt to work through the contradictions of his condition: male/female, human/divine, self/other. Yet language already bears the trace of the other, which is yet a further source of identification and difference. *Fort/da:* mother's body: anaclisis = Baby/o-o-o-o: own body: narcissism. Whether narcissistic or anaclitic, the choice of love object is always a rupture of the subject. The body is always simultaneously a body-for-the-self and a body-for-the-other, whether in the realm of erotics or politics.

The socialization of the infant occurs at the stage of narcissism, not only because the infant then enters into the symbolic matrix of language, but also because it is at this stage of development that the sexual instincts are unified in order to gain a love-object.[11] Just as the subject and the instincts are unified in order to be readily incorporated within culture, so too is the mode of sexuality unified from the polymorphous perversity of infantile auto-erotism to the genitality of adulthood. This genitality (indeed phallocentrism) is the limit of the body's dissimulation, and it serves as a primary paradigm within the symbolic. And yet, as we shall see, there are psychic strategies against this domination and reduction of the instinctual life.

> God . . . must have commerce only with cadavers.
>
> —*Daniel Paul Schreber*

> Narcissus . . . shall have commerce only with shadows.
>
> —*Plotinus*

> Certainly it is an interesting event we are dealing with: the putrescene of the absolute spirit.
>
> —*Karl Marx*

In March 1894, Daniel Paul Schreber began his relation with God.[12] Senatspräsident Dr. Daniel Paul Schreber, Margrave of Tuscany and of Tasmania, The Seer, Prince of Hell, The Hyperborean, a Jesuit novice at Osseg, Bourgmeister of Klattau, a young Alsatian girl defending her honor against a victorious French officer, a Mongol Prince, *Miss Schreber.* These were among the multiple identities within Schreber's psychotic drama, which began with a reverie in which he believed that it would be wonderful to be a woman submitting to sexual intercourse, and which culminated with the belief that he would be emasculated, changed into a woman, so that he could be impregnated by God and become the redeemer who would restore the world to a lost state of bliss by creating "a new race of men made in the spirit of Schreber." Almost every aspect of his daily existence was affected by "divine miracles," and his direct relation with God was affected by "Divine rays," which were also recognized by him to be nerves, semen, voices, and miraculous birds (the dove of the Holy Spirit, perhaps?), to which he gave girls' names. Yet in his role as redeemer he suffered: he was plagued by a ceaseless cacophony of voices in his head from which he could only gain respite by a "miracle of howling," in which his screams drowned out the voices. He was also to suffer numerous sexual abuses. And before he could redeem the world, not only would he have to die, but also the world would have to end. He read reports of his own death; believed that "soul murder" was being committed upon him; believed that God was trying to render him insane or kill him. For example, his head was full of minuscule speaking scorpions, resembling crabs or spiders, which plagued him, as did the miraculated "little men," cursory contraptions a few mm. tall, which were placed on his head to devastate him. As for the catastrophes which would signal the end of the world, they would appear in numerous forms: deluge, earthquakes, glaciation due to the diminution of solar heat, and epidemics of various sorts, some of the symptoms of which were visible on his own body: blue plague, brown plague, white plague, black plague, oriental leprosy, indian leprosy, hebrew leprosy, egyptian leprosy.

In paranoia, libido is withdrawn from the world as a defense mechanism (in the Schreber case, Freud claims, as a regression to the narcissistic stage in defense against sublimated homosexuality.) This withdrawal is symbolized by the catastrophes which mark the end of the world, and is counterbalanced by the utopia to follow, the cure. Concurrent with this withdrawal, the libido is fixated upon the ego, hence the megalomania; the suppressed internal meanings reenter consciousness in the form of external perceptions, that is, as delusions.

For the First Emperor Shih Huang Ti the world was a system of *pragma* to be modified as an expression of his megalomania; for Senatspräsident Schreber the delusional world was a sign of himself, an attempt at recovery, at a reordering of the psychic mechanism. Both cases are extreme: the First Emperor took himself for God in his vast megalomania; Schreber externalized his megalomania *as* God, a God who would torture, castrate and murder him, but who would also simultaneously offer him the greatest sensual pleasure ("voluptuousness") and the highest position in society—Redeemer. The lack of the Name-of-the-Father, (according to Lacan the cause of psychosis), is replaced by the Name-of-God in what we call a delusional, influencing system.

If, as Nietzsche claimed in *Thus Spoke Zarathustra,* the world is a cerebral fiction of God, we are compelled to ask, "What could one create if gods existed?" Nothing, of course, hence one must kill God in order to create: ". . . if there were gods, how could I endure not to be one! Hence there are no gods." And yet, we must note that according to the logic of the unconsciousness, which permits the cohabitation of contradictory significations, Nietzsche's realization is not a foregone conclusion. There are two possible solutions to this problem: one could either *kill* God or one could *become* God!

While Nietzsche heralded the problematic "death of God," Antonin Artaud lived this problem. He too recognized that "It was still necessary to kill God in order to live" (*OC*XVI;160). If, for Western theology, God was the supreme Being within a rationally ordered universe, in the modernist epoch God is, as Artaud recognized and suffered, the "monomania of the unconsciousness" (*OC*XV;315), where "immanence is a depot of God." (*OC*XVII;153) God, dethroned as absolute ruler of the cosmos, is reduced to the tormentor of that microcosm, the unconscious. The theological is subsumed within the pathological, but is no less real for that shift of *topos*. Indeed, Artaud's *Cahiers de Rodez* are among the most poignant, and in a sense the most typically modernist, examples of the attempt to exorcize God from His parasitic encrustation in the unconscious. The tragedy of Artaud's life was that during the period of his "madness" he couldn't simply purge himself of the God that tormented him. Rather, before he could forget Him, he first had to become Him. As Nietzsche entered his madness through the identities of Dionysus and the Crucified, so too did Artaud enter through the multiple identities of God and Satan, Christ and Anti-Christ. In a sense, the asylum at Rodez was the ultimate scene of Artaud's "Theater of Cruelty," an antimetaphysical and antitheological theater which proferred an art of difference, transgression and forgetting. If metaphysics functions as the science of the return of Being as memory and representation, then modernism, to the extent that it disrupts the classical *Logos,* entails an art of production and active forgetting. Thus the prolegomena to any "Theater of Cruelty," as well as its greatest work, is the exorcism of God from His last domain, the unconscious.

If the Rodez asylum was the stage for Artaud's "Theater of Cruelty," then the sanatorium at Sonnenstein was the scene of Schreber's interior passion play. Man and woman, living and dead, Messiah and man: Schreber too lived out a multiplicity of identities, which illuminate the general problems of sexual identity and difference, self-identity and origins, sovereignty and dependence.

What is evident in both cases, Artaud and Schreber, is not only the extreme interiorization of a God in a world where there is no longer a rational place for Him, but also the return of the repressed as a demoniacal God. The abstract, infinitely alien, mathematized God of Nicolas of Cusa and Leibniz is transformed into a personal, malicious, violent, lecherous, and foul God. What in previous centuries would have resulted either in condemnation as heresy or valorization as sainthood, is now no longer valued as prophesy, but as symptom. The modern epistemē no longer has a place for the miracles which governed Schreber's existence, so they are classified as psychopathological symptoms.

After Nietzsche, the productions of metaphysics and theology are recognized as totalizing, systematizing theorization, and are thus the sign of the domination of *Logos* and of the logic of domination; they can either be replaced by productive texts, signs of sovereignty and rebellion, or else they may be replaced by their own simulacra. In either case, the modernist text is a *poesis particularis,* and not a *mathesis universalis.* The texts of Schreber and Artaud show the breakdown of ontotheology in its final theatrical representation. Yet this representation is already dispersed by the multiplicity of subject positions which it engenders, by the differential of desire which it constitutes, and within the heterogeneity of the discourse which it brings out.

In Western culture, God is the classical influencing machine in His role as the guarantor of cosmic conjunction and personal identity. In mysticism God collects all libidinal cathexes; in the narcissistic megalomania of paranoia the self, the ego, collects all libidinal cathexes, only to project this aggrandizement as a personal God (a heresy!) But while the Eros of the cultural world strives to maintain the connections between the self, the other and the world, the Eros of the paranoiac mechanism strives to assume the greatest possibility of disjunctions and recombinations. Hence the multiplicity of Schreber's identities, the numerous catastrophes which will destroy the world, the many names of God, the multiplicity of meanings of the Divine rays. Schreber was self and other, man and woman, dead and alive. He could not "resolve as 'I' his discordance with his own reality," so he lived the discordance. Hence the Schreberian God functions in precisely the inverse manner of the classical Western God: as Deleuze and Guattari explain in *Anti-Oedipus,* one can only believe in God as master of the disjunctive syllogism. While oedipalization and phallocentrism are manifestations of a conjunctive apparatus, defining the origin of the self as the other, schizophrenia and polymorphous perversity (auto-erotism) are manifestations of a disjunctive apparatus, defining the autofiguration of the self. It is precisely the opposition between autofiguration and the influence of the other that structures the psychic destiny of the subject: this destiny is prefigured by the difference between the dramas of Baby/o-o-o-o and *fort/da,* making manifest the primal emotional ambivalence.

One such disjunction was made manifest to Schreber on the linguistic level by the "miraculated birds." Certain of the Divine rays appeared as birds which held the nerves of souls that had previously gained beatitude. These birds spoke to Schreber in the *Grundsprache,* the primal language (an archaic form of German full of ironic, hyperbolic euphemisms), and they spoke in homophonies, without knowing the meaning of what they said. An example of their speech:[13]

Santiago/Carthago
Chinesenthum/Jesus-Christum
Abendroth/Athemnoth
Ariman/Ackerman
Briefbeschwerer/Herr Prüfer schwört

This internal dialogue (monologue) of discrete differences between sounds indeed manifests the structure of the *Grundsprache*. In this primal language, the differences between sounds achieved in glossolalia and echolalia evoke a self and a world. The meaning isn't known, but is established in the very act of enunciation: the meanings of these homophonous disjunctions are explanations of Schreber's condition and call forth his attempted recovery. Simultaneously, these disjunctions signify the primal ambivalence of pleasure and pain. Thus, "Herr Prüfer schwört" ("Mr. Examiner swears") recalls the paranoiac delusions of observation, where God is continually watching Schreber and calling him a "slut." The "Briefbeschwerer" (paperweight) actually symbolizes the origins of his cure, since such a paperweight would be that which secured the papers on which Schreber wrote his autobiography: this autobiography opposes Schreber's discourse to the discourse of the God which curses him. God as Ariman; Schreber as laborer, writer, and Redeemer (Jesus Christ), awaiting the "twilight" of the impending apocalypse, which will smother him too.

We find a similar homophonic structure in the writings of the proto-Surrealist poet and linguist, Jean-Pierre Brisset:[14]

Les dents, la bouche.
Les dents la bouchent
L'aidant la bouche.
L'aide en la bouche.
Laides en la bouches.
Laid dans la bouche.
Lait dans la bouche.
L'est dam le à bouche.
Les dents-là bouche.

Here the homophony plays out the oppositions of possession/dispossession, incorporation/exclusion, acceptance/refusal, infant/adult. The very scene of language becomes the place of its exclusion: the infantile mouth is filled with milk, or the adult mouth closed, plugged, by the teeth. But when milk is lacking there is pain, and screams. Later, the teeth, which aid the mouth in speaking and eating, become ugly and painful within an ugly mouth because of the milk upon which it depended and choked, for which there is *ressentiment*. Finally, the teeth must be hidden, the mouth must be closed: this entails a rejection of language, of the "mother tongue." What was an overture to the other ends as a radical refusal, as silence. Indeed, if with Schreber we take the parts of the body and the bodily functions as cosmic metaphors, then we may agree with Antonin Artaud that, "Being has teeth."

> The Talmud warns against reading
> Scripture by so inclined a light
> that the text reveals chiefly the
> shape of your own countenance.
>
> —*Harold Bloom*

> . . . this imminence of a revelation
> which does not occur is, perhaps,
> the aesthetic phenomenon.
>
> —*Jorge Luis Borges*

We are all children of Schreber: Schreber, screaming at the sun, hoping for silence; Schreber in drag, trying to seduce God. All this as desire for beatitude, for "the grandiose triumph of the order of the universe" where "all legitimate interests end in harmony." But it is precisely this harmony of origins and ends which must always escape us: the unity of Schreber's beatitude as the spectacle of "the Perspective-that-God-be-with-us" entails the impossibility of a *"pensée de survol."* In fact, we are always caught between Narcissus and Oedipus, between autofiguration and the figurations of repression. The self is, as Merleau-Ponty claims, a "unity by transgression." But this is a dialectic of transgression, of possession and dispossession, between the self and the other. Always incomplete, always lacking.

In his parable, "The Great Wall and the Tower of Babel,[15] Kafka explains:

> . . . the Great Wall alone would provide for the first time in the history of mankind a secure foundation for a new Tower of Babel.

And yet, he asks:

> How could the wall, which did not form even a circle, but only a sort of quarter or half-circle, provide the foundation for a tower?

How indeed! Just as the First Emperor, Shih Huang Ti, walled in his empire and destroyed all the books of the past in order to establish and maintain his grandiose narcissistic unity, calling himself God—just as Schreber walled himself in an insane asylum and ceaselessly screamed to silence the voices that plagued him, in order to recover the beatitude that was due him within the order of the universe, within the order of the self—so too must the Great Wall as closure provide the foundation for the new Tower of Babel, the tower which would permit humankind a divine *"pensée de survol."* And yet that tower was never built, not due to a lack of technical efficiency, not due to theoretical ineptitude, but due to the lack of closure of the Wall. So too with the self: there is no complete self as center because there is no definable periphery of the self—the periphery of the self is the other.

The Tower of Babel reaching towards God; the First Emperor as God; Schreber having sexual intercourse with God: the entire sense of our culture reduced to the incantation, the interjection, "God!" Philipp Wegener[16] explains that such exclamations, while being emotional outbursts, are simultaneously "clauses not meant to be heard," hence a form of monologue, *and* "forms of prayer" which, since they address a deity, originate in "purposeful dialogic speaking." Simultaneously monologue and dialogue, addressed to the self and to the other, referring to the self and the other. And this is ultimately true of every enunciation. Even of the scream as an expression of pain, or of joy. As Schreber teaches us, "All nonsense is abolished," precisely because, as Wegener explains, there is,

> . . . a double transfer of monologic speech and dialogue. The purposeless utterances become purposeful utterances because of the effect they have; on the other hand, through the mechanization of movement, the meaningful utterances may change themselves into purposeless monologic outbursts of noise again.

As the reproductive, mimetic enunciations of infantile echolalia engender the outbursts which produce subjectivity, so do the private, repetitive enunciations of prayer aid in engendering the vast mechanisms of history. There is no nonsense, just a disquieting strangeness which we often encounter in art, in utterances, in situations. This strangeness is the Other, our muse.

Notes

1. For historical information about Shih Huang Ti, see Karl A. Wittfogel's *Oriental Despotism* (NY, Vintage, 1981); Jorge Luis Borges, "The Wall and the Books," in *Labyrinths* (NY, New Directions, 1964).

2. This is an attempt to examine the structure of narcissism as constitutive of subjectivity, and not the notion of narcissism as a type of character disorder. And yet, the Emperor Shih Huang Ti may certainly be categorized this way. Drawing upon Nathan Schwartz-Salant's *Narcissism and Character Transformation* (NY, Inner City Books, 1982), we may match the following characteristics of the narcissistic character disorder with some of the deeds and personality traits of Shih Huang Ti: (a) *lack of psychological penetrability and defense against relatedness to others*: the Emperor not only protected his nation behind the enclosure of the Great Wall, but he also secluded himself within a vast palace, and took the advice of nobody except his Prime Minister, Li Ssu. (b) *extreme self-reference*: the Emperor wanted to found an eternal dynasty, with himself as the First Emperor, and his heirs to be known as the Second Emperor, Third Emperor, etc.; he constructed enormous monuments for himself, palaces and a tomb, (in addition to the Great Wall), using vast work crews of over 700,000. (c) *rejects interpretation*: he imple-

mented standardized and objective laws which pertained to everyone without discrimination (this was the supremacy of Legalism.) He thus consolidated the centralization of power, which was accomplished by the destruction of the feudal barons and the suppression of local customs (i.e., of different worldviews.) (d) *cannot tolerate criticism*: all of the positions of power previously held by the feudal barons were given to his own functionaries, so as to avoid dissension. (e) *grandiose self-image (megalomania) and quest for perfection*: he spread the rumor that he was God. (f) *low empathetic capacity:* given to anger, rage, and envy: he was known to have "the heart of a tiger or a wolf," and was completely "without beneficence." He even forced his father to suicide and persecuted his mother. (g) *power drive*: he ascended the throne at the age of 12, and began to conquer and unify the states at the age of 25. (h) *lack of sense of history* (the historical process is assimilated only to the extent that it aggrandizes the ego) *and the desire to know ahead of time*: he insisted that history begin with him; in his old age, he wished to deny death, and not only forbade anyone to mention death in his presence, but also sought the elixir of immortality.

3.   From Elias Canetti's *Crowds and Power* (NY, Continuum, 1981), the section on "Rulers and Paranoiacs;" p. 417. In this regard, also consider the following lines of W. H. Auden:

Perfection, of a kind, was what he was after,
And the poetry he invented was easy to understand.
He knew human folly like the back of his hand,
And was greatly interested in armies and fleets.
When he laughed, respectable senators burst with laughter
And when he cried, the little children died in the streets.

4.   Maurice Merleau-Ponty, *The Visible and the Invisible*, (Evanston, Northwestern University Press, 1968); p. 217.

5.   Julia Kristeva, "Place Names," in *Desire in Language* (NY, Columbia, 1980); pp. 289–291 and passim.

6.   On the role of garbage in modernism, and in *Merz* in particular, see my "Ideology and the Problem of Style: The Errant Text," in *Enclitic* #14. On the glossolalic structure and the materiality of the text in modernism, see Annette Michelson, "De Stijl, Its Other Face: Abstraction and Cacaphony, or What Was the Matter With Hegel?" in *October* # 22. It should also be noted that in the first *Manifesto of Surrealism* (1924) André Breton suggests that echolalia and Ganser syndrome (beside-the-point responses), both techniques also utilized in the Zen *Koan* (question and answer exercise) as methods of enlightenment (Satori), are typical of the Surrealist enterprise. Yet, the difference between Schwitters and Breton, between Dadaism and Surrealism, must be noted. If the gutter with its garbage was the *topos* of discovery for Schwitters and the Dadaists, Paris with its bourgeois flea-markets and artifacts was the *topos* of discovery for the Surrealists. Deleuze-Guattari's claim in *Anti-Oedipus* (NY, Viking, 1977) is that Dada was a schizophrenic-revolutionary art, while Surrealism was a paranoid-oedipal-reactionary art.

7.   Merleau-Ponty, *op. cit.;* pp. 118–119.

8.   Ibid; pp. 255–256; The *locus classicus* of psychoanalytic studies on narcissism is Sigmund Freud's "On Narcissism: An Introduction" (1914), in *General Psychological Theory* (NY, Collier, 1970). A major recent analysis of the Freudian theory of narcissism is André Green, *Narcissime de vie, narcissime de mort* (Paris, Minuit, 1983). For an in-depth study of the constitution of the self and the ontology of Freudian metapsychology, see Marcel Gauchet, "Freud: Une psychanalyse ontologique," in *Textures* 72/4–5 and 73/6–7. See also Jacques Lacan, "The Mirror Stage as Formative of the Function of the I as Revealed in Psychoanalytic Experience," in *Ecrits* (NY, Norton, 1972.) Finally, for a critique of all of the above positions from the point of view of post-structuralist libido theory, see Deleuze-Guattari, *Anti-Oedipus.*

9.   Sigmund Freud, *The Ego and the Id* (NY, Norton, 1962); pp. 15–16.

10.   Jacques Lacan, *op. cit.;* p. 2.

11.   Sigmund Freud, "On the Mechanism of Paranoia" in *General Psychological Theory* (NY, Collier, 1970).

12.   All information on Schreber is from his *Memoirs of My Nervous Illness.* On the psychoanalytic interpretation of this case, see Freud's "Psychoanalytic Notes Upon an Autobiographical Account of a Case of Paranoia" (1911) in *Three Cases Histories* (NY, Collier, 1973.) See also Lacan, "On a Question Preliminary to Any Possible Treatment of Psychosis," in *Ecrits.* See also W. G. Niederland's work on Schreber. Still the classical text on the structure of the paranoiac mechanism is Victor Tausk, "On the Origin of the 'Influencing Machine' in Schizophrenia" in *Psychoanalytic Quarterly* Vol. II, 1933. An interesting account of these issues in relation to art can be found in Joan Copjec, "The Anxiety of the Influencing Machine" in *October* #23.

13.   Santiago or Carthage
           Chineseness or Jesus Christ
           twilight or dyspnoea (difficulty in breathing)
           Ariman or laborer
           paperweight or Mr. Examiner swears

See also Louis Wolfson's *Le schizo et les langues* (Paris: Gallimard, 1970) for the internal structures of schizophrenic language and homonomy, and the rejection of one's own language ("mother tongue").

14.   From Brisset's "La grande loi ou la clef de la parole," in André Breton's *Anthologie de l'humour noir* (Paris: Pauvert, 1972).

     The teeth, the mouth
     the teeth plug it (the mouth)
     helping the mouth.
     Help the mouth.
     Ugly (teeth) in the mouth
     An ugly mouth.
     Milk in the mouth.

Painful in the mouth.*
The teeth—hidden there**

15.   Franz Kafka, "The Great Wall and the Tower of Babel," in *Parables and Paradoxes* (New York: Schocken, 1975).

16.   Phillip Wegener, *The Life of Speech* (1885), in D. Wilfred Abse's *Speech and Reason: Language Disorder in Mental Disease* (Charlottesville: University of Virginia Press, 1971), pp. 172, 178.

---

*j'ai mal aux dents (I have a toothache)

**cache des dents-là, ferme la bouche (hide the teeth there, shut the mouth)

Michel de Certeau

6. The Institution of Rot

During the night [. . .] one single night, the lower God (Ariman) appeared [. . .] his voice resounded in a mighty bass as if directly in front of my bedroom windows [. . .] What was spoken did not sound friendly by any means: everything seemed calculated to instill fright and terror in me and the word "rotten person" (*Luder*) was frequently heard—an expression quite common in the basic language (*Grundsprache*) to denote a human being destined to be destroyed by God and to feel God's power and wrath. Yet everything that was spoken was genuine, not phrases learnt by rote [. . .] For this reason any impression was not one of alarm and fear, but largely one of admiration for the magnificent and the sublime: the effect on my nerves was therefore beneficial, despite the insults contained in the words [. . .]

—*Daniel Paul Schreber,* Memoirs of My Nervous Illness[1]

Don't write on the shitters, shit on writing.

—*Graffiti in the bathroom of a Paris movie theater, 1977*

Interspace: Psychoanalysis and Mysticism

I speak neither as an analyst nor as a mystic. I am accredited by neither of these two experiences, which have constituted, one after the other, inaccessible authorizations of discourse. To begin, I have only Saint-John Perse's Friday to invoke as my muse: the savage, transported to the kitchens of London, whose parlors his master Robinson Crusoe frequents, plays the soup spoiler and flirt.[2] Mysticism, especially, can only be dealt with from a distance, as a savage in the kitchen. Its discourse is produced on another scene. It is no more possible to conceptualize it than it is to dispense with it. Like Schreber's "basic language," it is "somewhat antiquated," "but nevertheless powerful."[3] It is like the phantom that returns to the stage.

The remoteness of this "basic" thing that returns in the form of mysticism, a hallucination of absences, is a mark of age, or a first death (the separation between its time and ours), and of a modesty to be retained (our distance from the place where this thing was written). The remoteness is also internal to me: I am divided by uncertainty when speaking of *that [ça],* of this relation between signifiers and an unknown, of this discourse, foreign yet near at hand, that is perhaps haunted by a maternal indeterminacy. This binds me even though I cannot believe to be in it, or what is worse, cannot pretend to have it. But after all, this is not unlike what psychoanalysis, along its borders and on its thresholds, tells to those who are determined not to *be a part of it* (of its institution), not to speak *from that place,* precisely because of what comes from it. There is thus, from the outset, a cleavage between the fact of being invested (captured?) in it, and the fact of not being there (neither in nor of that place).

It seems to me that Schreber's revelation, which is close to mysticism in so many respects, offers an approach to outlining the articulation between these two experiences, as well as their relation to the institution. In the course of that "unique night" in 1894, there rang forth a "mighty bass voice," not "friendly by any means," yet "beneficial" and "refreshing," and it said to the President: *Luder,* in other words, "harpy," "filth," "slut," or rather, since there is a certain familiarity to the insult, "*rotten* person." I propose to *meditate* upon this word, and that, according to Madame Guyon, means swallowing it. It appears in the interspace of mysticism and psychoanalysis, and demands attention even though it has nothing to justify it other than what it produces here and there: a "formula" that is heard, a "small fragment of truth"—a *splinter* of what?

A few global analogies can provide a framework, an admittedly fragile one, for Schreber's enactment of this *word* that is the archive of the subject (its corrupt document) and the saying of the subject's non-identity. I will mention only three points of convergence between psychoanalysis and mysticism. First, the distinction between a statement and a speech-act, a corpus and an act by the subject: that this distinction is central in Lacan does not alter the fact that it was precisely the mystic discourse of the sixteenth and seventeenth centuries that first established it.[4]

Second, Lacanian theory entertains relations of "separation" and "debt" with the mystics (Meister Eckhart, Hadewijch of Anvers, St. Teresa, Angelus Silesius, etc.); or, what amounts to the same thing, it rejects their goods, corpses of truths, and recognizes itself in the lack from which they received their name: something should be written about the return of these Christian phantoms at strategic points in analytic discourse, a movement that is homologous to the relation of "contestation" *(absprechen)* and "belonging" *(angehören)* that links the Freudian text to the Jewish tradition; something should be written about it—a zebrine patterning and labor of absences—to bide the time until what is written can be said in re-presentations of those strangers, who share responsibility for making Lacanian theory possible.[5]

Finally, in the mysticism of the sixteenth and seventeenth centuries, there is a desire analogous to that which Philippe Lévy discerned in Freud: a will to be done with, a death drive. With the mystics, a wish for loss is directed both toward the religious language in which the trace of their walk is imprinted and the course of their itinerary itself. Their voyages simultaneously create and destroy the paths they take. Or, more exactly, they take their course, but wish to lose the landscape and the way. Mysticism operates as a process whereby the objects of meaning vanish, beginning with God himself; it is as though the function of mysticism were to bring a religious *episteme* to a close and erase itself at the same time, to produce the night of the subject while marking the twilight of culture. It seems to me, in the context of our own time, that analytic trajectories have a similar historical function; they labor to expose the defection of a culture by its ("bourgeois") representatives, and through this diminishing of the signifying economy, they hollow out the place of an *other* that is the beyond of that which continues to support analytic critique. In this respect, mysticism and psychoanalysis presuppose—in the past in relation to "corrupt" Churches, today by way of "civilization and its discontents"—Schreber's feeling, so "perfectly clear" and intolerable, that, "in Hamlet's words, there is something rotten *(faul)* in the state of Denmark."[6]

This horizon of questions is not the subject I am addressing. It simply encircles the word *Luder,* which names the subject as a relation to the decomposition of the symbolic body, that identifying institution, and thus connotes a transformation in the status of the institution and in its mode of transmission.

Nomination: The Noble and the Rotten

Certain characteristics of the word Schreber heard are in consonance with the old mystic narratives, and are worthy of mention. First, there is a passage from sight to hearing. Sight blends into a voice-effect with the act of "perceiving speech" *(ich vernahm seine Sprache),* a "mighty bass voice" whose location, "in front of the window," is specifiable. The semi-blinding of the subject creates a void from which the word of the Other rings forth. Many of the auditory hallucinations that mark the path of mystic writings are like this. In fact, with Schreber, there is an inversion of content between the voice and sight. The voice assigns him a place that is the opposite of what he sees in God. The God whom he contemplates "in all His purity *(Reinheit)*" names him "rottenness." The oppositional terms symbolize within a rotten/pure, heard/seen structure. The word that condemns him to be annihilated *(zu vernichtenden)* comes during a spectacle offered by "God's omnipotence *(Allmacht).*" Speech nullifies the witness of glory. More exactly, this call to be carrion discloses the secret supporting the divine epiphany; Schreber carries its imprint *(Eindruck),* which is carved or written on his body as he stands in wonder before the "grandiose" and the "sublime." The decay of the subject, dictated by a voice, is the precondition for the theatrical institution of "omnipotence in all its purity." The basic language thus announces the *spoken* place at which the pure gold of a *shown* truth originates. In this respect, it converges with the knowledge that unfolds in mystical modes of narrative.

But this only concerns the content. The form of Schreber's experience is more important: it is one of naming. The naming in question is one of a series in Schreber's career; it is an additional one and is doubtless one too many. The year before (1893), Schreber had been named president of the appeals court in Dresden, *Senatspräsident.* That nomination, a promotion to a task and an application of the subject (he was addressed as "Mister President"), is replaced by the one imposed by the voice of the God Ariman: "Your name is rottenness, *Luder."* A play of identities in the empty space left by the original name, which is foreclosed, *expired.*

Is this the empty center of initiatory ruptures? Name changes and beginnings by the name are to be found everywhere in the mystics' tradition. For example, John of the Cross (Juan de la Cruz) replaces Juan de Yepes, his family name. In these onomastic substitutions, the new appellation is presented as a program for being, a clear program that takes the place of an earlier, obscure one—it is any "proper" name imposing upon the subject the duty-to-be of the unknown that is the will of the other; it introduces, through a switch of fathers, a filiation of meaning to replace filiation by birth. From this angle, naming is related to the family romance; it is an adoption into and by the noble family replacing the obscure one. In the case of Schreber, however "insulting" the name he received may be, it is still a sign that he has been adopted by the God Ariman, whom his "genuine" words and "expression of true feeling" brings close and renders "beneficial." To be called "rotten" or a "slut" is to be adopted by the noble family. This structure was operative in all religious "families" before it resurfaced in ideological, political, or psychoanalytic institutions.

In addition the name imposed by the other is authorized by nothing, and that is its special trait. "It signifies in itself something that refers first and foremost to signification as such."[7] The name is not authorized by any meaning; on the contrary, it authorizes signification, like a poem that is preceded by nothing and creates unlimited possibilities for meaning. But this occurs because the word *Luder* plays the role of that which cannot deceive. It compels belief more than it is believed. It has the status, Schreber says, of something veracious and authentic *(echt).* The basic language is here responding to a general necessity: "there has to be something somewhere that does not deceive"; science itself presupposes that "matter is not deceptive," so that even if we "deceive ourselves," at least "matter does not deceive us."[8] For Schreber, what guarantees the truth of all the rest and makes the interpretive proliferation of his discourse possible, as well as its slow metamorphosis into the body of a prostitute, is this name that he takes at its word, this signifier that comes from the other like a touch, this bass voice that affects his nerves and leaves an imprint on his body—a soothing effect produced by the "direct utterance of a real affectivity." Belief is founded upon the touch of a voice, which makes one believe that one is recognized, known, even loved. Here, it makes Schreber believe that it has finally established him somewhere, that it has fixed a place for him, that it has put an end to his drifting, that it has given him a place defined by the name by which it calls him.

Naming does in effect assign him a place. It is a calling to be what it dictates: your name is *Luder.* The name performs. It does what it says. Schreber's nerves immediately begin to obey it. And that is only the beginning. He will "incarnate" his name by believing it; he would like, he says, "to hand over my body in the manner of a female harlot.[9]

He hands it over the instant he believes. He executes himself in every sense of the word. He makes himself the body of the signifier. But the word that is heard designates precisely this transformation. It is more than a splinter of meaning embedded in the flesh. It has the status of a concept because, in circumscribing the object of belief, it also articulates the *operation* of believing, which consists in passing from a nameless, disintegrating body—a "rottenness" that no longer has a name in any language—to a body "remade" for and by the name: a "harlot" formed according to the specifications of the signifier of the other. The signified of the word, which oscillates between decomposition and slut, designates the overall functioning of the signifier, or Schreber's effective relation to the law of the signifier. It expresses the precondition and the result of believing in the word, when this belief operates as identification or well-being.

This madness is not a particular madness. It is *general.* It is a part of any institution that assures a language of meaning, right or truth. The only odd thing about Schreber, the jurist, is that he knows its hard and "insulting" secret. He is not someone who can go on knowing nothing about it. The same is true for many mystics, who do not extend to others, whom they consider "Pharisees" or "abnormal," the "insult" of the evangelical word targeting the "rottenness" that is presupposed by the "fine appearance" (institutional and sepulchral) of truth and justice;[10] they know it is addressed to them; their mystical nights have also taught them what shrouding conditions the verisimilitude of God, what (immemorial) error and (analytic) defection of the body underlies the recognition of the Name, and what unveiling of decay is both the effect and the "reason" of the belief in a justification.[11]

From Torture to Confession

The positioning of the subject under the sign of refuse is the point at which the institution of "true" discourse is imprinted. And this established discourse transmits itself by tirelessly producing, in "subjects," its condition which is the "soothing" and moreover truthful confession that those subjects are no more than putrescence. To this sly law of the tradition-transmission of a noble doctrine can be added an extreme procedure that has always proliferated along the borders of institutions of truth and which, far from diminishing, like an archaeological phenomenon of history, constantly develops, becoming more and more of a "regular administrative practice," or a political "routine": torture.[12]

It is necessary to examine the hidden alliances between mysticism and torture. They share features that are seemingly accidental, or tied to particular events. For example, certain old ascetic techniques and contemporary torture practices coincide: as one example, the forms of sleep deprivation used by Suso, the Rhenish mystic, are very similar to those found in Greek or Brazilian prisons. Neither is it purely by chance that work on mysticism develops in totalitarian periods, as was the case in France during the occupation under the Vichy regime. This fact must be set in relation to the differences among the historical figures produced by evangelical radicalism in the seventeenth century: it was particularly "mystical" in the Catholic monarchies like Spain and France, and "prophetic" instead in the more democratic, reformed monarchies of England and Scandinavia.[13] These mystic experiences assume the acceptance of an "absolute" power that one should not, or can no longer, change, and which reflects back toward the subject interrogations of which it is capable of being neither the representation nor the object.

This leads us to a more fundamental feature. The goal of torture, in effect, is to produce acceptance of a State discourse, through the confession of putrescence. What the torturer in the end wants to extort from the victim he tortures is to reduce him to being no more than *that* [*ça*], rottenness, which is what the torturer himself is and knows that he is, but without avowing it. The victim must be the *voice* of the filth, everywhere denied, that everywhere supports the *representation* of the regime's "omnipotence," in other words, the "glorious image" of themselves the regime provides for its adherents through its recognition of them. The victim must therefore assume the position of the subject upon whom the theater of identifying power is performed.

But this voice is also muzzled in the darkness of the prison cell, discarded into the night of torment, the moment it confesses that which, in the subject, makes the epiphany of power possible. It is a disavowed avowal. The voice can only be the other, the enemy. It must be simultaneously heard and repressed: heard because in saying the putrescence of the subject it guarantees or reestablishes a "belonging"—in secret, so it does not compromise the image upon which is based the institution's power of assuring its adherents the privilege of being recognized. The voice is required, but only as a whisper in the back halls of the institution. A murmurous scream exacted by torture, which must create fear without creating a scandal, legitimizes the system without toppling it.

What makes the victim right for this operation is precisely that he comes from outside. He brings a confession that is necessary for the internal functioning of the institution, but can at the same time be exorcized as something pertaining to the adversary. It is also true that the victim is the enemy. The stranger to or rebel against the institution displays an ambition that is intolerable within it (except hypocritically): he assumes, in one way or another, that a discourse—either a political discourse (a revolutionary project), a religious one (a reformist intention), or even an analytical one ("free" expression)—has the power to remake the institution. In opposition to this claim to reconstruct the order of history from a base in "adversarial" speech, torture applies the law of the institution, which assigns speech the reverse role of being no more than a confession linked to adherence.

Once again, torture is the perfect example of an *initiation* into the reality of social practices.[14] Its effect is always to demystify discourse. It is the *passage* from what is *said* outside to what is *practiced* within. This transit, the moment during which the torturer must *produce* assent from an exteriority, therefore *betrays* the game of the institution, but in darkness, under cover of night. While utopian (revolutionary) projects assume that modes of saying have the ability to determine modes of power, or that the institution can become the visible articulation of a "truth" that has been spoken or will be spoken—while this kind of project preserves an "evangelical" structure—torture on the other hand restores the law of what effectively *happens*. The voice, in torture, is no longer "prophetic"; it no longer aims for the transgression of following a desire. A name, *Luder,* dictates to the subject what he must be in order for the institution to be, in order for him to believe what it shows of itself, in order for it to adopt and recognize him.

The torture victim is surprised; he finds himself before a law he did not expect. For in the end, no one demands that he declare true what he holds to be false. The institution does not rest on the recognition of a truth it displays on the outside and in theory (on the inside, who takes it to be true?), but on its adherents' recognition of *their own* filthiness. Therefore, the subject seized by the apparatus of torture is faced not with the value or horror of the system—a ground upon which he would stand strong—but with a rift and intimate rottenness—a ground of weakness for him. The revelation of his own filth, which is what torture tries to produce by degrading him, should be enough to deprive him, like his torturers and all the others, of his right to rebel. The machinery of humiliation, through this reversal of the situation and this reverse use of speech (which no longer places the institution in question, but rather the subject), hopes to force the victim to accept the name by which his torturers address him: *Luder.*

What is perverse about the confessional procedure is that, no matter what, it is bound to hit the spot. Like Schreber isolated in the Sonnenstein mental hospital, the torture victim is deprived of the collective guarantees which ensure "normality"; he is abandoned to equipment that tears his body and unrelentingly works to prove to him that he is a betrayer, a coward, a pile of shit. He loses the alibi of the political, ideological, or social affiliations which in the past protected him against what the insulting name now teaches him about himself. Is this nomination not indeed the voice of what he is? "Yes, *that* [*ça*] is what I am, *Luder.*" What the name articulates in language is enough to make one forget past solidarities:[15] it is that "real" lurking behind a fragile self-possession and self-belonging. It is a mouth which opens to reveal what is rotten in the state of social relations or relations among militants. This thing that is pronounced and received is related to the hard revelation that mystic denuding and analytic elucidation adopt, in inverse modes but in the same solitude, as the beginning or principle of another voyage. We must inquire into what effects this confession has, what it enables the initiate to do, and what benefit an institution derives from such an enucleation.

There Is Some Other

Once he knows *that,* the torture victim may be annihilated, becoming the passive instrument of power; or he may allow himself any liberty, cynically exploiting his secret: these two types exist among the agents of the system— those who verify the revelation by conforming to the name, and those who exploit it by covering it over with a different, fine-sounding name. However, another outlet is open which is not resistance based upon the purity of militancy or the majesty of a cause, nor the game of the rotten within the institution of power. It is signaled in a movement that is neither denial [*dénégation*] nor perversion. It would be something to the effect of: "I am only *that* [*ça*], *but so what?*" Being rot does not necessarily lead the subject to identify with "that," or with an institution which "covers" it over. Some real survives this defection: a history, struggles, other subjects. It is perhaps even the case that the only thing real is what no longer seems liable to fix an identity or earn recognition for marchers.

Accounts by torture victims indicate the stage of breakdown at which their resistance intervenes. They "held up," they say, by maintaining (perhaps we should even say "enduring") the memory of comrades who, for their own part, were not "rotten"; by keeping in mind the struggle in which they were engaged, a struggle which survived their own "degradation" intact, and did not unburden them of it any more than it depended on it; by discerning still, through the din of their tortures, the silence of human anger and the genealogy of suffering that lay behind their birth, and from which they could no longer protect or expect anything; or by praying, in other words by assuming an otherness, God, from which neither aid nor justification was forthcoming, to which they were of no use and could not offer their services—exactly what an old rabbi means when he says that praying is "talking to the wall." This resistance eludes the torturers because it is ungraspable. It originates precisely in what eludes the victim himself, in what exists without him and allows him to elude the institution that takes him as its adopted son only through reducing him to *that* [*ça*], putrescence. Resistance such as this rests on *nothing* that could belong to him. It is a *no* preserved in him by what he does not have. Born of a recognized defection, it is the memory of a *real* that is no longer guaranteed by a Father.

The destruction of human dignity is also the beginning for the mystics—despite the fact that this corruption, which signs the subject and is often accompanied by the theatricalization of his body (wounds, infections, purulence, etc.), is unbearable for right-thinking commentators and is always disclaimed by "humanist" interpreters. In the words of Gottfried Benn,[16] the "stigmatized self" is the locus of breakdown and decomposition where "faith" arises. About this relation between contempt (you're nothing but rot) and faith (there is some other), we have a first indication in the form assumed by "pure love" for three or four generations of seventeenth century mystics: I love you no less for being damned. The subject does not stop looking toward the Orient from which he has been definitively separated, even after being rejected, cast away as waste. There is an outside—an *Out*—of what he *is*. But this moving, historical figure of faith conceived in terms of damnation is only a variant of the structure defined by Meister Eckhart with the concept of *Gelassenheit (gelâzenheit):* self-desertion based on the absolute (un-bound) of being, a "letting the Other be."[17]

Another example of this, of more classical inspiration (at least that is how it has come across in the written tradition that is all that remains of it), is to be found in the way in which St. John of the Cross characterizes the principle (nearly an *a priori*) that organizes the mystic voyage from start to finish. The principle of movement is "that which exceeds" *(aquello que excede).* It does not function as the presence and summation of all that is lacking. On the contrary, the excess and the unknown of an existence interface in every experience, just as in all knowing. Each stage arises out of the non-identity of the subject to the state in which he is. Perception, vision, ecstasy, deprivation, even putrescence, are one after the other cut off from a "that's not it [*ça*]," so that the discourse of St. John of the Cross constitutes an indefinite series of *not it, not it, not it.* The story he tells, as interminable as the events he classifies, in some way puts in narrative form the functioning of the signifier *God,* a source that introduces *always less* satisfaction and *always more* un-known in the subject's position. In short, what thus unfolds is the labor of what figures at the beginning of *The Ascent of Mount Carmel* as the postulate, or convention and rule of propriety *(conviene),* of an entire spiritual itinerary, to wit: *creer su ser.* Given the distinction between the verb *ser* (to be, ex-ist) and the verb *estar* (which is relative to a state), I translate this: to believe that there is some other.[18] In effect, for these mystics there is always some other, from which they in principle recover nothing. An other of no return. It ex-ists, nameless and unnaming.

Undoubtedly, the *there is some other* functioned on two registers which I am assuming we, unlike the mystics, can no longer hold to be identical. One is related to the role of the signifier, to a function of language: here, "God" is the meaningless fragment that breaks off all appropriation; it is the diamond splinter that restores an "always more" and an "always less" in relation to every act of knowledge and every pleasure. But the *there is* also expresses the meaning of Heidegger's *Es gibt:* "it gives." God in this case is the outside that is inside, the intimacy of Exteriority. It seems to me that the conjunction of these two functionings of the "there is some other," or of "God," was already problematical for the mystics. The certitude of the first often implies the verisimilitude of the second, or manages to hold it in suspense and make its uncertainty tolerable. However that may be, what I am able to conceive of it today (for reasons which I do not attribute to an anonymous and fictional contemporary *epistemē* but to much more particular fixations which, moreover, place my "masculine" approach to the mystics in question) is from the perspective that takes mysticism as the "science of the mere probability of the other."[19] This science assigns the recognition of a named putrescence (a calling, like a vocation) the role of an opening onto the indefinite probability of the other.

Tradition by Rotting

In this triangular sketch of "rottenness," whose revelation was heard by Schreber, the mystics and torture victims, I am simply exhibiting regions—psychoanalytic, Christian, and political—where I have encountered an identical problem. This geography of haunted itineraries has perhaps only subjective coherence. In truth, both our questions and the places where they are found precede us. The question at hand concerns either the *utopia* which, since the Reformation and the *Aufklärung,* has enacted the will to remake (rotten) institutions using fictions of "purity" as models, or the *realism,* the hidden figure of cynicism, which authorizes power by its ability to give recognition—or a noble adoptive filiation—to adherents who have already been convinced they are filth. In the first instance, the institution is the putrescence that must be reformed by recourse to more originary innocence, freedom, and purity. In the second, rottenness is something originary that the institution makes it profitable to recognize, and at the same time covers up. The resultant modes of initiation and transmission differ from one another and place the subject in opposing positions in relation to power and knowledge.

Looking back on the three experiences I have outlined, I am led to wonder whether there are outcomes other than reform based on a fiction of purity (where theory effects a denial), or conservatism based on an exploitation of putrescence (where the function of theory is to obscure its actual role). In the absence of a general reply to this question (there is none), I will limit myself to a few hypotheses concerning the features I have brought into focus.

President Schreber, whose name is rot, constructs a system *on the basis of* his degradation. He incarnates his name to become a filthy slut, or carrion—but the filth and whore of God, who "deals only with corpses,"[20] and is himself nothing more than a whore *(Hure)*.[21] The end of the world haunting this "prophet" of the absence of the other, the catastrophe of the Last Judgment in whose abyss he disappears, comes to a halt before 'the name of that which has no name."[22] "He rebuilds the world" upon this spoken place.[23] The genesis of a world on the foundation of a word. The production of a "delusional," fictional world on the basis of a genuine and authentic *(echt)* word. Schreber has to eliminate from the fiction he constructs any rifts into which universal disaster might seep. No nothing, no *nichts-denken* (thinking about nothing, conceiving nothingness) can be allowed to punch a hole in the corpus of his identity. He is at the last frontier—the putrescent—before total decomposition, and he can allow himself no rest and no absence, for *there is nothing other* than this discursive proliferation. In order to make this exhausting wager, he generates the *homogeneous;* he becomes a mother who loses nothing, and from within the network of divine rays he spins, he is able, in 1898, to consider himself "entitled to shit on the entire world."[24]

This discourse, which escapes the institution by substituting itself for it, can be likened to discourses that are termed spiritual, prophetic, or mystical, except that these often do not erect themselves upon so veridical a word. But this is not the case with the mystics of whom I spoke, to the extent that the *institution* itself *is the other* in relation to their delirium, and that is why the institution is relevant for them. In this context, there is no disappearance of the other, but an antimony between, on the one hand, naming, the poem that is authorized by nothing, and, on the other hand, the institution, which tends to control, rework, and alter the poem, allowing only interpreted or corrupt versions to circulate. But the debate is narrower. It is a question of determining whether, in refusing to replace the institution with a delusion, the mystic is not actually in the position of aligning himself with it, and by conforming to it in this way, of eliminating the other and returning to the same.

Such is the game of the institution. It *lodges* rottenness at the same time as it designates it. It assigns it a place, but a circumscribed one, constituted as an internal secret: between us, you're nothing but a slut, you're only a subject who is *supposed* to know. By lodging this "rottenness" within itself, the institution takes charge of it, limiting it to a truth that is known and pronounced on the inside, while allowing another discourse on the outside, the noble discourse of its theoretical manifestation. A piece of graffiti in a movie theater in Paris offered readers a transgression rejected by the institution: "Don't write in the shitters, shit on writing." Schreber went from one of these deviancies to the other. But for the institutional system, to shit in the shitters inside is the precondition for theory on the outside. Inside, "old fart" is a friendly term expressing the truth of a sodality: it is only said to those who are just that. This institutional "intimacy" is the only thing that makes it possible to qualify for engaging publicly in the discourse of and on the Other.

To put it another way, the institution is not only the delusional epiphany of an ideal ego which makes it possible to produce believers. It is not only a set of processes which generate credibility by withdrawing what they promise to give. It is not only a relation between something *known* and something *kept silent,* which is the mode in which Freud interprets the sacerdotal institution: that it is designed to keep a known murder silent. In addition, the institution is the assignation-localization of rottenness on the inside, which is what makes it discourse "grandiose"; it is a combination of the nocturnal *voice* which designates rotten people for itself, and the *manifestation* or "theory" of the sublime. This combination defines the relation to the master: call me *Luder,* so I can engage in your discourse. The transmission of knowledge takes the route of the rotten; tradition takes the route of a corruption that is recognized and allows the institution to remain the same.[25]

Thus, what goes on in the kitchen is quite different from what happens in the parlor. Perhaps the approach to take is the one traced in times past by St. Teresa and others, who wanted to join a *corrupt* order, and sought from it neither their identity nor recognition, but only the alteration of their necessary delirium. This would be to find in the institution itself both the seriousness of the real, and the mockery of the truth it displays.

Notes

1.   Daniel Paul Schreber, *Memoirs of My Nervous Illness*, tr. I. Macalpine and R. Hunter (London: Dawson and Sons, 1955), pp. 124–125. Translation modified. (*Denkwürdigkeiten eines Nervenkranken* [Leipzig: Oswald Mutze, 1903], pp. 136–137).

2.   *Collected Poems of Saint-John Perse* (Princeton: Princeton University Press, 1971), pp.58–69.

3.   Schreber, p. 50 (German, p. 13).

4.   See Chapter 5. (For "re-presentation," see Chapter 9, note 8—Tr.).

5.   See Michel de Certeau, "La fiction de l'histoire. L'écriture de 'Moïse et le monothéiseme,' " in *L'Ecriture de l'histoire* (Paris: Gallimard, 1975), pp. 312—358.

6.   Schreber, p. 164 (German, p.203).

7.   Jacques Lacan, *Le Séminaire III: Les psychoses* (Paris: Seuil, 1981), pp. 39–358.

8.   Ibid., pp.71–82.

9.   Schreber, p. 77 (German, p. 59).

10.   Matthew 23.27. In Greek it is *akatharsia*, in Latin *spurcitia*. In Luke a lawyer comments on the insulting nature of words such as these (11.45).

11. See for example Michel de Certeau, "Le corps folié: Folie et mystique aux XVIe et XVIIe siécles," in Armando Verdiglione, ed., *La folie dans la psychanalyse* (Paris: Payot, 1977), pp. 189–203.

12. There is an abundant literature on the subject. Cf. Amnesty International, *Report on Torture* (London, 1973) and *Torture in Greece* (London, 1977); Jean-Claude Lauret and Raymond Lasierra, *La torture blanche* (Paris: Grasset, 1975); Artur London, *L'Aveu* Paris: Gallimard, 1968); Bao Ruo-Wang (Jean Pasqualini), *Prisoner of Mao* (New York: Coward, McCann, Geoghan, 1973); Pierre Vidal-Naquet, *Torture: Cancer of Democracy, France and Algeria, 1954–1962*, tr. Barry Richard (Baltimore: Penguin, 1963); etc.

13. Cf. for example Steven E. Ozment, *Mysticism and Dissent* (New Haven: Yale University Press, 1973) for the sixteenth century; for the seventeenth century (and only if the reader makes distinctions between different kinds of experiences that are too closely equated by the author), cf. Leszek Kolakowski, *Chrétiens sans Eglise* (Paris: Gallimare, 1969). Cf. Michel de Certeau, *Politica e Mistica* (Milan: Jaca, 1975).

14. Cf. Pierre Clastres, *Society against the State*, tr. Robert Hurley (New York: Urizen, 1977), pp. 152–160 ("Of Torture in Primitive Societies").

15. Torture victims work not to "forget" their solidarities, like the resister who repeated the names of his comrades to himself while he was being tortured. The victory of torture is to efface the memory of any other name besides *Luder*.

16. Gottfied Benn, *Poémes*, tr. Pierre Garnier (Paris: Librairie Les Lettres, 1956).

17. For example, Reiner Schürmann, "Trois penseurs du délaissement: Maître Eckhart, Heidegger, Suzuki," *Journal of the History of Philosophy*, Vol. XII (1974), pp. 445–477 and Vol. XIII (1975), pp. 43–59; or Stanislas Breton, "Métaphysique et Mystique chez Maître Eckhart," *Recherches de science religieuse*, Vol. 64 (1976), pp. 161–182.

18. *The Ascent of Mount Carmel*, Book II, chap. 4, in *Complete Works of St. John of the Cross*, Vol. I, E. Allison Peers (London: Burns, Oates and Washbourne, 1934), pp. 73–78. On this text, cf. de Certeau, "Le corps folié," p. 193.

19. Jean Louis Schefer, *L'invention du corps chrétien* (Paris: Galilée, 1975), p. 141.

20. Schreber, p. 75. (German, p. 65).

21. Schreber, p. 278 (German, p. 384).

22. Jacques Lacan, *Ecrits: A Selection*, tr. Alan Sheridan (New York: Norton, 1977), p. 183.

23. Sigmund Freud, *The Case of Schreber*, in *Standard Edition*, tr. James Strachey (London: Hogarth, 1953–1974), Vol. 12, p. 71.

24. Schreber, p. 177 (German, p 226).

25. Must we recognize as a homologue of this structure the Aristotelian articulation of *form* and *matter*? Matter ($\dot{v}\lambda\dot{\eta}$) is, for Aristotle, at the same time what decomposes, dissolves (rots?), and what stands in opposition to form as a woman to a man. To give form to a certain "matter" (an indeterminacy in defection): the role of the institution?

Part II
Sexual Identity

Micheline Enriquez

7. Paranoiac Fantasies: Sexual Difference, Homosexuality, Law of the Father

O ur purpose in this work is to formulate some hypotheses and reflections about feminine paranoia and to attempt to encompass what could possibly constitute certain specific features and activities at work in the feminine aspect of the "illness."

A long detour by way of masculine paranoia will be necessary for us, even if we will only highlight certain aspects.

We will focus exclusively on the study of *paranoiac fantasies,* most notably those which form the Schreberian trilogy, namely:

- the fantasy of unmanning;
- the fantasy of redemption and the salvation of the world;
- the fantasy of supernatural procreation

At first then we will take up the analysis of this fantasmatic constellation, starting with the case of Schreber and masculine paranoia.

Secondly, we will devote ourselves more precisely to the study of the "case" of Valeria Solanas, a young American writer, author of a text as exceptional for its psychopathological elements as for its sociological and literary ones: the *Scum Manifesto* or Manifesto of the Society for Cutting Up Men.

The author, a member of the American Underground, has never pretended to write a "memoir of my mental illness," but rather a particularly violent pamphlet against American male-dominated society. The *Scum Manifesto* contains some of the most characteristic Schreberian themes, particularly the fantasies of unmanning, of saving the world and of unnatural procreation, but they are approached from a feminine angle. We will consider this typically fantasmatic paranoiac constellation which constitutes Schreber's delusional system and the theme of Valerie Solanas' text, a constellation whose effect manifests itself in the certainty *that a possible change in sex authorizes a possible change in the order of the universe and the order of life:*

1) in the relation it maintains with the originary fantasies, in particular with the fantasy of the primal scene.
2) in the relation it sustains with homosexuality, when it tries to specify the nature of this homosexuality, since if it remains true that the genesis of paranoia is dependent on a fantasy of homosexual desire (as in the letter of Freudian theory), the nature of this desire remains complex. To simply say that the love-hate couplet is by the same token implied here, says little about this "same-other," in this case.

Freud demonstrated an interest in paranoia from the beginning of his work, and tried several times to establish its genesis, referring in his first works to real events, memories, precise sexual scenes; and referring later on to fantasmatic constructions which he called at the time a "defense function."[1] In a letter to Fliess, he even spoke of defensive fabulations, that is, of some ensemble of stagings and imaginary scenarios of a secondary order, whose essential function was to allow for the recovery of experiences or memories which could be traumatic after the fact and stir up the appearance of pathological manifestations.

Freud perceived very quickly the complex involvement between what he called the sexual scene (at the time it was essentially a question of the scene of seduction) and the existence of fantasies focused on the same theme, whose appearance is only possible from bits and pieces to be traced and dated within the subject's own personal experience.

In effect, with regard to what he called at that time the psychoneuroses of defense (i.e., hysteria, the obsessive neuroses and paranoia), Freud tried to make diagnostic distinctions in terms of the date of the sexual scene, that is, the periods in which the decisive incident took place; the distinction is still valid currently.

From the very beginning, too, he stressed a relation between paranoia and the myths relating to childbirth and what was later to become the 'family romance,' which would in the end reveal itself to be a typical variation of the fantasmatic scenario that Freud then thought specific to paranoia.

What was merely an intuition and an incomplete reflection at the moment of the birth of psychoanalysis was to be elaborated progressively and resulted in 1911 in the study of President Schreber, and in 1915 in "A Case of Paranoia Running Counter to the Psycho-Analytic Theory of the Disease." The latter is a very interesting case because in a sense it is more exemplary than that of Schreber, in whose case the richness, complexity and intricacy of the themes are somewhat obscured.

Origin and Function of Fantasy

The fantasmatic Schreberian constellation consists:

- of a *fantasy of unmanning,* i.e., the possibility for a man to be transformed into a woman, with the suggestion of actual castration,
- of a *fantasy of redemption* and of the world's salvation.
- of a *fantasy of supernatural procreation.*

These fantasies, consciously formulated and which are symptomatic of psychosis to the extent that they belong to delusional conviction, only produce a structured and structuring ensemble (this is at least our hypothesis), when they are supported by an originary unconscious fantasy. This ensemble represents much more than a simple staging of desire. These fantasies appear more like some ultimate gropings for identifications, some *graftings of sense* necessary for the more or less successful emergence of subjectivity, and also for the emergence of a law, an order; graftings of sense, order and law, which find their source in something that Schreber describes as *"contrary to the order of the universe."*

In addition, desire always is articulated in a fantasy through which it appears veiled, denied, disguised, caricatured, or totally unveiled, but it is also the place of the most primitive defensive operations (much more primitive than repression) such as turning against oneself, reversal and its contrary, projection, denial, etc. The fantasy, then, has always a conservative, protective and defensive function and tends to maintain in another field and in another place an unknown or inexpressible secret.

In addition, (this is our second hypothesis) no imaginary formation is specific, nor is it itself determinative of a structure or of a process' dynamic. Freud reminds us of this in his article of 1908, on hysterical fantasies and their relation to bisexuality, a work in which he stated "that the paranoiac fantasies are of the same nature as hysterical fantasies, but that they have a direct access to consciousness, which they do not have in hysteria" and that they are "based on the sado-masochistic component of the libido."

Also, we should never reduce and too quickly establish a relation of cause and effect between a fantasy and a clinical structure. No fantasy has in itself either a nosographic or a diagnostic value.

Thus, Macalpine and Hunter's hypothesis about the fantasy of sexual uncertainty, for example, and the fantasies of pregnancy, which could account for Schreber's paranoia, is insufficient.

In fact,

- only *the articulation and combination of several fantasies,* of several imaginary formations, allow us to focus closely on clinical structures, since this combination always provides the key indices.

- *this fantasmatic constellation* is of a secondary order, belonging to secondary process. It makes sense for the subject but only takes its meaning from the relation it maintains with the originary fantasies. It is at this point that the delusional structure begins to make sense.

Starting with this, it begins to appear that *the origin of fantasies is integrated in the very structure of the originary fantasy,* a fantasy which belongs to both the myth and the history of the subject.

A well known example of the fantasy "A Child is Being Beaten," with regard to its place in the masochistic structure, will permit us to illustrate our account.[2] Freud presents this fantasy as a typical occurrence connoting the difference of the sexes, through the staging of positions

- active—passive
- or sadistic—masochistic.

This refers back to the masculine-feminine formations. They evidently do not overlap, but the confusion between active-passive and masculine-feminine is at the root of many pathological, neurotic or perverse manifestations, and indeed at the source of the Western and Judeo-Christian ideological and cultural tradition.

Such a fantasy, fully compatible with many clinical structures, is apparently more frequent in women, and by itself of little significance, except as the scars of Oedipus—remains of incestuous love for the father, without any obvious connection (Freud goes so far to say) to the genesis of true masochism. At the same time, Freud implies that this fantasy could be structural to the very organization of certain clinical structures where the paternal problematic is central.[3]

In a truly masochistic subject, the fantasy "A Child is Being Beaten" appeared to be sustained by *a fantasy of the primal scene—sadistic, violent and catastrophic.* In such a case, the body of an other (in this instance of the mother) invested by the subject (that is, the child) and by the father is subjected to violence and torture in a very particular context. In such a context, the date of the scene, what was heard and the history of the subject's "body" are of primary importance. Such an originary staging, where memory traces, bits of reality and imaginary formations are intermingled, acquires among other things a *fixity* which blocks all further metaphorization of the scene.[4]

Indeed, it seems that in such a context, where the data of lived experience and of history are obviously mixed, the fantasy "A Child is Being Beaten" becomes an attempt to escape, a search for identifications, for marks which found the alterity of the subject and enable him to mobilize his libido. In fact, this fantasy can play a structural role only to the extent that it is *supported* by an originary fantasy which presents a specified sadistic tonality in its relation to violence; a violence, however, which, even if it is related to the fantasy of anal-sadistic intercourse, is quite removed from it at another level. In any event, clinical experience shows us that no analysis of this fantasy can be done (understood, in the masochistic subject) unless one concurrently analyzes the primal scene. In effect it is only through a return to the primal scene that the identification can be reestablished, that the avatars of Oedipus (the incestuous positions in relation to the father, the positions with regard to sexual difference) can be analyzed.

Certain conditions are then necessary for the fantasy "A Child is Being Beaten" to truly refer back to a *subjective* masochistic position. If these conditions are resisted, it is merely a fantasy of masochistic desire, to be understood with Freud as a typical occurrence, an oedipal scar. It is only a symptom articulated in a process. Likewise, and even more so, the existence of a fantasy of desire, dependent upon repressed homosexuality, is clearly not enough to create paranoia.

Paranoiacs will encounter homosexuality in the course of their psychosis to the extent that it is caught up with their attempts at identification and the problematic of the father which is primordial for them:

- they are not aware of pursuing these attempts, nonetheless the demons who pursue them and persecute them set the father in question.

If it remains unanswered, this tormenting question gives rise to not only the vacillation of the subject, but also of the order of the world itself, hence of the order of the first marks referring to "to be or not to be" and "to be a man or a woman."

The originary fantasies bring to these two necessities related to the mystery of life, hence to the mysteries of procreation and death, not a response, but stagings which weave a plot to which the subject can then refer himself. All the delusional constructions, the medico-legal acts, even paranoiac crimes, have no other end than to witness this questioning of the order of the world. The paranoiac's "insane" responses are always attempts at a cure, and attempt to situate themselves in relation to *an order* in which their identity would be assured, as in a movement of counter-cathexis.

Seglas in 1895 defined paranoid delusion as follows: "The delusion presents itself like a sort of inexact perception of humanity, escaping from *the law* of universal consensus, like a particular interpretation of the external world in its relations with the personality of the diseased, who relates *everything to himself,* whether it is evil or good. The delusion is accompanied by a lack of criticism and of control, by an absolute faith, even though lucidity applies exclusively outside the delusion."

Let us add that the importance of chastisement to the system of persecution is symptomatic of an unconscious desire for punishment and self-chastisement; and that, at least according to classical theory, the persecutor is always of the same sex as the persecuted, and was previously a love-object.

The relation to law, to narcissism, to a certain type of *homosexuality,* are indeed the key points of paranoia.

As for Schreber, he maintains that a change in the order of sex, a change in the order of the world and of life must result.

It seems that such themes raise a question as to origin which in turn focuses on the question of paternity, and privileges the homosexual drives. But to say so sheds light neither on the originary fantasy, which sustains the relation of the paranoiac to paternity, nor on the nature of the homosexual drives in terms of sexual difference.

This is what we would like to clarify now.

The Schreberian Fantasies

Schreber is grappling with:

- *an "unmanning" fantasy,* which takes the form of "being changed into a woman," and thus a fantasy of sex change that goes far beyond the question of castration,
- *a fantasy of redemption,* the subject believing that he has a salvational and sacrificial mission, one which would bring about the good and happiness of humanity,
- *a fantasy of procreation,* which accounts for fecundation by means other than natural; supernatural divine means for Schreber, but also, more prosaically, means related to scientific techniques (artificial insemination, parthenogenesis, etc.) These means are in no way similar to intercourse, which implies a real, tangible relation between man and woman.

These fantasies can exist perfectly separate and not one of them of itself signifies paranoia. One could very well think of changing the world without for all that having to be changed into a woman; or inversely, of imagining systems of filiation which would not necessarily follow the route of ordinary genealogy, without being explicitly paranoiac (though in this case there arises a serious doubt).

Schreber himself writes: "I have been sick twice;

- the first time on the occasion of a candidacy to the Reichstag.
- the second following an extraordinary work that I had to provide in entering into my new function as President of the Dresden Court of Appeals."

The first illness lasted from the Autumn of 1884 to the end of 1885 and was completely cured. Schreber was sent to Flechsig's clinic where his state was diagnosed as acute hypochondria.

The second illness took place in october of 1893, after eight years of remission. This time it lasted nine years. Schreber left the clinic in July of 1902, if not entirely cured at least much improved, and in 1903 he published his memoirs, which were subsequently completely censored by Schreber's family. The court judgment which returned Schreber's freedom to him contains a summary of his delusional system in the following passage: "He thought he was called to save the world and give it back its lost bliss. But he could do so only after being transformed into a woman."

Schreber alleged that he was sworn to this mission by a direct divine inspiration. The essence of his mission of salvation consisted in this: that he first had to be *changed into a woman;* nothing or nearly nothing is said of this new order of the world. Schreber insists that this is a *necessity* founded on the universal *order,* not a matter of his own desire. He would rather remain a man, but neither he, nor the rest of humanity could attain immortality again unless he, Schreber, was transformed into a woman. This operation would be accomplished only after many years, and through divine miracles operating by way of *rays.*

One could think, says Freud, like the psychiatrists who had assessed Schreber, that the ambition to play a redemptive role would promote a whole set of delusional ideas, and that unmanning is only one means of attaining this objective. But Freud emphasizes that if one follows the *Memoirs* attentively, it turns out that the transformation into a woman and the correlative unmanning constituted the primary delusion, that it realized a serious prejudice, and that it is only secondarily related to the theme of redemption.

Thus, *the delusion of sexual persecution* is later transformed into "mystical megalomania."

Schreber's *fantasy of unmanning* can be formulated in a number of different ways:

For example:

I must be transformed into a woman.
I will one day be transformed into a woman.
or still yet,
I will become a woman.
But the form, in all cases, is *passive.*

The operation to accomplish, in this instance unmanning, proceeds from the desire of an all-powerful other (this is not me, this the Other, this is God). One sees that, in such a staging, the scenario is radically different from that of the ordinary transsexual who has the delusional conviction that he belongs to the other sex; hence his demand to the surgeon that the body be altered.

The male transsexual will say:

I want to be emasculated. I demand that my fantasy be realized, my castration is justified due to the existence of an error, and not by any necessary tie to a fault involving the order of the world. The fantasy of the transsexual is written in the *active form.*

In Schreber an invasive and diffuse notion of guilt is revealed: the transformation into a woman at once assumes the value of desire, of punishment, of desire for punishment, emasculation stemming both from the desire and from the punishment by law.

As for the *fantasy of redemption,* it is closely tied, as Freud stressed, to the *fantasy of unmanning.* It is expressed by the idea of a *sacrificial* vocation, a mission for which the *subject* is *chosen.* To become a woman is the price he must pay for the bliss of the world. Indeed, the subject finds there his reckoning, but he remains necessarily associated with the idea of sacrifice, sin and guilt, and redemptive punishment.

This is also a mission one has to accomplish alone, which quite obviously demonstrates megalomania, narcissistic omnipotence, and the delusion of grandeur.

But it is also a question of being the *sole elect of God,* since Schreber alone absorbs, thanks to his force of attraction, the largest number of divine rays that others are deprived of. Moreover, this mission demands patience and a long period of time (years, decades, says Schreber), a period during which the subject remains immortal and time remains suspended.

By virtue of his position in relation to God, Schreber becomes the instrument of his own omnipotence, the *incarnation of a sort of legitimacy.* This sacrificial and redemptive vocation restores narcissism, but introduces:

- a collusion between the ego-ideal and the ideal self
- a relation to temporality which manifests the negation of death
- a relation to the *law* where the subject becomes the instrument of an all-powerful law.

The narcissistic unity, however, is maintained at a very high price, that of the real sacrifice of a bodily part. Here the pound of flesh is not metaphorical and it is this which signifies indubitably the makings of psychosis.

As regards the fantasy of procreation, it is derived from the primal scene, in the sense that it poses the origin of the subject, and the relation between the parental union and what can result from it—pregnancy and childbirth.

In his work of 1909 on *family romances,* Freud separated fantasies of procreation. He thus designated a conscious group of fantasies through which the subject imaginarily modifies his relations with his parents (imagining that he is, for example, a foundling).

Freud's article of 1909 incorporated Rank's *The Myth of the Birth of the Hero,* and Freud thought at that time that the "family romances" were *characteristic marks of paranoia.*

He distinguished two stages, according to whether the child is or is not aware of the sexual determinants of procreation. In the phase of asexual ignorance, the child substitutes two idealized personages for the two parents, imagining himself to be the lost child. In the second phase, the sexual phase, the father alone is exalted, taking on a prestigious character, and the child's fantasies are oriented toward the mother and her infidelity and secret loves. This results in making the subject the *incarnation,* the depository of *legitimacy,* and in contesting the legitimacy of those brothers and sisters who preceded him, or are to come.

With the creation of such a romance, the subject fuels his desire to be the only one, *the elect of the father,* and he weaves, among other things, a certain desire for grandeur. This is certainly why Freud first pointed out these desires in paranoia, even if later on he discovered them in various forms in neurotics.

The formation by Schreber of the procreation fantasy is entirely exemplary in this respect. After many conflicts and ambivalences, he finally adopts a feminine attitude toward God: what happens to me, he says, is

> Something like the conception of Jesus Christ by the Immaculate Virgin—i.e., one who never had intercourse with a man—happened in my own body. Twice at different times (while I was still in Flechsig's asylum) I had a female genital organ, although a poorly developed one, and in my body felt quickening like the first signs of life of a human embryo: by a divine miracle God's nerves corresponding to male seed had been thrown into my body; in other words *fertilization* had occurred.

The Fantasy of the Primal Scene in Paranoia.[5]

These three fantasies encompass the essence of Schreber's delusion—to be called to save the world and return its lost blessedness, to be able to accomplish the mission only after having been transformed into a woman, and to give birth to Schreberian children. In our opinion, they form a system only to the extent that it is sustained by an originary fantasy of the specific primal scene. Moreover, this originary fantasy should be primarily defined as fixed, function as a point of appeal, constitute a force of attraction, and precipitate and impose certain responses and not others. What can be understood by 'fixed'—and how does this process of fixation operate? It is quite evident that not all primal scenes have this character and that they carry multiple issues, leaving the subject with a certain range of possibilities for his identifications and cathexes.

Now, what we call a fixed primal scene does not properly leave free range to the subject and impose on him a stereotypical issue.

In effect, to say point of appeal, force of attraction, is also to say fixation, a concept often invoked in psychoanalysis, but whose nature, significance and mechanisms are poorly specified. The concept seems to connote both the notion of inscription and memory trace, but the fixation of representations is not produced without the anchoring of excitation, without the participation of libidinal cathexis. As to the conditions for fixation, Freud insists that they largely depend on historical conditions, the first order of these being *trauma,* one which certainly depends on an event, but also on the subject's psychological condition at the time of the event.

When the analyst finds himself confronted with a fantasy of the "fixed" primal scene, what is clearly at issue is fixation and trauma.

Fixation and trauma, such as they were understood by Freud in "Inhibition, Symptom, Anxiety"—that is, as having a primordially anxiety forming and structural function—are the two essential means of repetition. While we need not recall their links to the death instinct, their relations to mastery and symbolization are no less evident.

Paradoxically, however, the paranoiac doesn't repeat much, at least in the classical sense of the term. He invests, creates and recreates, he interprets while leaning upon *fixation*—the recording in the purely visual sense of the term, and its corollary, blindness, *so as to graft sense upon non-sense, or to represent the unrepresentable.*

Such originary fantasies are very difficult to recover as such in analysis. They are recuperable from fragments, from traces, memories, clues, oneiric sequences, and it is often necessary to devote oneself to a reconstruction which, however, will never be arbitrary if one faithfully follows clinical procedure.

In the case of Schreber, Freud does not really make any allusion to the primal scene in his commentary. He will actually focus upon the primal scene in his study of the Wolfman, and in the case of 1915, "A Case of Paranoia Running Counter to the Psycho-Analytic Theory of the Disease." Nevertheless, it seems that in Schreber, the fantasy of the primal scene can be noticed when he tells us he was struck, in the days preceding the onset of his second illness, by the idea *"it must be rather pleasant to be a woman succumbing to intercourse."*

Much later, when his delusion was more systematized, Schreber claimed that God demands *a constant state of jouissance,* and that it is his duty to offer him this *jouissance* (that of God), and that hence he inscribes on his flags the *"cult of femininity"* which he takes as far as fetishism and transvestism. Or again:

> ". . . God would never attempt to withdraw . . . if only I could always be playing the woman's part in sexual embrace with myself . . ."

This disturbing proximity with the primal scene is not auspicious for later identifications. A lack of distance with the primal scene appears here as the part of the subject where blending, confused elements can be noticed, elements of fascination, negation and rupture, which are manifest as a sort of spatio-temporal disaster, that one supposes would be converted into a particularly violent and catastrophic angst. But Freud, at the time of the Schreber study, focused his work on the hypothesis that paranoia is connected with *repressed homosexuality,* an hypothesis which is no longer accepted today.

Only later would Freud see the importance of the primal scene, in the case of 1915, especially, but also mainly thanks to the Wolfman, who provided a paranoiac episode centered around hypochondriacal thoughts.[6] It seems that, from that point on, a certain primal scene fantasy is closely connected with paranoia.

The case of 1915 concerns a young woman, an only child living with her mother, the father having died many years before. During an affair with her employer, in the midst of sexual intimacies, she began to have persecutory delusions. She accused her employer of taking compromising photographs that might eventually cost her her job. She claimed that she heard a shutter click, which seemed to issue from behind a desk, where a heavily curtained window was located.

The problem confronting Freud was that this case *contradicted* his previous clinical remarks because the persecutor was not of the same sex. Apparently, homosexuality was not at issue here. But Freud finally succeeded in uncovering facts that the patient had kept secret, and which bring to light this young woman's strong fear that a director of her service division—a woman with white hair like her mother, who liked her—had been told of her relations and that she might resent her for this. Thus, in this instance, it was a *female persecutor,* thought to be an accomplice of the employer, and who represented a maternal figure capable of punishing, judging and eventually persecuting her.

Freud is once again reassured, and he can maintain his theory of repressed homosexuality and a maternal persecutor of the same sex. But in accordance with this observation, Freud invites us above all to refer, among the richness of the unconscious fantasies of neurotics, and probably of all humans, to "the one which is rarely absent and can be discovered by analysis and is related to the observation of the sexual relations between parents."

And in the case of the young woman in question, Freud proposes a "reconstruction." He indicates that the origin and the meaning of noise (the click, the shock, the trigger) is to be found in what he called at the time an originary fantasy *(Urphantasie),* the sound presenting a double aspect: first, revealing to the child the sexual relations of the parents, and, second, being the sound of the infant on the look-out and betraying him in turn.

We recognize, this time, the territory on which we ourselves are situated, says Freud. The loving one is always the father, and in relation to parental intercourse, the patient assumed the place of the mother. The act of overhearing must as as consequence be attributed to a third person, *and the identification to the mother is made at a regressive narcissistic level*—i.e., at the level of *identity* and not of *similarity.*

In effect, to make a choice of masculine love, the patient had to liberate herself from a homosexual dependence on her mother. To achieve this, she underwent a regression. Instead of considering her mothers as a love object (which would indicate her homosexual dependence, but would also posit the woman as desiring and desirable) she identified herself with her, she herself was transformed into a mother.

> "And the noise which reveals the parents as well as the child, in the case in question, ends in a rejection of the man, and gives to the *profound intentions of the maternal complex a means of coming to be.*"

Such a scene leaves no place for the father as a bearer of the phallus, indeed, but above all, it annuls all difference with the mother. There still remains an *empty place,* for the third person takes on the position of listener.

At that moment, the patient had worried about the sound she supposedly heard. It is only when she hurriedly left the apartment, having renounced sexual satisfaction, that, meeting two men on the staircase, she remarked that one of them was carrying a package, and that they were talking in low voices while looking at her. She constructed her delusion from this scene: the box became a camera; the noise heard as coming from the camera shutter, snapped by the two men behind the curtain of the apartment.

Freud, moreover, does not believe in the reality of the noise. According to him it is largely a projection, one whose origin is to be sought at the level of the body, a body prey to sexual excitation, which is neither admissible nor recognizable, and thus the body creates a mechanism of projection transmitting outside what is not sustainable from within.

Freud's clinical reflection on this originary fantasy is very fruitful. It highlights:

- the dreadfully traumatic aspect of such a fantasy
- the primordial importance of the heard (the noise)

and its two poles: to hear and to be heard.

- the primacy of the heard over the seen
- the secondarization of the trauma, its mastery or

rather its recovery, in the form of a delusional interpretation, which fixates a meaning

- this in turn materializes itself in something *seen,* whose primary function is to create a protective screen (a screen perceptible in the very discourse of the young woman, in the form of a curtain, a photographic plate, etc.)
- a type of "regressive narcissistic" identification with the mother whose consequences are the *"rejection"* of the male and the establishment of an empty place.

It is only this last point that we will take up more precisely.

The Narcissistic Identification with the Mother

The relation with the mother reveals itself to be of a narcissistic kind. The patient, says Freud, transforms herself into a mother, she is the mother. It is in this sense that he speaks of regressive narcissistic identification.

In his work, "Paranoia and the Primal Scene," Rosalato also takes up this term of narcissistic identification, as does Melman who calls it "an imaginary position captivated by the woman."[7] As for White, he interprets Schreber's feminine desire as a reemergence of a very precocious identification, one which would result from a particularly traumatic first moment of separation from the mother—a moment where Schreber's mother teaches the infant "the art of renunciation" (an art which, as is commonly known, the Schreber family cultivated, and that all paranoiacs lay claim to).[8]

The term narcissistic is not perhaps perfectly adequate. It might be more apt to refer to the notion of identification with the mother as a total body, as a *place* where investment and identification merge.

This type of identification provokes a rejection of the male and situates the relation with him in a space "outside sense," from where the imperative necessity of creating an imaginary formation makes sense.

The empty place—that of the third, which can be occupied by the subject himself—is occupied secondarily in the case of Freud's patient, by persecutors, which perfectly demonstrates that it constitutes a point of appeal, a force of attraction, i.e., represents what was rejected, foreclosed.[9]

It is quite clear that in this case what was rejected were the functions of the father and of the phallus as having an assignable place in the primal scene. And in the place of the *void regarding the father* there reemerges a *fantasy* which will always function to graft sense onto "non-sense," and place it in relation to the paternal order and the law, but in a fashion which differs according to the subject's sex.

The father and the law tend to evoke violence, even if "legitimate violence."

Every fantasy of the primal scene implies a relation of and to violence. Even if the sadistic conception of sexual intercourse is later abandoned, it is nevertheless operative for the mobilization and secondary elaboration of our relations to sexuality, life and death.

One could say that, when the neurotic is confronted by violence, he *represses* it, *does not recognize* it, does not want to be taken to task and resolves his problem more often by games of inhibition and withdrawal.

The sexually perverse personality stages violence either through a sado-masochistic scenario or in the form of visual, exhibitionist aggression, or voyeurism, etc. In a certain way, he *plays* with it, at best he speaks intelligently and subtly, like a masochist.

As for the paranoiac, he *rejects* it in the purest sense of the Freudian *Verwerfung;* according to the clearest mechanism of foreclosure, what was not symbolized reappears as real, the delusion of persecution being the most elaborate form, and murder the most naked. He rejects violence in his fantasy of the primal scene, where the narcissistic identification with the mother (or with the body of the mother as the totality of the scene) coupled with a powerful maternal investment leads to the *exclusion of violence.*[10] It seems plausible that such a fantasy is specific to paranoia.[11] Concerning the paranoiac, it is correct to say that what triggers the delusion, the madness, the act "outside the law," will always be centered on a traumatic situation; it imposes itself on the life of the subject and implies an irruption of "paternal violence."

The Schreberian Fantasies in Relation to Homosexuality

From this configuration of the primal scene where identification and maternal investment are confused, and where references to the paternal function begin to fail, the following states result:

- the impending threat of a return to narcissistic identification
- the presence of a void linked to primary, traumatic helplessness and the consequent states of fear and feelings of loss and imminent catastrophe which accompany it, and are easily detectable clinically in all paranoiacs.
- the absence of the idea of paternity, in its biological as well as its symbolic connotations.

Such an originary staging testifies to a blockage of meaning. How does the paranoiac attempt to get out of this void, this non-sense, and bring about some grafting of sense, counter-cathexis, and elements of certitude? What "defensive fabulations," what *system* will he put into place to constitute identifications, references that shelter him from the chaos of non-alterity and that will secure his conformity to the order of the universe?

A single solution seems to impose itself on the paranoiac: the option of homosexuality. In fact, the masculine paranoiac finds himself compelled to attempt paternal identifications and cathexes, an attempt which is properly a *narcissistic necessity* to constitute an Other, a mirror and a witness to his own alterity. This permits him to adopt a variety of libidinal identifications positions, and to construct a theory of origins.

To accomplish this, the paranoiac will employ a series of stagings and defensive fabulations, inserting them in the structure of the originary fantasy, where they will function to make visible his alterity and subjective positions. This, in turn, will privilege his homosexual urges and the libidinal cathexis of same. But what is the nature of this "same?"

A question is indeed asked here. Freud always claimed that the first relation of the boy to his mother is of a heterosexual nature. He will equally maintain that the original lack and a homosexual mother-daughter relation weigh doubly upon the daughter as she evolves toward femininity.

Can one really speak of heterosexuality, however, without recourse to an oedipal conflict, one which supposes a complex mechanism of separation and individuation, all the while passing through a process of decathexis and maternal disidentification?

To separate one's identity from the mother's, either as a boy or girl, constitutes the indispensable step for access to masculinity and feminity as such, and to the recognition of this difference. Failing this, the child will remain fixated on the mother, as common sense dictates, but chiefly to her "femaleness, i.e., all that turns around partial instincts, the symbiotic and fusional relation to the mother, and for some, this signals the era of bliss.

But this bliss—if that is indeed what it is—is destined to disappear. Schreber will nonetheless devote half of his life to recover it, even if he must suffer the "martyrdom of Christ."

Schreber maintains therefore "that it is possible to become a woman," and this supposes, as we have seen, a powerful maternal cathexis as well as a narcissistic identification with the mother. The grafting of sense operates secondarily by displacing the cathexis on the paternal figure, and by reinforcing progressively more perverse and mobile feminine identifications, with their fetishistic, masochistic, transsexual, etc. connotations. Since the father is invested libidinally, he takes on his specific sense according to the homosexual composition of the libido.

In the second place, Schreber thinks he has to save the world. His *"I must save the world"* presents an imperative character which must be emphasized (because it is more a question of saving himself than saving humanity). This allows him to achieve at least the minimal narcissistic adjustments, with their corollaries, of the ideal ego and the ego-ideal. Schreber also establishes, by means of this fantasy, a relation to the law, of which he becomes an instrument *(I must)*.

On the level of the primary process, it is the distress, the feeling of utter loss, of traumatic experiences, which are in question. The grafting of sense, then, is brought about by the necessity to sacrifice a real part of his body through the expedient of unmanning, which allows a *narcissistic reestablishment* of the subject.

At the same time, the father will be founded in regard to the law, of which the subject will become an instrument. This terrible paternal figure, the almighty persecutor, is that of the *idealized father* (a figure behind which maternal power is screened); it is the creator (not the representative) of the law, an incarnation of savage, arbitrary and irresistible violence. Nonetheless it assumes force of law for the paranoiac, allowing him to refer himself in an imaginary way to an Other.

Schreber believes equally that it "is possible to procreate in a supernatural manner," which for him denotes the meaninglessness of the elementary signifiers of paternity as well as excluding all manifest violence in the representation of the primal scene. He will thus invent a supernatural theory of procreation where the will of God is enough to impregnate at a distance.

The manifest violence that this process eliminates seems to reemerge in the passive form, with an acceptable, and accepted, homosexual transformation.

This fantasy also evokes the desire to bear the father's child, at the price of his own virility, as well as the desire to be sexually satisfied by him, which is clearly expressed for Schreber in the mode of anal eroticism, an intimate form of homosexual expression.

Another possible destiny for this fantasy resides in his desire to be the creator, and to engender himself; but to produce a work in this domain, however, writing appeared as a privileged resource.

Through all these fanciful stagings of supernatural procreation, the father is reestablished and serves as origin and antecedent. Nevertheless it is still a question of the triumph of homosexuality (but one can just as well say of bisexuality or unisexuality).

By reason of staging this delusional, fantasmatic constellation (the orders of sex, the order of the world, and the order of the creation of life) become significantly modified. It is in this way that the paranoiac recovers an order, certainty and meaning—all of which are established through the mobilization of the libido and homosexual identification.

The picture seems to be dominated by the compulsive and perfectionistic attempt to found or construct a figure of an *idealized father.*

It is to this almighty, castrating, persecuting, immortal, idealized father that the paranoiac identifies, submits and offers himself; he becomes its instrument. He can also go as far as Schreber, and ask him to prove his omnipotence and desire, ask for actual castration. But this fiction must be maintained at all costs, since it preserves a reference to the law, which, as soon as it is threatened, makes the risk of a tragic rupture (of killing, suicide, etc.) and its inscription in the space of illicit violence all too apparent.

But this idealized father is also a constant companion of the pervert, in that the confrontation with this arbitrary power responsible for the law is indispensable in maintaining the pervert's structure, that is, his transgression and disavowal.

However, this encounter with the idealized father in perversion and paranoia (even if this encounter is not yet constructed and elaborated for the paranoiac, whereas for the pervert, it is already in place) is not at all fortuitous. In fact, the frontiers between perversion and paranoia are not always easy to discern, since all perverts are capable of falling into paranoia, and all paranoiacs of stabilizing and disengaging themselves from psychosis by means of perversion.

The importance and weight of secrets asserting themselves as a major narcissistic reassurance may be found in the two structures. But this is where the resemblance stops. For the pervert, what is at stake in his relations to the other, what is at the core of his knowledge and power, are his secrets (secrets about the origins, knowledge of the other's desire, etc.). The paranoiac's secret is his own, he reserves and hides it from himself, because it concerns his homosexuality (with its connotations of *effeminacy*), as if this gave him the intimate acquaintance with a world before sin. Thus it seems that there is almost a narcissistic necessity for him to keep his homosexuality a *secret,* and to employ a variety of *logical contradictions* with regard to it. Such logical contradictions keep him in the space of desire, and in a certain relation to the law. Were these contradictions revealed to him, they could lead him back to chaos and to the primacy of maternal control, because they assure him of a minimum of sense, in the perspective, as Schreber tells us, of a certain conformity to the order of the universe.

Given this, one can maintain that the paranoiac has ceased to be perverse, because the pervert would, rather, have a tendency to defy to the order of the universe. He *wants* to be the source of the scandal, whereas the paranoiac wants to be the source of order—a continually new order, which promises the reign of good and of recovered bliss, even though to accomplish this he must impose a reign of terror and establish himself as the *exterminating angel.*

It is, in effect, the exterminating angel that we will confront in the case of Valerie Solanas.

The Scum Manifesto[12]

The Scum Manifesto is primarily a manifesto of the Society For Cutting Up Men, a fictive society of which the author is the only member, and one which invites women of all nations to ally themselves in a common effort to create a new, peaceful, unified, uniquely feminine society, one which might recover a lost bliss, following the radical elimination of men.

But SCUM used as a substantive, also signifies *scum, waste, refuse,* and on another level the SCUM Manifesto presents itself as an expression of this scum of society, otherwise called *woman.* For in effect: "in a society constructed by and for men, the woman is comparable to waste, which after being used up is thrown in the sewer along with the dishwater and the garbage."

We are talking, then, of a text, a work which in part treats a delusional neo-reality, and in part is a critique and indeed a denunciation, extremely violent in tone, but lacking "madness," of an objective reality—namely, the patriarchal, competitive and capitalistic society which imposes on woman a social condition of exploitation.

Paranoiac discourse, and this is not its least fascinating aspect, very often presents this double aspect of being at once a mad delusional discourse outside reason, and at the same time a passionate and often pertinent denunciation of disorders and evils "glaring within reality."

We ourselves are only concerned here with the delusional neo-reality which Valerie Solanas proposes, a neo-reality which indisputably raises a parnaoiac problematic, and what particularly interests us in this work is the paranoiac fantasies in their relation to the law, homosexuality and sexual difference.

Valerie Solanas is thus the author of a fiction, a fable, presenting all the characteristics of a paranoiac delusion. Nothing allows us to affirm that she is personally a paranoiac, because no literary text, no matter how pathological it may be, does in itself authorize a psychiatric diagnosis. The Scum Manifesto is to be understood as an attempt at sublimation and at self-analysis. Sublimation and an attempt at an abortive cure, since Valerie Solanas is, in the final analysis, an attempted murderer.

In 1968 (the year in which the SCUM Manifesto appeared) Solanas was 28 years old and vegetated in the American Underground, where she lived a marginal existence. She desperately sought work as an actress and she occasionally engaged in prostitution, as well as selling hand-printed copies of her work on street-corners. She lived in a hotel in Greenwich Village and associated with Andy Warhol, with whom she was more or less acquainted and from whom she sought to borrow money.

The SCUM Manifesto was written during 1967, at which time she tried to get it published. In June of 1968 she was evicted from the hotel where she owed 500 dollars. Girodias, an American editor, paid the 500 dollars in exchange for the full rights to her works, theater pieces, novels, and the SCUM Manifesto, and he proceeded to sell these rights to Andy Warhol for a film.

Valerie Solanas thus sold all her work for 500 dollars, and lost all editorial rights to it. She consulted a lawyer who confirmed that this was legal. She thought that there was nothing left to do than kill for the sake of justice. This is exactly what she attempted to do on the sixth of June 1968, firing five bullets into Andy Warhol. He barely survived. Solanas immediately turned herself in to the police. Warhol refused to press charges at the trial. Solanas pleaded guilty and received only a minor sentence.

But at the time of the trial and in the period directly following it, she was completely abandoned by everyone.

The SCUM Manifesto, which appeared for the first time in 1968, after the crime, was very coldly received and severely criticized. Later, it would be rediscovered by the most extreme feminist movements, but, at the time of its appearance, it was very far from being the Bible of the Women's Lib Movement, which judged it excessive and provocative. A second edition appeared in 1970, of which the French edition is a translation. Valerie Solanas was in prison when the first edition appeared, and the preface tries to make a martyr of her, but an abandoned martyr, of a sad sort.

Grace Atchinson, an American feminist akin to Kate Millet, who would finally break off with the feminists, was the only one interested in her after the trial. She returned many times to visit her in prison, and described Solanas as a strange creature, clearly a martyr for the feminist movement, a victim of the oppression against women, one who always gave the impression of having been totally isolated. Atchinson continuously returns to this impression of solitude, of distress around Valerie Solanas.

"She was alone, always alone," writes Atchinson, as alone and perhaps more alone that Schreber could possibly have been and, like him, she proposed to escape at last from indescernable distress and to change the order of sex (to annihilate the male sex), the order of the world (to found a new society), the order of life (to procreate in an unnatural fashion). On this, Valerie Solanas writes:

> Life in this society being, at best, an utter bore and no aspect of society being at all relevant to women, there remains to civic-minded, responsible, thrill-seeking females only to overthrow the government, eliminate the money system, institute complete automation and destroy the male sex.
>   It is now technically possible to reproduce without the aid of males (or, for that matter, females) and to produce only females.

The argument of the SCUM Manifesto is the following: the fact of masculinity and paternity are contrary to the order of the universe, the male being a biological accident, as the male Y gene is no more than an incomplete female X gene, an incomplete series of chromosones. In other words, the male is an incomplete female . . . Virility is an organic deficiency and men are atrophied beings, and *the profound, real but unrecognized desire of man is to be a woman.*[13] He does not want to recognize this, and as a result he compensates, overcompensates and is at the origin of social corruption which extends to all the institutions and to the American way of life. Thus, he is responsible for war, toil, politics, money, marriage, prostitution, mental illness, High Art, culture, sexuality, sexism (or the practice of discrimination and oppression on the basis of sex, as racism does on the basis of race), etc. Briefly, humanity is hastened to its own ruin, to the extent that it is in hands of men, more precisely, of *fathers, who have produced in the world the gangrene male spirit.* Certain females are both allied to and accomplices of these fathers, most notably the "mamas," the compliant mothers and the daddy's girls or female pimps, brutalized, passive, victims of the system. A female pimp is an *atrophied* woman, lacking assurance, suffering from insecurity, and who believes that men are beings on whom one can depend for help.

To these female pimps, to these daddy's girls, who have become Big Mamas, Solanas opposes the *SCUM*-women, or women's women, marvelous, dominating, independent women, who are devoted to the destruction of the masculine sex and of the paternal power embodied in the power of money.

When the male sex is destroyed, whether by mutual consent or by force, society will be purely feminine; women will reproduce among themselves. This destruction of the masculine sex will happen by way of the radical physical elimination of men, but "eventually, if the men have been reasonable, they will want to become women, having conducted intensive biological research which permits, by means of operations on the brain and nervous system, to transform men into women, body and soul."

"At that time there will be a fantastic new era, and work will be done in a festive atmosphere. In the program, all things considered, will be, primarily, *eternity* and *utopia.*"

SCUM is thus very much like Schreber's calling for the salvation of the world, to return to its lost bliss. She thinks she will only be able to accomplish her mission by sacrificing the masculine sex and its allies, and by eventually transforming men into women.

The Fantasies of Scum

1) *The fantasy of emasculation.* Remarkably this is precisely the same as that of Schreber. *"The desire of man is to be a woman."* But when the woman imagines suppressing the male sex, the mutilation envisioned is not carried out on her own body but on the body of the other. The problem is very complex. Is it a matter of having? Does a woman intend to deprive a man of what he has, and of what she does not and will never have? Or is it a question of something else altogether, located in the register of "being?"

Not being a man is indeed what Schreber is resolved upon. As for Solanas, she holds that *being a man, the very fact of masculinity is contrary to the order of the universe.* For SCUM there exist two categories of deficient females. The first are men "incapable of communicating, of identifying with others, totally egocentric, to whom sexuality is vast, diffuse, dispersed, and for whom the habitual psychic state is passivity. Their nervous system is boorishly constituted . . ." To prove that he is not a woman, he postulates that he is active, when he is in fact limp . . . But his deepest desire is to be a woman. The only honest men are the transvestites, the drag-queens (the converts), those who have crossed the line.

The second category of deficient women are simply those who discover in men a reason for being and who as a result become atrophied, dependent, submissive, etc.

This description evokes a woman who could have fashioned all misogyny and women after herself, and who at the same time subscribes to the most pejorative myths and stereotypes regarding feminity. For, if all masculinity is in effect contrary to the order of the universe, so is the fact of femininity.

The fantasy in the case of SCUM ends in the absolute annihilation of sexual difference (eventually in the subterfuge of a real manipulation). It is necessary to suppress, not only the masculine sex, but the *difference* itself, which is the source of all evil, and contrary to the order of the universe. This extends to both the male and female sexes and their embodiment in the couple, as well as the father on whose negative power the access to deviation and difference is founded. Like Schreber, Valerie Solanas shares the conviction that it is possible to change sex and that this change answers to a necessity from the perspective of the general good. But whereas Schreber claims a feminine desire, for Solanas it is sex in general that is contrary to the order of the universe, and those who are marked by it are going to be persecuted: "Sex is a refuge for the poor in spirit . . . The SCUM are women of leisure, quite prepared to assume an *asexual* being . . . In a future society, sexuality will be *bisexuality* . . ."[14]

2) *Scum's Fantasy of Saving the World.* Even if the style of the expression is extremely different, it is in all ways comparable to that of Schreber. It involves a salvational mission, a sacrificial and megalomaniacal calling, where one rediscovers the collusion between ego-ideal and ideal self, narcissistic omnipotence and the annihilation of time and death.

A completely automated society can be accomplished very simply and quickly once there is a public demand for it. The blueprints for it are already in existence, and its construction will only take a few weeks with millions of people working at it. Even though off the money system, everyone will be most happy to pitch in and get the automated society built; *it will mark the beginning of a fantastic new era, and there will be a celebration atmosphere accompanying the construction.*

The elimination of money and the complete institution of automation are basic to all other Scum reforms; without these two the others can't take place, with them the others will take place rapidly. The government will automatically collapse. With complete automation it will be possible for every woman to vote directly on every issue by means of an electronic voting machine in her house. Since the government is occupied almost entirely with regulating economic affairs and legislating against purely private matters, the elimination of money and with it the elimination of males who wish to legislate "morality" will mean that there will be practically no issues to vote on.

After the elimination of money there will be no further need to kill men; they will be stripped of the only power they have over psychologically deficient females.

> They will be able to impose themselves only on the doormats, who like to be imposed upon. The rest of the women will be busy solving the few remaining unsolved problems *before planning their agenda for eternity and utopia.*

But before the era of eternity, of utopia, there will be one of genocide, in the name of the coming good:

> Consequently, to get rid of any male whatever is a good and legitimate act, which is certainly to the advantage of women, and at the same time an act of pity . . . The few remaining men . . . can go off to the nearest friendly neighborhood suicide center, where they will be quietly, quickly and painlessly gassed to death.
> Finally, it will be possible to never grow old and live to eternity.

3) *Scum's Fantasy of Procreation* is very simple. It does not imagine divine or supernatural means of procreation, but more prosaically scientific means, excluding sexual union. Science replaces God:

> It is enough to set up sperm banks (the function of the man is producing sperm).
> The answer is laboratory reproduction of babies.

As in the case of Schreber, the reference to the paternal function, in the sense of a biological reality and symbolic truth, is discarded in such a fantasy of procreation. But the idea of maternity, as capable of being subtended by a *desire,* is also excluded and with it, the feminine connotation of maternity.

> Women have no interest in hatching swarms of babies, they shouldn't be obliged to serve the function of a rabbit for the needs of the species (laboratories can largely suffice).

Traces of the "regressive narcissistic identification" with the mother, an identification operative, as we have seen, in reference to identity and not to similarity, can be revealed in the SCUM Manifesto. In fact, Valerie Solanas claims that the deepest being of a man is *to be a woman:*

> His first experiences have been lived with his mother. He is tied to her for life. For the man, it is never very clear if he can be anything else than a part of his mother. All boys want to imitate their mother, to fuse with her, *to be* her.

This discourse brings us back to the complex paternal power of which Freud speaks, where maternal identification and investment are confused, and where the paternal order is foreclosed, insofar as it is that by which difference could come about.

But while the paranoiac man secondarily searches for an escape in the creation of a new delusional reality (sustained by a group of fantasies each of which pin him down and mark him in relation to a paternal order, and allow him to keep himself in relation to the law—precarious and persecuted, but also structuring), it seems that the female paranoiac, to the extent that she rejects the father at the level of the phallus, of the law and the symbolic function, keeps the father *outside sense.*

The major consequences of this foreclosure of the paternal signifiers will be for the woman, primarily:

- the impossibility of her access to femininity, the recognition of the paternal signifiers being a necessary, if not a sufficient condition of femininity, because they are the bearers of *sense* for the mother, the woman and the girl, at the level of sex, law, paternity and maternity.
- the creation of a reality of another order, which proceeds to exclude the paternal reference, for the woman as well as for the relation to the law. The staging of this other reality implies the *sacrifice of femininity.*
- a dire sacrifice, whose principle beyond the delusional rationalization of the absence of a sense of the paternal function, will be a *radical split of the feminine image,* which proceeds to institute a *female* femininity, embodied in the idealized mother, all-powerful, vengeful, terrifying, archaic, a mother of precocious sexuality, who becomes the creator of the law and is absolutely opposed to *femininity.*

This split reveals:

1) a homosexual confrontation which seeks to restore sense to the precocious sexuality and will savagely deny femininity, notably in its relation to law.

2) the choice, in all cases of feminine paranoia, of *two persecutors,* the one feminine (on the side of femininity) and the other masculine (on the side of the law of the paternal function), both returning to the sexual couple which recognizes difference and is founded upon it.

Feminine Paranoiac Fantasies in Their Relation to Homosexuality

The classical theory of such, with its supreme interest in femininity, in all cases of feminine homosexuality, including unconscious ones, does not appear to be able to totally account for the type of homosexuality implied in feminine paranoia.

In "normal" feminine homosexuality, where one chooses femininity, the idealized narcissistic object, the cult of Eve, one can certainly find a trace of feminine paranoia, but it will in no way constitute its full scope.

"Normal" feminine homosexuality can only be conceived of and referred to in terms of the oedipal problematic and of the phallic signifiers that it establishes. It involves a so-called "hysterical" homosexuality, such as we find in Dora or the young homosexual girl, reported by Freud, who tries to commit suicide by throwing herself off a bridge, to show that she fell by her father's fault.

This form of homosexuality is always interpreted as a rejection of Oedipus, of a more or less pathological scar. It is most commonly organized in the form of a challenge to the father, a father who is himself not very clear about the incest taboo regarding the daughter.

These types of homosexuals often nourish a number of aggressive and violent fantasies. There is a strong paternal identification in them, as well as an important fixation on the mother—a mother always lived fantasmatically as not accepting or considering as evil the girl's femininity.

But this type of homosexuality, being a relation of the mother-child, or husband-wife type, respects (in all aspects of the relation to the Other) the givens of the Oedipal game; namely, femininity as an object of desire, the father as a representative of the law, the identification with the two parents, and their libidinal investment.

In turn, the homosexuality of the female paranoiac organizes itself uniquely in terms of partial pre-genital drives, returning in the precocious feminine sexuality where the oral, anal and vaginal drives play themselves out. This, by way of an all-powerful maternal Other, who connotes the era of lost bliss and is sole bearer of sense and the law. In other words, her homosexuality is not articulated in terms of a desire for the other, but in terms of the "construction" and the compulsive search for a structurally and narcissistically necessary double, in a maternal identification, where identity and investment are confused in an original "Being woman."

This is most clear in the perspective of escaping or renouncing the maternal enterprise, an enterprise which is secondarily idealized, and in which the paranoiac—regardless of gender—feels obliged to choose an Other, which brings him closer to being the first-woman. In this regard, the homosexuality implied in this search privileges *femaleness,* in the sense that it connotes a primary Other, always maternal, and appertaining to a universe prior to sexual difference.

This is why the male paranoiac, who in choosing homosexuality must proceed to change his object, will establish an idealized father, whose figure is subtended by both a masculine and feminine element.

Regarding this same problem, the female paranoiac does not have to change her object or perform a displacement. For her, the masculine universe can eventually remain totally alien to her and appear contrary to the order of the universe. From this, she will *build*—rather than destroy—an idealized mother figure, who has no need of a masculine element for her fantasmatic elaboration.

In some manner, SCUM restores *Lilith,* Adam's first wife, with whom he bred a multitude of demoniacal children. Mythically, Lilith is a female demon of the Hebraic tradition. The legend tells of her having run away and being pursued by three angels. Lilith refused to reappear at Adam's side, and the angels told her that 100 of their children would die each day. In revenge, Lilith killed the children who were born in a sinful way. The old Jewish custom, when a woman was in labor, consisted of writing the following words on the wall: *"Let Adam and Eve be here; let Lilith stay outside."*

SCUM which defines itself as "women at ease, dominant, secure, nasty, self-confident, violent, selfish, proud, thrill-seeking, free-wheeling, arrogant females, who consider themselves fit to rule the universe, who have free-wheeled to the limits of this "society" and are ready to wheel on to something far beyond what it has to offer. Such a woman imaginatively constructs a world before sin, where there is no risk of losing the primordial mother love (since the masculine fact is against the order of the universe, women can't miss men), where paradise is regained and redemption assured under the iron law embodied by the idealized mother, where women reproduce themselves without the aid of men, until the day where even that will be no longer, for death and old age will be conquered."

Such a fantastic vision of the world, as a defensive fabulation, allows the paranoiac to recover *sense, certainty, reference* to a *system*—albeit a false one; he risks "remaining on a plane," as Schreber tells us.

This is why the paranoiac always wishes to be the instrument of a new and purified order, which he foretells.

We cannot stress enough the importance for the paranoiac of this *system,* a system which always refers him to an order, to a higher instance. Consequently, we should also stress the strange, subtle and strained relations that paranoia maintains with the social system and ideology. Ferenczi demonstrated this well, when he wrote: "the limited relation between the formation of systems and paranoia also perhaps explains why scientific theories or novel philosophical systems are always adopted—it is well-known—by a crowd of psychopaths."[15] This is why of all the clinical structures, paranoia is the one which can bring about the most social effects, and not least to the extent that the paranoiac knows how to reveal and denounce scandals and injustices.[16]

From this perspective, the SCUM Manifesto is filled with resonances and social consequences. SCUM is the sorceress of our time. Such is the iconography these particularly ill-favored witches show us; they are ugly, old and represent the last degree of moral and material solitude.

Poor witches, we accuse them of having entered into a pact with the devil, because he promised them gold. But they are poorer than Job. Jacques Bodin, a contemporary of Ronsard, founder of political science and a great witch hunter, remarked:

> What lures the misfortunate to devil worship is a depraved opinion he has, that Satan gives wealth to the poor, pleasure to the afflicted, power to the weak, beauty to the ugly. And nonetheless, one recognizes in a blink of the eye that there are none who are more miserable, more hated, more ignorant, more tormented than sorcerers.

Historically, the sorcerers and sorceresses were the scapegoats of civilization, having paid for the marginals, the heretics, those who did not wish to yield to a severely rigid social and spiritual order. They are just like the SCUM of our time, who declare themselves to be garbage, the dregs of society, but whose discourse also rings in our ears as the expression, the result of a sickness in civilization.

Michelet saw in witchcraft the expression of a revolt against servitude and contempt, the consequent indifference to power, and the abuses of Feudalism and the Church. *Forgotten by God,* incapable even of glimpsing the means of their liberation, the sorcerers and the witches invented a new cult which would save the disinherited.

The initiative for such an enterprise could only come from woman, doubly hated as a peasant serf and a daughter of Eve, as if in her were joined these two realities, one social, the other mythic.

These are the two realities that the SCUM Manifesto denounced and denied.

It is to the witches, the SCUM, that "Satan offers the frothing cup of life," finally allowing them to question the order of the world. Meanwhile, SCUM, the woman rebuffed by society, the garbage produced by capitalism, among the many others that America has unveiled and announced to us, puts in question our entire society and the forms of madness inherent in it. Valerie Solanas, presents in her delusion the signposts of a naive counter-culture, irrational, almost absurd, in which she poses as the first martyr and the messiah. But her message is so insane that it is impossible to reduce its meaning and interpretation to psychopathology, and an analytic study, rigorous as it might be, would not exhaust all its provinces. To say and prove that Valerie Solanas is a paranoiac is in a way reductive, for her "madness" is situated more in the answers she proposes than in the questions she raises.

Unfortunately, it is more often on the side of proposed answers that paranoia echoes across the social stage, and the insane solutions it proposes for some real problems can easily become collective, ratified by a social and political system.

Between the power of the imagination, the imagination of power, inspired madness, ideology, terrorism and holocaust, the frontiers are sometimes uncertain. It is the nature of power to desire limitlessness, and at that point, analysts or not, we are all involved.

Notes

1. The *Origins of Psycho-Analysis* (New York: Basic, 1954). Cf. esp., Drafts H, M, and K, and letters to Fliess, Nos. 39, 57, 61, 91.

2. "A child is being beaten" is a very well known phantasy, and can be articulated into three phases:

—My father is beating the child I hate (the unconscious sadistic phase).

—My father beats me (the unconscious masochistic phase).

—A child is being beaten (the conscious phase produced by the repression of my father's love for me. He only loves me; he doesn't love the other child, since he beats him). Cf. *Standard Edition*, 17:177ff. (1919).

3. *Ibid.*

4. Or, likewise:

—references which subtend sexual difference continue to persist within aggression, submission, sadism, and masochism.

—identifications are posed in reference to two poles of a dual relation (e.g., and most often, identification with the aggressor and with the aggressed).

We will return to the notion of fixity later on.

5. The work of Guy Rosolato ("Scène Primitive et Paranoia," in *Essais sur le symbolique*, Paris: Gallimard, 1969) is, to the best of our knowledge, the most complete and best contribution on the question.

6. "A Case of Paranoia Running Counter to the Psycho-Analytic Theory of the Disease," *S.E.*, 14: 261–272 (1915).

7. Rosolato, *op. cit.* Melman, Charles, "L'aventure paranoïaque: les cas Schreber," in Société française de psychanalyse, *Journée d'Autômne*, 1963.

8. White, R. B., "The Mother Conflict in Schreber's Psychosis," in *International Journal of Psychoanalysis*, 5– 5–73, 1961.

9. The Freudian term *Verwerfung* (foreclosure) is currently a very poorly understood concept. Freud himself never used it strictly in the same sense. It was used principally with regard to the Wolf Man to describe his relation to castration. Lacan conceived it as having to do with a complete absence of symbolization, of not symbolizing what should have been, i.e., as a mechanism of *asymbolization*. For Freud, *Verwerfung* always seems to involve a withdrawal of cathexis and at the same time, a withdrawal of signification, these two withdrawals being closely tied. Moreover, the foreclosure of the Name of the Father, doubtless at play in paranoia, doesn't cover all the aspects of foreclosure. The latter may involve other phenomena (e.g., the body, the sexual organs), and it is likely that it sustains a close relation to psychosis; but while an isolated phenomenon of foreclosure, by itself, may not validate the psychotic fact, it nonetheless does serve to bring it about.

10. This exclusion of violence might eventually lead back to "the hatred of hate," suggested with regard to paranoia by Jean-Luc Donnet and Andrè Green, in *L'enfant de ça*, Paris: Ed. de Minuit, 1973.

11.   This might allow us to eventually differentiate paranoia from other psychotic structures, most importantly, schizophrenia. In fact, for the schizophrenic, none of the figures in the primal scene are situated—no more the mother than the father—and the only issue for the subject is to be the thing, the partial object, for the mother. All this leads us to say that we can never with certainty give an account of schizophrenia by referring solely to the foreclosure of the signifiers of the father, to a uniquely paternal problematic. It is likely that the weakness of the maternal signifiers is just as important here, among which figure prominently:

—The establishment and recognition of an eroticized body.

—The access to auto-eroticism.

—The access to reassuring narcissistic positions.

—The establishment of an erogenous shift, or alteration, which would render the subject susceptible to pleasure.

The schizophrenic's void would be equally maternal as paternal, and his search for identity would follow the path of identification. The double void of the schizophrenic would lend brutal force to the death wish, something which would not occur for the paranoiac, for whom sadomasochism is very strongly libidinalized and rationalized. The schizophrenic is always at the edge of death and madness, and the polarities of life/death, full/empty, partial or complimentary object/total object, etc., structure his entire economy in a primordial way.

12.   Valerie Solanas, *Scum* (New York: Olympia Press, 1968).

13.   Like Schreber, who claimed to know about God's desire, V. Solanas claims to know more about men than they do themselves.

14.   We speak about annullment in the sense that the intended "myth" would be one of an initial indifferentiation, on the basis of which, perhaps, a considered sexuality could arise.

15.   Ferenczi, *Oeuvres complètes, tome II, 1913-1919,* Paris: Payot, pp. 109–116.

16.   Cf., on this subject, *Topique,* 11-12, E. Enriquez, "Le Pouvoir et la mort."

Alphonso Lingis

8. The Din of the Celestial Birds or Why I Crave to Become a Woman

N ow you understand why I craved to become a woman.[1] Use your imagination, please, for a moment, gentlemen, and put a man's voice in that sound-field; you will see immediately what I mean. Male eyes over which the tears no longer flow, male voice that therefore guffaws, chuckles, with a dry throat, but cannot trill, titter, giggle, laugh like a woman. Virile male throat that can arrest, restrain, bawl allegiance to the State, but cannot warble, whimper like doves, coo like a woman. Negating voice of the virile spirit that can order, but cannot command the bird-calls. Everywhere in the skies miraculous feathered gusts called me to the voices of women.

Trebling over the base of male voices advancing upon me from past and future generations, not conveying beneficently intelligible information-bits, but in their raw physical reality as blows hurled against me. For I do not hear in them the law-ordered divine or cosmic or civic logos, but the strident cacophony of a creaking and collapsing cosmic edifice. Virile voices muttering, legislating, ordering me about, virile blows hammering against the bones of my skull, for nine years my nerves compressed under the bone-crushing agony.

They have not stopped. Just yesterday, this woman's voice in El Salvador:

"What you have heard is true. I was in his house. His wife carried a tray of coffee and sugar. His daughter filed her nails, his son went out for the night. There were daily papers, pet dogs, a pistol on the cushion beside him. The moon swung bare on its black cord over the house. On the television was a cop show. It was in English. Broken bottles were embedded in the walls around the house to scoop the kneecaps from a man's legs or cut his hands to lace. On the windows there were gratings like those in liquor stores. We had dinner, rack of lamb, good wine, a gold bell was on the table for calling the maid. The maid brought green mangoes, salt, a type of bread. I was asked how I enjoyed the country. There was a brief commercial in Spanish. His wife took everything away. There was some talk then of how difficult it had become to govern. The parrot said hello on the terrace. The colonel told it to shut up, and pushed himself from the table. My friend said to me with his eyes: say nothing. The colonel returned with a sack used to bring groceries home. He spilled many human ears on the table. They were like dried peach halves. There is no other way to say this. He took one of them in his hands, shook it in our faces, dropped it into a water glass. It came alive there. I am tired of fooling around he said. As for the rights of anyone, tell your people they can go fuck themselves. He swept the ears to the floor with his arm and held the last of his wine in the air. Something for your poetry, no? he said. Some of the ears on the floor caught this scrap of his voice. Some of the ears on the floor were pressed to the ground."[2]

That voice was my own. And do you not think that those amputated and shriveled ears which no tears bathe, are my own?

I had my virile honor, erected in contempt of death. This monumental death, this prodigious absence was my identity. For I had an identity, was an identity. An identity wholly addressed to the appeal of the other, wholly a demand put on the other—I was this vertiginous sign: Herr Senatspräsident Schreber. Out of this identity I identified the vibratory and phosphorescent filaments of time. By that I do not mean that I compacted the dissipating ripples of reality into molten primary substances with the alchemy of my imagination; I mean I detached my nerves, with all the centripetal force of the compact mass of my identity, from the silken filaments of the real, and held fast to, and was held to, the signs, the univocal and intransient symbols, my own identity disseminated over them. I do not mean I created their identity, or my own. I rather identified myself with the empty place of death, which was designated to me by the death of my father. The code for this individual indivisible absence I made myself, these terms "I," "Herr," "Senat," "Präsident," already existed; the presidency established long ago with bullets, the avenues to the Senate paved with concrete, the mastery of the misters, a bonded and insured capital accumulated by the capitalization of the circulation of women, the words preserved by taxidermists on the shelves of libraries. My place at the presidency of the senate was prepared by the unification of the Prussian, Napoleonic and Saxon Codes by the Triple Alliance made with Bismark's guns. One sun in the cosmic spaces about me ascended each morning to efface the pale light of the planets and the raging stars which my sleeping eyes had not seen. One God was the sign, ideality and value, that immemorially grounded the black hole of my identity.

Do you understand the operation of causality between signs and nerves? Am not I—this sign "I"—itself nerves? Is not the sign "God" himself nerves? Sir

Charles Sherrington's discovery of synapses proved that the nerves are not merely conduits for the transmission of sensa—they are loci of creations. Could it be that unrelenting intellectual toil, such as that of an imperial jurist, could produce nervous sickness? That is what happened to me.

There are signs, there is language, in nerves. The I knows its power in the power to formulate signs with nerves—with a driving will. But nerves themselves alone know how to formulate the signifiers, and it happens that they do so themselves, without or against the will. And one day they formulated the suggestion that I, Herr Schreber erected at the center of codes, economies, police, planets, galaxies, was so much flesh being auctioned off to be carried away for abominable uses. The signs circulating about me were in fact the Deutschmarks the bidders were shouting. In the meter of my vibrating nerves I heard—was it an objurgation formulated by the nerves themselves? was it the voice of some long dead Zoroastrian god—the hissing word *"Luder!"*—whore! slut!

Do you understand the causality between signs and nerves? This sign, like ptomaine poison, mortified my substance—paralyzed my nerves, immobilized, putrified me. They took me away and laid me in a bed in a padded cell. They entombed me.

And now the forcing, the unrelenting intellectual toil, that had produced the nervous collapse, started again. The force of the I was now unrelentingly its victim. My thought now spreadeagled on my nerves, its lewd erections forced by them. One July day under a scorching sun prostrate on the auction block, the sky reeling with the shrieks of invisible birds, I tore loose the stones of the Devil's citadel of Sonnenstein and built an altar. From the most remote antiquity I heard this voice: One need only build an altar and a god appears. I became its temple prostitute. Into my voluptuous substance the god discharged the unbearable excesses of his own voluptuousness. This is the transfiguration I stand before you to tell.

You are a century too late to put in your bids for my body. You will no longer find the bile of its corruption in the earth in which it was buried. I have become—out of that totally different kind of forcing which I must begin to explain—a sign, wholly addressed to the appeal of the other, of you, wholly a demand put on the other, on you. Will the signs which you attribute to me, Herr, Senat, Präsident, Schreber, really be able to tell this strange issue of my destiny? Yet you are able to understand my book, which has lost none of its syntax, grammar, syllogistic consistency, science, metalinguistic control. You are able to understand it with your intelligence. Can you also understand it with your nerves?

You can, on the occasion of the sign I am now for you, cursorily improvise images. You could imagine my body as a physico-chemical mass, and speak of the noxious and pharmaceutical substances I ingested in the "Devil's kitchen" of Coswig, and of their effects. You could, like the superintendent von W., make a drawing of my substance as an uncouth axis of posture and awkward dynamic diagrams of position, apprehension and movement. You could draw too the outer opaque face and surfaces, with their blotched colors and wrinkled patterns, arching eyebrows and grimacing cheeks, striking mustaches and formal handsomeness, which do not correspond to the layout of the musculature or the inner, biological operational systems, any more than the stripes of a zebra outline its nervous system or intestines. But now the sign "I" shall designate a palpitating mass of nerves. Each nerve taken separately can express the whole system.

I know it by the vibratory phenomena that traverse it like radiating pulses of energy, and which witness themselves in the distensions of pain and the concordances of pleasure, and which remember themselves. These can originate from within, but also from without. By reason of nervous sensibility my body substance finds itself exposed in a universe where the nodes of substance are likewise vibratory and radiant, travelling in parabolas and curves like spermatozoa about my nervous substance. These sensa pour upon me with the beams of light, they resonate in my system the secret racket of the universe. These radiations are of the same nature as my own fibrous substance; they are the elements by which one sensitive substance such as my own communicates with another across distances of space and time. They are creations, and creative. And they contain bliss. And they compose the real order of the universe, and not only its ideal laws.

They are creations, and creative. Essentially transitory, gyrating modulations of time. Not *causa sui*, to be sure, theophanies of extrahuman forces. The skies about me are full of them—black dew of sperm, showers of silverfish, phosphorescent and powdery moths, reeling din of celestial birds.

There is joy *in the universe;* it would be impossible for a rational mind to suppose that the joy, which is the voluptuous force in all our energies, is only some effect produced by the chemistry in our organic batteries only. The sensa bring bliss into our nervous substance, and without them the gratitude that swells voluptuousness is not possible. They are detached radiations, free-flying birds, but they come out of bliss, and they are attracted to voluptuous homelands. They are engulfed, absorbed, in the voluptuous wombs of organisms. You will confirm this oblivion into which they lose themselves, thinking of the most convulsive orgasms you have known, which can be remembered later less than the precise words of some insignificant slogan in the shopwindow. But voluptuousness in my body is not appetite, is not voraciousness and rapacity, but the very substance of consecration. For laughter, weeping, blessing and cursing are sensation itself, and not reactions released once the neutral sense data, pure messages, are synthesized, interpreted and evaluated by a second, intellectual, instance. For one must not imagine, with the old epistemologists, that the nervous sensibility is a purely passive substance upon which the active forces of material nature imprint traces of their encounter with it, which can serve as data for an intellectual cognitive interpretation, and which could materially produce abrasions or concordant harmonies, pain or pleasure, that would be biological mechanicams of regulation for the organism. On the contrary the nervous sensibility is as active, as radiant, as the world-rays that encounter it; there is no original moment when it is passive and the sensa left on it are neutral. It is our sensibility, and not first our judgment, that weeps and laughs, consecrates and imprecates; these are the very mode of contact with which sensibility encounters not mere appearances but the forces of things. My nervous substance caught up in the nerves of the worlds is a merry, howling, exalting and execrating substance.

Do there exist radiations that are divine? Do you believe that all the remote things, the worlds and the earths, the mortals, the vestibules of death, the *lumina naturalia*, the gods, are but symbols, significations posited merely by the linguistic consciousness regulated by the phallus that an Oedipal infant makes of himself? Have you, with Dr. Weber, already barricaded yourself behind the hypothesis that what one takes to be insights concerning cosmological and religious matters arise in fact out of a disturbed imagination? If so, it is evident that the life that I had had to lead will be of no interest to you. I won my release from Sonnenstein asylum many years ago. What I am saying today can be understood only by those whose minds have not been asbestosized by that hypothesis, such that their nerves still might conduct other, deviant and fractured, rays. Which, like all rays, are rays of beatitude. I affirm that what is bracketed upon our nervous substance is not only the atomic dust of sense-data which electrical trade winds have made contiguous with our nervous surfaces. I affirm that if a physical organism can be the place where alone the worlds and the earths as such, the *Platzhälter, lieu-tenants,* of death, and the gods can show themselves, then they are themselves attracted by our nervous substance, not because it is an empty place and a corpse, but because it is living voluptuousness which irresistibly lures their bliss. The divine comedy and the divine tragedy, the blessing and the malediction that are fate and destiny themselves, are attracted by nerves, by this mirthful, sobbing, exalting and execrating substance. "All the examined souls . . . found as it were the fundamental source of their existence in the force of attraction developed in my body due to the intense hyperexcitation of my nerves; I mean that I was for them the means by which they could intercept the divine rays brought close to the trajectory of my force of attraction; they then adorned themselves with them like a peacock does with strange feathers, thus obtaining miraculous powers." "Thus they find in my body an absolute or approximate substitute for the celestial beatitude they lose and which probably consisted in a voluptuous pleasure of the same kind." (111, 180) But my substance is porous and will not contain them; creations come out of the still waters of its sleep.

If the sensibility is not merely a passive surface where sense data are auto-matically delivered over to the understanding, the relations between sensibility and understanding have to be reconsidered. Understanding is not simple sponta-neity arising over this passivity; it is subject to *forcing*. The great Kant over-turned epistemological naturalism, biologism and pragmatism by declaring that the mind does not think because it has a natural tendency to think; on the contrary, as soon as there is the first movement of thought, thought finds itself under an imperative. To think is to have been afflicted with the imperative for the universal and the necessary. One does not think because one wants to; one thinks because one is commanded.

Unrelenting intellectual toil, the forcing, which I as jurist and legislator had continually intensified, preceded the nerve sickness that resulted in my incarcer-ation. I have not explained, have not understood the causality in effect there. Henceforth my smouldering nervous substance became the point of convergence of a disproportionate quantum of radiating elements of the universe. But to the extent that the flux of radiations concentrates on an entity in any remote corner of the universe, there is danger for the order of the universe, departure and rending of the radiant substance of deity. By reason of the order of the universe inscribed in its own inner essence, out of its necessary egoism, the deity must necessarily strive mightily to disengage its filaments from my substance. As they plummeted upon me, I understood that their banshee cries demanding signs of life from me were those of the cosmic coroner who wanted to return to the management of his own affairs. Thus I understood the tactics devised against me, manoeuvering to reduce me to a corpse, such that the extravagant quantity of cosmic nerves could be extracted from me.

A policy wholly based on a misunderstanding. No thought extracted from an organism, and no voluptuousness, essentially nocturnal, admit the opaque or-ganic transubstantiations of pregnant sleep. For them sleep is equivalent to cre-tinism and to the horrifying hardening of the corpse hidden under the voluptuous caress. I came to realize that the warped rays of cosmic time inces-santly rail and poke at my nerves in order to verify whether their silence is not that of demented *rigor mortis*. For alien intelligence cannot penetrate the opaque and vibrant ardor of voluptuous substance, and can only understand a corpse.

No philosopher of our time imagines that the mesh of human reason is the natural product of an imperative *Logos endiathetos* ruling every radiation of the universal electromagnetic field. Reason is forced. That of which I have become certain, through the most extreme experiments performed on my substance, is that however brutally the cosmic cacophony bombards a living organism, it is unable to reduce it to insanity; on the contrary, all strategems, however diaboli-cally contrived, have the paradoxical result of forcing sane discourse. To be sure, the unhinged universe has the power to undermine and destroy that organ-ism entirely, to reduce it by nerve murder to putrefying bile.

I exhibit to you my sane discourse, product of an absolutely unprecedented forcing. I do not hesitate to act on the conviction that you can understand my words. Not because you have made your intellects in the image and likeness of a God, observing only the empirical externals of an organism as from extrasideral distances. It is through your own voluptuous substance that you shall know me.

I played for you a recording; did you listen in? What did you hear? A female voice. And a field of exanimate noises, tingling, shocking, clattering, molesting, discordant Irian Jaya jungle clammoring with forty-three species of birds-of-paradise. Infinity of tones of the one hundred and two elements of physics converging on the female vocalization whose transfinite virtuosity no other organic species is capable of. A female discursion produced by a conceptual intellect constructing ideal essences, mental identities, which are then coded in audible signs? Surely not: provoked by the radiations of metallic reeds, blocks and plates whose meter and syncope have not the character of signs, elements of a code, but that of appeals, summons, pressing outcries for assistance, and that of demands, imperious requisitions, exactions. Nowhere does the female voice regulate itself into the formulation of a phrase of any code, and yet this voice has expressed all that any voice, stentorian, logical, law-regulated, symbolic or indicative could utter—all the whimpering, giggling, sobbing, crying, screaming, glorying, squalling, ullulating, rending, haranging, harrowing—epic, comic, tragic, farcical, sacred, demonic, possessed. You have heard the speech that speaks to one or in one, the *Grundsprache.* And, from time to time, you have heard a single coded vocalization, of a metalanguage: you have heard *parole.* You have heard the female animal hunted down, beset, trapped, harried, subjected to relentless mechanical and electronic forcing—emitting the wolf howlings, compulsive hiccupping, weepings, jackal laughters, whoopings of birds—and that same voice, voice of Brooklyn-born Cathy Berberian shifting into metalanguage, understanding and identifying itself, in a foreign tongue—identifying all that as *parole:* words.

Thought takes, apprehends, comprehends, time; the tempo is not its own. Where the tempo is given, there can be thought. I distinguish between the slow wail of trains, the groaning that runs the length of paved avenues, the earth-swells of rolling and falling substances, and the animate voices that dwell in the skies. Voices of insects and birds, of men or of human images, or of the exanimate utterances of those far away or long ago. *Grundsprache* glittering in the voices of the light, of the sun, for my sensibility has lost its compartmentalization and become synesthesic.

Miraculous birds! Compulsively swooping about me their worthless phrases learnt by rote and empty of all information. But when they discharge their venomous phraseology, they sink into the voluptuousness that fills my substance, and turn into outcries of joyous gratitude and admiration. For the singing in the skies is nonrepresentational production, nonreferential gratuitous expression of nervous systems charged with excess libidinal energies.

Yet the birdcalls have a strange affinity for the meaningful signals of human discourse. A material affinity: a tendency to homophony. They vocalize on the meters and tempos of my own sensibility when it is formulating my thoughts, or to the things said in the talk at large in the world. Unlike parrots, which also repeat words meaninglessly, but the very sounds of meaningful phrases, and when their own impulses stimulate them, as it were freely, the celestial birds compulsively reverberate sounds analogous to words, Chinesenthum for Jesus Christum, Abendroth for Athemnoth, Santiago for Cathago.

I have never heard this homophonic quasi-speech out of the throats of the pigeons that prattle all day in the courtyard of Sonnenstein, nor of the canary in the common room, nor of the chickens, geese and ducks. It is not the birds whose domestication has made their behavior conform to and corresponding to the behavior of men that utter sounds analogous to human signals, but the free-flying sky-birds. Descartes reasoned that in fact dogs have no speech, and put forth, as the proof, that they do not speak to us. Did you understand his proof? From the fact that they do not speak to us, he concluded that they do not speak to one another either. For speech is not a means of communication between beings already familiar, but a means for addressing aliens, of making contact with that with which one shares no commonplaces. It is only through speech that we can make contact with worlds as such beyond the landscapes laid out within the reach of our eyes, with the spaces between the stars, with the stars turning in the black vortices of galaxies, with birds calling libidinally from the corridors of the heavens. I, Daniel Paul Schreber, from the stone walls in which they entombed me, from my long rotted-out skull, am speaking to you eighty five years after I was sequestered from kin and fellow-men. None of my kin or contemporaries heard me.

The birdcalls are not the code for the messages; they are vested for me with understanding of the nature of things.

Freedom of thought is the freedom to think about nothing. Thought's opposite is not imbecility or idiocy, but sleep—and that fact, which could never be derived from the internal analysis of the concept of thought but only from the nature of an organism as such, is what pure intellects, such as gods, never arrive at. The paths laid out by thought do not branch on indefinitely; a thought is a finite movement. Every well-formulated thought concludes. The formula sinks into sleep and its voluptuous pregnancies. The order of thought is not extended in interminable horizons, in the spherical world of the dreamer Columbus, whose thoughtful sailors knew that every well-charted path ends in the vortices of a maelstrom.

I had to protect thought, the freedom of thought, from writing down, from note-taking. Thought had to delineate its paths to its sleep out of the repetition-compulsion that is the very mode of existence of the *Grundsprache*. I found that cursing is an essential mode of grammar and is intrinsic to the purposes of thought. You, for example, in ordinary human intercourse, if you hear someone mutter "If only that which . . ." and you immediately badger him with "Well what exactly do you mean?" will most likely hear him mutter back "Fuck you." The insult is not grammar emptied of its cognitive content and turned into aggression, mimicry of blows struck; it is one of thought's essential methods to deflect the forcing into the lower depths of voluptuousness and torpor. In my forced insomnia I turned to reading books and newspapers, which are not means for the provocation of thought in the masses, but devices fabricated to produce thinking-about-nothing. Another strategy I used was committing poetry to compulsively repetitive memory. I found powerful mantras in the rhyme and rhythm of the most banal verses. Om padme hum. Counting in a silent voice I learned the mantric effect of numbers. I spent many hours at my piano, turning my thoughts into the continuities of thoughtless music. I learned to repeat the birdcalls like an opium-eating parrot; whenever I heard a "And then . . . ?" "However . . . ," "Rightly . . . ," I repeated these vocalisations slowly, operating thereby on them a conversion that reduces them to thinking-about-nothing and voluptuousness. Thought is contained in tempo. "Senatspräsident," for example—it has the wrong tempo. Into my collapsed and withered lungs I conducted the prana with mantric meter.

I will speak now of the maelstrom at the end of all the paths of thought, and the transubstantiation I underwent in its acids. From midnight skies magnesium-white with the cold rays of the nocturnal sun, shrieking birds of prey descended upon my body-carapace, my legislator body, dashing into the acids to tear off shreds of my muscles, reeling in the skies their hooked beaks bleeding with my virile honor.

Will your nerves be able to see my transubstantiation? My surface-body, that organ-for-being seen, that for-others of exposure, was no longer sustained by eyes turned upon it; I encountered only images of men, the very eye of the sun ceased to delineate and make the patterns of my surfaces glow, but only scorched, excoriated me. My surface-body, that form, *formosa*, containment and contour and beauty, that zebra-striped, peacock-patterned diamond-faceted surface reality which has its own logic and is incomprehensible biologically or vitally as the mere patterned delineation of the vital systems of an organism, as the stripes of the zebra do not derive from the acupuncturist's diagram of motor filaments in the musculature, or from the anatomist's diagram of its skeleton and glandular coils—that body-surface dissolved like the cirrus-striped morning sky upon the ascent of the night sun. I was an invertebrate mollusk, having lost the stand and the stance of legislating virility, of the self-steering and ordering muscular axes. I lay a decomposing corpse, spasmodically shaken by the imprecations of the frantic and hysterical birds. The virile, soldierly contempt for death that erects the body and holds it hard in its commanded commanding stand left me; I longed for a watery death with the vertigo of a beached sun-scorched octopus using its flaccid tentacles only to return to the primal brine.

My inner body itself, I mean that organized, functional assemblage of respiratory, nutritive, circulatory, filtering and excretory organs, got dismembered, disconnected, I became a butcher's table of severed organs, still palpitating, like a frog's leg, still miraculously alive, without stomach, without intestines, practically without lungs, with an esophagus in shreds, without kidneys, my pharynx having swallowed itself. My soft and shriveled penis was a worm in the sludge of my sodden lungs.

Like every man, I had always known I had another body, a fibrous substance of voluptuous sensation; like every man I had been in touch with it in my scrotum, that sack containing spheres squirming with spermatozoa, of vital spirals, those warm and life-emanating suns, that amorous couple between the strong levers of my locomoting skeleton. Two suns suspended in a fibrous and crackling tissue of nerves. Here there are nerves that are not just a communication system of coded information-bits, nerves that are not just the pre-wired channels for motor impulses.

The prodigy that, in my mineralized immobility, my butchered dismemberment, I then witnessed was this: my scrotum withdrew into my body, like the clitoris, the penis of a woman, into the closed labia; the night sun made me eternally prepubescent Apollo. But I knew they had not been severed, I had not been castrated; they were inside. Inside, this sack of voluptuous nerves, like a sun extending its rays, pushed its filaments outward into all the milky expanse of my substance. I felt the extremities of this tintinabulating mass of filaments just under the skin wherever I touched. My flesh had been stripped of its virile carapace, excoriated of its gritty and leathery male skin, animal hide, and was wrapped in skin soft and diaphanous as that of a baby, as that of the membranes of the vulva.

My testicles had become as invisible to me as my rump, and my hand seeking them found my buttocks. My caressing fingers explored my buttocks, perceiving neither a muscular pulley-system nor a surface destined for display. My buttocks were swollen testicles laid out to the wanton fingers of the night's sun.

When I turned over, my hands folded back upon themselves, and found my other buttocks, my other testicles, my breasts. What would you say of your chest? Would you say this: "More than the arms, more even than the back, the chest is the seat of upper body strength. It is the bear's muscle—whose main and converse functions are to push things away from the body and hug things to it—and when developed properly it is very beautiful: two clean downward sweeps from the windpipe to the armpits and then an open flaring into the shoulders that give the body ovalness and depth above the waist. For some reason, maybe because they lie so close to vital organs, or because of the warm, dense, quick pump they take, the pectorals are probably the most satisfying part of the body to work." I had said things like that in the long years spent on bench presses in my father's gymnasium. It is in his chest that every male invests his virility.

But this virile investment makes him female. Over his ribs are not abducting and adducting thongs, but mountings for teats. Males do have breasts, and can give milk; in Bali, fathers home from the rice paddies at midday nurse their infants. I felt in the erected teats the viscous nerves I had felt in my now retracted penis; I felt in the carnal padding of my breasts the squirming filaments that I had felt in my now interiorized scrotum. I spent many hours looking at my breasts in mirrors, seeing them swell with the afflux of my yoga respiration, under my caresses and those of the lascivious nocturnal sun. My wife had not, as I had for her, kissed, kneaded, suckled my breasts—how few women understand that a man is a woman! That when a woman reduces her partner to an erected penis for which her vaginal hole craves, she makes herself an appetite, a need, a lack, and not a voluptuous consecration. Every infant understands that one satisfies need in order to refuse the demand for love, that is, the demand to receive the absolute and unconditional love the baby has to squander. Mother-love is cynicism: she smooths out all the wrinkles, shelters him with soft blankets, gives the baby his bottle, leaves no need unsatisfied—in order to detach herself from him, in order to abandon him for another. But she will treat the other, to whom she now goes, in the same way: she now makes herself a baby, a need, a gaping, craving hole, and demands of the other not love but the penis she lacks when she makes herself a lack. Her cynicism cannot recognize that the one who does not only pull out his erection but takes off all his clothes is amorously coupled suns in the nervous nets of the scrotum, is round and flaccid buttocks, is breasts with teats, and that all sex is lesbian.

I was long horrified to leave the tombs of Sonnenstein into the devastated world order identified by the sign woman. A woman is an object of social commerce, and can be used as a key sign in the constitution of social codes, as wealth in the economy, as an icon or idol in the rituals of prestige. In short, a prostitute. I do not deny that when I was forced to witness my transubstantiation into voluptuous substance, I dreaded being delivered over to depraved human beings for their own needs and appetites, delivered over to the gods for ignoble usages. I thought I was being divested of every power and right to be an agent and not only an object of social legislation and law-regulated rational discourse, to be an administrator and not an object in the economic arena. But I made this marvelous discovery: that the most malevolent alchemical experiments made on the substance of its body, by intentional or exanimate and stupid interventions, do not have, of themselves, the power to disintegrate the rational faculty in an organism. I found my reason completely intact. All the aggressions and demands made on my substance I incessantly heard as forcings, imperiously forcing my mind to continue, to supply the cause or the consequence. Reason: the very power to continue, to establish the inapparent continuities.

But all the momentum and indomitable powers of my reason were in fact thrown into the ultimate enigma of the discontinuity. I mean the ultimate and initial discontinuity: that severance that is life itself, the life which reason in an organism must serve. With this shortcircuiting of human reason upon the ultimate and initial discontinuity, reason reaches its highest, religious form. The place of this shortcircuiting is named with the word creation. The nerves of life do not extend by derivation nor by assemblage; they are the locus of discontinuity, entropy, creation. Real seeing is not drawing, is not the reifying of one's own signs; seeing is seeing hierophanies in the skies illuminated by the day sun and by the night sun, skies whose nerves quiver with the outcries of gratitude of celestial birds. I believe that the sight of creation has the power to negate and annihilate all the noxious poisons of the radiations. In the paralysis of my virile and motor body, in the vivisection of the tubes and glands of my vital, functional organism, insomniac eyes bathed by the tears of the night sun, I saw in my body not a corpse the gods would at last penetrate and use for their own purposes, I saw in the decomposing brines of my substance an equatorial ocean of creations. I came to understand that creation was a rational idea and that continuous transmission was not, and my reason itself became religious.

I took my pen and wrote: "The concept of eternity is beyond man's grasp. Man cannot really understand that something can exist which has neither beginning nor end, and that there can be a cause which cannot itself be traced to a previous cause . . . If God created the world, how then did God himself come to be? This question will for ever remain unanswered. The same applies to the concept of divine creation. Man can always only imagine that new matter is created through the influence of forces on matter already in existence, and yet I believe—and I [have] prove[n] . . . by means of definite examples—that divine creation is a creation out of the void." (2–3)

Voluptuousness is not torpid satiety; the caressing hand searches insatiably. I long fondled the orifices of my body, found everywhere my substance porous, full of apertures and tubes designed to conduct substances forcibly and firmly to their release. I came to understand that a body is not a mechanism that welds itself together, or a plenum whose agitations compensate for accidents, that is, losses of its substance through remediable collisions. I came to understand that the voluptuous nervous substance radiant with gratitude, bliss and blessing, is full of chutes and tubes for the release of rays, rays that are creations and miraculously creative. I felt the day sun and the night sun in lesbian embrace in my testicles, my buttocks, my breasts. And I came to finally formulate for myself too the idea that out of the wreckage of my body would be born a heliolithic and blessed race.

Do my gods appear strange to you? Is your religion orthodoxy and your inquiry into me inquisitorial—decreeing in advance that to make gods one's own is to make oneself a god, that is, an idol? Is it your faith that on the stones and ashes of the holocaust of my body, on the burning bush of my nerves, no prophetic flames can blaze rays of light into the future?

From the greatest antiquity I heard the immemorial mantra: One need only build an altar and a god appears.

Notes

1.   Opening passages are a reference to Luciano Berio's musical composition, *Visage* (VOX-TURNABOUT, TV 331 027).

(In response to a request for a page of the score of his composition, *Visage,* Luciano Berio replied with the following letter: "I am very sorry that I cannot be helpful as I would like to be. There is no score of *Visage.* All my working sketches were left behind at the studio of the Italian Radio in Milan, when I composed *Visage* in 1960–61: they were obviously misplaced, lost or stolen. Anyway, it may be interesting for Professor Lingis to know that an important aspect of the project was to expose non-articulated vocal sounds and then to move to the "discovery" of vowels, the consequent opposition and interaction between vowels and consonants, the syllables, the vocal inflections (emotions) and finally "words" (PAROLE in Italian). From then on, there are constant references to vocal gestures and language stereotypes: television-English, Italian, Neapolitan dialect, Hebrew, etc., each with various associations to emotional states. The electronic sound expands and develops these vocal and language gestures, giving a musical reason to the experience. In composing *Visage* I learned a lot about language, phonetics and phonology (I knew Prof. Roman Jakobson). The first performance took place in a large concert hall in Milan. In complete darkness, the audience was surrounded by loudspeakers. One young lady passed out and her husband attacked me. Thus I had to learn how to defend myself physically.") (Editors' note.)

2.   Carolyn Forche, *The Country Between Us,* (New York: Harper & Row, 1981), p. 16.

Jean-François Lyotard

9. Vertiginous Sexuality: Schreber's Commerce with God

Intensities and Names

The use of the proper name exemplifies the way in which the *tensor* both dissimulates and is dissimulated within the semantic field. This concerned Frege and Russell, and it remains problematic for the logician because it points in principle to a specific reference, and does not appear to be exchangeable with other terms in the logico-linguistic structure. The proper name has no intra-systematic equivalent, since, in pointing toward exteriority, like the deictic, it has no connotation of its own, it is interminable. Logicians (having scant choice of means) solve this problem with a concept: the existential predicate. Hegel was already quite aware of this: the *Meinen,* as well as the obstacle that is posed by the supposition of existence (i.e., by flesh and blood, as Husserl would say, in turn) could be opposed to the systematic ordering of signs. Thus, when asked: what about Flechsig? We might answer: there is at least one existing individual who could be called Flechsig—Schreber's doctor—and who would be referentially maintained as an anchor point. But the name of this same individual tends to *dissolve* when it is seized upon by Schreber's madness. It produces a multitude of incompatible propositions about the same compatible "subject." Flechsig will be predicated simultaneously as cop, God, a lover seduced by Schreber's feminine charms, someone who prevents the president from shitting, and a member of a noble family which has known the Schrebers for a long time. In what sense is that mad? Only in what it states.

This is the same madness as Proust's, the latter scarcely more prudent for having interposed a narrative subject between himself and his text—naming it Marcel—much the same madness having to do with the proper name 'Albertine.'

143

It is the same as Octave's madness about the proper name 'Roberte;'[1] whorish legislator, virtuous libertine, undecidable-body-offered-refused, she is the very embodiment of dissimulation in two distinct senses. On the one hand, the Huguenot and the tart can operate as signs within the equally intelligible networks of respectability and sensuality. On the other hand, each of these assignations hide something: not the other as such, i.e., insofar as it belongs on the side of the regulated network. Rather, what occurs is that each assignation dissimulates the sign in its function as tensor, not just as sensible sign. The tensor-sign consists in the fact that Roberte's name covers a region where two "orders" (at least two, there must be others) are not two, but are indistinguishable; where the name *Roberte* is like a disjunctive bar turning quickly around some point— around, for example, the look, the vulval slit, the gloved hand, an intonation— and which changes place with the segment that forms the bar. If "Roberte" is a tensor, it is not because she is both a harlot and a capable woman, but because she *exceeds, goes beyond the one and the other* of the respective assignations. This takes place in the vertigo of an intensity where, if the skirt slips up over the inner thigh, if the fat thumb is raised before the seducer's mouth, if the nape of the neck turns under his teeth, it is most certainly through authentic prudery and sincere sensuality. But over and above any reasonable explanations it is through an *instinctual* formation *(figure)* that the impulses are arranged and dispensed, impulses which do not belong to Roberte, or to anyone. Roberte is not someone's name (an existential predicate), even as a double. Rather, it is the name of the unnameable, the name of the Yes and No, of neither Yes nor No, of the first and second. If the proper name is a good example of the tensor-sign, this is not because its singular designation is problematic when one thinks conceptually, but because it covers a region of libidinal space given over to the open-endedness of energy impulses, a region ablaze.

The above would apply to Schreber as well. In taking account of the *Memoirs of My Nervous Illness,* we see just how much vertigo is fixed, so to speak, on the name of Flechsig. It is necessary, Schreber thinks, that I become a woman so that God can impregnate me, and, by my giving birth to a new race of men, accomplish humanity's salvation through me. This sex change is miraculous: but for Schreber all bodily modifications are miraculous and must be imputed to an uncommon power, in any case, to the remarkable decision of a power (in this regard Schreber's religion is entirely Roman, akin to that penetration of divine instances in the simplest, most commonplace events; it would be the secularization of the sacred or the sacralization of the secular.) Thus the mystery of defecation: it gives substance to dissimulation, which spreads to Flechsig (through God). If we can describe these perpetual ambivalences of the instinctual objectives, then the important thing nonetheless remains the indiscernability of contradictory terms, e.g., giver and retainer of shit, Flechsig protector and executioner, loving and persecuting God, my male and female body, my divine and human ego; and still something *more*.

Defecation is not natural, but miraculous. Now, here, apropos of the *"miracle of shitting,"* which Freud quotes in full,[2] we see that delusion can pile up on a single name. What is *signified* by the fact that defecating requires the miraculous intervention of a "One" who is both Flechsig and God? Does it signify the love that *one* brings to Schreber, or the assistance *one* lends him? No, or rather, yes, but very indirectly. This tender love appears only allusively in the President's discourse, and in an inverted form. If God-Flechsig renders defecation miraculous, and releases Schreber's body from the natural aspect of this function, this is, really, for the purpose of 'demiraculating' *in extremis* the act of shitting and thereby of persecuting the President: "some other person in my environment is sent to the lavatory."[3] In this way, they cut short "a very strong development of soul-voluptuousness"[4] which accompanies a successful defecation. And if they use him in this way, it is because a similar pleasure *threatens* God-Flechsig, in that it subjugates them to the President's body, as is the case with all extreme pleasure. For example,

> The experience of years has confirmed me in this view; indeed I believe that God would never attempt to withdraw (which always impairs considerably my bodily well-being) but would follow my attraction without resistence, permanently and uninterruptedly, if only I could *always* be playing the woman's part in sexual embrace with myself, *always* rest my gaze on female beings, *always* look at female pictures, etc.[5]

It is thus not out of love that *one* miraculates the Schreberian defecation, but rather, to defend himself against the seduction it exercises. Flechsig is a lover on the defensive. But Flechsig is also a hellish persecutor who asks Schreber: "Why do you then not shit?" Thus Flechsig humiliates his victim. All the same, however, God-Flechsig is even more stupid than his victim, since he is incapable of understanding that a human creature needs no miraculous intervention by the Almighty to defecate.

> The pen almost resists writing down the fantastic nonsense that God in His blindness and lack of knowledge of human nature in fact would go so far as to assume that a human being could exist who—something every animal is capable of doing—cannot sh. . for sheer stupidity.[6]

We shall see whether all these contrary properties merely are puns upon the name Flechsig. But first we must deal with two preliminary remarks. To begin with, let's observe the "sheer stupidity," which extends well beyond Bataille's notion of bestiality—one which is quite self-aware, even if not self-conscious. This notion is the secret *mindlessness* of petty eroticism, whereas with Schreber we have to wade through swamps of ambiguity working over the instincts themselves, like animal montages. Here we are outside of the mindless *animal* knowledge, since the "body" no longer shits when it "needs" to, and even shit no longer knows its way out. This is the incredible stupidity of the mad body, into which Flechsig plunges Schreber. Unlike the organic body—montage of montages, functional assemblage, erotic edifice—this libidinal body seems to lack established channels for the circulation and discharge of impulses. There is no depth to this stupidity, but only immensity, absence of measure. This *libidinal stupidity* is entirely different from the stupidity of Bouvard and Pecuchet, which consists in repetition—e.g., in quoting *ad nauseam*, always within the realm of common places. Yet it is very close to it, since, like it, it rests on the destruction of the subject, i.e., one who remains capable of responding through word and deed to the loss of identity (this is indicated in Flaubert by the *duo* which serves to form the dumb hero). This stupidity is inseparable from the kind of dissimulation we are talking about here.

A second remark is that this stupidity resurfaces in the odd acceptance of femininity involved in President Schreber's quote above. In *having the properties* of a woman rather than being a woman, this *having the properties* is indifferently translated as playing the role of the woman in copulation or *being the male partner of that woman* ("playing the woman's part in sexual embrace with myself"),[7] looking at female beings, always looking at female pictures, and, doubtless, again, always being seen as woman, etc. Here again is the immense stupidity of the libidinal band.[8] Corresponding to the proper name Flechsig, then—tensor par excellence—is Schreber's anonymous body, one without regulated organic functions, without sex, or with too many sexes. Can we say at this point that the name Flechsig is only the predicate of some few statements which would have it that certain incompatible instincts come together? *Flechsig loves me,* since he lets me shit-enjoy. *Flechsig hates me,* since he won't let me shit-enjoy. *I love it when Flechsig hates me,* because my own persecution is necessary to accomplish mankind's future salvation. *I hate it when Flechsig loves me,* because I wish that defecation would be as natural for me as it is for others.

Let's stop enumerating statements which are themselves already oversimplified. Also, let's pass over the reading that Freud makes of Schreber's relation to Flechsig. Freud's is an exemplary semiotic or conceptual reading, since it does take into account all the statements and even other intermediate propositions which result from variations on a unique nucleus or root phrase: *"I (a man) love him (a man)."*[9] These are necessary variations of instinctual displacements (as in the elaboration of the fantasy "A child is being beaten"), and they involve a use of negation—hardly a generative use, but nonetheless one which is fully engaged.

It would be preferable to discuss the following point: Do these statements (whether there are four or x number of them, it is not important; who could possibly exhaust the potential series?) represent what we are searching for, under the name of dissimulation? Don't they rather provide a play of meaning; on the one hand homonymous (Flechsig the lover was the homonym for Flechsig the executioner), on the other, synonymous (Flechsig lover and executioner was synonymous with God—a synonymous group to which Freud does not fail to add the Father)? These are the kinds of relations the semiologist knows and accepts, not as objections, but as encouragements to his method. While the preceding considerations do lead up to these various transformations, they scarcely enable us to approach the libidinal economy. If Flechsig, like Roberte, is a tensor-sign, and not just a "sensible" individual, this is not due to the propositional play of meanings that belong to his name; rather, this occurs through the vertiginous state of anal eroticism that possesses the Schreberian libidinal body, and of which Flechsig's name is the extension. Vertiginous, because, once again, the disjunctive bar turns so furiously around the anus that the President's asshole becomes a solar incandescence. Henceforth, to promote or to forbid the passage of matter (whether of feces or the Divine member) becomes indecidable, the two moments being invested and released at once: "this is done by forcing the faeces in the bowel forwards (sometimes also back-vards) and when owing to previous evacuation there is insufficient material present . . ."[10] Through this drawing and quartering in place—towards constipation and diarrhea, towards hetero- and homosexuality, towards virility and femininity—the positions of the sun, the gods, the doctors, and men, begin to revolve, forbidding any stable distribution and "thought." This incandescent vertigo carries the name Flechsig, and as such assumes the value of a tensor-sign.

The tensor-sign extends the spin of the top beyond Schreber's organic body to the unexpected regions of the libidinal band. The name Flechsig takes hold of these regions, or rather, lets them exist as pieces of a vast *anonymous*-maniacal-erectile-labyrinth. Ah! You think you're a doctor in the process of restoring my solar anus to its miserable proportions of pregenital Oedipal regression? In saying Flechsig, in building my metaphysical and historical novel on Flechsig, in putting Flechsig at the beginning and end of my loves and hatreds, I am using you, doctor, not as a piece in *my* paranoiac game, as you believe, but as an unexpected scrap of the *immense band, where anonymous flows circulate.* Your name is the guarantee of anonymity, the guarantee that these instincts *belong to no one,* that nothing, not even the "doctor" is outside their range, safe from their investment. That's what you are afraid of, and why you lock me up. What gets spun out under the name Flechsig is thus not only the happy play of words found in the tamest of statements, but also the incandescent bodily part that is no longer assignable because of the simultaneous investment of the pro and con.

Even more so, this unthinkable searing would be transmitted to other libidinal regions, namely, to the languages of history and religion, their invention and containment within this anal vertigo, their sexualization, as they used to say, their plugging into the mad anus, their extension from this to that. Thus, the so-called frontier of Schreber's body is violated by Flechsig's name (just as much as is the so-called frontier of Flechsig's body). This limit is itself pulverized by the vertiginous spiral, the President's body is broken apart and its pieces projected across libidinal space, mixing with other pieces in an inextricable patchwork. In this case, the head is nothing more than some odd butt-end of skin. Flechsig, my ass! Beyond synonymy and homonymy, anonymity.

Use Me

What if God's proper name were *pimp?* Let's reread Schreber:

> It was mentioned in earlier chapters that those rays (God's nerves) which were attracted, followed only reluctantly, because it meant losing their own existence and therefore went against their instinct of self-preservation. Therefore one continually tried to stop the attraction, in other words to break free of my nerves . . . Always the main idea was to "forsake" me, that is to say abandon me; at the time I am now discussing it was thought that this could be achieved by unmanning me and allowing my body to be prostituted like that of a female harlot, sometimes also by killing me and later by destroying my reason (making me demented).[11]

And, like a real "whore," Schreber adds:

> But with regard to the efforts to unman me it was soon found that the gradual filling of my body with nerves of voluptuousness (female nerves) had exactly the reverse effect, because the resulting so-called "soul-voluptuousness" in my body rather increased the power of attraction.[12]

Would this be like a real girl, or rather, to be carried away by the power of dependence?

But, to begin with, who really wants this scandal, this feminization?

> From the human point of view, which on the whole still dominated me at that time, it was in consequence very natural for me to see my real enemy only in Professor Flechsig or his soul (later in von W.s soul also, about which more will be said below) and to regard as my natural ally God's omnipotence, which I imagined only Professor Flechsig endangered; I therefore thought I had to support it by all possible means, even to the point of self-sacrifice . . . that God himself must have known if indeed He was not instigator, of the plan, to commit soul murder on me, and to hand over my body in the manner of a female harlot.[13]

The prostitute accepts prostitution in the name of a higher calling. She wants it in much the same way a martyr does: she bears witness to her humiliation, just as Mary Magdalene did before Jesus. She begins by testifying against her procurer. But this break with her procurer remains naive in two senses, namely, in its affective and political, or economic, aspects. The naiveté is affective in that it is to God's eyes that one delivers up one's suffering, and oneself to his heart. Politically, or economically, since it's the pimp, here Flechsig, but Herod or Pilate as well, who cashes in on this suffering, who profits by it, and thus, ignores it as such. Then, in retrospect (i.e., while writing the *Memoirs:* "It occurred to me only much later, in fact only while writing this essay did it become quite clear to me . . .")[14] the two names, Flechsig and God, merge. On reflection, he realizes that his own appeal is at least as criminal, as that of the initial crime. It's at this point that the pimp-God-doctor takes on his full libidinal dimension: the order of the world, Schreber says, is really violated by the project of my transformation into a woman (into a prostitute). There is no appeal, since God, too, is my persecutor; he is not the impartial judge who receives my suffering, he is still the pimp who demands it and uses it to make a profit, and in this way, exposes and exploits it in the duplicity of suffering-pleasure.

Schreber protests this situation, and we have to see in his struggle to get out of mental institutions, where *they* have locked him up, the same fight that a girl has to escape the whorehouse or red-light district where they have sequestered her. But this protestation is ambivalent. For, as we have seen, Schreber wants to be God's prostitute, to take pleasure in being a woman, and to give pleasure, if not as his lover, at least as his master. This is why he wants to be *all women and woman all the time,* and the "incessantly," the "continually," which occur throughout his writing, define the condition for Flechsig-God's pleasure, namely, *that there be women all the time.* This is the creature's effort to attain the level of the divine omnitemporality: "Even when I was living alone in my studio," says Xavière Lafont, a former prostitute of rather great notoriety, "the phone would ring all hours checking if I were home [. . . the pimps] have all the time they need to get you. Even in America if they want." And even when she quit her job: "Sometimes the phone would ring even in the middle of the night, and on the other end, there would be nothing, just the sound of heavy breathing, and then, they would hang up."[15]

In the formation of this ambivalence, which serves to confuse God and the pimp, God and Flechsig, "punishment" is a decisive element: Schreber calls it persecution. Nonetheless, it is identical to the kind of punishment undergone by Xavière: being locked up, being placed in a state of dependence, the asylum works like the whorehouse or red-light district. Xavière sums it up: "The punishment is again the way to get a human being to accept the unacceptable. But it is also this sadomasochistic link that in the end makes you feel something toward your procurers. This something has no name. It is beyond love and hate, beyond sentiments. A savage joy mixed with shame, joy to endure and to hold out, to belong and to feel freed from freedom. It must exist for all women, in every couple, at least on a minor or unconscious level. I cannot really explain it. It is a drug. Like the feeling of living your life several times all at once with unbelievable intensity. The pimps themselves feel that 'something' when they punish, I'm sure."[16] This nameless something, why call it "sado-masochism," as she suggests? Here, we are in the midst of pure dissimulation. If Flechsig is the name for this *vertigo,* so too, is pimp or gang of pimps. What succumbs to punishment, regarding this vertigo, is the illusion of self: "They have succeeded since, from then on, I existed through them."[17]

But naturally, as in the good old master/slave dialectic, this extreme dependence can be manipulated by "the woman" as a weapon against the master. In love, the female orgasm may well draw the body towards blind union. That is why Schreber elected to become womanly; more, a prostitute, and thus, more and more mad, more and more "dead"—to better seduce Flechsig and God. Is it more a matter of intention than intensity? And at the point, where with Xavière, we thought we have found *strength,* i.e., the strength of *powerlessness* ("I wouldn't say I regret this life. But you miss it forever. It is like cocaine. You never find this intensity in . . . normal life.")[18], should we make room for *power* and its complicity with every form of weakness? Assuredly. But this is no reason to eliminate the former; intensity is hidden in signs and events. If the proper name is pimp or God, it is also the occasion for this unnameable "something." If the self succumbs to dependence, this is not only due to the wretched fluctuations in the preoccupations of power.

In the dead of the night, when palms and glances are exhausted, when penis and vulva are in tatters, when the earth is senselessly scorched, this command may be born in the raw and intimate throat of a woman: "Use me." This means, there is no me. Prostitution is the political aspect of dependence, but the latter has, in addition, a libidinal dimension. This is missing in Sade. The demand for "passivity" is not a demand for enslavement, and the demand for dependence is not a plea to be dominated. There is no slave dialectic here, neither Hegel's nor Lacan's dialectic of the hysteric, since both presuppose *role permutation within the space of domination.* All this is virile bullshit. "Use me" does tend in the direction of the rod raised over the flanks, the enticement of power, the relation of domination. But something different and so much more important transpires within those flanks, namely, the prospect of abolishing the *center,* the *head.* When the man Flechsig, the pimp, avails himself of this "demand," flaunting its "employment," to make himself head, to give himself power—he is really defending himself, he doesn't dare grasp the import of this offer and follow it up. The passion for passivity, which causes this demand to be formulated, is not a *single* force, a complementary power in a conflict. Rather, it is power itself and as such, it liquefies all those stases which occasionally block the flows of intensity. It would be wrong to think that the offer of spread buttocks and inviting orifices by the woman bent over like a gleaner, is some kind of potlatch challenge—"here's what I've got for you, now show me what you have for me." This offering is the opening up of the libidinal band, and this opening, this instantaneous extension and invention, is precisely what the power-brokers, the pimps, the politicians, deny. They are quite content to capitalize on these libidinal intensities, to generate surplus value, to over-exploit the forces of pleasure, sinking back into the mire of an overly shrewd form of speculation. This interest, this intervention by a third party, is undoubtedly true of intellectual eroticism as well. At least, one is bound to ask—just as one ought to, as concerns the subject of that baroque machinery which ties Schreber's body to Flechsig's—whether the erotic consists in refashioning, hoarding, or indeed, capitalizing on force, as is more than sufficiently suggested by certain oriental texts, or even in *Les liaisons dangereuses.* One might also ask if, in setting aside this sort of intelligence, by incorporating a degree of "cool detachment" (i.e., the heat of tense calculation) to these orientations of energy, this doesn't have the contrary function of *intensifying* overlooked regions and passages. This intensification does not occur by way of a *secondary formation* (i.e., by way of calculation, a different space-time, or the organic body), alternating with or standing in contrast to a primary order, but by raising the intensities themselves, by injecting libido into the very process of intelligence, by *incorporating the head* into the libidinal band, by running capital and the capitalist machines to profit instinctual circulations, by eroticizing understanding. Just imagine the small businessman, the vapid little accountant, placing his ignoble art in the service of his glands.

This was the Sadean kind of silliness that Klossowski could never shake, even in his "The Philosopher-Vilain."[19] But at least this was the silliness of a Sade. There is another Sade—the one who is Spinoza and Lucretius—the one of "Yet one more effort, Frenchmen, if we are to become Republicans." This is the libidinal materialist, the one we want, the kind we want to draw out here.

"Use me" is an order and a supplication, an imperious plea—but what it demands is the abolition of the I/Thou relation (the reversable master/slave relation) and, evidently, also, the relation of *usage.* This plea seems purely religious, inasmuch as it demands dependence. This is what Jesus said on the cross, no? But Jesus could demand dependence *because* he offered his pain as compensation for sin. The pricelessness of his suffering, of his abandonment, the terrible Schreberian *demiraculation* that he underwent, a release perpetrated and accomplished by the beloved, who is thus almighty—Jesus posed this pricelessness as the price to be paid for the redemption of sins. By this token, Jesus is a calculating prostitute. You make me die, and that hurts, but everyone is in the same position: perverts and cretins ("they know not what they do") will be saved, within the gracious body of creation, i.e., of capital. God is a pimp who says to his girl, Jesus, as he says to Schreber: "do it for me, do it for them." What, you might ask, does Jesus get out of all this? I would answer, what would a prostitute get by selling her most incongruous bodily parts, her looks, her flashy dress, even her high boots? What would Schreber get? But this is not the question. The prostitute, just like Jesus and Schreber, invents and projects herself as *subject* by means of a kind of calculation, even if this be pure fantasy. Her own imposition is enough to *convert perversion,* and thereby, to circumvent it. And don't forget that, just as Jesus is also God, the prostitute *is* indeed her client, but she is also her procurer. The Trinitarian mystery of similitude is the machinery which both produces the sensible sign and dissimulates the tensor-sign. Once again, don't be taken in.

"Use me" is a statement of vertiginous simplicity; it is not mystical, but materialist. I'll be your imprint, your very tissues, you be my orifices, palms and membranes. Let's get lost, let's leave the power, the foul justification, behind, through the dialectic of redemption. *Let's get dead.* Unlike what Sacher-Masoch said, this doesn't mean that I die by your hand. Precisely here lies the supreme ruse, intended or not, namely, that out of the highest order—emanating from that body exhausted by caresses and insomnia—the subject-function might be resurrected, in the din of unleashed partial drives. To gloss the Hegelian plea: be my master, may your will be done. This is how Sade, Freud and Bataille understood it, introducing the political right here; and thus, once again, order, strategy, and the rationality of war, i.e., Laclos and Clausewitz.

In the aridity and exasperation of all her bodily parts, what does this one-woman band want, when she asks for all this? Do you really believe that she wants to be mistress over her master, and all that? Come on, now, give me a break! She wants you to perish with her, she wants the limits pushed back, the full sweep of all this tissue, that immense tactility, to feel an inner intimacy without being stifled by it, a feeling that continually exceeds itself, yet with no sense of conquest. In the face of this, what can possibly hold for the tight-skinned mediocrity of the hard guys? They sneer, all the while thinking they unmask, exploit, the hysteric or the woman's pretended lie. Just like the politicians' mediocrity, as inscribed in the note Lenin passed to Trotsky across the halls of the Winter Palace (and we're not making this up!) "Say, if the White guards kill us, do you think Sverdlov and Bukharin can make it on their own?" This is a kind of street jargon, and one of the best commentaries on this comes, once again, from Xavière: "At first sight, they seem to be quite jovial fellows. They are well-dressed, often with an effeminate flair. They are not necessarily homosexual, but they almost could be. Anyway, they are not very good lovers. They always move in packs"[20]—packs, because these small-town perverts need an organization, as Deleuze and Guattari say.

"What does a woman want?" asked Freud. She wants man to become neither man nor woman, that he no longer want anything, that she and he, however different, become identified through the insane junction of their very flesh. Schreber wrote that "it would be more in conformity with the realization of desire, in the afterlife, that one be finally delivered from the difference between sexes." He went on to quote Mignon's song from *Wilhelm Meister:* "Und jene himmlischen Gestalten/Sie fragen nicht nach Mann und Weib" (And these celestial figures don't ask whether you are a man or a woman.) And as for the intellectuals' wish that all rapture, all incandescence, be called the death instinct, well, sure, sure! These intellectuals, under the guise of affirming life, merely want to totalize, unify, capitalize, conquer, expand, constrain, and dominate. The same holds, too, for those "Greeks," Lenin and Trotsky, and for those wandering packs of pederasts, who prostitute the masses-women. Since they are duped by the unspeakable proper names of their rulers, the crazed plea of the masses is not "Long live the Social!" nor even less, "Long live the Organization!" but rather, "Long live the Libidinal!"

Notes

1. Lyotard here refers to Pierre Klossowski's *Robert ce soir,* (New York, Grove Press, 1969) (translators' note).

2. Sigmund Freud. "Psycho-analytic Notes Upon an Autobiographical Account of a Case of Paranoia (Dementia Paranoides)" in *Collected Papers,* Vol. 3 (New York, Basic Books, 1959), pp. 406–408.

3. Daniel Paul Schreber. *Memoirs of My Nervous Illness,* p. 178.

4. *Ibid,* p. 178.

5. *Ibid,* p. 210.

6. *Ibid,* p. 178.

7. *Ibid,* p. 210.

8. The reader should recall that for Lyotard the "libidinal band" usually signifies the continuous flow of libidinal processes. The term "bander" also has the colloquial meaning in French of having an erection. (translators' note)

9. Freud, *op. cit.,* p. 448.

10. Schreber, *op. cit.,* p. 177.

11. *Ibid,* pp. 98–99.

12. *Ibid,* p. 99.

13. *Ibid,* p. 77.

14. *Ibid,* p. 77.

15.   Quoted from *Semiotext(e)*, 10, 1981, p. 83. (Translators' note.)

16.   *Ibid*, p. 83.

17.   *Ibid*, p. 83.

18.   *Ibid*, p. 83.

19.   Lytard here refers to Pierre Klossowski's *Sade mon prochain*. (Paris, Editions du Seuil, 1967) (translators' note)

20.   *Semiotext(e)*, *loc. cit.*, p. 85.

Janine Chasseguet-Smirgel

10. On President Schreber's Transsexual Delusion

I would like to begin by responding to a question concerning paranoia posed by Robert Knight[1] and cited by Stoller[2] in his article, "Facts and Hypotheses: An Examination of the Freudian Concept of Bisexuality." To quote Robert Knight:

> Many analysts have long been aware that Freud's theory leaves something to be desired in the way of completeness. It begins with the fully developed homosexual wish, the first step of the formula, "I love him," and proceeds with the various ways in which this repressed wish is denied and projected. It does not explain why the paranoiac developed such an intense homosexual wish phantasy, nor why he must deny it so desperately. Other men also develop strong homosexual wishes which are repressed in other, non-psychotic ways or are acted out in overt homosexuality, perhaps even with a minimum of psychotic conflict. Why does the developing paranoiac react so frantically to the dimly perceived homosexual drive in himself? Is the homosexual wish so much more intense in him than it is in other men who successfully repress it without forsaking reality testing, or is it that the need to deny the homosexuality is so much greater? And if the latter is true, why is this need to deny so terrifically strong? Why is the thought of homosexual contact with another man so completely intolerable?[3]

Rather than take up Stoller's explanation right away, which in the meantime seems to have the ample approval of Christian David, I would like to turn first to Schreber's *Memoirs*. There we find that in 1893, on the fringe of Schreber's second psychotic episode (the one that became the principal object of Freud's interpretation, a brilliant interpretation if ever there was one, even if it is still open to criticism on certain points), in a state halfway between waking and sleeping, he has the idea that it would be "lovely" (in German: *"recht schön'*)[4] "to be a woman succumbing to intercourse." To my knowledge, none of the commentators on the *Memoirs* or on Freud's interpretation of them have turned their attention to the singularity of this expression. He does not say that this would be amusing, pleasant, or voluptuous, but instead uses an epithet with a clear *narcissistic* connotation, putting his wish in the category of aesthetics. It is on the question of narcissism that I wish to concentrate here—a question central to Freudian theory of paranoia in general, and to Schreber's delusion in particular. But Freud, clouded by the "biological bedrock" of the "repudiation of femininity" common to both sexes,[5] does not pursue it to its final consequences. He vigorously states that transformation into a woman, constituting Schreber's primary delusion, was experienced at first as a "persecution and a serious injury," and also that the "voices" heard by the patient never treated this transformation as anything but a "sexual disgrace." "He . . . looked upon his transformation into a woman as a disgrace with which he was threatened from a hostile source. But . . . (in November 1895) . . . he began to reconcile himself to the transformation and bring it into harmony with the higher purposes of God," writes Freud, citing Schreber's famous statement: "Since then, and with full consciousness of what I did, I have inscribed upon my banner the cultivation of femaleness."

Thus, after the persecutory phase of the illness, dominated by shame and insult inflicted by Schreber's narcissism, and after the attempts to transform him into a woman, to unman him "for purposes contrary to the Order of the World," as he puts it (which must be understood as "contrary to his ego"), there follows a religious phase in which the man Flechsig, the object of desire, is replaced by God, and Schreber, elected by Him and transformed into a woman, gives birth to a new race of men. He says himself, and Freud cited him, "I shall show later on that emasculation for quite another purpose—a purpose *consonant with the order of things* (read: in consonance with the Ego, ego-syntonic)—is within the bounds of possibility, and, indeed, that it may quite probably afford a solution to the conflict."[6] We know that this statement represents an essential part of Freud's theory, served to him, so to speak, on a silver platter by Schreber himself. Still, Freud had to understand it, and according to him, this reconciliation with the fantasy of feminine desire amounts to a "kind of healing," by reason of the compensation that the ego gets from the delusion of grandeur. Certainly, the central position thus assigned to narcissism softens to some degree the criticism directed at Freud with regard to the overly "evolved" level of the conflict. Let us note, in passing, that though Freud based the paranoid delusion on sadomasochism,[7] he did not, in his study of the Schreber case, speak of fixation at the anal-sadistic stage in paranoia. On the contrary, Abraham, in his classification, did designate the anal destructive phase (expulsive phase) as this morbid entity's point of fixation, and Freud reproached him in a letter for not having taken the fixation and regression to narcissism into account. Still, since we now know more about Schreber's childhood, especially about his father's personality (thanks essentially to Niederland),[8] I think we are in a better position to respond, at least partially, to Knight's question cited at the beginning of this paper. I say this because historical factors and parental relationships are of decisive importance in this case. And I think this point of view corresponds with the position taken by Christian David in his work.

Robert White,[9] in his study on "The Mother-Conflict in Schreber's Psychosis," allows us to take another step toward solving the problem, with his review of new theories concerning the president's paranoia, and by his personal contribution to the problem. (At this point, allow me to recall that, in an effort with which he kindly associated me, P. C. Racamier[10] conducts a "Revision of the Schreber Case," which gives the essentials of post-Freudian research concerning this illustrious patient). Taking up Niederland's discoveries on the subject of Schreber's father, White notes a few of the formulas that Dr. Schreber proffered lavishly through guides and manuals intended for the use of parents. These formulas have the aim, among others, of dispelling any trace of insubordination in the child—which might appear, for example, as bouts of weeping "for no reason." Harsh words and corporal punishment will quickly get the better of such childish whims, and then, says the good doctor, "one is master of the child forever." Training in "the art of renouncing" is no less edifying. It is certain that the baby will cry for food if placed on the knees of the nurse or the mother, who eats and drinks all she wants. But under no circumstances must one give in to the infant. A nurse, who did not refrain from giving a bit of pear to one of the Schreber children under these circumstances, was immediately dismissed by the learned pedagogue. Among many practices designed to harden bodies and souls there was that of having the children sleep in unheated rooms, and that of treating them with cold ablutions. All traces of bitterness toward whoever administered punishment had to be eliminated—infractions chalked up on a blackboard once a week, got the punishment called for, and the child had to hold the hand of whoever had struck him, etc. The contraptions invented by Schreber *père* are also known: devices designed to straighten slouched backs, drooped heads, and the children's somewhat neglected postures, were to be used daily for at least two hours. Though these facts are by now widely recognized, I bring them up again because White uses them to support his argument (taken up in large part, admittedly, by Stoller) "Schreber's image of his mother was fused with that of his father. The mother was, to a great extent, an agent of the father, who clearly was the higher power behind her." The father had usurped the maternal powers, as Niederland had already stated. The breaking off of the relationship of oral dependence on the mother, which was too brutal and came too early, created in Schreber an intense need to identify with the pregenital mother, to regress to an undifferentiated fusion with her by magically incorporating her, by *"becoming* her." The function of the pre-Oedipal father is to help his son emerge from the primitive fusion with the mother by offering himself as a support for identification. (White draws here upon the work of Loewald, Fairburn, and Erikson.) But usurpation of the maternal prerogatives of Schreber's father made it impossible for him to fulfill this function a guide toward individuation. Schreber's delusion thus united him with the mother that was torn from him too early.

Fine. This argument sounds convincing. But if this was the basic cause of the president's illness, one may still wonder why he did not regress to the autoerotic stage, according to the definition of 1911—that, precisely, of "the Schreber case, where self and non-self are confused."—that is, why he did not become an outright schizophrenic. Moreover, identification with the mother, as a lost object would put the development of the illness in an essentially depressive register. But even if the diagnosis presents a few uncertainties, the schizophrenic and depressive aspects sometimes overriding the systematic delusion, the whole of the illness, as it emerges from reading the *Memoirs* and some of its annexes, appears to be in an essentially paranoid register. Furthermore, in my opinion, White's argument makes a serious omission: how does one explain Schreber's (relative) "reconciliation" with his delusion of transformation into a woman, starting from the point when he becomes the sexual object of God; or in other words, what happens to narcissism in this business?

Stoller, in the article cited above, tells us that those "who dread homosexual impulses dread them partly because they fear lest their wishes reveal their weakness (weakening of the feeling of being truly anchored in one's own sex)." This proposition, too, is very interesting, but is deficient in my opinion because it does not make for a good enough understanding of the annihilating feelings of shame, of insult, of dishonor, and of the degradations that are associated with feminine identification in paranoiacs, and to a varying extent in most males, regardless of any envy they may feel, on another level, toward maternal procreative attributes and capacities.

At this point, I will take the liberty of reviewing a few hypotheses that I have had the opportunity to advance elsewhere, including the paper, "Freud and Female Sexuality," presented at the London International Congress (July, 1975). It appears to me that *human prematuration,* the primary impotence that derives from it, and the child's absolute dependence on the mother for survival, lead the child to wish to free himself from the archaic mother, to become more autonomous in relation to her particularly because of the aggressive projections of which she is the object. This, which amounts to a growth factor, moves the child of both sexes to project power onto the father and his penis and to withdraw cathexes, more or less, from the specifically maternal capacities and organs. If the relationship with the mother is good enough (for reasons which are external as much as internal), the male child will take his father as a model, and as the supporting medium for his own ego-ideal, so as to become one day like his father, and to possess his mother ("Later on, I will marry Mommy.") He will then invest his own penis with a current and, especially, future sexual value. He will still, however, reserve a portion of his narcissistic (and not only erotic) cathexes for the maternal capacities and organs—breasts, vagina, the ability to bring children into the world. This process will lead him to develop according to the characteristics of his own sex and to integrate his femininity. In other words, he will not depreciate feminine capacities in a reactive way. But if the relationship with the archaic mother is very bad, the child will be able to remove all narcissistic cathexes from the maternal prerogative and transfer them entirely to the father's penis and to his own. As a result, the integration of his femininity will be particularly difficult or even impossible, so great will be his contempt for femininity. The resexualization of passive homosexual drives will be repulsed with horror as unacceptable for the ego, insofar as reactive cathexis of the penis will have taken up all the narcissistic libido thenceforth withheld from femininity. The homosexuality that then inclines the subject toward the father is precisely a function of the depreciation of the mother and femininity, and therefore, of the subject. *In such a case, there exists a maximum tension between erotic desire and narcissism; the celebrated "repudiation of femininity" (Freud, 1937) is intrinsically linked to a homosexuality that is narcissistically despised on account of this same repudiation.* This situation can be relieved, if not resolved, only if the father presents a good support for the ego-ideal's projection. In which case the desire that has him as its object will be more readily accepted, since it is less disgraceful. But the intensity of the mother conflict will still preclude a genuine integration of femininity. This integration presupposes the absence of any counter-cathexis of maternal capacities or any overly radical decathexis of them, and at the same time, the ego-ideal's projection onto the father. It seems to me that contempt for women is never "normal," contrary to what Freud says, other than as a passing attitude which later changes into protective feelings toward them—a moment in the development of the little boy that mothers are in a position to observe; a pronounced contempt generally hides fear and envy regarding women, as well as *uncertainty concerning the possession of valid virile personal attributes.*

I am sketching the image of the paranoiac who seeks to escape a powerful maternal imago narcissistically countercathected in a reactive way, and who fails at the same time in his effort to hang on to the father's virility; the latter, in turn, does not lend itself to adequate narcissistic cathexis. This image hardly applies in President Schreber's case, as much for specific data concerning his mother, which is completely obliterated, as his father, whose power and glory could not possibly be doubted. But it seems to me that without being too paradoxical, it is possible to clarify both the absence of narcissistic cathexis of the mother's femininity *and* the impossibility of projecting the ego-ideal onto the father as an identifying projection. We have already seen that Schreber's mother had no existence of her own. She was only the enforcement agent of the father, who had taken over her prerogatives. "Father discussed with our mother everything and anything; she took part in all his ideas, plans, and projects, she read the galley proofs of his writings with him, and was his faithful, close companion in everything," writes Schreber's sister in a letter cited by Niederland.[11] Dr. Schreber echoes this: "When the man can support his opinions by reason of demonstrable truth, no wife with common sense and good will wants to oppose his decisive voice."[12]

Conversely, the household, far from emblazoning its banners with the cultivation of femininity, devoted itself to the cult of virility, as did, in a way, the people of Germany as a whole who followed Dr. Schreber's precepts. This virility could be called "virility as masquerade," paraphrasing the title of Joan Rivière's famous article, or virility defined with some irony by Stoller[13] as a "preoccupation with being strong, independent, hard, cruel, polygamous, misogynic, and perverse." In the case of Schreber *père,* though, perversion as a conscious sexual behavior pattern and polygamy may be deleted from this list. In any case, Dr. Schreber fought forcefully against abandon, pride, and spiritual weakness through the precepts that he lavished in his role as a "Friend of the Family [who serves] as Pedagogue and Guide to Family Happiness, National Health, and Cultivation of Human Beings: *for Fathers and Mothers of the German Nation,*" to quote from the title of one of his works. On the one hand, we can assume that having been raised in the absurd cult of a caricatured virility, symbolized by the *erect* postures of children held by iron collars and leather straps, and without any mother image distinct from the father that could command recognition, Daniel Paul Schreber was not able to narcissistically cathect his mother's femininity. He was led, on this account, to repress and narcissistically counter-cathect his own femininity, which was, in fact, deeply despised by his father. On the other hand, it was also impossible for him to be a man, like his father, by projecting his ego-ideal onto his father in an identifying projection. It is really very difficult to identify with a man who develops such a "repudiation of femininity" and who, to achieve this effect in his children, submits them to constant restraint, immobilizing them and squeezing them in the sphincter formed by his dictates, his rules, his constant monitoring and control, and his orthopedic devices. Thus, this repudiation of femininity, particularly of its tender, soft, enveloping and nourishing aspects, was accompanied in Schreber's father by an identification with an archaic anal-sadistic image that demanded absolute submission. Identifying with Dr. Schreber would have implied, for his son, identifying with a terrifying composite figure. This would have provided a way out of the conflict and an opportunity to become more independent with respect to this "father-mother," had this identification not also implied an incorporation, i.e., an acceptance, of the feminine desire banished from his ego. "That which has been abolished within, returns from without," according to Freud's famous formula. And what was abolished within, as being narcissistically intolerable—for precise historical reasons linked with Schreber's family life, and not because of a universal castration fear that would necessarily be equally distributed—was femininity. And it returned from without in delusional form.

It may be noted that masochistic identification with the turd molded by the father's rectum (Flechsig and then God) to his own liking is constantly present at the heart of Schreber's delusion. Doesn't Flechsig want to perform certain "repugnant manipulations" on him? Isn't there a "plot" to "hand me to another human being . . . in such a way that my soul was handed to him, but my body—transformed into a female body . . .—was *left* to that human being for sexual misuse and simply *'forsaken,'* in other words, left to rot?"

I emphasize "leave," "forsake," and "left to rot;" the anal-passive character of these expressions is evident. Note, moreover, that God addresses only sleeping men or *corpses,* that during the hypochondriacal stage of Schreber's illness—whatever the overdetermination of his symptoms significations—he believes himself dead and *decomposed,* and that in his *Memoirs,* references to the body's fecalization abound. For example, there is a description of the *rotting of the guts,* a miracle produced by the soul of von W: "It threw the putrid matter which caused the abdominal putrefaction into my belly with such ruthlessness, that more than once I believed I would have to rot alive, and the rotten smell escaped from my mouth in the most disgusting manner."[14] Christian David is right to stress that passivity is not equivalent to femininity. It is nonetheless true, in Schreber's case, that femininity is constantly associated with anal passivity (not only to the extent that he is penetrated, but especially manipulated) and with masochism. The fantasmatic here appears in a precise historical context, and tends to depreciate the feminine component of bisexuality.

To briefly summarize, in terms that the president himself would not have denied, "To be a woman in the Schreberian universe is to be shit." A chasm separates this proposition from that other one about how beautiful it would be "to be a woman . . ."

I have in fact recognized a similar kind of problem in a certain number of subjects with paranoia or who present a persecutory fear of feminine identification, arising for historical or even cultural reasons, since the ego-ideal, as Freud says, is located at the interface between the individual and collective.[15] Specifically, femininity in these cases is narcissistically decathected or countercathected, without the father having been able to furnish the child with a valid model for identification. Whether the father engulfs the mother, or the mother the father, the result is the same. Whether the mother is an object of depreciation because of her own characteristics or the family's attitudes, or whether she is so in a reactive way, because of the powerful and terrifying image to which she has given rise—when it is not a combination of both factors that come into play—the result is still the same; that is, the son's femininity cannot be integrated. The example of August Strindberg comes to mind here, whose first, terrible, mother image is coupled with another one of a profoundly depreciated mother. Doesn't he entitle his autobiography, *The Servant's Son,* his mother having worked as a maid in his father's home before becoming his wife? One of his patients, born in an Islamic country in the Mid-East, who presented a number of hypochondriacal disorders, such as fears of anal hemorrhage, pregnancy fantasies, and persecutory fears, and who early on in his analysis had an anxiety dream in which he was afflicted with two holes, said to me one day, "When my sister was born, everyone detested her." I stupidly asked him, "Why?" He answered as if it should have been obvious, "Because it was a *girl.*" At that point I asked myself how a man could integrate his femininity when women in his culture are such objects of hate and scorn. It goes without saying that the familial constellation can aggravate this state of affairs, or, to the contrary, correct it.[16]

One patient was going around from analyst to analyst with a dossier containing documents that he deemed compromising concerning his previous analysts. He had undergone psychotherapy abroad with an analyst with whom he said he was satisfied, and who was of the same nationality as his father. Unhappy with his French therapists, he was in search of a (finally) legitimate French analyst—a type of person, he had been told in his native country, that was simply not to be found. In his quest, he seized with rare talent upon the manias and shortcomings of those that he had consulted. Once in front of an analyst, he would sketch a gallery of particularly entertaining portraits, the listener's pleasure tempered only by the uneasy feelings that would crop up at the thought of the picture for which he himself was going to be the model, all to the great amusement of those colleagues whom the patient would later consult. Now this patient, when I saw him, told me, as if in passing, that his father utterly scorned his mother, who was . . . French.

The general pattern I am proposing may present variants and complications. (A case comes to mind in which a patient who feared he might change sex—sometimes inspecting the appearance of his chest in the mirror, and imagining that he had a feminine bottom—had a family formation that presented the particularity, among others, of being dominated by an overpowering grandmother figure, with a completely obliterated mother and a depressed father, who passed his days in bed, letting his son play with his penis.) Even so, I think it is always possible to make out a constant: the inability to integrate one's femininity because of a lack of narcissistic cathexis of maternal femininity or a reactive countercathexis of it, and the eventual return, by way of delusion, of this abolished femininity. In these cases, it is indeed only in the middle of the psychosis that it becomes truly LOVELY—i.e., takes on considerable narcissistic value—to be a woman submitting to intercourse, and to identify with the mother in the primal scene.

The thesis I am proposing by stressing the role of narcissism follows the Freudian line, but departs from it in the importance accorded the negative or positive cathexis of man's femininity, rather than only the cathexis of the penis. For me, this viewpoint is complementary to Stoller's, and not exclusive of other elements—aggressive drives, for example—the details of which would, however, overwhelm our present subject.

It seems to me that, in radical opposition to the negative narcissistic cathexis of femininity in the future paranoiac, there is a possible cathexis of it by the future transsexual, with a withdrawal of narcissism from his own virility. If, as Christian David says, the transsexual thus represents *the borderline case of a psychic bisexuality asymptotic to zero,* the paranoiac, for his part, reaches desperately for a virility devoid of any trace of femininity, before it can make a delirious return to his ego. It seems to me that in the case of the transsexual, the accent should again be placed on narcissism. Kathy Dee, whose moving confession recently appeared on television, has written a book, *"Travelling: A Transsexual Itinerary"* (1974), which makes instructive reading. It is true that this is a case of a rather sophisticated character who lacks neither talent nor breeding. Although dealt with in large part by Freud, some new accents are unmistakable. I do not have the time to cover in any great detail this work that, could, to a certain extent, serve as a counterpart to Schreber's *Memoirs.*

Kathy Dee, waking up after "the operation," says:

> Mommy . . . You were supposed to love me for two . . . You have lost your child, the first one. I am here like an echo of she who is no longer here, like an echo of your own desire, of your own flesh that no noise will ever cover . . . Then I will have given in to the demand always present in your eyes where so often our soul flooded prayer to give you back she whom you lost the first with whom and for whom you have never stopped clinging to life and of whom I was the substitute in your heart pale glimmer of her intelligence of her beauty . . . Mommy had said yes at the piano, blacks and whites; enroll him in the girl's class, boys are too unruly, he is intuitive and nervous. Her diaphanous hands twisted, broke up *Rhapsody in Blue* and the image of these . . . extraterrestrial dream girls . . . I followed the proposed model, she was beautiful, intelligent and mythic . . . Ill at birth, she destroyed me in leaving. She studied too well. Too sensitive, too beautiful, too obedient, too wise, too perfect, too distant . . .

The first time Kathy Dee, then Jean-Marie, put polish on his nails, he used the bottle from his sister's purse, preciously conserved by the mother in remembrance. It is clear how much being a girl meant, not only replacing the lost object adored by the mother, but also being invested with all its qualities, whereas virility was rejected by the child's narcissism. So, enrolled in the Scouts like the sister before him, after the discovery of high heels and a G-string that he had made for himself, Kathy/Jean-Marie recounts:

> I trembled with shame before these crude beings, stinking of man, these plunderers of little girls with no respect for denied congenital beauty, horrible puppets virile before their time. I trembled with rage to see them exist to fight each other. It was said, they shouted as strongly as their throats could that they were men. Filthy men!

(Note, that here the idea of virility is fecalized). And also: "I wished the old man had spoken true. Disappeared, all the men, DIS-APPEARED."

I agree with Stoller in thinking that the transsexual is not mad. His femininity has not been eliminated within, and therefore does not return from without. Nonetheless, the scorn and hate for men really amount to a "repudiation of virility," the transsexual thus forming the borderline case where it is possible to observe a near symmetry to the "repudiation of femininity" common to both sexes that reaches its heights in paranoia.

In a statement cited twice by Christian David in his paper, Leon Kreisler lays stress on the fact that "the biological forces . . . can be submerged by lived experience." Exactly—and the transsexual who I agree is not mad, but who seeks to match her anatomy with her profound psycho-sexual identity, lives in constant danger that her repudiated and submerged virility, as well as her psycho-masculinity—which, after all, must amount to something—may resurface like a drowned corpse? I am thinking here of an observation recorded by Paulette Letarte concerning a transsexual, after surgery and hormone treatment, who had her eyebrow arch planed, her Adam's apple ground down, and had chromosome tests done, acting on an impulse that can be interpreted as a veritable persecution by the anatomical sex that had disappeared. So it is that certain transsexuals manage to mimic the very quintessence of an exquisite femininity. In their midst, most women, no matter how beautiful and charming, feel like slow-witted bags, clumsy and crude. One journalist recently supported the claims of a transsexual who was imitating Marilyn Monroe in a stage production, to the effect that only a transsexual was able to identify with a woman so suavely feminine.

In the case of Kathy Dee, there is scarcely any mention of the father, and any narcissistic projection on him is out of the question. As one sexual partner told him/her before surgery: "You think all the virtues belong to women and detest your own sex." "And I detest my own sex, my fucking idiotic sex, my stupid sex," and also: "I love women so much that I strive to be just like them." Before the operation, homosexuals reproached him for loving women too much, because in fact what mattered to him/her was not primarily a search for pleasure, but rather, as Stoller points out, a search for identity. On television, Kathy Dee explained that since her operation, her sexual sensations have been almost nil. But it still *seems like heaven*. Which just goes to show that what dominates at this deep level is not a fear of castration, as loss of the penis, nor even the *aphanisis* that Jones postulated, based on the example of the transsexual (before the term existed), intending precisely to accord women a counterpart to the fear of castration. It is instead a sense of identity which is at stake. An identity with links to narcissism that I wish to stress; for the parental influence's impact itself stems from the basic, primitive desire for congruence between sexual identity and narcissism, between the ego and ego-ideal. In other words, narcissism oversees the process and tries to turn an identity using whatever comes to hand, even if what the family makes available is warped and twisted.

This outlook seems to me to make the child more the subject of his own desire, and permits us to grasp the mother's primary influence other than as an "imprint," in the ethnological sense of the term—which is an idea that Stoller has introduced into psychoanalysis, mistakenly it seems to me, regardless of the undeniable interest his work holds.

An absent, seriously depressed father, and a beautiful and fascinating mother, according to what the patient says. A middle-class climate from which the mother wished to escape through an unusual (for her milieu) love for art and music, and a sister of hers in the home, feeding her daydreams on movie magazines. An older brother, the twin of a blind sister, who wanted to "feminize" his little brother, who told him fairy tales, and who set up puppet shows for him to watch, with movie stars cut out from photos in the leading roles. All this would be more than enough to make a small, sensitive boy's sexual identity waiver. "I didn't know if I was in love with the actresses or if I wanted to be like them. I began to make myself up and to dress unisex. My mother wouldn't make me cut my hair . . . I wanted to be a girl." Given a free and open, seductive, shimmering femininity, with an absent and scorned virility ("I have a memory of my mother pushing away my father's hand that wanted to settle on her."), the "biological forces" risk being submerged. Pushing the point, it might be said that one seeks to be like the parental *persona* which most lends itself to narcissistic cathexis.

Both Stoller and David, it seems to me, think that primitive symbiosis with the mother has the effect, in both sexes, that the child's sexual identity is primarily feminine; the boy has to win his virile identity, an effort that is spared the girl. I think this perspective sets the problem in a light that clarifies many aspects of the psycho-sexuality of both sexes. But in my opinion, pushing the hypothesis even further would allow us to better understand the famous dissymmetry implied by the "repudiation of femininity" common to both sexes, and by the primacy of the phallus and the symbolic elements associated with it. As I have had occasion to point out elsewhere, the phallus, being the organ the mother lacks, indicates triumph over the omnipotent mother on whom the premature human child depends for survival. Its effect is to precisely allow the child to differentiate himself from the mother, and consequently, to become independent of her. At the archaic level, it is the father whose attributes make it possible to gain a hold over the mother, not only for the boy, but also for the girl. I doubt that the girl's sexual identity is much more secure than the boy's; a result of the symbiotic relationship with the mother, it does not enable her, any more than it does the boy, to win her own specific sexual identity, which is, in fact, a product of secondary identifications, in a process that is by no means exempt of conflicts. It seems to me that it is chiefly as a result of this absence of differentiation from the primitive mother that penis envy first arises in the girl. That the phallus's symbolic significations are objects of an inflation that occurs because the phallus is propped up on the grave of the mother's primitive power helps us, in my opinion, to understand the disparity which exists between *the mother's image according to the unconscious and woman's image according to Freud.* This viewpoint does not seem to destroy Freudianism, and restores a fundamental role to the castration complex, even if this role covers the vestiges of a ruined city where the Mother/Goddess reigned.

Freudianism, as David says, is neither a dogma nor a religion. But such is not the case for Lacanianism, whose entire theoretical edifice rests upon a single pillar: the phallus. If that is removed, the edifice crumbles. David has recalled the recent misfortunes of a certain female follower of this school. But to be both feminist and Lacanian attests to an inconsistency which well deserves to be punished.

I would like to conclude by commenting on the main thesis supported by David—that is, the gap between psychological bisexuality and biological bisexuality.

Surely, the principle of economy—Occam's razor—demands that we not multiply concepts. Lacking further discoveries, however, most of the phenomena studied by David cannot be broken down to biological factors. Human prematurity once again, and the gap between the ego and the ego-ideal that derives from it, as well as the child's long period of dependence within the family, and the resulting importance of object relations can all explain the strengthening of the psycho-affective factor relative to the biological, and the latter's possible straying, or even, in some cases, its total subversion. [17]

To those who would reproach Christian David, in the name of Freudian orthodoxy, for neglecting the biological roots of the drives, it may be answered that Freud himself, so as to preserve the questionable theory of phallic sexual monism and the primacy of the phallus that springs from it, did not hesitate to deny the instinctual attraction between the sexes and to make of the girl's wish for motherhood not an essentially feminine desire, biologically founded, but the ersatz version of an insatiable masculinity, thus making the wish to have the father's child more direct on the boy's part than on the girl's . . . So . . .

Notes

1.   Robert Knight, "The Relationship of Latent Homosexuality to the Mechanism of Paranoid Delusion," *Bulletin of the Menninger Clinic*, No. 4, pp. 149–159.

2.   R. Stoller, "Faits et hypothèses. Un examen du concept freudien de bisexualité" (Facts and Hypotheses: An Examination of the Freudian Concept of Bisexuality), *Nouvelle Revue de Psychanalyse*, Vol. 7, pp. 135–155.

3.   Knight, *Op. Cit.*

4.   Although the common translation of *"recht schön"* would be "rather beautiful," it is translated in Schreber's *Memoirs* as "rather pleasant." We suspect that Dr. Chasseguet-Smirgel is here referring to the distinction that Kant makes, in his *Critique of Judgment,* between what is beautiful *(schön)* and what is merely "pleasant," "attractive," etc. Hence her reference to the "category of aesthetics." (eds. note).

5.   See Sigmund Freud, "Analysis Terminable and Interminable," (1937) *Standard Edition*, Vol. XXIII.

6.   Sigmund Freud, *Psycho-Analytic Notes on an Autobiographical Account of a Case of Paranoia (Dementia Parnoides)* Standard Edition, XII.

7.   See Freud, "Hysterical Fantasies and their Relation to Bisexuality" (1908), *Standard Edition*, Vol. IX.

8.   Here I refer to the works written by William Niederland between 1951 and 1963 on the relationship between Schreber and his family, particularly his father.

9.   See Robert White, "The Mother-Conflict in Schreber's Psychosis," *International Journal of Psychoanalysis*, 42, pp. 55–73.

10.   See P. C. Racamier and Chasseguet-Smirgel, J., "La révision du cas Schreber," *Revue Française de Psychanalyse*, Vol. 1, pp. 4–26.

11.   See W. Niederland, "Further Data and Memorabilia Pertaining to the Schreber Case," *International Journal of Psychoanalysis*, Vol. 44, pp. 202–207.

12.   Cited by M. Schatzman in *Soul Murder* (London: Allen Lane, 1973). This book, which shamelessly uses documentation collected by various authors, and especially by Niederland, has the merit of grouping together in one volume the work done by others over the years. Furthermore, its anti-psychiatric orientation gives its reasoning a truly naive aspect. Doesn't Schatzman claim, among other things, that suspending repression would be enough to make one hallucinate?

13.   Stoller, *Op. Cit.*

14.   Schreber, *Memoirs of My Nervous Illness*, p. 154.

15.   See Freud, "On Narcissism: An Introduction" (1914), *Standard Edition*, Vol. XIV.

16.   This culture itself furnishes a possible model for the resolution of certain unconscious conflicts. It seems to me that the psychoanalyst should consider cultural phenomena as projections of our drives and of our defense mechanisms into the social space. In this instance, in this type of civilization, depreciation of the woman is itself tied up with the existence of overwhelming maternal power. In this case, who can explain the chicken and the egg?

17.   One might say, in the final analysis, that there is a fundamental biological factor, specifically human, that, by its consequences, would be capable of overriding the biological factors related to sex.

Prado de Oliveira

11. Schreber, Ladies and Gentlemen

The problem of the relations between homosexuality and paranoia seems extremely complex. In an earlier work[1] I tried to clarify the circumstances under which Freud (with Ferenczi's emphatic support) insisted that paranoia corresponds to the repression of homosexuality.[2] It would be prudent, nonetheless, to stress that, among all the founders of psychoanalysis, Freud and Ferenczi are the only ones who attach value to this relationship between paranoia and homosexuality. None of the other early psychoanalysts approached the question in quite the same way—a way which has not been without consequence for subsequent elaboration of such a theory.

In dealing with paranoia, Abraham, Stärcke, and Ophuijsen preferred to speak of anal eroticism. More recently, Macalpine, Hunter and Lacan question why the presence of homosexuality in paranoia necessarily entails a feminine transformation, as, for example, in the case of Schreber. After all, the question is not entirely clear-cut. There are many psychotic homosexuals or paranoiacs who are perfectly well-adjusted people—"normal," so to speak—who have never felt the slightest urge to be transformed into a woman. Conversely, there are numerous cases of individuals who do experience the desire to be transformed into a woman without being psychotic, and without, for all that, being worse off than anyone else.

However it is put, the problem of the relation between homosexuality and paranoia, of their connections, persists. Freud had stated emphatically that homosexuality was present in all forms of neurosis, and maintained this sort of articulation when it came to paranoia. He even evolved four purportedly logical formulas for our consideration. Following Abraham and Lagache's remarks on the subject, and using these formulas, I have tried to introduce others as well. In any case, we could easily produce other examples of homosexuality and paranoia which would be equally suggestive.[3] On the basis of Freud's formulas, for example, it is quite possible to introduce a kind of homosexual erotomania or even—to court a psychoanalytic heresy—a feeling of heterosexual persecution. Lagache, in some astute clinical observations, has spoken of homosexual infidelity, without, however, drawing out the theoretical consequences that seemed to ensue.[4] My purpose here, then, is to attempt to study some clinical cases which will shed light on the subject, and try to draw from them conclusions pertinent to our pursuit, namely, the question of the presence of homosexuality in paranoia and its modalities.

Ladies

In 1915, Freud was stung. Not by a fly or wasp, but by a woman, a young woman who, even if wasp-waisted, did not literally sting him. She stung him to the extent that her case seemed to contradict standard psychoanalytic theory. Let us try, then, to establish if this theory must accommodate itself to Freud's patients or if it is the other way around. Freud had been stung, and he felt challenged to bring the young woman's case into line with psychoanalytic theory. He would try anything to accomplish this, even, as Macalpine and Hunter have said, to become a veritable acrobat. But he did not have to go quite so far. It would have sufficed to have been aware of the potential forms of homosexuality within the feeling of persecution.

How, then, does this young woman's case unfold? A woman of thirty, with uncommon grace and beauty—and a "wasp-waist"—visits a young man in a room which used to be called a *garçonnière,* and they engage in sexual intimacies. The young woman, still inexperienced, tends to jump at the slightest sound. Thus, upon hearing a slight noise, she begins to question the young man. He is, somehow or other, able to convince her that it is nothing. The young woman then composes herself and leaves the room. She runs into two men on the staircase outside. They whisper something. One of them is carrying a package, a small box, perhaps a camera, the woman says. And it is at this point that the delirium is tripped, as one might trip the shutter of a camera. From this point on, the young woman will feel threatened by her lover; she will be jealous of him at work, suspecting all sorts of things, convinced that he is using the photos to blackmail her. She will wind up going to a lawyer, who sends her to Freud. All this will in turn trigger Freud's interpretive apparatus. The cliché is obvious: the young woman felt drawn to her supervisor at work—who was so much like her mother. Besides, and even before the affair with the young man, the young woman expected that he had an affair with this older woman. In short, all this amounts to no more than a typical scene, entirely plausible in turn-of-the-century Vienna.

We see, though, that the woman was delusional. Just imagine the conditions necessary to take a photo indoors, curtains drawn, without a flash. The camera aperture would have to admit such an enormous flash of light that the young woman, blinded by the flash, might have lost her virginity (along with that of the unexposed film). But this consideration did not at all impress her, nor did it calm her, nor even stifle her feelings of persecution. It will only be later, after having composed herself and left the room, that the delusion erupts. Why? Because she meets two men on a staircase. She meets these two men and—I stress—the whole delirious mechanism is set in motion. These two men trigger it with such intensity that the young woman remains quite blinded by it.

A question arises here as to the relation between this encounter (which will give rise to a deferred elaboration) and the event that was properly the occasion for the entire episode, one scarcely mentioned by the young woman—namely, a barely detectable sound behind the curtain of the room she had just left. I will return to this question after examining two other examples of feminine paranoia drawn upon by Freud, for whom cases of feminine paranoia are more frequent than masculine paranoia.

Twenty years prior to being stung, Freud made some other clinical observations. In collaboration with Josef Breuer, he subjected an intelligent woman of thirty-two to psychoanalytic therapy. Her case was comparable to chronic paranoia. Six months after the birth of her first child, the first signs of the disorder appeared. She became introverted and distrustful. Relations with her husband and family became repugnant to her. She also complained of the lack of regard and the rudeness shown her by her neighbors. She was quite certain that someone had something against her, that everyone was trying to harm her. Shortly after, the woman became aware that someone was watching her, reading her thoughts. One afternoon, she was struck by the idea that, at night, someone was watching her undress. One day, when she was alone with her maid, she sensed in her genital region that the maid had had an indecent thought. This sensation became increasingly frequent and she also began to imagine naked women with exposed genital regions and pubic hair. Occasionally, the woman imagined male genitals; she also heard voices discussing her movements and addressing her reproachfully. Under analysis, Freud claimed that the patient acted just like an hysteric (this remark will bear upon our next example). In the first therapy session, the analysis unveiled the fact that the onset of visual hallucinations referred back to an earlier attempt at treatment, conducted at a hydrotherapy clinic, where the woman saw other women nude and was able to mingle freely among them. When analyzed, the hallucinations appeared to stem from the reproduction of real images, which were repeated because they were of some interest to the woman.

We can see that Freud had at his disposal an entire range of elements to emphasize the presence—actually, a massive presence—of homosexuality in paranoia, but did not. Instead, he pushed the analysis further, up to the point of reducing the woman's current problems to her infantile play with her brother. What appears to indicate that such an analysis was well-founded is that, during its course, the woman no longer saw female organs with pubic hair, that is, adult female organs, but, rather, hairless female organs, children's genitals. Freud's analysis goes as follows: brother and sister played at "mommy and daddy." Having read a certain book prompted the woman to recognize her present sexual difficulties with her husband. The woman no longer wanted to play at "mommy and daddy." Incest, and what will later be called "the primal scene," are the two axes of Freud's analysis of the case. There is no question of homosexuality at this juncture, even if it seems flagrantly obvious.

But here's something surprising: If the onset of the disorder is owed in part to the absence of the brother so dear to the woman, it is due even more to what provoked that absence. The woman's husband and brother had argued. Two men then were once again, at the origin of a feminine paranoid crisis, though it would not be justified to insist upon their exclusive role here. While, in the preceding case, it was the two men who gave rise to the elaboration, after the fact, of what had until then been a heterosexual relationship, in the present case the argument between the two men is the occasion pointed out by the woman, on the basis of an event after the fact. In truth, it seems as though this argument only assumed importance several days later after a visit by one of the woman's sister-in-laws, who, in discussing her own difficulties with her brother, made the following remark: "In every family lots of little things happen that we gladly cover up. But when something like that happens to me, I take it lightly." And, she further insisted: "when something like that happens to me, I treat it with disdain." A few moments later, the woman convinced herself that the remarks were addressed directly to her; that she was being accused of taking things lightly, and that she should have made light of her past and present history with her brother, even to the point of joking about it. In effect, she believed that she was being accused of frivolousness, as was the case with Schreber as well. What do these paranoiacs have against frivolity? And what must have happened to this woman (aside from her sexual relations with her husband and infantile play with her brother) that these simple words affected her so? Not much, I expect. Let us note only that in this case the deferred effect follows a scene between two women, a scene which in turn refers one of them back to a scene between two men.

We now have two scenes, each with its couple of men: one on a staircase, the other in the middle-class home. Here is another scene which takes place in a shop. Freud presents it as a case of hysteria, but this should not bother us. We have already seen him treat the case of the one woman (characterized as chronic paranoia) as if it exhibited symptoms of hysteria. And in examining the following case we will find numerous symptoms of paranoia, even of phobia.

Emma cannot enter a shop by herself. She absolutely must be accompanied, even if only by a young child (Freud does not specify the child's sex). She traces this fear back to age twelve, when she went shopping and saw two salesmen burst out in mocking laughter. They teased her and joked about the way she was dressed. Freud's analysis of the case allows us to trace this fear back to a still earlier memory. At the age of eight Emma went to a store to buy some candy. While there, the grocer slid his hand through her dress and onto her genitals. She immediately fled the store, but returned once again. Unable to confront the grocer, she admitted defeat and left the store never to return again. Granted, this is practically a fairy-tale. But, all considered, we once again find two men here, laughing behind a counter, who are utilized in a deferred elaboration of an event that occurred several years earlier.

This observation dates from 1895. We have additional reasons to stress the presence of paranoiac elements in this case, which is presented as one of hysteria. The mocking laughs are obviously there, but, also, when Freud evaluates the subsequent effect of the events on Emma's psychic functioning, on their deferred elaboration, he evokes the period when they occurred—puberty. Now, a year later in *letter No. 52* to Fliess, Freud attributed the constitution of the paranoid syndrome to this displacement of events in time.

Two men, then, cast their somber light on two so-called women paranoiacs, who, according to classical psychoanalytic theory, have repressed their homosexuality. Is this sufficient to draw some theoretical conclusion? Perhaps, but only on the condition that we refuse to generalize these conclusions and that it be possible for us to verify them in cases of masculine paranoia. This theoretical conclusion would take its place among other examples of paranoia I have discussed elsewhere,[5] with what is subject to the following formula: *No, there's no homosexuality in me. It's in them, the homosexuals.* And, by projection: *They upset me, a heterosexual, with their homosexuality, to the point of madness. These pairs of men, on a staircase, at home, in a store, they remind me that there is homosexuality, and I don't want to know anything about it. They persecute me with their homosexuality.*

And even, perhaps, to generalize what certain psychoanalysts might themselves say about homosexuality: *There's no homosexuality in or between psychoanalysts. It's in them, in the paranoiacs.* Didn't Freud himself feel disconcerted by the similarities between his own theory and Schreber's?

The formula for this particular example would be: *Homosexuality can present itself in an inverted form in paranoia.* For example: *this isn't me, a man who desires another man. These are really women who desire one another.* And, by projecting the object-shadow within the Ego, by narcissistic identification: *It's me, a woman, who desires her, a woman.* Simple homosexuality cannot explain the need to be transformed into a woman, as Macalpine, Hunter, and Lacan have stressed. It is necessary that, following the projection of homosexuality, a narcissistic identification take place.

Other cases of paranoia might very well invalidate this mode of psychical functioning. In *Draft H* or in his *Introductory Lectures on Psychoanalysis,* Freud introduces some cases even more difficult to clarify from this particular angle, though the possibility of doing so is not ruled out. It nonetheless remains that the fantasies subjacent to these three cases of feminine paranoia can apparently be reconstituted from a fantasy reported by Schreber: ". . . it really must be rather pleasant to be a woman succumbing to intercourse."[6] It is enough for us to consider that the event which triggers the deferred elaboration retains an analogical relation to the event itself *(événement coup).* Meeting the two men on the staircase would have awakened in the young woman her fantasy in the garçonnière: "It would have been rather pleasant to have been a boy with the young man in this room." As for the second woman, she might have said to herself, while listening to her sister-in-law: "It really would have been rather pleasant to be a man with my husband. He would see who he was dealing with when he argued with my brother; as for her—my sister-in-law—I would show her what games with brothers are all about." Emma might have said: "It really must be rather pleasant to be a boy with the grocer." Without taking any risks, she could have helped herself to lots of candy. They could even have laughed together like the two clerks in the shop did.

Gentlemen

It is extremely curious that the great majority of writers who are interested in Schreber place a disproportionate stress on the relations between the father and the son. Perhaps Niederland's discoveries, their scandalous character, and the rather striking relationship between the father's books and the son's memoirs, contributed to the situation.[7] Most work on the Schreber case appears to proceed as if the fundamental question posed by Katan simply had not been understood. What question does he ask? He says that all the data on Schreber and his father may be true; that perhaps everything happened just the way Niederland reconstructed it; perhaps Schreber's childhood was exactly the way Niederland and many of his followers imagined it to be. But why do these memories reappear in the form of psychosis, of hallucinations, and not simply as childhood memories?[8] After all, if all the suffering children in the world—and here it is not a question of the degree of suffering—went mad, the psychiatric hospitals would be hard-pressed to cope. The question of Schreber's father's own methods is quite evidently an historical one, of great interest to a certain kind of psychoanalysis (badly in need of psychiatry's dignity), but it is not, I think, a legitimate psychoanalytic issue. It is even more curious to see the question treated as a psychoanalytic issue by those very people who venture an appeal to the "Name of the Father," when, in the theory in which this idea appears, the whole question is largely a function of the mother's utterance. Since in the present context, this question might lead us astray, I propose we defer it and follow out our examination of feminine paranoia. I would also propose that we limit ourselves to what concerns female figures in the Schreber case.

Freud's exercise around the word *sun,* in German, seems to us today somewhat untenable (this word itself is feminine in German). In the course of analyzing Schreber's *Memoirs,* Freud maintained that psychoanalysis need not concern itself too much with word gender. Now, while this is certainly true with regard to primary process, in the case of secondary process, e.g., as with writing, this claim is less admissible. We should recall that Schreber was not himself certain of the sun's nature. Might it simply be an organ of God? Or, rather, would it be the very equivalent of God? By the requirements of his own thesis, Freud was obliged to reduce the whole complex to the masculine: he wanted God the father. Now the problem is not just that Schreber's God is often rigged out with female attributes—for example, the famous cry "God is a whore!" Nor even that a masculine God is rigged up with a female organ (a father with a vagina? one might ask). But, even more crucially, and to stick to this sort of grammatical analysis, the article which designates the plural in German is the very one which designates the feminine, *die.* Instead of writing, as in French, *les,* to designate both God and Sun, Schreber had to write God and Sun in the feminine, *la.* Even more incredibly, he had to use *die* for male genitals—which, at a stroke, and independently of their masculine character, could only be designated by an article which suggested the feminine. Strange language: Schreber would have had to create a basic language, one suited to calling a dog *(un chien)* a dog or a bitch *(une chienne)* a bitch.

However, this kind of grammatical acrobatics, just like genealogical acrobatics, has no real place in psychoanalysis. On the other hand, the fantasms which circulate within the family, and especially those preferentially retained by a particular family member, seem far more important. Some recent discoveries in Schreber's writings—particularly those of Han Israëls—as to the respective position of each of his family members may serve to help in the above regard.[9] Not only did Pauline Schreber (Daniel Paul's mother) come from a family of higher social status than her husband, Dr. Moritz Schreber, but the same situation prevailed with her parents as well. Pauline Haase's (her maiden name) mother was from a far more distinguished and wealthy family than her husband, Moritz Schreber's father-in-law. Israëls notes the profound effect of this difference in status: "Thus in all the stories told by Pauline about wealth and distinction, of the life led by her parents, we can perhaps detect a silent reproach against her husband, who had not even attained the rank of professor."[10] This silence can turn into quite an uproar: for example, we learn, as Israëls tells us, that Mendelssohn frequented Pauline's parents' home; that she married just one year after he did, and that, in old age, she wrote letters complaining that his compositions were not played often enough. Or, again, that the only place in Leipzig from which you could see Goethe's student quarters was from Pauline's original home. There are many more examples. In psychoanalytic terms, we could say that the "ego-ideal" left by this woman to her children referred principally to her mother and herself, always leaving the man in either an idealized or devalorized position. Poor Dr. Moritz had a lot of trouble rivaling Goethe and Mendelssohn, as later Schreber could not rival Flechsig's portrait placed on the newlywed's nightable. What could "bedroom gymnastics" do against that kind of music?[11] So little, that a feminine ego-ideal became dominant. Pauline's presence was so weighty, and with it, that of her mother, of her family, and her efforts to idealize her husband, that practically none of her children were able to leave home for any extended period of time. Even when their chosen professions required that they move to another town, the streets they chose always reflected some aspect of the maternal residence. Hence Leipzigerstrasse in Chemnitz and Moritzstrasse in Dresden.[12] And when Schreber left the asylum in 1902, he went to live with his mother for almost two years.

These remarks would be of little interest if we did not find their echo in Schreber himself. They resound in some poems that Schreber dedicated to his mother, and which were recently discovered by Israëls. Regarding his mother's choice of a place to live:

"It was not chance that you took residence there:
Usually only professors were renters.
The Princes' House! How proud the name
Laden with memories that echo in your soul![13]"

Regarding what Schreber understood of his mother's childhood:

"School was disdained; it was considered elegant
To retain a tutor instead.
He praised, scolded when necessary,
He taught you, and long with you, your siblings.
Your head was burdened almost more than proper
With everything that belongs to education,
With world and natural history, foreign languages;
It is still noticeable now in your old age.[14]"

Regarding what Schreber understood of his parents' marriage:

"Thus now and then a suitor also appeared
Ready to attach himself to you for life;
One rapturous one swore solemnly that
Only united with you could he find happiness.
Rejection was then distressing for the poor man,"
"For you it was not agreeable either;
Yet it doesn't do to take up the yoke of marriage
With an unloved person solely out of pity.
So on it went until the right one came;
When he, a young doctor, spoke of love,
When he took courage to propose,
There was, of course, no more lengthy pondering.[15]"

In the first part, we can recognize what Israëls indicates: Schreber's father, being neither a prince nor a professor, does not deserve his mother. In the second, the mother appears as an ideal, entitled to all the material cultural riches. In the third, we sense a certain slippage. Many men courted his mother, but when it came time to choose, she was no longer able to think twice. Was it because of her age, some deception or other due to Mendelssohn, or an entirely different, more banal, reason? We just do not know. We only know that, among all the statements in Schreber's *Memoirs,* the only one whose construction closely parallels one of the statements crucial to the onset of his madness— ". . . it really must be rather pleasant to be a woman succumbing to intercourse"—is one in which he speaks about birds: ". . . how nice it would be if man could also fly like the birds." Towards the end of her life, when his mother gave two swans as a gift to her grandson, Schreber again wrote a poem to commemorate the event:

And I don't think of transforming myself,
Much preferring to wander always as a swan.[16]

Provided we admit an equation between birds and little girls, or one between birds and women, Schreber is always left with a remembrance of the latter. But a remembrance of what?

Fairbairn was the first to stress that the absence of female personalities from Schreber's delusions proved their omnipresence.[17] This thesis corresponds to Abraham's, for whom the paranoiac must become the love object introjected by himself, and also for Klein, for whom, if things happen this way, it is because the paranoiac is unable to separate love from hate. The mother's sadistic desire for knowledge would result in short-circuiting the possibilities of establishing symbolic relations. What would have been denied within by hate, reappears on the surface in the form of love. The formula would be simple: *I am or I must become he (or she) towards whom my hate is lovingly carried.*

Schreber felt that he had to remain a memory, had to always remember. For his wife, as I have suggested elsewhere, on to whom everything was transferred, and to whom his book was dedicated, he had to become a woman. For it was she—with an entirely excusable curiosity—who insisted on seeing him dressed up in woman's clothing. She also insisted on exchanging female gossip with him.

But maybe I am wrong. Schreber was much more insistent on being a woman in his mother's presence. In fact, he tried to become his own mother, who had never accepted the woman he had chosen, from a social position inferior to his own, just as his mother had done with his father. Better to become a woman than to die, as Schreber would have said, in opposition to his brother Gustav.[18]

To be a woman for another woman. The inversion of masculine homosexuality is comparable to the inversion of feminine homosexuality. Homosexuality is never found precisely where we expect to find it. In the banality of its everyday expressions, it is only found in its inverted forms. Men love women, women love men. Each believes that homosexuality is located in the other. However that may be, Ladies, Gentlemen, don't you recognize yourself in this pattern?

Notes

1.   See Prado de Oliveira, "Trois études sur Schreber et la citation" in *Psychanalyse à l'Université,* v. 4, No. 14 (Paris: Editions République, 1981).

2.   It should be noted that, in this work, I never pretended these circumstances could in any way justify the clinical practices or methodology or either Freud or Ferenczi.

3.   See Prado de Oliveira, "La libération des hommes," in *Cahiers Confrontation,* No. VI, (Paris: Aubier-Montagne, 1981).

4.   See Daniel Lagache, "Contribution à l'étude des idées d'infidélité homosexuelle dans la jalousie et Erotomanie et jalousie," in *Oeuvres* (Paris: Payot, 1977).

5.   Prado de Oliveira, "Trois études . . ."

6.   Daniel Paul Schreber, *Memoirs of My Nervous Illness.*

7.   Here I refer specifically to a series of articles dating from 1951 through 1963 by William Niederland. The most important of these articles was probably "Schreber: Father and Son," *Psychoanalytic Quarterly,* 28, 151–169.

8.   See M. Katan, "Childhood Memories as Contents of Schizophrenic Hallucinations and Delusions," *Psychoanalytic Study of the Child,* Vol. 30, 1975: pp. 357–374.

9.   Hans Israëls, *Schreber: vader und zohn,* dissertation, University of Amsterdam, 1980.

10.   *Ibid.*, p. 44, n. 6.

11.   "Bedroom Gymnastics" is a reference to the title of one of Moritz Schreber's most popular monographs. (trans. note).

12.   Israëls, *Op. Cit.*, p. 180, n. 92.

13.   Psychosis and Sexual Identity: Toward a Post-Analytic View of the Schreber Case (Albany: State University of New York Press, 1988), p. 240.

14.   *Ibid.*, p. 238.

15.   *Ibid.*, p. 241–242.

16.   *Ibid.*, p. 222.

17.   See W. R. D. Fairbairn, "Considerations Arising Out of the Schreber Case," *British Journal of Medical Psychology,* Vol. 19, #2, 1956, pp. 113–127.

18.   This is a reference to Gustav's suicide, which occurred in 1877. (trans. note).

Octave Mannoni

12. The Pathogenesis of Creation or the Liberation of Women

Dear Distinguished Professor: [Freud]

I take the liberty of writing to you upon the advice of my new friend, Dr. Gross,[1] who says you know him and who admires you greatly. He has sent me an issue of your *Jahrbuch* which he just received containing an article of yours which interested me very much as you will see shortly.[2] I discussed with him at length the content of this article and surprised him very much with my knowledge of the material—all the more as I did not tell him from where I learned of it. He is convinced that what I would tell you about it would be of great interest to you. He may be deluding himself, but all this will become clear if you will read further.

I live incognito in Munich, more precisely in Schwabing. My name is Jaochim Fuchs and when I write "my name," it is not a figure of speech. I decided on the name myself—in other words, it is a false name. In fact, I escaped like a prisoner from a university clinic in Leipzig where I was under treatment. Upon reading your article, it seems that you do not know Professor Flechsig—in any case, I could not get a recommendation from him considering the way I departed, on a particularly dark night, a feat that you would appreciate if you knew his clinic. I had asked the Professor to cure me of a very painful sciatica and he spared no pains: hydrotherapy, mecanotherapy, electrotherapy, chemotherapy, heliotherapy—my sciatica had become his personal enemy—and I could ascertain that if a sciatica prevents the patient from sleeping, it can prevent the neurologist from doing so also. I admired his zeal and devotion. I even started to feel sorry for him. He told me, however, that upon trying everything in vain he could only recommend the cauterization of the sciatic nerve, a procedure that he had never done before but which he longed to try. When he insisted that we take advantage of this opportunity, something happened that no other medical doctor—except you Dear Distinguished Professor—would believe: my leg stopped hurting immediately. Astonished, I assured him that I was cured and that my torments and his had come to an end, but he refused to admit it. I insisted, nonetheless, on being discharged at once and thinking that I pleased him, congratulated him for the brilliant success of this "moral treatment." Well, would you believe it, Dear Distinguished Professor!, instead of sharing my joy, he fell into a cold fury as if I had been gravely disrespectful to him. Since I tried to flee, he called his attendants and I found myself in what I believe was a small cell, though I cannot describe it because there was no light. I escaped via the roofs and gutters in the middle of the night, and if he could have seen the perilous acrobatics that I had to perform in total darkness, he would have had proof that I was actually completely cured. I reached Munich by freight train, since I did not have enough money on me to both buy a ticket and set up in Schwabing. The free, joyous and even slightly crazy life one leads there, with so many eccentric men and, especially, women, talented or totally unproductive artists, has only contributed to reinforce my cure. Otto assures me that this admirably confirms your concept of illness. As a matter of fact, he enjoyed my story of the escape, all the more as he himself escaped one night from another university clinic in Zurich, but he only had to scale one wall. He was being treated there for *dementia praecox.* You know him, he is as mentally sound as you and I, or at least as much as I, although you might think that this isn't saying much . . . He explained to me, however, since he is quite witty, that one cannot be a good judge of sanity in Schwabing: here, those who are not mad pretend that they are and there is nothing more comfortable for one and all.

I have important things to tell you and I do not want you to get discouraged and stop reading. You must have already noticed that I have a certain difficulty in posing a question directly and simply. I have to make every effort since there is always so much to say and being clairvoyant I always see so well the usefulness and the uselessness, the importance and the insignificance of each detail. Being artistic, too damn lucid, I am so cramped by it that I produce very little and even, so to speak, nothing at all. And if I have so much trouble writing a simple letter like this—which I promised Otto—it is because I see with almost painful precision all I should put into it and all I should omit.

Perhaps you think that Joachim Fuchs is my *nom de plume?* Yes, of course it is. Whatever I publish or exhibit will appear under that name. But now, I only use it to hide myself. You may tell me that it is unlikely that Professor Flechsig would be looking for me, but you would be mistaken. Certainly, he will not do it directly. Still, it is upon the advice of an uncle of mine that I went to consult him, since in my family the Professor is considered a genius, the God of neurology. Everyone admires him even if they have only seen him in a photograph. Yet he is not handsome, with an eye deformed from constantly peering into a microscope, and bushy eyebrows which nearly meet his enormous sideburns. But if he should have the unfortunate idea of telling any member of my family—they are close—how I parted company with him, I would be in deep trouble. Even without that, if they should discover that I live in what they imagine to be a place of debauchery, and certainly outward appearances give them good reason, they would do everything in their power to save my soul. But the salvation of my soul is the loss of my individuality *(personne)!* I feel that in reading me, someone like you might already suspect something; well, do not doubt it any longer! My real name—do not betray me—is D. P. Schreber. Yes, yes, of the family. Daniel Paul's family! He is a cousin of mine. My given names are David Peter. Now my letter must interest you more. I hope that you have not abandoned it before reaching this point. An absurd remark, since, if you have read it, the question is resolved, and, if not, the question does not exist; but I like absurdities.

Otto could not guess why your article interested me so much. But be assured that I am the only member of the family—absolutely the only one—who is capable of reading it, not only with sympathy and understanding, but also with a tender sadness. You did not know my cousin personally and that's a pity. He was a distant cousin and we are a rather complicated family. Sometimes I even have trouble identifying them, which probably means I do not like them very much. Ours is a family of magistrates and physicians, much more so than Otto's. I remember when I was still young what a seductive man my cousin could be. From his early childhood he had been raised with the most rigorous methods which seemed to have produced a kind of perfection. He had nothing of that strict and authoritarian coutenance then, no bushy sideburns, as was still the fashion, to emulate the "great man," himself a magistrate and physician, but on the grander scale, who communicated his ambitions and used to make us swallow his martial medicine.[4] This would rather be a model for Professor Flechsig or for Hans, Otto's father. Daniel Paul, who died recently as I think you know, since you certainly waited until that moment to publish your article, was slim and vigorous, with a fine head and a sometimes dreamy and penetrating look— never suspicious or haggard—but thoughtful and immediately precise and attentive. He gave you the impression that you were important to him because he was interested in you, and at the same time of no consequence to him, as though he could regally do without you. His moustache was thin and floated a little as is seldom customary with us—perhaps in the English style. He was very cultivated, reading Thucydides as well as Horace in the original, which impressed me thoroughly. Yet, all these qualities did not prevent him from being very competent in his work.

Since Otto is a psychiatrist working with Kraepelin at our town's Königliche Clinic, he agreed, at my request, to question an attendant who happened to work at the asylum where my cousin died. But he only related insignificant information. All hospital attendants behave like hospital attendants, all psychiatrists like psychiatrists, and all mad people, necessarily, like mad people. I am therefore led to believe that Otto was told exactly what is said about all mad people: that he had to be spoon-fed and that his arms were tied for that purpose. Otherwise, if he was not watched carefully, he would grab the spoon and try to force-feed the attendant. Anyway, nobody ever questions the meaning of such common behavior. In any case, this is all I know about the end of this delightful man. It is acknowledged, however, that except for the matter of the spoon he had become, alas, sweet and docile.

I can appreciate how you described the beginnings of his illness in a penetrating and exact way, and it seems that I, too, although I make no use of it, possess many qualities of mind that help me to appreciate yours. In a certain way I am sensitive to the mad sides of almost everybody. I acquired this ability, or this defect, from my family naturally, and this is why Schwabing suits me so well and I like Otto so much. I am not very interested in associating with people who are called rational. In truth, this question remains obscure to me, because Professor Flechsig also has a crazy side which makes him odious to me.

Yes, the madness of Flechsig, of Daniel Paul's father, of Otto's father, are repulsive to me. I like Daniel Paul's, Otto's and my madness very much. I would not want to be deprived of mine, and perhaps this is clearer to you than to me because of your vast knowledge.

Daniel Paul's father, Dr. Daniel Gottlob (everybody in this family will end up being called Daniel, since it is a first name used as a common denominator, as the mathematicians would say), Dr. Gottlob, then, gave his children a very strict education according to principles that I find questionable. But I am not competent and I would rather tend to judge them according to the results, which seems legitimate in matters of pedagogy. Based on these results, the principles are not good. I have read his books—without ever finding any proof or demonstration— and still Dr. Gottlob had such prestige and influence that people believed in his doctrine like it was Gospel. All considered, one would become skeptical about any doctrine which rests on its author's prestige. I know Gottlob's arbitrary methods only in an abstract way, although they were also applied to me, like to all the children in the family. You must bear in mind that there is a considerable difference between a method fanatically applied by its inventor and one applied by a disciple, even a faithful and dedicated relative. Let us recall that many devices were to be built with bars, belts, loops, specially shaped wooden pieces, and you can well imagine that even those who believed that they were applying the rules and admired the inventors were either too negligent or too thrifty to get the proper material. Once—Gottlob had died a long time ago but his ideas were still worshipped—out of curiosity I asked an orthopedist in our town whether people would order these types of instruments. He gave me a contradictory answer—and contradictory answers are always revealing—in the sense that, first, he would never manufacture such horrors and, second, his clients were far too miserly and ignorant to order them. When a doctrine relies upon only the reputation of its author, this always happens. As for me, I recall once having been tied to my chair with an ordinary string—a grocer's string probably, I remember its color—or in my bed, with a bathrobe cord. Happily, Gottlob was unaware of how badly people followed him, and he believed that his doctrine was applied all over Germany when it was not applied in the Kingdom,[5] nor in our town, nor even in his own family. However, he was admired everywhere. It is so nice to have a marvelous doctrine at your disposal which one is not so much obliged to apply. There lies perhaps the foundation of religions. But the sole victims of these barbaric concepts—and I feel like saying it serves them right, if it were not so uncharitable—were his own children. I am happy to relay this detail since I have been surprised, when reading your work, not to find any mention of my uncle's pedagogical methods; it is precisely on this point that Otto wanted me to let you know what I told him. I believe, however, that Otto is wrong when he thinks that you did not know about Gottlob's pedagogy, for it is quite well known. He has written and published so many works that they can be found in any library and nothing, certainly, was easier than finding them in Vienna. My cousin's *Mirabilia,*[6] on the other hand, which you managed to obtain, are impossible to find, although they are in my opinion rather more interesting. Why this injustice? Because Gottlob's works have a utilitarian aspect (even if nobody applies them), while Paul has written the epic poem of neurology. If this tendency holds, only practical and utilitarian manuals will soon be written. I made this remark to Otto who started laughing: "Nobody will put them into practice," he said, "this will be a new literature of the imagination. Such was already the case with devotional books." Otto is very intelligent but, in my opinion, has no common sense.

He has a particular turn of intelligence which makes me think that he suffered in the past from obsessional neurosis. One day, he had come to pick me up while I was finishing washing and he inquired like an examiner: "Why is it necessary to shave before taking a bath?" I did not know what to answer. Would you? Well, it is "because there is no steam yet on the mirror." I did not want to admit defeat and answered: "One can shave after bathing, the hair is softer." He added dryly: "Zero, this is not the answer to the question. It is the answer to another question, which is: Why is it necessary to shave *after* bathing? An uninteresting question indeed: and much too easy." What do you think? Isn't it absurd? Someone who reasons like this is certainly very clever—but isn't he . . . just a little too much?

I wondered why you did not show more interest in all of Gottlob's manuals. I would not like it to be the result of discretion, human respect, or good manners. It is unworthy of you. There is a sentence in your article where you more or less imply that someone who knows my family could make the connection between my cousin's madness and its actual causes. But you add—and this has troubled me—that this would require someone bolder than you. Is it possible that you lack courage? I cannot believe it. Were you afraid to be sued for libel? I know that the risk exists, but Paul was not afraid of being exposed to a libel suit, which, by the way, never took place. Flechsig did not dare—with a jurist! Or do you simply mean that it is up to your readers to inform themselves because you are not interested in this facet of the question?

I have a copy of the *Mirabilia* with me. It means a lot to me. Just think, it's Flechsig's, with a dedication. And what a dedication! I had borrowed it from the clinic's library and took it along when I escaped. My family, on the other hand, is looking for every copy so as to destroy them all. They even had copies stolen from hospital libraries, when possible—that's why I had no scruples. My copy, flatteringly dedicated to me, has of course mysteriously disappeared. I never had any other source than this text to understand what happened to Paul, nor, for that matter, did you. Thus I had no advantage over you. But I do have the impression—since I dealt personally with Flechsig himself—that he is directly responsible for my cousin's madness. I have not studied medicine, except for three months when I learned the names of the bones—it is contrary to an artist's nature to work in medicine. Thus I cannot say anything worthwhile medically about my cousin's madness. But I think that he started to become mad because Flechsig resembled Gottlob so much. Certainly, Flechsig made a strong impression. Didn't he cure me of sciatica, and isn't it true that he who is most capable of healing is also most able to cause sickness? I believe Socrates said that. But since I am not even able to explain the cure of my sciatica, although I understand it very well in a way, I cannot say more on the effect that Flechsig might have had on Paul. What you and I know, by reading *Mirabilia,* amounts to very little: the first time, Paul suffered from insomnia. This is less painful than sciatica. Flechsig kept him for six months and released him cured. But my cousin complained that he had not been treated with enough consideration. He was proud of having paid a considerable honorarium. This nevertheless was a lesson which he had given the Professor, a lesson in "consideration." What a pitiful revenge! I only stayed five weeks and payed nothing with the exception of my watch and tie pin (my bottom-hook was even removed), and during these five weeks I strongly felt the lack of consideration of which the other patients complained. And how could I have made a good appearance, without a tie, with unbuttoned boots, in front of the Professor? But I had more energy, or more madness—it is the same thing, and I escaped via the roofs and with unbuttoned boots! Paul was too courteous, too well behaved, too respectful of titles, laws and rules. He was also less agile. And, mostly, I believe that he had conceived of another plan of revenge. I will come to that. But, first, I realize that I have not told you enough about myself. Who, in our time, does not like to talk about himself?

Besides, Otto claims that, whatever one does, one always speaks about one-self. He also pointed out a sentence in your article, the importance of which I had not realized. It is on the last page: you draw a comparison between my cousin's theory and yours. At a congress, or in Vienna, I'm not sure, he introduced you to some humorous verses where Heine suggests that the cause of the creation is an illness, and that God shit the world one day to recover from a stomach ache.[7] You asked Otto to dictate these verses to you. Some idea! People in good health have no need to invent. Otto is cunning, but he is the most generous man I have ever known.

Me, I am a "great painter." I put quotation marks, because I have never painted anything. With quotation marks I could even be the greatest painter of all times. But I know my limitations. For instance, even with quotation marks, I will never be a great musician.

A great musician, whose works have never been performed, nor even written, may have an entire sonata in his head or even a complete symphony which would gain nothing from being transcribed on paper. If I were a musician (and I could only be a great musician), I would return from my walks in the nearby woods (you know, there are beautiful lakes within a few kilometers) with an original work. And in the evening, if I could resist the habit of meeting Otto, or some other person (preferably, a female person) in a tavern or Weinstube, I could dictate a great symphony, or at least a little chamber music, hotel chamber music in this case, at my leisure. But how could one imagine me returning in the evening with a complete painting in my head and summoning a copyist to dictate to? This is because music, unlike painting, can be written. Which proves that, in the scale of the arts, painting is far superior to music.

Nevertheless, people who know nothing about it believe that a painter could have a painting in his head. When I saw the *Isle of the Dead* for the first time, a painting that so many of our crude compatriots blindly extol to the skies these days, I understood immediately, by having reflected on all these questions for a long time—I am also an exceptional art critic—that this painting was ridiculous precisely because Böcklin had composed it in his head! He should have been a musician, he missed his vocation. In painting, one always improvises with colors, brushes, the fingers of both hands, one never executes. A great poet may have nothing to say: a hero may have no exploit to accomplish; and someone like me might need to suffer from sciatica to discover, on the roofs of a university clinic, unsuspected acrobatic talents. I told Otto that no motive moved me. Why copy nature? It's already there. It's self-sufficient. I should use colors according to my inspiration, without worrying about representing anything, so as to be myself and to be amazed enough by the result to respect it and leave it alone. In the arts, one calls this perfection. Otto begs me to try. But even in Schwabing I would look mad. Otto encourages me. He compares me to Bernard Palissy, but that is stupid. Palissy was passionate, free of any scruples, someone who squandered his wealth and burned the household furniture, much to the despair of Mrs. Palissy, no doubt. In compensation, though, he supplied her with plates and dishes. No, I'm not going to nip in the bud any hope of future glory with experiences which would ridicule me.

In fact, music and painting differ because music is written and painting is not. And this brings me back to you, Dear Distinguished Professor. You have invented a system of concepts, a topology, a nomenclature to write up my unfortunate cousin's case. One can, then, teach it and give it to students to learn. As for me, I see his case like a painter. I understand it in one glance, but cannot talk about it the way you do. In fact, I am a painter, and you are a musician. Otto did not tell me what kind of instrument you played. If we could collaborate, me with my clairvoyance and you with your writing, how many great things might we do? But can a collaboration be conceived between such opposed faculties? Each of us must resign himself to sorely lack what the other possesses in abundance.

To explain my point of view to you, I should perhaps resort to concrete facts; otherwise I would be embarrassed like someone who must explain verbally (to a blind person, for example) the difference between a Van Dyck brown and burnt Sienna. My unfortunate cousin's madness, provided it is madness and not just the inspiration that spurred him to write, is perfectly clear to me in the *Mirabilia*. I understand, even admit willingly, that you wish to make it clearer, understandable for all of us, but doesn't it mean precisely that you give a reasonable and logical version of it, which is perhaps a kind of treason? We will never know what Paul would have thought of your article, but it can hardly be doubted that he would have protested, in one way or another. I would like to do it in his place, respectfully—as he would certainly have done himself, most respectfully—if he were able to do it. I propose, because of my incapacity, to offer you a case history of the same kind as those you yourself exhibit with so much talent, but shorter and simpler. For greater formality, I am even going to give it a title.

The Case of Artillery Lieutenant Bückingfresser

Never has any family name so ill-suited its bearer, since Heinrich was the nicest and most well-bred of my high school friends. His father, like the rest of the town, believed naturally in Gottlob's methods, but applied them much too gently for them to be disastrous. Both our fathers were friends. His, occupied a rather lofty position in the postal services of the kingdom, and mine, of course, was a judge at the tribunal. They met every evening to drink a bottle of Rhine wine and gamble its price at a French game, the name of which I have forgotten but which was played very quickly. The other patrons played complicated and extremely slow games—because they did not converse, my father said. But they did not look favorably on the cavalier way my father and his friend quickly played their game. I recall that one evening—I was eleven and there was a snow storm—I had come to fetch my father because my mother was worried by his lateness. The bottle and colored glasses were empty, the game had already started and my father was dealing. He put the trump-card on the table and simply said: "King, that makes five." He at once took his fur hat and left hurriedly, without saying goodbye to anyone. The others remained speechless, their mouths agape. One of them, who was lifting his mug to his lips, stared, motionless, his mug at a finger's breadth from his nose. They were undoubtedly thinking that all the men in our family were a little touched in the head. They probably had no opinion about the women, whom they only saw at church. I did not understand their point of view then, but today I fear that they were right.

Heinrich left high school at fifteen, his father intending that he enter the military. I had to stay in school since my father naturally wanted me to go into medicine. During the first days of vacation—it was a sweltering beginning of August, almost like the one that brought us the comet[8]—Heinrich had gone with his father to a tailor specializing in military uniforms so as to have a cadet uniform made. He told me about it later when his memory had returned to him. Personal tastes hardly matter as far as uniforms are concerned, and the tailor would have never dared to ask him, according to tailor's customs of the time, whether he "carried" on the left or right, for fear of making him blush. However, some technical questions must have bothered the father, for the tailor led them to his workshop to show some pieces of uniforms in the process of completion. Heinrich had completely forgotten the rest and remembered it only after his father's death. Perhaps you could explain that? Undoubtedly because of this temporary forgetfulness, the memory that came back to him was preserved with an extraordinary precision. The workshop was located in a garret, with a large glassed bay, lighted by a late afternoon sun. Four or five employees—I cannot remember the exact number, contrary to Heinrich who remembered everything—were busy sewing, sitting cross-legged, on a high and very wide table. They were bare-footed because shoes, I guess, may dirty the fabric. One of these workers was an apprentice about Heinrich's age, who had stripped to the waist because of the heat. He was—or appeared to my friend—of a celestial beauty, an angel with light blue eyes, long, golden hair, amber-colored skin illuminated by the sunset. Heinrich remained, he said, as though hypnotized for a moment or two, without thinking about anything. Then his father, who had settled with the tailor, took him by the hand and led him away. Heinrich walked submissively like a sleepwalker and, like a sleepwalker, he had forgotten all about it when he awoke. His mother asked him if he liked the color of the uniform and he answered: "very likely." His answer seemed inadequate but no remark was made because the color was regulation, and his mother recognized that her question was trivial. A truly extraordinary case of amnesia, for which you will certainly find an explanation or at least an adjective. I know nothing about it, but I understand it very well, without being able to explain it.

I did not see Heinrich again at the beginning of the term. The Cadet School was in Dresden, and he later went from garrison to garrison. Because of his great interest in mathematics, he had requested to be assigned to the artillery, a less noble arm than the cavalry, where his father would have liked to see him. A model soldier, a brilliant lieutenant, he was about to be promoted to captain, which would have made him the youngest captain in the army of the Reich, except for two or three princes who are never seen in the barracks, when he learned of his father's death. He was of course granted a leave for family reasons and left for the funeral, but to everyone's surprise, in civilian clothes! One accepted the inevitable, as he had already shown a few peculiarities: he had studied non-Euclidean geometry which is of little use to artillerymen, publishing a scornful and insulting pamphlet against the professors at the university and in defense of a certain man named Cantor, of whom nobody had ever heard. Indignation had not been too extreme, because most of his officer friends asserted that the university scholars, if they were unhappy, could always challenge him to a duel, and that would settle everything. At the end of his leave, however, he never returned to his quarters and nobody ever knew what became of him. It seems that he was never pursued for desertion, and simply decommissioned as a *de facto* resignation, which was in accordance with peacetime customs and regulations.

I had met him, always by chance and rarely, when he was a lieutenant, but did not hear a thing about him after his resignation. I did not even recognize him with his beard when he stopped me in the street near his new lodgings, where we walked together. He explained what he was doing.

He had a grandiose project: to completely revolutionize the art of clothing. He claims that it is impossible to dress curved bodies correctly with fabrics whose weft and warp cross at right angles. He used terms such as "Mercator projection," "loxodromics," "geodesics" and others which I do not know. He demonstrated on mannequins, over which he had spread colored threads, and I understood much less than an artilleryman who juggles trigonometry, which I never knew anything about. It is on this occasion that he told me what had happened at the tailor's and how its remembrance obsessed him and interfered with his work. I suggested that perhaps this memory was responsible for his passion for the art, or rather the craft, of tailoring. He replied that my supposition was absurd: he was interested in weaving, not in tailors. If he succeeded, he would become rich. It seems that his goal was to invent a kind of diagonal weaving about which I understood nothing. I wonder whether he had gone mad or whether he was on the trail of a great invention. In any case, I did not hear anything about him for years.

End of the Story of the Ex-Artillery Lieutenant

You will ask me why I told this story. It is not only to show off my talents as a story-teller. It would be simple for me to invent a subject, even more so to tell a true story, though reality is never, never sufficiently artistic. This remark might make you think that I invented this story. No, no, my account is very faithful. You are bound by professional confidentiality, and if you wish to use this case history in one of your works, do not fail to change the names. Would I bother to take this precaution if this story were invented?

But I told you this story for still another reason. The point is that when I told Otto about it, he answered: "He is working on his cure? will he succeed?" This was not very clear . . . What did he mean? He tried to explain it, saying that it was your idea of sublimation, and also something similar to what Heine meant about creation; that if Heinrich succeeds and becomes rich, he will overcome his difficulties. If not, he will pass for a madman and perhaps even become one. He added that Paul did the same thing when he wrote his *Mirabilia,* but he did not succeed. I wonder if you would agree with Otto.

This, Otto told me, is also what happened to a certain Bertha Pappenheim, a person who was supposedly cured in this way. I have vaguely seen the name in the newspapers, though I do not know who she is.

In any case, his remarks made me think of many different things. Did he imply that you did the same thing by inventing psychoanalysis? He answered without hesitation: "Yes, absolutely," but added immediately that there was a major difference, that you had invented a model, initiated a work that all those who were incapable of invention could resume, after you and according to you, to be cured in that way. While Heinrich, if he were to succeed and become rich, would only bring to others a new kind of fabric, which would undoubtedly be a service, but he will never cure anyone, besides himself. I do not know exactly what to think since Otto, as I told you, has no common sense but does have very original, exciting ideas. Perhaps you will consent to let me know what you think of them.

I dreamed a little about Otto's strange ideas and seriously reflected; I too was on the point of being an inventor but, thank God, I escaped this nonsense and did not know, before my talk with Otto, where I had acquired this strange whim. I am fully aware that this letter is excessively long, considering that it is only the first one, but I am reassured by the idea that it must interest you. It is therefore necessary that I also include this story, which is hardly to my credit—I am not speaking out of vanity. I will try to be brief. It is really difficult, because I have so much to say. I had invented—this is incredible—a cannon. Otto claims that it is because Heinrich was in the artillery at the time. There is a strange coincidence here, I agree, but my inspiration came from somewhere else; I am sure of it. My cannon now, do not laugh, was open at both ends, the charge was incorporated in the projectile like a rocket, and the firing was done with a flashlight battery, etc. When I told this story to Otto he raised an objection that I had not thought about. My cannon, he said, would have many qualities. Its range would depend only upon the strength of the charge; but he feared that the velocity at the start would be too small, which would harm its accuracy. But, I said, it does not matter since there is no recoil! We spent hours discussing these questions while drinking beer, and I could notice once more how clever Otto was. These discussions were useless (except when it rained, since they helped pass the time) for I had long ago renounced the actual use of my idea. I had been too ashamed of myself. And I had never been so afraid as at that time. They could steal my invention. How and through whom could I get the job carried out? Could I trust the Grand General Staff or the Krupp family? Wouldn't I suffer the same unfortunate fate as Dreyfus, if they falsely accused me of intending to deliver my plans to the French? Dreyfus was tried, indeed, and returned from Devil's Island. Me, they wouldn't try me, just declare me insane, as always happens with inventors, and I would end up in an asylum, hands tied behind my back, spoonfed by a devoted attendant. I was getting thinner every day.

Well, I must admit that these fears would not have stopped me. It was on the day when I bought everything—pens for drawing lines, India ink to make the necessary drawings—that I understood that I had become really insane. Me, a painter, render such a drawing? Sign it with my name? Impossible. Leonardo drew war machines, yes, but freehand, and today this would not be taken seriously! No, my name will never appear on a list that already includes a Johann Dreyse and an Antoine Chassepot. My place is on a list which is not closed and starts alphabetically and chronologically with Apelle; there's still some room left, and there should be when you see the number of candidates here in Schwabing alone. I might gain a modest fame, like that of Paolo Ucello or Gustave Moreau, but that is much more honorable than being the first on Chassepot's list. (What a name: Nachttopfsjäger!)

*   *   *

I was interrupted by Otto, who came to pick me up and share his distractions, always the same. Nevertheless, I do have to tell you about Daniel Paul since this is the purpose of my letter. Let me also explain what made me fall into my mania for invention, as well as the distractions that I share with Otto, and the questions which do not come to mind at the moment but which will come along the way.

I see now that what transformed me into an inventor is the same thing as happened to Heinrich: an impossible love, but much more ridiculous. The girl was an imbecile who, without having read Goethe, believed firmly in the perfidious advice that Mephistopheles sings to Gretchen: first, the conjugal ring. The

Devil knows what he is doing. If he were not somehow mixed up in the affair, how can you explain the absurdity of girls rushing into the slavery of cooking or housework when, on the contrary, they are given the chance to enjoy themselves a little. Unfortunately I did not know Otto or Schwabing at the time, and things were less clear to me or I would not have fallen into this folly of wanting to perfect an artillery piece! Otto is much more serious and practical, and he has already been working with great success for the liberation of women. This, he says, should be the primary purpose of psychoanalysis and he complains that you unfortunately do not quite agree. In any case, you see that I am in a good position to understand what happened to Heinrich, to God according to Heine, to Gottlob according to his *Memoirs,* and probably to you and to Otto—for why would he want to liberate all women? One at a time is good enough. He, too, must be trying to escape something to undertake such an enormous task!

Let us now try to settle a question which cannot wait any longer, since my letter has become too long. If I could come to Vienna to be psychoanalyzed, I would talk in this way, I mean, like I write—in total freedom. It is therefore only fair that I pay you your fee for a session for the time you spend reading this letter—I almost wrote "that you waste" but, to be accurate, it will really not be lost. Perhaps you could even send me a diagnosis or an interpretation—and also your bill. You will be paid by return mail.

Now that I have settled this question, my mind is at ease and I can go on.

What a pity that my cousin is dead. I would have liked him to have read your article and to have responded according to his own inspirations. I think he would have felt more confident than you in understanding the *Nervensprache.* But he certainly would have agreed that, based on a few bits, you have achieved a quite remarkable reconstitution, although, of course, without nearly the direct knowledge he had of it.

He would justify himself by invoking the Order of the World. Perhaps, since he had a suspicious nature, he would have suspected you of a certain professional complicity with your professorial colleague, Paul Emil Flechsig. You are, after all, a neurologist by training, like him. My cousin is also a neurologist, but by avocation, and it is for this reason that he investigated things further than both of you. His book is the most grandiose enterprise ever attempted at writing a total, human, cosmic and divine neurological treatise.

But he did it to humiliate Flechsig and had nothing against you, obviously. I am almost certain that he did not know your name.

You both made, separately and simultaneously, the same fundamental discovery. He developed and extended it further—in an inevitably adventuresome way, as inventors are wont to do. You were limited, and rightly so, in your brilliant intuitions, by the legitimate concern for scientific verification and you should not be blamed for this excess of caution. His basic discovery (which is yours as well) is found almost everywhere in his *Mirabilia,* particularly on pages

130 and 187, and is worded as follows: "rays must speak, by nature . . . they are forced to speak." And you, better than anyone else (at least now that he is dead) know that in his usage "rays" and "nerves" are perfectly synonomous. *Nervensprache*—why didn't you dare say it in your article? Perhaps from fear of being accused of plagiarism? *Nervensprache* is precisely the same thing that you call primary process in your own nomenclature. After all, America was discovered by Columbus, but we kept the name Amerigo Vespucci, to whom it gives much honor. At any rate, both of you succeeded simultaneously and almost brilliantly in the adventurous navigation which was to lead you from the neurology of the microscope (where Flechsig was engulfed) to the neurology of speech.

Perhaps if Daniel Paul were alive, he would have, as you admittedly fear, started proceedings against you over the issue of priority. As a good jurist he was aware that it is the date of publication which counts, and that is in his favor. It would not help you, as you propose, to invoke the testimony of a colleague! The tribunal would not have taken it into account; the law is formal, jurisprudence is invariable, and only publication is evidence as far as dating is concerned. I know this because I have studied these questions in the past, so as to be able to defend my rights when I publish something.

Your moderation—all relative since you fearlessly defied your opponents—and the fact that you did not break as radically with all current opinions, earned you a success, I dare say not greater than his, but which cannot compare with his miserable failure. But imagine that he were more skillful, political, devious, and he succeeded in getting appointed as *extraordinarius* at a university to teach the *Nervensprache*. With his gift for oratory and the magnificent classical language he used (less elegant than yours, but more colored), he might have been quite a success. And he also would have been cured, according to Otto. It is inconceivable, you might say; but you know better than anybody how difficult it is to make an a priori judgment. At any rate, lacking a medical background, he would never have thought to make a therapy out of it. Here, the advantage is on your side.

By trying to present his defense in this way, I foresee what brought on his misfortune. It is Flechsig! Upon coming back to the clinic, hoping to receive more consideration, after the prestigious nomination with which he had been bestowed, Daniel Paul faced an intractable neurologist who continued to place neurology far above the juridical sciences. Surrounded by his assistants, interns, attendants and patients, he reigned as an absolute master in his domain—exactly like my cousin with his assessors, ushers, court clerks, constables and judges could reign in his domain, the tribunal.

It was therefore an insoluble conflict between two specialists, without any possible mediation other than mutual consideration, courtesy and respect, which unfortunately, as I learned at my own expense, Flechsig knows nothing about. I found out about it when I realized the ruse with which my cousin tried to lure him on to his terrain (that of criminal law) by accusing him of *murder*. Since he was not actually dead, he could only accuse him of soul murder, a crime which unfortunately does not figure in the penal code. Anyhow, once he was in the clinic it was extremely difficult to bring the question before a tribunal. People suspected of insanity are exposed to the most revolting denial of justice while those accused of the greatest crimes can vindicate themselves at their leisure. This is a frightening state of affairs which demands of everyone, myself in any case, the greatest prudence. If I manage to escape a fate like Paul's, it is thanks to Art: I take it seriously, and everything else is unimportant.

I have naturally carried out investigations some time ago in the various hospitals where my poor cousin stayed, but without success. Unfortunately, an artist has no clerical experience and I only found uninteresting documents: bromide or chloral prescriptions, inventories of confiscated objects (belt, penknife, suspenders, laces, etc.), and nothing else. I had hoped to find clinical observations, prognostics, at least diagnoses . . . nothing. Otto tells me that it is the same everywhere, even Kraepelin is only interested in a dozen of his patients, those who are most likely to supply him data for his works. And if there is someone who looks like a criminal, he is sure to be part of his work, so my friend, who is a bit of a rumor-monger, claims. Having discovered that Flechsig would advocate castration in serious cases, I wanted to be sure that my unfortunate cousin had not been mutilated. Luckily, he was no longer at the university clinic. It is impossible to know, anyway. And do not believe that it is because the files are confidential and secret. I was allowed to rummage everywhere. In fact, I had sneaked a few visitor passes from my brother, the doctor, and my family likeness probably made things easier. At any rate, I was welcomed like a colleague and had access to the most classified files.

Indeed, an extraordinary trust prevails in our country among the "respectable people," and it seems as though the spies, crooks and other brigands have not yet noticed it. When I told Otto about it, he laughed—which surprised me—and said that this was one of his father's concerns. There is a Frenchman, whose name he had forgotten, who thought of using fingerprints to identify criminals. Otto's father, Hans Gross, a magistrate in Graz, thinks that the system should be generalized since, he says, not being registered is insufficient grounds for not being a criminal! You can see to what absurdities the most rigorous logic can lead! All the subjects of your emperor, according to Otto, could thus one day be required to carry with them a card with their fingerprints! I really laughed at that idea! Otto's father is a bit crazy like Flechsig or Gottlob. But Otto assures me that this will happen in time, since insane people, he claims, have more influence than others on the course of history. Besides, he adds, criminals will not find themselves any worse off, since the police will be too busy with all these fingerprints to bother with them any longer. He has no sense of reality! I do not think that you in Austria will one day have to carry a ridiculous card bearing your fingerprints like a poorly washed glass. In any case, all of us in Germany are too attached to the liberal ideology, too civilized, to risk anything of this kind. The proof, moreover, is that this Austrian father tried to have his son arrested on German territory, creating an enormous scandal. Laws are respected in our country more than in yours.

Otto had in fact written an essay on the "sadistic personality." I have not read it. Obviously, I do not know his father, nor do I know if he was drawing his father's portrait in that essay. He contends that his was a purely scientific work and that if his father recognized himself, it is a "projection" phenomenon. In any case, Otto was arrested and taken away by a *Bavarian* policeman, holding a certificate from a *Helvetic* psychiatrist, by the name of Jung, at the request of an *Austro-Hungarian* magistrate. This was inadmissible, as the rules of international law were scoffed at. (I was not here yet at the time.) Lawyers of some note took this affair in hand, the press spread it all over the Reich and Otto was returned to us. Since then, when he resumed his talks against patriarchal power, he is better understood on one hand, and on the other, a little less convincing since his impartial theories seem a *pro domo* presentation for the defense.

I teased him a little about it, by asserting that there was also a matriarchal power. My great-aunt Frederica, whom I didn't know, or was perhaps too young to remember, is well-known in our family as Frederica "the Great." Undoubtedly the streak of madness in her descendents' constitution—Gottlob especially—comes from her. If you had pushed your inquiry in that direction, you might have understood Paul's case better. She was not insane, simply terrible. It is true that Gottlob also was not considered insane; he had succeeded. Here is a person who, I believe, slightly resembles my great-aunt. She is a baroness, wife of a Bismarckian general, who caught our attention, largely because of her three daughters who are charming in every respect. (In our family, it is either law or medicine. I am an unfortunate exception; Otto does the best he can. The General and the Baroness's families are big landowners, or in the army to avoid dividing up inheritances). Otto claims that if there are women as monstrous as Frederica or the baroness, it is always because of men's exorbitant power. The Bismarckian general, however, even though he puts on really proud airs, cannot completely hide the fact that his wife makes him quite submissive. But Otto is intransigent on that point, and for my part I agree with him: it is up to men to liberate women, for if they liberate themselves, they might become like the baroness or Frederica. This would be a pity.

*   *   *

I have trouble ending this letter. I write when I have a spare moment, and I am always being disturbed. Yesterday, I was interrupted again by Otto. He came to pick me up to go to the general-baroness's daughters. He saw the letter on my table, and I could not prevent him from glancing at it. Something—perhaps a remark about him—must have irritated him a bit, and he frowned. On the way (it's a fairly long trip, since I live on the outskirts of town, at the widow Schlinge's, who is an insufferable blabbermouth; I am moving at the end of the week, fortunately)[9] he delivered one of his pedantic speeches, as unfortunately happens to him rather frequently.

He acknowledges the way I apprehend things intuitively, even admits that it is indispensible, and that everybody does it. But, he adds, it has always been done and, plainly, has served no purpose. First, in this way, I do not leave the impression that I speak better than others, and this is already very important. Secondly, there will be no possible verification, nor even any communication, etc. I do not remember everything . . . But he said that as far as he is concerned, without his theoretical works he would not have gotten the consideration from Kraepelin that he now enjoys. And then, he concluded, in a way that seemed contradictory, "as soon as one speaks, one is necessarily doing theory—necessarily, you are yourself doing theory."

When I told him: paradox, paradox, he went one tone higher to tell me: the first man, paleolithic or neolithic, who stated that stones fell downward laid the theoretical foundations of physics. The next step (after centuries!) was to discover that plumb-lines were not parallel, and that the "bottom" was a point. The rest? It was to understand that a body which rolls on a slanted plane is one that falls, just like the neolithic stone. Such is also the case for the pendulum, for it is as if it rolled on a slanted, but cylindrical plane. "You see! You see!" he said, he was incredibly excited. It is not possible to be that excited over such simplistic theoretical ideas. Since I was amused, I said "So what?" There is a certain naiveté in him. "There was an apple, Newton's apple. It was not a falling apple, which would have been uninteresting, there had already been Galileo. It was a swinging apple."

"Just like a pendulum, then?"

"Yes, but Newton's genius is to have understood suddenly that, if gravity just stopped when the apple was at its lowest, it would turn indefinitely around its connecting point. He had made his great discovery!"

Is that true, dear distinguished Professor? One never reads about these things anywhere. How would Otto know all this? Is he mocking people? Irritated, I reminded him: "But you, you established the theory of sadism and that only got you thrown in jail." It proves that it was true! he said. But then you understand nothing about psychoanalysis: my theory was correct because it was affectively supported by the idea of harrassing Daddy. The notion of a disinterested truth is a joke! Kraepelin never understood anything about this."

He resumed his speech by saying: "Freud is the Galileo of psychoanalysis, he told me so himself. That is why he made so many enemies." And after a short while, he added: "It is not over with Newton, there will still be an apple or a stone.[10] It is me, Otto, who, after Freud-Galileo, will become the Newton of psychoanalysis. My apple will be the liberation of women. Freud did not dare." He irritated me more and more, and I replied: "If you make an apple out of the liberation of women, it will be to devour it." He laughed and said: "Obviously, a theory has meaning only if it is put into practice." We just happened to arrive at the General's house.

Dear distinguished Professor, my letter will be even longer than I had anticipated. I do not see any other remedy than imploring you to count it for two sessions. Otto told me that he once had a twenty-four hour session with Jung—he did not say how he paid for it, perhaps he jumped over the wall for fear of the expense? But you need not worry about that sort of thing with me, and I beg you to read on with confidence: send me your bill, it will be honored. In any case, I continue.

One of the general's daughters is, as everyone knows, the mistress of a professor from the University of Heidelberg—it is quite close, a little bit over two hours by train. She, too, had some ideas, naturally quite narrow, on the liberation of women, so Dr. Gross took on the task of expanding them. She devoted her efforts to improve the conditions of women factory workers, because the professor—we all call him by his first name, Max, and I will not, out of discretion, divulge his name—sees progress only in the realization of democratic ideas, while, for Otto, the progress of humanity consists in recovering the "polymorphic perversion" (he owes you this expression and acknowledges it) which is repressed by socialization, and he asserts that democratic ideals will not change this repression in any way. He maintains that, to convince Max and recover a certain kind of *Gemeinschaft,* he did half the work by seducing his mistress; but judging by the fury of their theoretical discussions, their opposition is sharper than ever. Otto sent Max into a rage when he accused him of doing nothing else but perfecting the Heidelberg Catechism, the effects of which Otto blamed for the unbridled development of the economic activities in the modern world, while the true cause of this development, according to him, results from the frustration of perverse drives provoked by the appropriation of women by men. I will not go into the details of his reasoning; he sees in economic activity less a "sublimation" than a "compensation." These discussions are very scholarly and I do not always follow them very well. Since Max is quite jealous and makes a point of hiding it, he suffers from attacks of depression all the more severe since Otto is the very picture of happy contentment. I observe all this with a mixture of great sadness and amusement which—how shall I put it?—makes life more interesting, indeed. When the widow Schlinge makes advances, I really do not feel any inclination to liberate her. Still, she is in great need of it. Even more than the baroness's daughters. Otto urges me to undertake the liberation of the general's third daughter. He is in charge of the other two. To tell you the truth, I am not very tempted by it. To begin with, she is hardly interested in me, but rather in Otto, if he were not so busy already. Then I told myself: what if both of us were successful in liberating all three of the general's daughters; would it be enough for so many millions of enslaved women? Then I must confess that the general's wife frightens me. And even the general, a little. I live an easier, and also freer life than Otto, thanks to a few charming girls from Schwabing, but they do not need to be liberated, which is clearly why they do not interest Otto. Maybe I should be working on my own liberation. Yes, that is certain, and I will add, to be fair, that I owe Otto a great deal on this point.

It seems to me that Otto has not realized that he has two discourses on sexuality, one for women and one for men. To men, he contends that only love is a value, and the effective exercise of sexuality does not have the importance generally attached to it. In our alienating civilization, the torments of love are the reason why we try to get rid of them through sexual relations, which, as past humanity shows, never solve anything and are performed over and over. He relates a personal experience on this subject: a professor had asked him a question on what becomes of a number "raised" to the zero power. This was insoluble for him at the time. He was so disturbed by it that he masturbated. This, he said, taught him a lot. The curious thing is that I didn't know a thing about the zero power, but didn't masturbate. It is, he said, because I do not care, while he had taken the question to heart on account of the professor. He claims that this continually happens: the other is a problem, to which we have no solution—hence this behavior. I do not know if you will agree. Perhaps, you will prefer the discourse he holds with women, without himself noticing the difference, it seems.

To women, he says that love results only in useless torments. Only physical pleasure brings satisfaction; vaginal orgasm (and he is capable of describing its manifestations with great precision, although I have never heard any woman confirming it; isn't it strange?) is the supreme remedy to all evils.

I see clearly that the reason why he does not notice the difference is that both theories are basically identical. But he shifts the emphasis of value: he makes men more tolerant and women more desirable.

But sometimes he maintains that the difficulty is insoluble and lies at an inaccessible depth. In the past, he says, in obscure eras, when a holy man met a woman who troubled him, he would not identify it as love, nor would he be sexually aroused; on the contrary, it made him "sick" and if he reached a conclusion, it was that he was dealing with a witch who should be burned as soon as possible. The major problem therefore is to know if there is something formidable between human beings, a terrible difficulty which could lead equally to murder, anthropophagy, rape or persecution. For love would then be an institution, a characteristic of socialization, or civilization, intended to overcome this original difficulty. Or could it be that it is love which is original, innocent, "natural," and which has been perverted by society's demands? For the moment, Otto remains embarrassed by this question, but does not acknowledge any practical interest in it. In practice, he says, if love is an institution which favors socialization, its great value is to be recognized and it is to be practiced as much as possible. On the other hand, if it is something rooted in our nature and oppressed by civilization, it is also therefore quite important, and oppression should be overcome to devote oneself to it unreservedly. He is thus not as worried about theory as he leads us to believe. And I myself wonder how much one must oppose nature to society, like he does. When he restricts himself to preaching the recapture of the polymorphic perversion of childhood, suppressed by the effect of educational repression, it is much simpler. And it is, in my view, entirely sufficient; I even fear that if it were brought to life again integrally, one would surely be a little inconvenienced in practice.

He says something else, even more surprising: that overcoming repression or prohibitions is not enough. The liberation of women is *political* because it is up to women to destroy the world such as it has been organized by men so as to redo it differently. His numerous adventures are not only "pedagogical," according to him, but also revolutionary.

As for me, I would be tempted to believe that, of the two of you, it is you who are right; I am eager to put his theories into practice, as I do all the time, but I do not dare confess to him that it is only because I find pleasure in it. I have the curious impression that I lack any political ideal. But if this theoretical work aims, no matter how, at making us freer, it is marvelous and one should perhaps not be all that particular.

I believe that, unlike you, that, after all, there is nothing to renovate. Those who want to fight the illusion of the broken stick in the water will be obliged to twist it without gaining anything. This was what Gottlob was doing with his children, Flechsig with my cousin, Hans Gross with his son—this is what almost everybody does. We, painters, are against the "renovators" who want to maintain our illusions. You show us, much better than Otto, the truth *in* error. You will not always be understood. There will be "renovators," I'm afraid, who will rely on the authority of your works . . . But I must stop, as the Philosopher would say, without having devoted much thought to whether one had to stop because one had enough of it or if a Stop, such as God, was a necessary end. I have to stop because I think that you really must have enough of it.

With my most respectful admiration,

Joachim Fuchs

P.S. You might think that I should not have signed my letter with a name that is not mine. But in a sense, it is mine. Besides, it is the name to which you must send your reply, in care of Dr. Gross, at the Königliche Psychiatric Clinic, Munich. I do not know as of yet where my new address will be after I leave the widow Schlinge. But then, who, besides myself, knows which of my two names is the true one? And still, would I have falsely taken the name of Schreber? For what purpose? Simply so you would read my letter to the end, otherwise you would have thrown it out? Perhaps it was just a ruse. Unless there is another ruse, for I can guess what you are about to do now: you are going to read it again to find some sign which will remove your doubt. Thus you will have read it twice. Because of this second reading, I will owe you for four sessions instead of two. Please let me know the amount of your fees. You will receive a check by return mail, and thus see with which name it is signed.

Respectfully,

J. F. alias D. P. S.

Notes

1.   Otto Gross (1877–1919) was a doctor and an assistant to Kraepelin. He was considered a brilliant but erratic young psychoanalyst, who contributed some significant monographs to the movement, among which "Anti-social Personality Disorders" is perhaps the best known. In early life he was a teetotaler and vegetarian, but later became addicted to cocaine. It was during this period that Freud began his relationship with him, soon subjecting Gross to an intensive psychoanalysis. Freud determined that Gross would have to undergo detoxification, and subsequently sent him to Jung's clinic. He escaped from Jung's clinic (reference in the text) and from that time onward had only sporadic contact with the psychoanalytic movement, which vigorously opposed his idea that sexual immorality could be used as a therapeutic method. Gross died in an asylum in Vienna.

Hans Gross (1847–1915), also mentioned in the text, was indeed Otto Gross's father and a criminal psychologist of great renown, who was perhaps most responsible for the notion that frustrated sexuality leads to crime. He is also generally considered as the founder of juridical psychology. His most famous book is *Kriminalpsychologie* (1898). (E.T.)

2.   This is the *Jahrbuch für psychoanalytische und psychopathologische Forschungen* of 1911, which allows us to approximately date the letter. (F.T.)

3.   In French in the German text. (F.T.)

4.   The word "martial" has a meaning in medicine alluding to *the iron* chancellor. (F.T.)

5.   Of Saxony (F.T.)

6.   After having thought of *Memorabilia,* the translator considered *Mirabilia* as a more accurate rendering of *Denkwürdigkeiten.* (F.T.)

7.   Freud indeed quotes four verses by Heine, at the beginning of Chapter II of *Narzismus,* and mentions the *pathogenesis of creation.* (F.T.)

8.   1910 (F.T.)

9.   The translator's attention has been brought to a discovery which may not be coincidental: *Fuchs,* the fox, wants to escape from the widow *Schlinge,* the trap. However, if the entire letter is constructed on plays of signifiers, the author has mixed things up too much to recognize it. (F.T.)

10.   *Ein Stein* means "a stone." The translator does not believe in premonitions, but this curious coincidence must be pointed out. (F.T.)

Part III
The New Schreber Texts

Han Israëls

Introduction to the New Schreber Texts

The most important chapter of Schreber's *Memoirs of My Nervous Illness,* dealing with "miraculous events" in his own family, was never printed with the original text because it was considered "unfit for publication," and has subsequently been lost. (See Fig. 5) In 1976, when writing a paper on Schreber, I decided to visit Leipzig in an attempt to recover this lost chapter. I did not, of course, find it, but I did come upon something else of great importance. What I found were descendants of the Schreber family, living in and around Leipzig, who gave me completely unknown texts by Schreber—texts which are printed here for the first time in English. What follows is a brief account of this significant discovery.

As is commonly known, Schreber's father wrote a number of books on medicine, orthopedics, gymnastics, and education. "Victory Gardens" in Germany were and still are called Schreber gardens in his memory. Occasionally articles are written about these gardens, which explain why they are called Schreber gardens and just who Dr. Schreber was. In one of these articles, written in 1960 and published in East Germany, the author expressed in a footnote his gratitude to a descendant of Dr. Schreber who gave him access to the family papers. When I was in Leipzig in 1976, I visited the author of that article. I asked him if this descendant was still alive, and, if so, whether he had her address. He was unable to answer these questions, as nearly twenty years had passed since he last spoke to her, and even then she had been quite elderly. He was, however, able to tell me that she had been a teacher at the Leipzig conservatory. Upon visiting the conservatory, I learned that the woman had died nearly ten years ago, but that they still had her last address. I visited the apartment, and the people who were currently occupying it gave me the name of someone who had something to do with the woman's estate when she died. This in turn led me to a woman who proved to be Dr. Schreber's great-great granddaughter, and who was able to direct me to older living members of the family. These people provided me with a number of Schreber's writings (some poems for family occasions, and a speech for a Christening) which formed part of the basis for my doctoral thesis.[1]

Not all of the new Schreber texts, however, came from these East German descendants of Moritz Schreber. One text was published in a journal about Schreber gardens in 1907. The poem dated 1907 comes from a psychiatrist's estate, who originally acquired it from Schreber's adopted daughter. And I came upon Schreber's last writings while checking through his psychiatric file at the mental hospital at Leipzig-Dösen.

The basic historical context of these writings cannot, of course, be presented here, since that would require an extensive biographical account of Schreber's childhood and family life in general. I will, however, try to supplement the texts themselves by adding a few edifying notes—mostly ones containing details regarding names and dates. The information for these notes is derived largely from three extremely accurate family trees drawn up by G. Friedrich, a grandson of Schreber's sister Anna. The three genealogies consist of: (1) The Schreber family itself. (2) The Haase and Wenck families (Schreber's mother was born Haase, and her mother, Wenck). (3) The Jung family (Schreber's sister Anna married Carl Jung).

A. Poem for the Silver Wedding Anniversary of His Sister Anna (1889)

The first text is a poem that Schreber wrote in 1889 to commemorate the silver wedding anniversary of his sister Anna. This is not the earliest of Schreber's writings, for we have a ruling written by him in 1864 about the different kinds of membership of a student society, which is quoted in a text about that society.[2] (This is also discussed in my thesis).[3] There were also several letters about him, written in 1864 and 1865, and found in a personnel file which the Saxony ministry of justice opened on Schreber, and which were discovered by Devreese.[4]

Schreber writes in his *Memoirs:* "I was by no means what one would call a *poet,* although I have occasionally attempted a few verses on family occasions."[5] The present poem, to the best of my knowledge, is the only one written prior to the *Memoirs,* that is, before 1903. The title of the poem refers to the date on which his eldest sister Anna and her husband, Carl Jung, celebrated their silver wedding anniversary. (see Fig. 6)

The poem is written in the first person plural, and the "we" undoubtedly involves Anna and Carl Jung's five surviving children (One child, Friedrich Moritz Heinrich, died in 1868, and his death is mentioned in line 23 of the poem).

In line 24 a dead father and mother are mentioned; that must refer to parents of Carl Jung (Anna's father had died prior to her marriage, and her mother was still alive in 1889; in line 34 we read that she was recovering from an illness.). Carl Jung's parents were Friedrich Jung (d. 1884) and Anna Margaretha Jung (nee Mengerssen) (d. 1877).

We read in the poem that the children gave the parents a picture of themselves. The children are enumerated from line 57 onward. The first one, described as the "tall rural economist," is Carl Friedrich ("Fritz") (b. 1867). "Rural economist" was formerly a term used to describe an estate manager, which was Carl Friedrich's profession. This line of work might in turn explain line 58 "The light stripe in his hair shows his craft" *(Sein Handwerk zeigt der lichte Streifen unterm Haar).* As a gentleman farmer, he must have done a lot of outdoor work, which would account for his tanned skin and lighter hair.

In line 60 we read about two daughters: Anna Pauline Helene, called "Helene" (b. 1868), and Anna Pauline, called "Paula" (b. 1870). Paula married Paul Friedrich, who became professor of medicine at Kiel. He is mentioned in Schreber's *Memoirs* as "the husband of one of my nieces, now Professor Dr. F. in K."[6]

In line 61 Carl Wilhelm, called "Wilhelm" (b. 1872), is mentioned, and Schreber refers to his musical activities, which later resulted in a career. He was conductor and music critic in Leipzig, and his second wife, Meta Jung-Steinbrück, was a famous opera singer.

In line 65 the youngest child, Carl Woldemar Felix, called "Felix" (b. 1882), is mentioned. Felix was later in contact with Franz Baumeyer, author of two informative articles on Schreber. Baumeyer indicates that Felix Jung was "one of Schreber's nephews (son of sister Anna), Solicitor Dr. J."[7]

The poem concludes with a statement that it was read aloud by Paula. It was probably neatly transcribed by her sister Helene.

B. Poem About Swans Which His Mother Gave as a Gift to His Nephew Fritz Jung

This text is undated. It was probably written soon after the publication of the *Memoirs,* that is, after 1903. The reason I am so sure of this dating is that Schreber's mother, Pauline, gave two swans to Fritz Jung (the eldest son of Schreber's sister Anna, mentioned above), and the undated poem accompanied this gift. Now there is a photo of the estate managed by Fritz Jung which shows the two swans given to him by Pauline Schreber, and this photo was most likely taken in 1905. (see Fig. 7) It is probable, then, that the swans were given and the poem written about this time.

To properly explain the first lines of this poem, it is necessary to invoke one of Wagner's operas. The *Memoirs* attest to Schreber's interest in Wagner (See, for example, pages 52 and 143). Wagner's *Lohengrin* has as its locale the beach of the river Scheldt near Antwerp in Belgium. The knight Lohengrin arrives there in a boat carried by a swan. He frees the heroine and breaks the spell over the swan, who then turns out to be the heroine's brother. The first two stanzas of the poem hint at these events.

The Pleisse in line 4 is a river near Leipzig. The children *(Sprossen)* in line 13 are probably the eldest children of Fritz Jung.

C. Christening Speech for a Granddaughter of His Sister Anna (1904)

This text does not require special explanation. Schreber recited it on December 26, 1904, when Fritz' daughter was baptized. Born September 30, 1904, her name is mentioned in line 72. Obviously, at this time—two years after his release from the asylum—Schreber was functioning relatively normally; otherwise he would not have been asked to recite on such an important occasion. The text had been very quickly jotted down and nearly without correction (see, for example, lines 11, 12 where the word *"empfunden"* (felt) has been written twice.). (see Fig. 8)

D. Poem for His Mother's Ninetieth Birthday (1905)

This is by far the most important text of all. It is the only piece of biographical material on Schreber's mother written by Schreber himself. Up to the present, a great deal has been written on his mother, but it was largely the result of speculation.[8]

The text was printed, so I assume other copies were struck. But I am only aware of the existence of the one copy from which the English translation was done. The poem itself was intended to accompany an album of photographs illustrating places that had played some part in Pauline Schreber's life (see lines 3, 4). (see Fig. 9)

The first paragraph (line 23 ff.) deals with the *"Feuerkugel"* (Fireball), a famous house that is often mentioned in books on the history of Leipzig.[9] Pauline Haase was born here just after the battle of Leipzig, where Napoleon ("the Corsican" in line 30) was soundly defeated.

Lines 35–50 deal with the following course of events. As a child living in the Fireball, Pauline had often been shown the windows of a room, in an adjoining house, where Goethe made his student quarters. Many years later, when the local Goethe Society wanted to put a memorial plaque between the windows of his old student rooms, she was the only one who knew which were the right ones.

The second paragraph (line 51 ff.) deals with two other houses where Pauline lived: *"Hohmanns Hof"* (Hohmann's Court) and *"Schwarzes Bret"* (Black Plank). Both houses are mentioned in histories of Leipzig.[10] From line 77 onward we read that the children did not go to school: it was held to be "elegant" (line 77 *"vornehm"*) to have a private tutor at home. I have argued elsewhere[11] that it was important for Pauline to have an "elegant" grand-parental home— even grander than that of her husband Moritz. Aside from Pauline, the children were: Eduard (1812–1864), Therese (1817–1883), Gustav (1822–1871), and Fanny (1827–1895). Of all Schreber's uncles and aunts, the least is known about Eduard and Gustav. Both are mentioned in Friedrich's genealogy, but only to the extent that they remained bachelors. We can also doubt whether both uncles held conventional jobs, since Schreber's sister Anna, from whom most of the genealogical information was obtained, was extremely careful about listing the occupations of family members. Pauline's sister Therese married a Leipzig physician, Dr. Döring, in 1841. He died in 1849. Fanny married Gustav Loesch in 1851. He was the owner of an estate called "Beerendorf," and he died in 1874.

The third paragraph (line 99 ff.) deals with the next house where Pauline lived, the *"Fürstenhaus"* (Princes' House), a house that is also mentioned in literature on the history of Leipzig.[12] In line 121 we read how learned men visited the family of Pauline's parents. Among these learned men were Professor J. C. A. Heinroth, still famous for his work in psychiatry, and the professor of criminal law, C. J. G. S. Wächter.[13] When Schreber studied law, Wächter was one of his professors. In the *Memoirs* Schreber mentions "Dr. Wächter, who was to take up a position of leadership on Sirius" and who "knew me personally."[14]

In line 123 Pauline's father is mentioned: Wilhelm Andreas Haase (1784–1837), professor of medicine at Leipzig, who married Juliana Emilie (nee Wenck) (1788–1841). The "Gewandhaus" with its famous Gewandhaus orchestra still exists today (line 125). The conductor of this orchestra from 1835 onwards was Felix Mendelssohn (I have written at length in my thesis about the relationship between Pauline and Mendelssohn). The Gewandhaus may have been mentioned here because Pauline liked to hear grand stories; when she was quite old, a granddaughter-in-law wrote: "Dear Grandmama used to look down on the present Gewandhaus concerts with great scorn. In her day, Mendelssohn conducted in person, as did Schumann."[15]

Waiting for the "right one" which eventually brought a "young doctor" (line 145) is of course a reference to her husband Daniel Gottlob Moritz Schreber. Moritz Schreber had studied medicine at Leipzig, and Pauline's father was one of his professors.[16] In the time frame of the poem, Moritz Schreber was a *Privatdozent* (university lecturer) on the faculty where Pauline's father was a full professor. The poem tells us the exact location where Moritz Schreber proposed to Pauline: under a railway viaduct. The lightning *(Blitz)* of line 149 is no doubt the name of the railroad engine passing by. I do not fully understand the course of events in line 149 through 159: Moritz Schreber proposed to Pauline Haase in the beginning of 1838. One is led to believe that Pauline's father died after that, since his death is mentioned after the proposal. But in fact he had already died in 1837, according to Friedrich's genealogy of the Schreber family.

The Nikolaikirche (St. Nicholas Church), where the wedding of Schreber's parents took place, is still extant in Leipzig. The period of happy marriage did not last very long; Moritz Schreber died at a relatively early age in 1861, and during the last ten years of his life he suffered from a severe head ailment which is mentioned at the end of the seventh paragraph. When the poem first appeared in 1905, Pauline had been a widow for nearly half a century (line 185). Line 214 refers to the first-born child: Daniel Gustav, called "Gustav," born in 1839.

The sixth paragraph refers to the next houses where the Schreber family lived: in the Church of St. Thomas Square (Thomaskirchhof) and King Street (Königstrasse) (line 222). It covers the period of approximately 1841 to 1847. Schreber mentions many events during this period. "Your mother died" (line 227) refers to the death of Pauline's mother in 1841. "It meant taking in your youngest sister" (line 228). Pauline's youngest sister was Fanny Haase, but I am unable to find any reference to her living with the Schreber family, apart from this line in the poem. The apartment became too small for the family and they moved to Thomaskirchhof 22. Pauline already had two children, Gustav and Anna. And "before it had been really thought over" (line 241) the third child was born. This of course refers to the poem's author, Daniel Paul, called "Paul," who was born July 25, 1842. A few years later the family moved again (line 247). I do not know what Reklam, Engelmann and Drechsel in line 250 refer to; the only thing that seems to fit is that the Schreber's new address, Königstrasse 4, is sometimes referred to in Leipzig guidebooks as "the house of Dr. Drechsel." A fourth child (line 254), Sidonie, was born in 1846. Pauline also had to care for "unrelated" children. In 1844 Moritz Schreber took over an orthopedic clinic and moved it to his own home at Königstrasse 4. Among the patients at the clinic were a number of children who boarded there. Thus the household grew larger and larger (line 259). It consisted of Pauline, her husband, the four children, possibly Pauline's sister Fanny, the in-patients, and a small domestic staff. Once again it was necessary to look around for other places (line 261).

Paragraph seven deals with Pauline's last house, the house in the Zeitzer Strasse (line 263). (see Figs. 10 and 11) The Schreber family moved there in 1847. Pauline remained at this address, along with her unmarried daughter

Sidonie, (see Fig. 12) until her death in 1907. The other children, Gustav, Paul, and Klara, also lived there at different intervals during their lives. Schreber's sister Anna lived in a house that was virtually next door with her family. The house at Zeitzer Strasse was originally situated outside the city proper. It was designated by several addresses and finally called Zeitzer Strasse 10. The house was demolished in 1915.

Lines 280–291 are among the most important passages in the poem. They deal with the head ailment which affected Moritz Schreber during the last decade of his life, and about which much has been written. Ritter dates the onset of the illness at the end of the fifties.[17] Most later authors have accepted this date. I have, however, shown elsewhere that the illness began in 1851.[18] In the poem Schreber even describes the effects of the head ailment on the family itself: "The world was avoided, even in the house there were off-limits areas." There were times that Moritz Schreber did not even want to see his own children. Similar reports have come down from Schreber's sisters. Anna once said about her father "that in the last ten years of his life he suffered from an exceptionally severe head complaint, so that at times his family feared for his sanity." His wife was "the only one allowed to be with him when the nerves in his head tormented him too much. Then not even the children he loved so much were allowed to see him."[19] Moritz Schreber died from a perforated intestine in 1861.

Lines 292–323 deal with Pauline as a widow. One night in May of 1877 her son Gustav shot himself (line 297). Pauline was very concerned about family illnesses (line 298). Anna suffered from a stomach problem, Paul was a psychiatric patient, and Klara was described by a nephew as "ailing." There were, however, some pleasant events as well. The coming of the three in-laws (line 302) and the grandchildren (line 303) are discussed. The three in-laws were Carl Jung (Anna's husband), Sabine (Schreber's wife) and Theodor Krause (Klara's husband). The grandchildren are Anna's (see commentary to text A).

Following these lines there are seven fragmentary vignettes, from line 324 onwards. The first is about the Arts (the municipal theater) and nature (Beerendorf and Schenkenberg). Beerendorf and Schenkenberg are two country villages where estates owned by the Haase family are located.

Rudelsburg and Kösen (line 345) are places about thirty miles south of Leipzig, and Kösen is a spa.

The third vignette deals with the commercial street "Brühl" (line 353). The businesses on the street consisted mainly of Jewish-owned fur shops. The Schreber family apparently owned a commercial building on this street. Several companies were located in the building, among which was a "chemical factory" owned by Gustav Schreber. There is, however, virtually no reliable historical information about this factory.

Pauline and Moritz once took the children to Lausche and Klosterberg Oybin (line 361), located about seventy miles east of Leipzig. Oybin is a spa. Because of his intestinal problems, Moritz Schreber visited a number of spas at the end of his life. The "border stone" on which Schreber liked to "sit straddled" (line 364) must have demarcated the border between Saxony and Bohemia (Austria).

The fifth deals with Dresden, the municipal city of Saxony. Line 387–394 refer to a house in Dresden that Schreber had built for his family (with his mother's financial help). This house, Angelikastrasse 15a, still exists in Dresden. Line 393 and 394 could be interpreted in the following way. In 1902 Schreber first left the asylum at Sonnenstein, returning to live with his aged mother (87) in Leipzig. His wife, possibly afraid of living with a mental patient, stayed behind in Dresden. He did not return to Dresden until 1903. In lines 393 and 394 Schreber expresses the hope that the person who helped him return to his home in Dresden would visit him there. This quite obviously refers to his mother.

The last and seventh vignette offers two riddles. The solution to the first one is "Fireball" (Feuerkugel); the solution to the second is: "Princes' House (Fürstenhaus). Both houses were mentioned earlier in the poem (lines 23 and 99).

E. Poem for the Fiftieth Birthday of His Wife (1907)

Sabine Schreber's birthday was on June 19, 1907. (see Fig. 13) Line 15 mentions her parents: her father, Heinrich Behr, was artistic director of the municipal theater; her mother was the daughter of Roderich Benedix, a comic playwright.

In line 16 Schreber mentions the death of his mother, which took place about a month earlier, on May 14, 1907. In lines 36 and 37 Schreber speaks about the new house in Angelikastrasse, (see Fig. 14) which was also mentioned in the previous poem. Lines 39 and 40 indicate that Sabine Schreber played an active role in decorating the new house. I have often lamented this fact, since it would have been much more interesting if Schreber himself had been responsible for some of the striking details on this house, such as a musical melody carved into the lintel above the door (see Fig. 15)—a melody from Wagner's *Siegfried*.

In line 44 a child is mentioned. Baumeyer was the first to write about this adopted daughter.[20] (see Fig. 16 and 17) Apparently, she was already living with Sabine when Schreber returned from Leipzig in 1903. At some later date, Schreber and his wife legally adopted the child. She died in 1981, and it was she who originally possessed this poem.

F. Declaration About Schreber Societies (1907)

This declaration by Schreber was originally published in the journal *Der Freund der Schreber-Vereine* (Friends of the Schreber Societies), Vol. 3, 1907.

(see Fig. 18) I am aware of the existence of only one copy of this extremely rare issue, and that is in the Gartenbücherei of the Technical University in West Berlin.

The text is the result of a rather complicated affair, which I have described at some length elsewhere.[21] Briefly put, the affair is as follows. A few years after Moritz Schreber's death a Schreber society was founded in Leipzig to honor this rather distinguished educator. This began primarily as an educational society that owned a playground. Small, high-yield gardens were eventually planted on the playground, and the educational society expanded into a kind of horticultural club, in which each member owned a small garden. Later on, in and around Leipzig, more Schreber societies were founded. They consisted of little garden plots grouped around a playground. A number of these societies were incorporated into a league which was called "Verband Leipziger Schrebervereine" (commonly referred to as "Verband" or "Leipziger Verband").

Now the text written by Schreber deals with donations that Pauline Schreber left to societies which were members of the "Verband." These donations to the official league members were, however, contested by societies not belonging to the official league, and they complained vehemently. As a result, they also received donations from Pauline's descendants, and it was Schreber who was responsible for this. The gesture of giving gifts to non-member societies was used for polemical purposes by these societies against the official league members. I am not exactly sure where they published these polemics, but I suspect that it was in their own journal, *Der Schrebergärtner* (I have never found the 1907 volume of this publication). At any rate, the effects of this affair on Schreber are probably reflected in a remark entered in his psychiatric file in 1907: "After his mother's death, he made many calculations concerning numerous legacies, overworked himself and slept badly some nights."[22]

G. Texts Written in the Leipzig-Dösen Mental Hospital (1907–1910)

The last documents are some short notes (sometimes just a word or two) written by Schreber in the mental hospital at Leipzig-Dösen, where he spent the last years of his life. The hospital's archives contain Schreber's psychiatric file. This file has been conscientiously published by Franz Baumeyer.[23] An envelope in the file contains these notes, and I am not entirely certain why Baumeyer did not publish them along with the rest of the material in the file, or why he made no mention of them.

One of the notes is cited in a file on Schreber dated December 11, 1907: "Writes a letter to the senior medical officer in which he asks if he may be allowed to make 'arrangements for his burial'."[24] This refers to the first of these notes. (see Fig. 19)

The next note, undated, probably belongs to the same time period as the first; it seems to be thematically connected. (see Fig. 20)

Let me quote from Schreber's psychiatric file once again: "February 1, 1909 . . . Now and then writes in barely legible characters, 'Miracle' (after he was asked the cause of his groaning) or 'Tomb' or 'Don't Eat'."[25] Without this last clue I would never have been able to decipher the final two words of the fourth note: *"nicht essen"* (Don't eat).

There is nothing much I can say about the later notes. The psychiatric file dated 1910 states: "From time to time writes something on his note pad, his scribble only resembling characters (see Figs. 21 and 22)." That a few of these "scribbles" have been deciphered at all, is the result of the great skill of Dr. Annemarie Hüber. (We do not, however, claim that the deciphering is either perfect or in any way definitive.)

I must conclude by saying that the commentary has, unfortunately, remained rather fragmentary. This is due mostly to space limitations. But, hopefully, what little is here will be of some help to the interested reader.

Notes

1. Here I refer to my dissertation: *Schreber: Father and Son* (Amsterdam: 1981), republished in a new English-language edition by International Universities Press, Madison, Conn., 1987. All further references will be to the present edition.

2. Adolf Hirschfeld and Franke, August, *Geschichte der Leipziger Burschenschaft Germania 1859–1879: Festgabe zum zwanzigsten Stiftungsfeste am 25., 26., 27., und 28. Juli 1879* (Leipzig, 1879) p. 18.

3. Israëls, *Op. Cit.,* p. 133.

4. Daniel Devreese, "Adelstolz und Professorendunkel" in *Psychoanalytische Perspektiven 1: Schreber-dokumenten I* (Ghent, 1981) pp. 131–163.

5. Daniel Paul Schreber, *Memoirs of My Nervous Illness* (London: W. Dawson & Sons, 1955), p. 80.

6. *Ibid.,* p. 96.

7. Franz Baumeyer, "The Schreber Case" *International Journal of Psychoanalysis,* No. 37, 1956, p. 69.

8. See, for example, Robert B. White, "The Mother-Conflict in Schreber's Psychosis," *International Journal of Psychoanalysis* No. 42, 1961, pp. 55–73; Harold Searles, *Collected Papers on Schizophrenia and Related Subjects* (London, 1965), p. 432; Heinz Kohut, *The Analysis of Self, The Psychoanalytic Study of the Child,* No. 4 (Monograph), New York, 1971, p. 255.

9. See, for example, Karl Grosse, *Geschichte der Stadt Leipzig von der ältesten bis zu die neueste Zeit* (Leipzig, 1898), p. 272.

10. *Ibid.,* p. 361 and p. 288 respectively.

11. See Israëls, *Op. Cit.*

12. Karl Reumuth (ed.) *Heimatgeschichte für Leipzig und den Leipziger Kreis* (Leipzig, 1927), p. XXI.

13. Richard G. Siegel, "Frau Pauline verw. Dr. Schreber," in *Der Freund der Schreber-Vereine* 3 (1907).

14. Schreber, *Op. Cit.*, p. 72.

15. Israëls, *Op. Cit.*, pp. 333–334.

16. Ernestus Henricus Weber, *Annotationes anatomicae et physiologicae* Prol. XX, Lipsiae, 1833.

17. Alfons Ritter, *Schreber: Das Bildungssystem eines Arztes* Dissertation, University of Erlangen, Erfurt, 1936, p. 14.

18. Israëls, *Op. Cit.*, pp. 347–348.

19. Hugo Fritzsche, "Aus Dr. Moritz Schrebers Leben," *Garten und Kind: Zeitschrift der mitteldeutschen Schrebergärtner* 6 (1926), p. 13.

20. Franz Baumeyer, "Noch ein Nachtrag zu Freuds Arbeit über Schreber," *Zeitschrift für psychosomatische Medizin und Psychoanalyse*, No. 16, 1970, p. 244.

21. Israëls, *Op. Cit.*, pp. 183–185 and 237–239.

22. Baumeyer, "The Schreber Case," p. 65.

23. *Ibid., passim.*

24. *Ibid.*, p. 65.

25. *Ibid.*, p. 67.

26. *Loc. Cit.*

The New Texts

A. [Poem for the Silver Wedding Anniversary of His Sister Anna][1] (1889)

July 26, 1889

This day, on which you want to renew the

2 Faithful union made twenty-five years ago,[2]

The crowds of well-wishers will certainly soon be thronging,

4 And many will come to join your celebration.

Many a wish for blessings will ring in your ears,

6 Many a good word will sound at the festive table,

But none of them will bring you such joy

8 As this first greeting from the mouths of your children.

We are certainly the most closely, indissolubly bound

10 To you through gratitude and love and faithfulness,

And therefore today's happy consecration

12 Will be felt by no one more deeply than us.

So let us, too, united with you, first direct

14 Our gaze upward and, our hands devoutly folded,

Praise God thankfully for the benevolent fate

16 With which he has mercifully administered over you.

Yes, dear parents, the course of the past years has flowed

18 More rich and beautiful for you than for many others;

Not for all who wander the pilgrimage of life

20 Is the cornucopia of happiness poured out as it is for you.

Nonetheless—how could it be otherwise on this earth—

22 You were not completely spared suffering and pain:

The first child was taken at a tender age,[3]

24 You put your father[4] and your mother[5] on a bier.

Not seldom did illness, a sinister and unwelcome guest,

A. *[Gedicht zur silbernen Hochzeit seiner Schwester Anna (1889)]*

Den 26. Juli 1889.

Zum heut'gen Tag, an dem vor fünfundzwanzig Jahren
2   Der treue Bund geschlossen, den ihr wollt erneuern,
Da drängen sich wohl bald der Gratulanten Schaaren
4   Und viele werden kommen, Euer Fest zu feiern.
Da wird manch Segenswunsch an Euer Ohr erklingen,
6   Manch gutes Wort ertönt an froher Tafelrunde
Und dennoch wird wohl keins Euch solche Freude bringen
8   Als jetzt der erste Gruss aus Eurer Kinder Munde.
Sind doch auch wir durch Dankespflicht und Lieb und Treue
10   Am engsten, unauflöslichsten mit Euch verbunden
Und wird daher des heut'gen Tages frohe Weihe
12   Von Niemand inniger, als wie von uns empfunden
So lasst auch uns zuerst, vereint mit Euch, die Blicke
14   Nach oben richten und, die Hände fromm gefaltet,
Gott dankbar preisen für die freundlichen Geschicke,
16   Mit denen über Euch er gnädig hat gewaltet.

Ja, liebe Eltern, reich und schön vor vielen Andern
18   Ist der vergangnen Jahre Wechsel euch verflossen;
Nicht allen, die des Lebens Pilgerpfade wandern,
20   Wird, gleich wie Euch, des Glückes Füllhorn ausgegossen.
Zwar blieb—wie könnte es auf Erden anders kommen—
22   Auch Euch nicht alles Leid und jeder Schmerz erspart :
In zartem Alter ward das erste Kind genommen,
24   Den Vater und die Muttei habt Ihr aufgebahrt.
Nicht selten ist, ein finstrer, unwillkommner Gast

26 Appear to you at the bedside of your children,

In many a night and frighten sleep away

28 From your anxious faces with a heavy burden of care for us.

But everything has always ended well,

30 Upon troubled days followed sunshine,

And today when you glance back

32 You can certainly be satisfied with destiny;

Your life is free from everyday needs and cares.

34 New force returns even to the mother who was sick;[6]

You are surrounded by a lively throng of children,

36 So that in almost everything happiness smiles on you.

That is why, when we express our wishes in words today,

38 Let us say, in short, how we feel at heart:

If only fate would leave everything thus in your old age,

40 When time without resting flies at a rapid pace.

Yes, may God's blessing continue to govern visibly

42 Over you and all those dear to you, as now,

And what it pleases Him in his grace to bestow upon you

44 Last yet many a year until the most distant time!

But it is not fitting on such days,

46 Which are comparable to the birthday of a marriage,

To dare approach the birthday child empty-handed, with words only;

48 A meaningful gift delights any child.

Therefore we have decided to present a gift also,

50 And just because we haven't found anything better,

We, somewhat impudent and bold, finally

52 Present all of ourselves as gift.

May you regard us kindly in this picture,

54 All of the young Jungs. Come here, observe us well.

26 Die Krankheit an der Kinder Bette Euch erschienen

Und hat in mancher Nacht, mit schwerer Sorge Last

28 Um uns den Schlaf verscheucht von Euren bangen Mienen.

Und dennoch hat noch alles immer gut geendet,

30 Auf trübe Tage folgte wieder Sonnenschein,

Und wenn ihr heute Eure Blicke rückwärts wendet

32 So dürft Ihr mit dem Schicksal wohl zufrieden sein,

Frei ist von Alltagsnoth und Sorge Euer Leben,

34 Der Mutter selbst, die krank, kehrt neue Kraft zurück;

Von einer munt'ren Kinderschaar seid Ihr umgeben,

36 So fast in allen Dingen, lächelt Euch das Glück.

Drum, wenn in Worte heut' wir uns're Wünsche fassen,

38 So sei es kurz gesagt, wie's uns am Herzen liegt :

Hier mög nur das Geschick beim Alten Alles lassen,

40 Wenn ruhelos die Zeit in raschem Wechsel fliegt.

Ja möge über Euch und Euren Lieben allen

42 Wie jetzt, so ferner Gottes Segen sichtbar walten,

Und, was zu schenken Euch in Gnaden Ihm gefallen,

44 Noch manches Jahr bis in die fernste Zeit erhalten!—

Doch nicht mit Worten nur geziemts an solchen Tagen,

46 Die dem Geburtstag einer Eh' vergleichbar sind,

Sich händeleer an das Geburtstagskind zu wagen,

48 Ein sinniges Geschenk erfreut ja jedes Kind.

So haben denn auch wir zu schenken uns entschlossen,

50 Und weil wir just nichts Besseres herausgebracht

So haben schliesslich, etwas dreist und unverdrossen,

52 Wir selber zum Geschenk uns Alle dargebracht.

In diesem Bilde mögt Ihr freundlich uns betrachten,

54 Die ganzen jungen Jungs. Kommt her, beseht uns recht.

A la bonheur, wouldn't you say, we are not to be disdained;

56 We are a stately, impressive lineage.

This one here at the far left is the tall rural economist;[7]

58 The light stripe in his hair shows his craft;

And there—I stumble here in the flow of my speech—

60 You see your wonderful pair of dear daughters.[8]

Then another offshoot,[9] not quite grown up, it seems to me.

62 Only it's a pity that his voice doesn't sound out from the picture,

Otherwise you would soon hear, accompanied by piano or fiddlestick,

64 The fundamental power of his bass.

And finally that one, the littlest hanger-on in the nest,[10]

66 Of whose deeds there isn't yet much to say,

But we hope for the best from his growth still to come,

68 That he will one day measure up to his siblings.

So now you have all five of us together,

70 Hang us up carefully on a nail,

So that when another one of us departs, as Fritz has already,

72 Or, as it sometimes happens in the ways of the world,

One of your daughters wants to part from you in a bridal wreath,

74 You know how it was at home before we scattered,

And that, remembering past times, you then

76 Delight in the present happiness of your children.

And now to conclude, dear and honored guests,

78 Join voices with me in a loud cheer, won't you,

This united us today for this happy wedding celebration:

80 Long live our dear parents and silver anniversary couple!

Written by Dr. Paul Schreber, Chief Administrator, District Court,
Recited by my sister Paula.

A la bonheur, nicht wahr, wir sind nicht zu verachten,
56   Wir sind ein stattlich, hochgewachsenes Geschlecht.

Der hier ganz links, das ist der lange Oekonome
58   Sein Handwerk zeigt der lichte Streifen unterm Haar;

Und da—hier möcht' ich stocken in der Rede Strome—
60   Erschaut Ihr Euer Töchter wunderlieblich Paar.

Dann noch ein Spross, mir scheint, noch nicht so ganz erzogen
62   Nur schad', dass aus dem Bild nicht auch die Stimme schallt,

Sonst würdet zu Klavier ihr oder Fiedelbogen
64   Vernehmen bald von ihm des Basses Grundgewalt.

Und endlich der, das kleinste Häkchen in dem Neste,
66   Von dessen Thaten noch nicht viel zu sagen ist,

Doch hoffen wir von seinem Wachstum noch das Beste,
68   Dass er dereinst sich auch mit den Geschwistern misst.

So habt Ihr uns dann nun beisammen alle Fünfe,
70   Hängt uns fein säuberlich an einem Nagel auf,

Dass, wenn noch eines sich, wie Fritz schon, auf die Strümpfe
72   Macht, oder, wie's nun mal so geht im Weltenlauf,

Der Töchter eine wollt im Brautkranz von Euch scheiden,
74   Ihr wisst, wie's bei Euch war, bevor wir uns zerstreut,

Und dass Ihr dann, gedenkend an vergang'ne Zeiten,
76   Am gegenwärt'gen Glück der Kinder Euch erfreut.

Und nun, zum Schluss, Ihr lieben hochverehrten Gäste,
78   Jetzt stimmt Ihr mit mir ein zu lautem Ruf, nicht wahr,

Das uns vereinte heut' zum frohen Hochzeitsfeste
80   Hoch lebe unser liebes Silber-Elternpaar !

Gedichtet vom Landgerichtsdirektor Dr. Paul Schreber,
82   Gesprochen von meiner Schwester Paula.

B. [Poem About Swans Which His Mother Gave as a Gift to His Nephew Fritz Jung] (Undated)

I don't come from the banks of the Scheldt[1]

2   Like one of my ancestors

Who rowed Lohengrin:[2]

4   The Pleisse[3] is my native land.

And I don't think of transforming myself,

6   Much preferring to wander always as a swan,

Bringing my mate along with me,

8   And I make only one request of you:[4]

That if this pair of swans

10   Gives you joy and pleasure,

At the same time you will thankfully

12   Remember the donor many a year to come.

May they also, any of your offspring,

14   Who are close to the hearts of ours,

Not dare to come too near;

16   Because I've heard it said at times

That the waters which refresh us swans,

18   Have, however, no planks for people.

Above lines written

by my uncle Paul Schreber (d. 1911)

B. [Gedicht über Schwäne, die seine Mutter seinem Neffen Fritz Jung schenkte]

Nicht wie Einer meiner Ahnen,

2 Der den Lohengrin thät kahnen,

Komm'ich von der Schelde Strand :

4 Die Pleisse ist mein Heimathland.

Denk' auch nicht mich zu verwandeln,

6 Will vielmehr als Schwan stets wandeln,

Bring' auch meine Schwänin mit

8 Und stell' an Euch nur Eine Bitt':

Dass wenn Euch das Schwanenpaerchen

10 Freud' Euch und Vergnügen schenket,

Ihr dabei noch manches Jährchen

12 Dankbar auch der Geberin gedenket

Möchten auch, wenn je von Euren Sprossen

14 Welche von den unsrigen ins Herz geschlossen

Sie Sich nicht in allzu grosse Nähe wagen;

16 Denn ich hörte nun einmal zuweilen sagen

Dass die Wässer, die uns Schwäne laben

18 Drum für-Menschen doch noch keine Balken haben

Vorstehende Zeilen schrieb

mein Onkel Paul Schreber (†1911)

when Grandmother Schreber

gave us two swans

July 8, 1937 Fr. Jung[5]

C. [Christening Speech for a Granddaughter of His Sister Anna] (1904)[1]

Very honorable baptism gathering,

2   Dear friends and relatives!

As the oldest one invited to the christening and besides,

4   the only godfather to appear, it is fitting

for me to first thank our host and baptismal pastor for

6   his friendly words of greeting and

then to toast the health of our godchild.[2]

8   In this connection Pastor B. has already

taken the words out of my mouth, so to speak,

10   and thereby encroached a bit on my pre-

rogatives as godfather. But that which is deeply

12   felt can well be said twice.   [sic]

Esteemed christening guests! It certainly did not

14   happen without intention that the parents of the infant chose

precisely Christmas as the date of the christening.

16   Not only for the obvious reason that

at Christmas-time relatives and

18   friends from farther away can also gather together

in larger number, but certainly also

als Grossmutter Schreber uns

zwei Schwäne schenkte.

8. Juli 1937 Fr. Jung.

C. [Taufrede für eine Enkelin seiner Schwester Anna (1904)]

Hochansehnliche Taufversammlung ! Liebe

2 Freunde & Verwandten !

Als ältestem der zur Taufe geladenen und obendrein

4 dem einzigen erschienenen männlichen Pathen geziemt

es mir wohl zunächst für die freundlichen Begrüssungs-

6 worte unseres Wirtes und Taufvaters zu danken und

sodann die Gesundheit unseres Täuflings auszubrin-

8 gen. In letzterer Beziehung hat allerdings HPastor B

mir bereits sozusagen das Wort vom Munde weg-

10 genommen und damit ein wenig in meine Prä-

rogative als Pathe eingegriffen. Allein was tief empfunden

12 empfunden wird, kann ja auch wohl zweimal gesagt

werden

14   Werthe Taufgenossen ! Es ist gewiss nicht ohne Ab-

sicht geschehen, dass die Taufeltern gerade das Weih-

16 nachtsfest als Zeitpunkt der Taufe gewählt haben.

Nicht bloss aus dem äusserlichen Grunde, dass

18 in der Zeit der Weihnachtsfeier Verwandte und

Freunde auch aus weiterer sich in grösserer Zahl

20   because they were mindful of the deeper

meaning that Christmas has as a celebration of

22   joy for all of Christianity.

And since Pastor B., as I just

24   pointed out, meddled somewhat in my job of

godfather, then he will perhaps not hold it against me

26   if I, in return, venture

somewhat into the ecclesiastic realm, linking my

28   words to the pronouncement of the prophet

by which was foretold the more sublime

30   meaning of the Christmas celebration:

For unto us a child is born, and

32   unto us a son is given, and His name shall

be called "Wonderful," "Glory, the Prince of Peace."

34   *"For unto us a child is born."* Thus

resounded the shout from this house[3]

36   about three months ago to the joy of all

who take part in its destiny

38   in sorrow and in joy. To be sure, the following part

doesn't correspond; not a

40   son is born to us, but rather, this time

a girl is bestowed upon this house.

42   Only I am surely not mistaken when I assure

that because of this the parents'[4] joy was

44   all the greater. For even if

normally at the first expectation of a growing

46   family a boy is what people

20 zusammenfinden konnten, sondern sicher auch

weil sie der tieferen Bedeutung eingedenk

22 waren, die das Weihnachtsfest als ein Fest der

Freude für die ganze Christenheit hat

24 Und da Herr Pastor B. nach dem, was ich bereits

bemerkte mir etwas in das Handwerk des Pathen

26 gepfuscht hat, so wird er mir vielleicht nicht übelnehmen

wenn ich mich zur Vergeltung dafür etwas auf

28 das pastorale Gebiet begebe, indem ich meine

Worte anschliesse an den Ausspruch des Prophe-

30 ten womit er jene erhabenere Bedeutung des

Weihnachtsfestes im Voraus verkündigt hat

32   Denn es ist uns ein Kind geboren, und

ein Sohn ist uns gegeben, dess Name wird

34   heissen "Wunderbar" "Herrlichkeit der Friedenfürst"

"Denn es ist uns ein Kind geboren." So

36 erscholl der Ruf vor etwa einem Vierteljahr

aus diesem Hause zur Freude aller derjenigen,

38 die an dessen Geschicken in Leid und Freude

Antheil nehmen. Der Fortgang stimmt ja

40 allerdings nun nicht; nicht ein

Sohn ist uns geboren, sondern ein Mägdlein

42 ist diesmal diesem Haus bescheret worden. Al-

lein ich irre wohl nicht wenn ich annehme

44 dass die Freude der Eltern deshalb nur eine um so

grössere gewesen ist. Denn wenn auch

46 bei der ersten Erwartung einer Fami-

especially long for,

48   in our case the maintenance of the

family line and genealogy

50   has already been assured with two strong male

offspring,[5] and so it may be considered

52   as a welcome enlargement of the

family picture that now

54   the eternal feminine, too, has attained

importance in it.

56   *"Wonderful."* In a higher sense

this word is meant only for that other

58   child who was born during the holy night

as saviour to the world. Only again,

60   in a certain other sense every child

could be called wonderful. For

62   a great wonder is contained in the origin

of every new human life, in the appearance

64   of every new human soul, a wonder

that we are only capable of contemplating,

66   or at most, describing, but can

never completely comprehend in its deeper

68   implications.

"Glory." Contained in this is

70   for the moment only a draft for the future

applicable to our godchild. For our

72   Ilse Anna Elisabeth yet lies small and

helpless in her little bed; for long years

lienver[m]ehrung in der Regel wohl ein Knabe

48 besonders heiss ersehnt zu werden pflegt so war

doch in unserem Falle für Erhaltung des

50 Stammes und des Stammbaumes bereits

durch zwei kräftige männliche Sprossen hin-

52 reichend gesorgt, und es durfte daher

als eine willkommene Ergänzung des

54 Familienbilds betrachtet werden, dass nun

mehr auch das ewig Weibliche darin zur

56 Geltung gelangt ist

"Wunderbar." dies Wort gilt in

58 einem höheren Sinn nur von jenem andern

Kinde, das in der Weih-Nacht als Heiland

60 der Welt geboren worden ist. Allein wiederum

in einem gewissen andern Sinne durfte jedes

62 Kind wunderbar genannt werden. Denn

ein hohes Wunder ist in der Entstehung

64 jedes neuen Menschenlebens, in der Erscheinung

jeder neuen Menschenseele beschlossen, ein Wun-

66 der, das wir nur anzuschauen oder allen-

falls zu beschreiben vermögen, niemals aber

68 in seinen tieferen Zusammenhängen voll

begreifen können.

70 *"Herrlichkeit"*. Darin ist ja auf unsern

Täufling angewendet vorläufig nur eine

72 Wechsel für die Zukunft enthalten. Denn noch liegt

unsere Ilse Anna Elisabeth klein und

74   to come she will still need the loving

care of her parents and the support

76   of other people; yet her

little body already contains the

78   seed of all the abilities and propensities

which we today hope and wish

80   might one day unfold

in full bloom and glory.

82   *"The Prince of Peace."* When I speak

of our godchild I would indeed like

84   to substitute for this word the other

expression, "angel of peace." If the

86   combative element finds a strong

representation in her brothers, if they themselves

88   are perhaps one day called to battle as fighters

for the country,[6] then it will be

90   her task to be active

in the more narrow household and

92   family circle, to lovingly reconcile

existing or newly arising oppositions,

94   to alleviate unaccustomed troubles and

pain, and thus, corresponding to

96   the woman's vocation, prove herself

as a true angel of peace.

98   But here, too, the black and the bright

destinies lie in the hands of the

100   future. Only if the environment

74 hülflos in ihrem Bettchen; noch wird sie

auf lange Jahre hinaus der liebevollen

76 Fürsorge der Eltern und der Unterstützung

anderer Menschen bedürfen; allein doch sind

78 auch in ihrem kleinen Leibe schon alle die

Fähigkeiten und Anlagen im Keime ent-

80 halten, die wie wir heute hoffen und wün-

schen, sich dereinst zu voller Blüthe und

82 Herrlichkeit entfalten sollen

"Der Friedensfürst." Dies Wort möchte

84 ich wohl, wenn ich von unserem Täufling

rede, mit dem andern Ausdruck, "Friedensengel"

86 vertauschen. Wenn in ihren Brüdern

das streitbare Element eine kräftige

88 Vertretung finden mag, wenn dieselben

vielleicht einmal berufen sein könnten

90 selbst als Streiter für das Vaterland in Kampf

zu ziehen so wird es ihre Aufgabe sein

92 mehr in dem engeren häuslichen und

Familienkreise zu wirken, vorhandene

94 oder neu entstehende Gegensätze in Liebe

zu versöhnen, fremden Kummer oder

96 Schmerz zu lindern und so dem Beruf

des Weibes entsprechend, als ein wahrer

98 Friedensengel sich zu erweisen

Noch liegen ja auch hier sie in der

100 Zukunft Schosse, die schwarzen und die

and the external circumstances under which

102   she saw the light of the world soon

appear to guarantee a successful

104   development, then we also hope that in a more distant

future a merciful fate and

106   the love of her parents might smooth

the whole path of life for her

108   into one that is as sunny and happily formed

as possible.

110   And let us voice these hopes

and wishes by raising our glasses

112   and drinking to the well-being of our

godchild. Our little Ilse Anna Elisabeth, may she

114   grow, blossom and thrive; long may she live.

D. [Poem for His Mother's Ninetieth Birthday] (1905)

For the 29th of June, 1905

Youth may dream of a golden future,

2   Old age lives in the past,

That's why we have dedicated to you a book

4   Of dear old places, of old times.

It is to freshen your memory

6   Of sites known to you during your long life.

    As you turn its pages you will see many a thing

    8   That reminds you of earlier happiness and sorrow.

heitern Loose. Allein wenn die Umgebung

102   und die äusseren Verhältnisse unter denen

sie das Licht der Welt erblikt hat zunächst

104   eine gedeihliche Entwicklung zu verbürgen

scheinen, so hoffen wir auch von einer fern-

106   ren Zukunft, dass ein gnädiges Geschick und

die Liebe ihrer Eltern ihr die Pfade des Lebens

108   ebnen möge, ihr [den] ganzen Lebensweg

zu einen möglichst sonnigen und glücklichen

110   gestalten

und diesen Hoffnungen und Wünschen lassen

112   Sie uns Ausdruck geben, indem wir unsere

Gläser erheben und auf das Wohl des Täuflings

114   leeren. Unsere kleine Ilse Anna Elisabeth sie

wachse, blühe und gedeihe, sie lebe hoch.

D. [Gedicht zum neunzigsten Geburtstag seiner Mutter (1905)]

Zum 29. Juni 1905.

Die Jugend mag von goldner Zukunft träumen,

2   Das Alter lebt in der Vergangenheit,

D'rum haben wir von alten lieben Räumen,

4   Von alten Zeiten Dir ein Buch geweiht.

Es soll Dir der Erinnerung Frische geben

6   An Stätten, Dir bekannt aus langem Leben.

Wenn Du es blätterst, wirst Du manches schauen,

8   Was Dich an früh'res Glück und Leid gemahnt.

For life's light path was not only cleared for you

10 Across sunny spring meadows;

No, you have also borne a full measure

12 Of cloudy, troubled days of existence,

Poor in joys, rich in pain and sorrows,

14 As not many other people have.

Yet the course of time works soothingly;

16 It lets what was beautiful always appear beautiful,

It readily dissolves the pains into wistfulness.

18 So may the pictures, too, which we bring together

Into an unassuming book bring you joy

20 In looking at them. Although the art is scant,

You will not completely disdain the gift:

22 It is as fine as we were able to make it.

I. Fireball[1]

24 At the beginning, as is fitting, is the house

In which you yourself began life.

26 It looks quite unchanged

Although generations have already gone by.

28 The thunder of Waterloo had hardly faded away,

The happy news flew from mouth to mouth:

30 The Corsican[2] has been defeated for the last time.

"The world is at peace" sounds all around;

32 There—happy cries of victory still resounding to the ear—

There in the Fireball almost at the same hour

34 Haase's first little daughter was born.[3]

Denn nicht allein durch sonn'ge Frühlingsauen

10 War Dir der leichte Lebensweg gebahnt;

Nein, auch von neblig-trüben Daseinstagen,

12 An Freuden arm, an Schmerz und Wehe reich

Hast Du ein vollgeschüttelt Mass ertragen,

14 Nicht allzuvielen And'ren darin gleich.

Doch mildernd wirkt auch hier der Zeiten Lauf;

16 Er lässt, was schön war, immer schön erscheinen,

Die Schmerzen löst er gern in Wehmut auf.

18 So mögen auch die Bilder, die wir einen

Zu anspruchslosem Buch, Dir beim Betrachten

20 Zur Freude dienen. Ist auch die Kunst gering,

Wirst Du die Gabe doch nicht ganz verachten :

22 So schön just ward's, wie's nach den Kräften ging.

I. Feuerkugel

24 Den Anfang macht, wie billig wohl, das Haus,

In dem Du selbst das Leben angefangen.

26 So ziemlich unverändert sieht es aus,

Sind auch drei Menschenalter schon vergangen.

28 Der Donner Waterloo's war kaum verklungen,

Von Mund zu Munde flog die frohe Kunde :

30 Der Korse ist zum letzten Mal bezwungen.

"Der Welt wird Friede" tönt es in der Runde:

32 Da—Siegesjubel schallt noch in den Ohren—

Da, in der Feuerkugel, fast zur selben Stunde,

34 Ward Haase's erstes Töchterlein geboren.

After years your thinking returned anew

36   To the house in which it happened.

It was in order to finally tell the correct place

38   Where Goethe had found his student lodging.

In the picture you see the mounted plaque

40   Which now clearly proclaims the poet's fame.

To those in the know it might say in addition

42   That your merit is also bound to it.

The places where the great man trod

44   Are sacred, according to his own words,

That is why the crowd of admirers

46   Likes to search out the spot where his path of life left traces.

That he be saved from oblivion here,

48   That this trace not be blotted out,

Your memory diligently succeeded

50   In preserving it faithfully for decades.

II. Hohmann's Court and Black Plank[4]

52   To write poetry about "Hohmann's Court" and "black plank"

Is somewhat difficult for me, I admit.

54   A city chronicler who takes his material

From the houses could report on them;

56   He knows how to narrate with great ease

What there was of the construction to change,

58   What the occupants inside were diligently engaged in,

Whether it was more expensive in one year than another;

60   About "Hohmann's Court," perhaps, that relatives

Of the present count once occupied it;

Dem Haus, in dem's geschah, hat noch nach Jahren

36 Dein Denken sich von neuem zugewandt.

Den rechten Fleck galt's endlich zu erfahren,

38 Wo Göthe die Studentenwohnung fand.

Im Bild siehst Du die Tafel angeschlagen,

40 Die's nun zum Ruhm des Dichters deutlich kündet.

Dem Kund'gen mag sie ausserdem noch sagen,

42 Dass Dein Verdienst sich auch damit verbindet.

Die Stätten, die der grosse Mann betrat,

44 Sie sind geweiht, nach seinem eig'nen Worte,

Darum, wo Spuren liess sein Lebenspfad,

46 Forscht der Verehrer Schar gern nach dem Orte.

Dass hier er dem Vergessen ward entrissen,

48 Dass diese Spur nicht ausgelöschet ward,

War Dein Gedächtnis mit Erfolg beflissen

50 Das sie, Jahrzehnte, treulich aufbewahrt.

II. Hohmanns Hof und schwarzes Bret

52   Von "Hohmanns Hof" und "schwarzem Bret" zu dichten,

Das fällt mir, ich gesteh's, ein wenig schwer.

54 Ein Stadtchroniste mag davon berichten,

Der von den Häusern nimmt die Stoffe her,

56 Und der, was baulich d'ran zu ändern war,

Was die Bewohner trieben d'rin mit Fleiss,

58 Ob's teurer war in dem, als jenem Jahr,

Mit viel Behagen zu erzählen weiss;

60 Von "Hohmanns Hof" etwa, dass ein Geschlecht

Von jetz'gen Grafen einst darin gesessen,

62   Indeed the earliest ancestor, if I heard rightly,

        Still measured out the cloth with the yardstick;

64   About the "black plank," that whoever was not able

        To spend more on his physical needs could eat his fill,

66   As well as may be, for fifteen pennies,

        As the students often did at the time

68   —Of course now it could hardly be done for that.

        Yet all of this, to be sure, doesn't concern you much.

70   With a few words I want to enlarge upon

        What these old houses mean to you

72   As well as I can.

        They saw the happy days of your childhood

74   Dedicated to learning and to lively play,

        Where there are no cares, except for the torment

76   That ABC's and arithmetic bring.

        School was disdained; it was considered elegant

78   To retain a tutor instead.

        He praised, scolded when necessary,

80   He taught you, and along with you, your siblings.[5]

        Your head was burdened almost more than proper

82   With everything that belongs to education,

        With world and natural history, foreign languages;

84   It is still noticeable now in your old age.

        Nevertheless you have always loved books;

86   But who your valiant teachers were

        Aside from Hauthal, from Reichardt, Kruger,

88   Indeed I could only find out from you yourself,

62 Der Ahnherr allerdings, vernahm ich recht,

Das Tuch noch mit der Elle zugemessen;

64 Vom "schwarzen Brete", dass so schlecht und recht

Für fünfzehn Pfenn'ge satt sich konnte essen,

66 Wer, wie schon damals öfters die Studenten

—Jetzt wär' es freilich kaum damit getan—

68 Ein Mehr an seinen Leib nicht durfte wenden.

Doch alles dies fieht Dich wohl wenig an.

70 Was diese alten Häuser *Dir* bedeuten,

Darüber will ich mich, so gut ich kann,

72 Mit ein'gen Worten nur verbreiten.

Sie sahen Deiner Kindheid frohe Tage,

74 Dem Lernen und dem heit'ren Spiel geweiht,

Wo's keine Sorgen gibt, bis auf die Plage

76 Die's ABC und Rechnen beut.

Die Schule ward verschmäht, für vornehm galt's :

78 Man hielt an ihrer Statt sich den Magister,

Er lobte, tadelte gegeb'nenfalls,

80 Er lehrte Dich und mit Dir die Geschwister,

Mit allem, was zur Bildung so gehört,

82 Mit Welt-, Naturgeschichte, fremden Sprachen

Ward mehr als billig fast Dein Kopf beschwert;

84 Man merkt's noch jetzt in Deinen alten Tagen.

Von jeher liebtest trotzdem Du die Bücher;

86 Wer aber Deine wack'ren Lehrer waren,

Von Hauthal abgesehn, von Reichardt, Krüger,

88 Das könnt ich wohl nur von Dir selbst erfahren,

Because other witnesses are hardly living anymore.

90 They have all long since gone;

It has been nearly eighty years or more

92 Since your education was begun.

So may the old houses which we have presented

94 Tell in pictures

What else occupied your mind

96 And touched your heart in those early days;

And should the houses remain silent, too,

98 Perhaps this and that will occur to you.

III. Princes' House

100 The childhood years had flown by swiftly,

You gradually grew into a young lady.

102 You moved into another new house

In which your young life now passed.

104 It was not yet necessary to move far away

From the previous home. The old city was cramped;

106 If one wanted to flee the summer's heat there,

A plot of land right next to the "Kauz" was to be found.

108 It was not chance that you took residence there:

Usually only professors were renters.

110 The Princes' House! How proud the name

Laden with memories that echo in your soul!

112 Your life had come to bloom,

The fragrance of youth like a rosy luster

114 Flowing over even everyday things;

How could it be otherwise at the age of twenty!

Denn and're Zeugen leben schwerlich mehr.

90 Sie alle sind schon längst dahingegangen;

Schier achtzig Jahr und drüber ist es her,

92 Seit man mit Deiner Bildung angefangen,

D'rum, was Dir sonst in jenen frühen Tagen,

94 Den Geist beschäftigte und das Herz gerührt,

Das möchten nun die alten Häuser sagen,

96 Die wir in ihren Bildern vorgeführt;

Und sollten auch die Häuser schweigsam sein,

98 Vielleicht fällt selbst Dir dies und jenes ein.

III. Fürstenhaus

100   Die Kinderjahre waren rasch verflogen,

Zur Jungfrau wuchsest mälig Du heran.

102 Ein neues Heim ward wieder 'mal bezogen,

In dem das junge Leben nun verrann.

104 Weit weg vom früh'ren Heim zu ziehen,

War noch nicht not. Die alte Stadt war eng;

106 Wollt' man aus ihr des Sommers Hitze fliehen,

Fand man ganz dicht beim "Kauz" schon ein Terrain.

108 Kein Zufall war's, wo man die Wohnung nahm :

Meist nur die Professoren waren Mieter.

110 Das Fürstenhaus ! Wie hallt der stolze Nam'

Erinn'rungsvoll in Deiner Seele wieder !

112 Dein Leben war zu seiner Blüt' entsprossen,

Der Duft der Jugend wie ein ros'ger Schein

114 Auch über das Alltägliche ergossen;

Wie könnt's mit zwanzig Jahren anders sein !

116   The house was also very congenially located,

          Quite close to the city gate; in between colonnades,

118   A garden where flowers could be tended,

          Grapevines may have even spread on the walls.

120   In the house, as well, happy pastimes;

          Learned men went in and out;

122   It was the joy of the parents to converse[6]

          In a lively and sociable way; the father did not spurn

124   A tasty meal with a glass of wine.

          Hardly a concert in the Gewandhaus was missed;

126   At times, but less frequently, you went to the theater,

          Five of you! That cost a lot of money.

128   Music was also cultivated diligently at home,

          Aesthetic things were perceived with warmth,

130   You had an ever awake sense

          For everything new, whatever excited the epoch.

132   However, when they wanted to teach you skat[7]

          and whist, they didn't encounter much talent;

134   But when a man of intellect stepped into the house,

          Your intellect, too, gladly found refreshment.

136   Thus now and then a suitor also appeared

          Ready to attach himself to you for life;

138   One rapturous one swore solemnly that

          Only united with you could he find happiness.

140   Rejection was then distressing for the poor man,

          For you it was not agreeable either;

142   Yet it doesn't do to take up the yoke of marriage

116   Gar freundlich war anoch das Haus gelegen;

Ganz nah das Tor; dazwischen Kolonnaden,

118   Ein Garten, wo man Blumen konnte pflegen,

An Mauern mochte selbst der Wein geraten.

120   Dazu im Haus ein fröhliches Verweilen;

Gelehrte Männer gingen ein und aus;

122   Sich heiter und gesellig mitzuteilen,

War Freud' der Eltern; einen guten Schmaus

124   Beim Glase Wein verschmähte nicht der Vater.

Konzerte im Gewandhaus wurden kaum verfehlt;

126   Bisweil', doch selt'ner ging man ins Theater,

Fünf Köpfe hoch ! Das kostete schon Geld.

128   Mit Fleiss wurd' auch daheim Musik gepflegt,

Schöngeistiges mit Wärm' empfunden,

130   Für alles neue, was die Zeit bewegt',

Ein stets geweckter Sinn bei Dir gefunden.

132   Zwar als man lehren wollte Dich den Skat

Und Whist, stiess man auf nicht zuviel Begabung;

134   Doch wenn ein Mann von Geist das Haus betrat,

Fand auch der Deine gerne darin Labung.

136   So ab und zu erschien auch 'mal ein Freier,

Bereit sich Dir für's Leben zu verbinden;

138   Ein Exaltierter schwor wohl hoch und teuer,

Vereint mit Dir nur könnt' er Glück noch finden.

140   Abweisen war dann peinlich für den Armen,

Zählt' auch für Dich nicht zu dem Angenehmen;

142   Doch ging's ja auch nicht an, blos aus Erbarmen

With an unloved person solely out of pity.

144 So on it went until the right one came;

When he, a young doctor,[8] spoke of love,

146 When he took courage to propose,

There was, of course, no more lengthy pondering.

148 Near Machern under a viaduct*

—The "Lightning" was just passing by under full steam—

150 Your heart twitched strongly one more time:

A "yes" came forth, you promised your life.

152 And when the cloud of steam cleared,

It quickly became plain to others

154 That cupid had once again drawn his bow,

That Miss Haase was now to be a bride.

156   Soon after—you followed your husband—

The house that was home to you was left behind.

158 To be sure, even here the light was not without shadows

—You saw your father go to an early grave[9]—

160 To be sure, subsequent times brought much happiness,

When the waves of life rose and fell,

162 To be sure, your gaze likes to rest on many another,

However—if you recall those times

164 So full of joy and bliss,

Which I was only able to paint with feeble brushstrokes,

Note (in text) for outside readers: The railway from Leipzig to Dresden was only completed as far as Machern at that time (beginning of 1838). Now and then excursion trains were sent out to give the people of Leipzig a chance to try out the great novelty of the railway.

Des Ungeliebten Eh' joch aufzunehmen.

144 So ging es fort, bis dass der Rechte kam;

Als der, ein junger Doktor, sprach von Minnen,

146 Als zu 'nem Antrag er den Mut sich nahm,

Da gab es freilich nicht mehr lang besinnen.

148 Bei Machern, unter einem Viadukt*

—Der "Blitz" in vollem Dampf passierte eben—

150 Hat heftig noch einmal Dein Herz gezuckt :

Heraus war's "Ja", versprochen Du fürs Leben.

152 Und als des Dampfes Nebel sich verzogen,

Da ward es rasch auch And'ren klipp und klar,

154 Dass Amor wieder 'mal gespannt den Bogen,

Dass Fräulein Haase eine Braut nun war.

156   Bald wurde jetzt—Du folgtest Deinem Gatten—

Das Haus verlassen, das Dir Heimat war.

158 Zwar war auch hier das Licht nicht ohne Schatten

—Den Vater saht Ihr auf der frühen Bahr'—

160 Zwar bracht auch spät're Zeit noch manches Glück,

Wenn Lebenswogen gingen auf und nieder,

162 Zwar ruht auf manchem and'ren gern Dein Blick,

Und dennoch—ruf'st Du jene Zeiten wieder,

164 So voll von Freuden und von Wonne,

Die nur mit schwachem Pinsel ich konnt' malen,

Anmerkung für dritte Leser : Die Eisenbahn von Leipzig nach Dresden war damals (Anfang 1838) nur bis Machern fertig. Ab und zu wurden Vergnügungszüge abgelassen, um den Leipzigern Gelegenheit zu geben, die grosse Neuerung der Eisenbahn zu erproben.

166   Then it would surely seem to you that the sun

Could never again shine as brightly as in the Princes' House!

168   *IV. St. Nicholas Church*[10]

Now a house of God is next in line;

170   The picture shows you the nave and the altar.

The quiet consecration which fills it

172   One day manifested itself to you in a very special way.

Before that altar you gave your hand

174   To the man who offered his to you,

Who from then on stood faithfully at your side

176   Until he was gathered to the dead.

From that time on you were bound to each other in love and faithfulness,

178   Together you bore every happiness and sorrow;

If ever two hearts had found each other,

180   Then yours did, for all time and eternity.

Alas, that only modest duration of untroubled

182   Marital happiness was granted this union!

Alas, when he himself still walked below,[11]

184   How far back that time is already!

As a widow you have been mourning going on fifty years;

186   The world has almost become another world in the meantime,

Your own hair has already paled long since.

188   Never have you forgotten him, nor your love!

V. Dove

190   When you exchanged the bridal wreath for the bonnet

And said farewell to your parental home,

166 So dünkt Dich's wohl, als könnt' so hell die Sonne,

Als, wie im Fürstenhause, nie mehr strahlen !

168 *IV. Nikolaikirche*

Ein Gotteshaus folgt jetzo in der Reihe;

170 Das Bild zeigt Dir das Schiff und den Altar.

Die es erfüllt, die ernste stille Weihe,

172 Sie tat sich Dir einst ganz besonders dar.

Vor jenem Altar reichtest Du die Hand,

174 Dem Mann, der Dir die seinige geboten,

Der fortan treu zu Deiner Seite stand,

176 Bis er versammelt wurde zu den Toten.

In Lieb und Treu war't Ihr seitdem verbunden,

178 Vereint ertrugt Ihr jedes Glück und Leid;

Wenn je zwei Herzen hatten sich gefunden,

180 So Ihr für alle Zeit und Ewigkeit,

Ach, dass nur mäss'ge Dauer war beschieden,

182 Dem Bund in ungetrübtem Eheglück !

Ach, da Er selbst noch wandelte hinieden,

184 Wie lange schon liegt diese Zeit zurück !

Als Witwe trauerst Du an fünfzig Jahre;

186 Die Welt ward fast 'ne and're unterdessen;

Schon längst erbleichten Deine eig'nen Haare,

188 Nie hast Du Ihn, nie Deine Lieb vergessen !

V. Taube

190 Als Du vertauscht den Brautkranz mit der Haube,

Dem Elternhause Lebewohl gesagt,

192   At first the path only went as far as the "Dove;"

        Wedding trips were not taken then.

194   Only with difficulty do you recognize the house

        In the picture; then it looked so different from now.

196   Next to it whole houses were torn down;

        Indeed, another floor was added to the top.

198   However, the old rooms are still there today,

        Though it has become different since the springtime of your life;

200   Maybe lovely kind of flowers on the path of life,

        "The springtime of life," I should say,

202   The lovely kind of flowers on the path of life,

        "The springtime of life," I should say,

204   It is called honeymoon,[12] but whether rightly,

        It would be proper to first ask.

206   For true love should not shine for only a short time

        With a false shimmer, like sequins;

208   Real gold keeps its shine always,

        In spite of time and rust, until life's limits.

210   So it was with you from those happy days onward,

        Hardly touched yet by sorrow and cares;

212   When two hearts beat thus together,

        A beautiful today is followed only by a more beautiful tomorrow.

214   To enjoy the delight of motherhood for the first time,[13]

        To dedicate one's all to the beloved man,

216   Truly, when such blossoms unfold,

        What could be more beautiful on earth!

218   Every wish and every hope fulfilled;

192 Da ging der Weg zunächst nur bis zur "Taube",

Noch wurden Hochzeitsreisen nicht gemacht.

194 Notdürftig nur erkennst im Bild Du wieder

Das Haus; so anders sah es aus als jetzt.

196 Daneben riss man ganze Häuser nieder;

Ihm wurde wohl ein Stockwerk aufgesetzt,

198 Indess die alten Räume sind's noch heut';

Wo's anders ward seit Deines Lebens Lenze,

200 Ist Phantasie vielleicht in Dir bereit,

Dass sich's zu früherer Gestalt ergänze.

202 Am Lebensweg der Blumen hold Geschlecht :

"Des Lebens Lenz", so durfte ich wohl sagen;

204 Man nennt's die Flitterwochen, ob mit Recht,

Das wäre billig wohl erst noch zu fragen.

206 Denn nicht für kurze Zeit in falschem Schimmer,

Dem Flitter gleich, soll wahre Liebe glänzen;

208 Das echte Gold bewahrt den Glanz sich immer,

Trotz Zeit und Rost bis an des Lebens Grenzen.

210 So war's bei Euch seit jenen heit'ren Tagen,

Noch kaum berührt von Kummer und von Sorgen;

212 Wo so zwei Herzen miteinander schlagen,

Folgt schönem Heute nur ein schön'res Morgen.

214 Die Mutterfreud' zum ersten Mal geniessen,

Sein Alles dem geliebten Manne weihn,

216 Fürwahr, wo solche Blüten sich erschliessen,

Was könnte wohl auf Erden schöner sein !

218 Erfüllt schien jeder Wunsch und jedes Hoffen;

Only one wish, unfulfillable, remained open still:

220   O, that time would stand still for once,

Hindered in its course, for the marriage is young!

222   *VI. Church of St. Thomas Square and King Street*

In the foregoing it was a pleasant idyll

224   Still without dissonance that I took the effort

To trace; then the first grief

226   Sounded shrilly into your young married life.

Your mother died.[14] The house became too small;

228   It meant taking in your youngest sister;[15]

You had to accommodate yourselves

230   To a new residence, it couldn't be otherwise;

Your choice was Church of St. Thomas Square. The picture

232   Came to be in my list only by chance.

In the meantime fate was realized;

234   You see the framework ready for demolition.

Modesty forbids me to compose

236   Many lines about this house;

So I only want to briefly report on the fact,

238   As the habit of completeness enjoins me.

You had already brought along two little children,

240   A boy and a girl were already there,[16]

When, before it had really been thought over,

242   The stork dared to come again.[17]

I myself, namely, appeared at that time,

244   He who is now perpetrating these verses on you,

Nur ein Wunsch, unerfüllbar, blieb noch offen :

220 O, dass die Zeit nur einmal stille stehe.

Gehemmt in ihrem Lauf, weil jung die Ehe !

222 *VI. Thomaskirchhof und Königstrasse*

Im vor'gen war's ein freundliches Idyll,

224 Das ich zu zeichnen Mühe mir gegeben,

Noch ohne Missklang, da ertönte schrill

226 Ein erster Schmerz ins junge Eheleben.

Die Mutter starb. Die Wohnung ward zu klein;

228 Die jüngste Schwester galt es aufzunehmen;

Ihr musstet, anders konnt's einmal nicht sein,

230 Zu einer neuen Wohnung Euch bequemen,

Den Thomaskirchhof traf die Wahl. Das Bild

232 Kam nur durch Zufall noch in meine Liste.

Inzwischen hat das Schicksal sich erfüllt;

234 Zum Abbruch fertig schon siehst Du's Gerüste.

Von diesem Hause allzuviel zu dichten

236 Verbietet mir wohl die Bescheidenheit;

D'rum will ich kurz das Faktum nur berichten,

238 Wie mir's Vollständigkeit einmal gebeut.

Zwei Kindlein hattet Ihr schon mitgebracht,

240 Ein Knabe und ein Mägdlein war vorhanden,

Als sich, bevor man's noch so recht gedacht,

242 Der Storch zu kommen wieder unterstanden,

Ich selbst bin nämlich dazumal erschienen,

244 Der diese Verse jetzt an Dir verübt,

Hardly worthy of earning your approbation, to be sure,

246 A rascal, still, who gives beyond his capability.

After a few years came another change.

248 How will my muse now succeed

In singing a not all too sober song

250 Of Reklam and of Engelmann and Drechsel?

I won't attempt this, and from King Street

252 Only touch upon the growth of the family,

Which, although not an immodest multitude,

254 Had nonetheless already attained the number of four.[18]

Added to that the care of unrelated children

256 Brought in to you by the clinic[19]

There was no less annoyance and trouble with them,

258 Yet they were watched over like your own.

Thus the household had become larger and larger

260 Together with the number of servants;

It was necessary to look around for other places

262 Where you could live thereafter on your own.

VII. Zeitzer Street[20]

264   A home on your own land was decided upon;

Now it was time to consider carefully and cleverly

266 How the house should be constructed

And what kind of shape it would be given.

268 The location was still practically in the country at that time,

Only scattered isolated houses, where today

270 The tumult of the big city is almost torment.

Kaum wert zwar Deinen Beifall zu verdienen,

246 Ein Schelm jedoch, der übers Können gibt.

Nach wenig Jahren kam von neuem Wechsel.

248 Wie wird es meiner Muse nun gelingen

Von Reklam und von Engelmann und Drechsel

250 Ein doch nicht allzu nüchtern Lied zu singen ?

Dies geb ich auf, und von der Königstrasse

252 Sei der Familienzuwachs nur berührt,

Der, wenn auch nicht in unbescheidnem Masse,

254 So immerhin zur Vierzahl schon geführt.

Dazu nun noch die Sorg' um fremde Kinder,

256 Die Anstalt hatte sie Dir eingebracht;

Verdruss und Mühen gab's um sie nicht minder,

258 Doch wie die eig'nen wurden sie bewacht.

So war der Haushalt gross und grösser worden,

260 Mit ihm die Zahl der dienenden Personen,

Man musste umsehn sich nach andren Orten,

262 Wo man auf Eig'nem künftig könnte wohnen.

VII. Zeitzer Strasse

264 Beschlossen war ein Heim auf eigner Scholle;

Nun galt es klug und emsig zu bedenken,

266 Wie man das Haus darauf errichten solle,

Und welcherlei Gestalt ihm wär' zu schenken.

268 Fast ländlich noch war damals seine Lage,

Vereinzelt nur die Häuser, da wo heut'

270 Gewühl der Grossstadt nahezu schon Plage.

As it was being built—that was a happy time!

272   Planning out for ourselves every corner and space,

How it should soon become attractive and useful,

274   Being delighted about each tree in the garden,

Perhaps even about each potato!

276   Also when you had moved in, there were still years

When life proved to be mostly happy;

278   A little girl with blond hair[21]

Was added to the children.

280   But then suddenly the sky darkened

Long drawn out illness gnawed at your husband;[22]

282   From then on it threw deep shadows on life's path,

At the same time being a test of your love.

284   What you suffered and did without in those days

—The world was avoided, even in the house there were off-limits areas—

286   Truly, no one else need say it,

You yourself often linger there in your thoughts.

288   And finally, just when you were allowed to hope,

Recovery, as the reward for sacrifice, seemed to beckon,

290   Then you were hit the hardest:

You saw him suddenly swallowed up in an early grave.[23]

292   What further happened was, at that time,

Surely bearable, yet hardly a gain;

294   The world seemed bleak and lonely, without joy,

The charm and spice of life were gone.

Im Bau ! Das war noch einmal frohe Zeit !

272 Ausmalen sich für jeden Fleck und Raum,

Wie's hübsch und nützlich künftig werden solle,

274 Sich freu'n im Garten über jeden Baum,

Vielleicht selbst über die Kartoffelknolle !

276 Auch als Ihr drinnen waret, gab's noch Jahre,

Wo heiter sich das Leben meist gezeigt;

278 Von einem Mägdelein mit blondem Haare

Ward Anschluss an die Kinder noch erreicht.

280 Da aber ward der Himmel plötzlich trübe,

Langwier'ge Krankheit nagte an dem Gatten;

282 Fortan, zugleich ein Prüfstein Deiner Liebe,

Warf auf den Lebensweg sie tiefe Schatten.

284 Was Du gelitten und entbehrt in diesen Tagen

—Man mied die Welt, im Hause selbst gab's Schranken—

286 Das wahrlich braucht ein and'rer nicht zu sagen,

Oft weilst Du selbst dabei noch in Gedanken.

288 Und endlich, da man eben durfte hoffen,

Genesung schien als Opfers Lohn zu winken,

290 Da wurdest Du vom Härtesten betroffen :

Ins frühe Grab sah'st Du ihn jäh versinken.

292 Was dann noch weiter kam, das war zu Zeiten

Erträglich wohl, doch kaum noch ein Gewinn,

294 Die Welt schien öd' und einsam, ohne Freuden;

Des Lebens Reiz und Würze war dahin.

296   Cares and sorrow multiplied,

      A harsh blow, a painful end for your son,[24]

298   Children's illness, strain on yourself,

      Much gloom wherever you cast your glance.

300   Of course there were better hours now and then,

      Since, in addition to the children who didn't remain at home,

302   Three in-laws now numbered,[25]

      The troop of grandchildren added to your loved ones.[26]

304   On trips the world still offered many a beautiful thing,

      Yet you still had to do without many other things.

306   It is not easy for man to get used to

      Living mainly on past events.

308   Therefore I don't want to linger on details;

      Following is a disordered mixture of pictures

310   Which, without the commentary of rhyming lines,

      Are meant to portray what you experienced and saw.

312   But at this festivity we don't want to complain;

      We can celebrate thankfully

314   To see you still mentally active and alert,

      Although sometimes ear and limbs fail.

316   Children, grandchildren and great-grandchildren

      —And look, the number is quite impressive—

318   Joined today in love rejoice over your ninety years,

      Be it in silence or, if so, over the goblet,

320   Let us beseech God's merciful blessing

      For the remainder of your life's path

296 Des Kummers und der Sorgen wurden mehr,

Ein herber Schlag, des Sohnes schmerzlich Ende,

298 Krankheit von Kindern, eigene Beschwer,

Des Trüben viel, wohin Dein Blick sich wende.

300 Zwar gab es dann und wann auch bess're Stunden,

Da sich zu Kindern, die im Haus nicht blieben,

302 Der Schwiegerkinder Dreizahl eingefunden,

Der Enkel Schar vermehrte Deine Lieben.

304 Auf Reisen bot die Welt noch manches Schöne,

Doch vieles andre musstest Du entbehren.

306 Nicht leicht ist's, dass der Mensch sich d'ran gewöhne,

Zumeist nur vom Vergangenen zu zehren.

308 D'rum will ich nicht bei einzelnem verweilen;

Es folgt ein regellos Gemisch von Bildern,

310 Die, ohn' Erläuterung gereimter Zeilen,

Erlebtes und Geseh'nes sollen schildern,

312 Zum Feste aber wollen wir nicht klagen;

Wir dürfen es mit Dank erfüllt begeh'n;

314 Ob manchmal Ohr und Glieder auch versagen,

Dich geistig frisch und rüstig noch zu seh'n.

316 Die Kinder, Enkel und Urenkel freu'n sich

—Und sieh', recht stattlich schon ist ihre Zahl—

318 In Lieb' vereint heut' über Deine Neunzig

Sei's still, sei's, wenn es angeht, beim Pokal,

320 So lass uns flehn um Gottes gnäd'gen Segen,

Fürs übrige von Deinen Lebenswegen,

322   And hope that, if His will is not otherwise,

        You will perhaps also attain a hundred.

324   *Addendum*

        1.

        Only a few pages ago I promised, indeed,

326   That I didn't want to ride Pegasus anymore,

        And that a rhymed commentary should

328   No longer accompany the pictures still to come.

        Yet at the picture of the old city theater,

330   Of Beerendorf's and Schenkenberg's fields,[27]

        My poetic vein swells once again;

332   I must form what I perceive into verses

        In which you may enjoy many a beautiful

334   Fruit of art full of enthusiasm

        Both villages were often visited,

336   Nature presented itself here in field and meadows.

        Nature and art, who would like to do without them!

338   They are the two sides of human life

        Which, in combination, lend it true charm

340   And give strength and freshness to daily toil.

        So an aspect of the happiness of youth

342   Is portrayed to you also in the above pictures,

        In each one faithful and true

344   —Thus I don't need to describe it first in words.

        2.

        In Rudelsburg and Kösen[28]

322 Und hoffen, dass, ist anders nicht Sein Wille,

Vielleicht auch noch die Hundert sich erfülle.

324 *Anhang*

1.

Nur wen'ge Blatt zuvor versprach ich zwar,

326 Dass ich nicht mehr den Pegasus wollt' reiten,

Und nicht mehr ein gereimter Kommentar,

328 Das, was noch kommt von Bildern, sollt begleiten,

Doch bei dem Bild vom alten Stadttheater,

330 Von Beerendorfs und Schenkenbergs Gefilden

Schwillt mir noch einmal die poet'sche Ader,

332 Zu Versen muss ich das Empfund'ne bilden,

In jenem durft'st Du manche schöne Frucht

334 Der Kunst voll von Begeisterung geniessen,

Die beiden Dörfer wurden oft besucht,

336 Natur bot sich dort dar in Feld und Wiesen.

Natur und Kunst, wer möchte sie entbehren !

338 Sind's die zwei Seiten doch im Menschenleben,

Die, im Verein, ihm wahren Reiz gewähren,

340 In Tagesmühsal Kraft und Frische geben.

So stellt sich denn auch Dir in ob'gen Bildern,

342 In jedem einzelnen getreu und wahr

—In Worten brauch ich's d'rum nicht erst zu schildern—

344 Vom Julgendglück je eine Seite dar.

2.

In Rudelsburg und Kösen

346   You were there too,

You in the carriage, the bridegroom on foot,

348   Therefore you receive a poetic greeting from there too.

    3.

Although your heart is hardly set on fur and skins,

350   And you have perhaps only moderate liking

For those who eat kosher and for Poland's Jews

352   Let me, however, put a photograph of

A building in Brühl[29] together with the others,

354   On which not seldom did your cares rest.

The magnificence of its appearance was not all too great,

356   Not always a pleasure to supervise it;

Yet sixty years it belonged to you and yours,

358   And let one thing be said in its praise:

When it was no longer ours, it was a loss

360   That we cry over less than others.

    4.

To Lausche and to Klosterberg Oybin,[30]

362   You went there once with three children.

It was a great amusement for me at the time

364   To sit straddled on the border stone.

When I went there for the second time

366   I took pictures of it,

After fifty years. One notices

368   That everything was almost as it was earlier.

Only the people have grown somewhat older,

346   Da bist Du auch gewesen,

Zu Wagen Du, der Bräutigam zu Fuss,

348   D'rum werde auch von dort Dir ein poet'scher Gruss.

3.

Hängt auch Dein Herz wohl kaum an Pelz und Fellen,

350   Hast Du vielleicht nur mäss'ge Sympathie

Für das, was koscher isst und Polens Juden,

352   So lass mich doch den andern zugesellen,

Vom Brühl ein Bauwerk in Photographie,

354   Auf dem nicht selten auch die Sorgen ruhten.

Nicht allzu gross war seines Anblicks Pracht,

356   Nicht immer's zu verwalten eine Lust;

Doch sechzig Jahr war's Dir und war's den Deinen

358   Und eins sei ihm zum Lobe nachgesagt :

Als es uns nicht mehr war, war's ein Verlust,

360   Den weniger, als and'res, wir beweinen.

4.

Zur Lausche und zum Klosterberg Oybin,

362   Da zogt Ihr einstens mit drei Kindern hin,

Spreizbeinig auf den Grenzstein mich zu setzen

364   War dazumal mir höchliches Ergötzen.

Alks ich zum zweiten Male hingekommen,

366   Hab' ich die Bilder davon aufgenommen,

Nach fünfzig Jahren. Man nimmt wahr,

368   Dass alles beinah noch wie früher war.

Die Menschen nur sind etwas älter worden,

370   In these as well as in other places.

    5.

      The artistically famous Residence of Saxony[31]

372   Is now presented to you in several pictures;

      In addition to Leipzig, it drew dear to your heart long ago,

374   Since it was the destination of your first trip.

      But I have undertaken to show you

376   Not what has been photographed many times already

      With that art of light since invented,

378   And of which nicer ones could be bought in commerce,

      But rather, only what may especially touch you:

380   The New Market, where you stayed as a guest.

      The Saloppe,[32] where the coffee led you,

382   And where one can see the towers of Dresden in the valley,

      Also a few classical reminiscences

384   Of Schiller and Körner. From the big garden,

      Palace and pond where white swans gleam,

386   All sorts of other things pay their respects to you.

      Last you behold a modest house[33]

388   Which only recently came into existence with your help;

      It still looks unfinished in some respects,

390   The windows are not even in place.

      But when your son has moved into it,

392   Why should hope already be lost completely,

      That she who helped us find the way to our own home

394   Should once more stay there as guest?

370   An diesen wie wohl auch an and'ren Orten.

    5.

    Die kunstberühmte Residenz von Sachsen

372   Stellt sich Dir jetzt in einigen Bildern dar,

    Nächst Leipzig Dir von je ans Herz gewachsen,

374   Seit sie das Ziel der ersten Reise war.

    Doch nicht, was sonst schon vielfach aufgenommen,

376   Mit jener Kunst des Lichts, seitdem erfunden,

    Was man im Handel schöner mag bekommen,

378   Hab' ich mich Dir zu zeigen unterwunden.

    Nur was etwa besonders Dich berührt :

380   Der Neumarkt, wo Du gastlich abgestiegen,

    Saloppe, wo der Kaffee hingeführt,

382   Und man im Tal sieht Dresdens Türme liegen,

    Auch ein'ge klassische Reminiszenzen

384   Von Schiller, Körner. Aus dem grossen Garten,

    Palais und Teich, wo weisse Schwäne glänzen,

386   Sonst allerlei, um Dir noch aufzuwarten.

    Zuletzt erblickst Du ein bescheid'nes Haus,

388   Mit Deiner Hülfe kürzlich erst entstanden,

    Unfertig sieht es noch in manchem aus,

390   Noch nicht einmal die Fenster sind vorhanden.

    Doch wenn es erst bezogen von dem Sohne,

392   Warum soll gänzlich schon die Hoffnung schwinden.

    Dass *Die* noch einmal d'rin zu Gaste wohne,

394   Die Weg und Steg zu eig'nem Heim liess finden ?

6.

A while ago chance brought me two pictures
396   Perhaps not unwelcome to you;

That is why they also have been put into the book;
398   I thought there might be space for them at the end.

A verse for them is almost necessity.
400   I didn't want to mention names in explanation,

Who knows if you yourself wouldn't recognize
402   The object again after a long time.

But here our rich mother tongue fails,
404   For, even if I asked all scribes,

What in the world could rhyme with "Klitzschen"[34]
406   Besides "Hitschen," "Pritschen," "Titschen"?[35]

So let the pictures be sufficient to you,
408   Lines up not to your displeasure, I hope,

As that which otherwise gives delight after years:
410   A bit of remembrance from old times.

7.

Two Riddles

412   *a) Four syllables*

The first two are in the older sense an element
414   that gives us warmth after the light of the sun.

The two last ones are the shape that everyone knows,
416   In which another element acquired its form.

The whole is an old building in Leipzig's streets,
418   Famous because of a student who was once its inhabitant.[36]

6.

Zwei Bilder, Dir vielleicht nicht unwillkommen,

396   Bracht' mir vor ein'ger Zeit der Zufall ein;

D'rum sind sie in das Buch mit aufgenommen;

398   Platz, dacht ich, mag für sie am Schlusse sein.

Ein Vers dazu ist fast Notwendigkeit,

400   Da, wollt ich nicht zur Deutung Namen nennen,

Wer weiss, ob nicht selbst Du nach langer Zeit

402   Den Gegenstand nicht wieder würd'st erkennen.

Doch hier versagt die reiche Muttersprache,

404   Denn was in aller Welt könnt wohl auf "Klitzschen",[1]

Und wenn ich alle Schriftgelehrten frage,

406   Sich reimen ausser "Hitschen", "Pritschen", "Titschen"?

D'rum lasse an den Bildern Dir genügen,

408   Dir nicht zum Missfall, hoff ich, eingereiht,

Als das, was sonst nach Jahren schafft Vergnügen :

410   Ein Stück Erinnerung aus alter Zeit.

7.

Zwei Rätsel

412   *a) Viersilbig.*

Zwei erste sind in ält'rem Sinn ein Element,

414   Das uns die Wärme spendet nächst dem Licht der Sonnen.

Die beiden letzten sind die Form, die Jeder kennt,

416   Worin ein and'res Element Gestalt gewonnen.

Das Ganze ist ein alter Bau in Leipzigs Gassen,

418   Berühmt durch einstigen Studenten als Insassen.[2]

b) Three syllables

420   First are two syllables which refer to men

Of high rank and noble descent;

422   Because in old times they were first

In war and battles, they were so named.

424   The last syllable is what protects us

In the storms of weather, as in those of life

426   Even if everyone today unfortunately

Does not own one as a possession any more.

428   The whole word you could translate well enough,

According to the meaning, as "dynasty."

430   Yet in a certain other sense you must

Transport yourself mentally to Leipzig.

432   Here, as always, an edifice of not little beauty

Which has its name, so I have heard,

434   In that it shelters the first sons

Desirous of learning as sons of the muses.[37]

E. *[Poem for the Fiftieth Birthday of His Wife] (1907)*

Dedicated to his dear little Sabine
for the nineteenth of June 1907
from her Paul

Since I last spoke to you in verses

2   Many a fleeting year has disappeared.

We both became gradually older,

4.   Gray has already found its way into our hair.

So I am making this effort today in vain perhaps

b) Dreisilbig

420   Zuerst sind es zwei Silben, die auf Männer

Von hohem Rang und hoher Abkunft weisen,

422   Weil sie in alter Zeit die Vordersten

In Krieg und Schlachten waren so geheissen.

424   Die letzte Silbe ist, was in den Stürmen

Des Wetters, wie des Lebens uns beschützt,

426   Wenn schon es leider heutzutage

Nicht jeder mehr zu Eigentum besitzt.

428   Das Ganze könntest Du dem Sinne nach

Mit "Dynastie" so ziemlich übersetzen.

430   Doch musst Du in gewissem and'ren Sinn

Im Geiste schon nach Leipzig Dich versetzen.

432   Hier stets, ein Bauwerk nicht geringer Schöne,

Das seinen Namen—hört ich—davon trägt,

434   Dass es der ersten lernbegier'ge Söhne,

Als Musensöhne oft in sich gehegt.[3]

E. [Gedicht zum fünfzigsten Geburtstag seiner Frau (1907)]

Seinem lieben Sabchen
zum neunzehnten Juni 1907 gewidmet
von Ihrem Paul.

Seit ich zuletzt in Versen zu Dir sprach,

2   Ist manches flücht'ge Jahr dahingeschwunden.

Wir Beide wurden älter allgemach,

4   Schon hat im Haupthaar Grau sich eingefunden.

So mühe ich mich denn heut' vielleicht vergebens

6   —Since the stream of my songs flows more tiredly—

With the wreath of rhymes, which in the springtime of life

8   Sprouts full of fragrant blossoms all by itself.

Also—should I direct a glance backwards,

10   Should I speak to you of things past—

Not joy alone is there to relate in verse,

12   Not only about happiness and cheer can I sing.

Several times we closed up our hope in a coffin;

14   Some of those dear to us have been lowered into the grave.

Both of your parents have long since perished,

16   Nor have I remained son to a mother.[1]

The full force of youth, which may not know

18   Limits for its goals and wishes,

Oh, it sometimes even wavered, and

20   Suffered now and then because of little things.

And worse yet: my mind, disturbed for a second time,

22   Was in the bonds of heavy illness;

The bitter cup of separation and sorrow,

24   Full of grief and suffering, was yours again.

Nine heavy years passed in that way,[2]

26   You could almost consider yourself a widow;

Hope of returning hardly came to mind,

28   Prospects for recovery hardly seemed to beckon.

But for that very reason we musn't complain,

30   Since much changed for the better;

We once again saw light after troubled days,

32   Old love's bonds were newly knotted.

6   —Da matter meiner Lieder Bächlein fliesst—

Am Kranz der Reime, der im Lenz des Lebens

8   Voll duft'ger Blüthen ganz von selber spriesst.

Auch, —soll ich rückwärts Deine Blicke richten,

10   Soll ich Dir reden von vergang'nen Dingen—

Nicht Freudiges allein ist da zu dichten,

12   Nicht nur von heit'rem Glücke kann ich singen.

Wir sargten mehrmals uns're Hoffnung ein;

14   In's Grab versenkt ward Manches uns'rer Lieben.

Dir gingen längst schon heide Eltern ein,

16   Auch ich bin keiner Mutter Sohn geblieben.

Die volle Kraft der Jugend, die nicht Schranken

18   Für Ziele und für Wünsche kennen mag,

Ach, sie gerieth zuweilen schon in's Wanken,

20   Litt, ab und zu, durch Kleines Ungemach.

Und schlimmer noch : verstört, zum zweiten Male,

22   War mir der Geist in schwerer Krankheit Banden;

Der Trennung und des Kummers bitt're Schaale,

24   Voll Sorg' und Leid, war wieder Dir erstanden.

Neun schwere Jahre gingen so dahin,

26   Fast mochtest Du Dich schon als Wittwe dünken;

Kaum kam auf Rückkehr Hoffnung in den Sinn,

28   Kaum schien Genesungsaussicht noch zu winken.

Doch g'rade darum dürfen wir nicht klagen,

30   Da Vieles auch zum Besseren sich wandte;

Wir sahen wieder Licht nach trüben Tagen,

32   Neu knüpften sich der alten Liebe Bande.

And if everything that once embellished

34   Our life with charm could not be returned,

What right do we have to complain about it,

36   In place of that we were permitted to found[3]

Our own home, which brought us new happiness,

38   Your complete pride and joy;

To combine nature with taste here,

40   You create sensibly for the pleasure of the eye.

And if, where we were formerly living,

42   You greeted a guest from time to time,

Now you can speak of higher responsibilities:

44   A child is permitted to accompany us into our new house[4]

Therefore we can also celebrate this day,

46   Your birthday, with glad spirits.

We don't know what the future might bring:

48   May what exists long continue to exist as it is!

And as the autumn, soothing with its mild warmth,

50   Still brings pleasure through many a sunny day,

So let a grain of joy be scattered now and then

52   On our path in the evening of life.

But if nothing else remains according to our wishes,

54   May one thing stand beyond all time:

That you keep your past love for me

56   As mine is faithfully dedicated to you.

Und konnte auch nicht Alles wiederkehren

34 Was unser Leben einst mit Reizen schmückte,

Wie sollten wir uns d'rob mit Recht beschweren,

36 Gab's doch dafür auch, was uns neu beglückte

Ein eig'nes Heim war uns vergönnt zu gründen,

38 Dein ganzer Stolz und Deine ganze Freude;

Natur hier mit Geschmacke zu verbinden,

40 Schaffst sinnig Du, woran das Aug' sich weide.

Und wenn, wo sonst wir Wohnung aufgeschlagen,

42 Von Dir begrüsst ward wohl ein Gast zu Zeiten,

Jetzt kannst Du noch von höh'ren Pflichten sagen :

44 In's neue Heim durft' uns ein Kind begleiten.

So dürfen wir denn auch den heut'gen Tag,

46 Dein Wiegenfest, mit frohem Muth begehen.

Nicht wissen wir, was Zukunft bringen mag :

48 Mög', was besteht, noch lange so bestehen !

Und wie der Herbst, mit milder Wärme labend,

50 Durch manche sonn'ge Tage noch erfreut,

So sei uns auf den Weg am Lebensabend

52 Ein Körnlein Freude ab und zu gestreut.

Wenn aber sonst Nichts nach den Wünschen bliebe,

54 So steh' doch Eines über aller Zeit :

Erhalte Du mir Deine alte Liebe,

56 Wie sie Dir treulich wird von mir geweiht.

F. *[Declaration About Schreber Societies] (1907)[1]*

Declaration

In connection with the execution of the will of Mrs. Pauline Schreber, widow of Dr. Schreber, by which she left 500 marks to each of the existing Schreber societies in Leipzig, a letter with the following content was printed some time ago in one or more Leipzig papers:

"As is generally known, Mrs. Schreber bequeathed 500 marks to each of the Schreber societies that belong to the Leipzig League. The societies which do not belong to the League, but which function according to the ideas of Dr. Schreber, felt discriminated against by this, and they turned to the Schreber heirs. In their behalf Senate President Dr. Paul Schreber in Dresden informed the petitioners that no objections could be made to the proceedings of the Leipzig League in the distribution of the sum offered. He has been instructed by the heirs, however, to send the petitioning Schreber societies a one-time amount of 250 marks each in recognition of the fact that they worked conscientiously like the League societies in the spirit of their deceased father, Dr. Schreber-Leipzig."

The mentioned letter came to my attention only at a late date. In the meantime the question as to what extent we, the heirs of Mrs. Schreber, should bestow of our own accord certain gifts on the Schreber societies in Leipzig which do not belong to the League has been most completely settled between us and the participating societies. Yet, I feel obliged, in order to counter misunderstandings in the circles of the League societies, to explain that the above letter contains quite a preponderance of objective errors.

I never said in the letter directed to the concerned societies that we, the heirs, "could make no objections to the distribution of the League of Schreber Societies,"—for, as the League of Schreber Societies had absolutely nothing to distribute, the amount of the bequests was, rather, paid out directly to the individual societies in our charge.

I have in no way offered the explanation to anybody at all that the petitioning societies should receive a one-time sum of 250 marks each—the sums awarded in reality were indeed quite different amounts.

Finally, it never occurred to me to express myself as is claimed: "recognition that the petitioning Schreber societies worked conscientiously like the League societies in the spirit of our father." Rather, I

F. *[Erklärung über Schrebervereine (1907)]*

Erklärung

In Betreff der Ausführung des Vermächtnisses der Frau Pauline verw. Dr. Schreber, wonach dieselbe die in Leipzig bestehenden Schrebervereine mit je 500 Mark bedacht hat, hat vor einiger Zeit eine Einsendung folgenden Inhalts in einem oder mehreren Leipziger Blättern Aufnahme gefunden :

> "Bekanntlich hat Frau Dr. Schreber den Schrebervereinen, welche dem Leipziger Verbande angehören, je 500 Mark testamentarisch hinterlassen. Dadurch fühlten sich die dem Verbande nicht angehörigen Leipziger Vereine zurückgesetzt, die doch ebenfalls im Sinne Dr. Schrebers wirken, und sie wendeten sich an die Schreber'schen Erben. In deren Auftrag teilte nun Herr Senatspräsident Dr. Paul Schreber in Dresden den Anfragenden mit, dass gegen das Vorgehen des Leipziger Verbands bei der Verteilung der ausgesetzten Summe keine Einwendungen gemacht werden können, doch sei er von den Erben angewiesen worden, den anfragenden Schrebervereinen in Anerkennung, dass sie im Geiste ihres verstorbenen Vaters, Herrn Dr. Schreber-Leipzig, gewissenhaft wie die Verbandsvereine arbeiteten, ihnen einen einmaligen Betrag von je 250 Mark zukommen zu lassen."

Die erwähnte Einsendung ist erst verspätet zu meiner Kenntnis gelangt. Obwohl inzwischen die Frage, inwieweit wir, die Erben der Frau Dr. Schreber, auch den nicht zum Verbande gehörigen Leipziger Schrebervereinen aus freien Stücken gewisse Zuwendungen zuteil werden lassen sollten, zwischen uns und den beteiligten Vereinen nahezu vollständig zur Erledigung gebracht ist, so sehe ich mich doch, um Missdeutungen in den Kreisen der Verbandsvereine zu begegnen, zu der Erklärung veranlasst, dass die obige Einsendung ganz überwiegend sachliche Unrichtigkeiten enthält.

Ich habe in den an die betreffenden Vereine gerichteten Schreiben niemals davon gesprochen, dass wir, die Erben, "gegen die Verteilung des Verbandes der Schrebervereine keine Einwendungen machen können,"—wie denn der Verband der Schrebervereine überhaupt nichts zu verteilen gehabt hat, des Betrag der Vermächtnisses vielmehr an die Einzelvereine in unserem Auftrage unmittelbar ausgezahlt worden ist.

Ich habe keineswegs gegen irgend jemand die Erklärung abgegeben, dass die anfragenden Vereine einen einmaligen Betrag von je 250 Mark erhalten sollten,—die wirklich gewährten Beträge sind in der Tat der Höhe nach ziemlich verschieden.—

only used the phrase for two societies that do not belong to the League as motivation for the donation made to them, that we, after all, had the impression from the information we received that "your esteemed society, in view of its aims and purposes, may not be unlike those belonging to the League."

Therefore, I have an objection to raise against the thoroughly one-sided coloring which has been given to my statements.

Dresden, November 1, 1907
Dr. jur. Paul Schreber, retired Senate President

G. [Texts Written in the Leipzig-Dösen Mental Hospital] (1907–1910)

I.

12/11/07

I am ready to sign a

2   declaration with firm hand, which, as has

somehow become known to me, is to be

4   required of me by the authorized supervisory board

of the Dösen Mental Hospital in view of a

6   in reference to my proposed particular   [sic]

method of interment, request therefore

8   presentation or notification of the

essential contents of an order submitted to

10   that effect.

D. Schreber retired Senate President

Es ist mir endlich nicht beigekommen, einer "Anerkennung, dass die anfragenden Schrebervereine im Sinne unseres Vaters gewissenhaft wie die Verbandsvereine arbeiteten", in der behaupteten Form Ausdruck zu geben, sondern ich habe nur bei zwei Vereinen, die dem Verbande nicht angehören, zur Motivierung der ihnen gemachten Gabe die Wendung gebraucht, wir hätten aus den uns gewordenen Mitteilungen immerhin den Eindruck gewonnen, dass "Ihr geschätzter Verein hinsichtlich seiner Bestrebungen und Ziele den zum Verbande gehörigen Vereinen nicht fernstehen mag."

Ich habe daher gegen die durchaus einseitige Färbung, welche meinen Erklärungen gegeben worden ist, Widerspruch zu erheben.

Dresden, den 1. November 1907.
Dr. jur. Paul Schreber, Senatspräsident a.D.

G. *[Texte, geschrieben in der Heilanstalt Leipzig-Dösen (1907–1910)]*

[Erster Text aus Dösen]

11.XII.07

Ich bin bereit mit fester Hand eine

2 Erklärung zu unterschreiben, die wie mir

  irgendwie bekannt geworden, von der der

4 Heilanstalt Dösen vorgesetzten Aufsichtsbehörde

  hinsichtlich einer in Betreff meiner vorzuneh

6 menden besonderen Bestattungsweise von

  mir erfordert werden soll, bitte also um

8 Vorlegung oder Bekanntmachung des

  wesentlichen Inhalts einer deshalb eingegangenen

10 Verordnung.

D. Schreber Senatspräsident a.D.

II.

I cannot

2   arrange my burial

myself

4   A hospital management

or authority must be

6   available who will make the

necessary prepar-

8   ations even

if it should only

10 be a question of

some decay (of the) living body

symptoms of decay

III.

12/11/07

Should I expect

more information of some

sort this evening

Schreber

IV.

8/9/09

Don't eat

Strawberries

V.

8/9/09

[Zweiter Text aus Dösen]

Meine Beerdigung

2 kann ich nicht selbst

anordnen

4   Es muss eine Anstalts

leitung oder Behörde

6 vorhanden sein die die

erforderlichen Vorbe-

8 reitungen trifft selbst

wenn es sich nur

um irgend

eine Verwesung (am) lebende Körper handeln sol

Verwesungserscheinungen

[Dritter Text]

11.XII.07

Habe ich heute Abend

noch irgendwelche Mittei-

lung zu erwarten

    Schreber

[Vierter Text]

9.8.09

Erdbeeren

Nicht essen

[Fünfter Text aus Dösen]

9/8.09

stays eternally

trust

our Lord

VI.

11/13/1910

do research

on causes

VII.

11/13/1910

[attempt to decipher the text only partially successful]

am eternally damned

am wrong?   [diagonally:]

    and   don't know

[diagonally:]   how to

suffer[1]   continue

VIII.

[Written on the edge or   have really good qualities

between the lines:]   in myself

nor   was always *honest*

lusty   + ha[ve]

debaucheries   *righteously*

                          yielded

                          Dutiful civil servant

                          have not been able

                          to speak to my sisters

                          because the [?] to me

bleibt ewig

unserm

Herren vertrauen

[Sechster Text aus Dösen]

13.11.1910

Ursachen

erforschen

[Siebenter Text aus Dösen]

13.11.1910

[Entzifferungsversuch innerhalb des Textes nur z.T.gelungen]

bin ewig verdammt

habe Unrecht ?

und

[schräg :]

leide

[schräg :]

weiss

nicht

weiter

[Achter Text aus Dösen]

[Am Rande, bzw.

zwischen die

Zeilen geschrieben :]

auch nicht

wollustigen

Ausschweifungen

habe doch recht gutes

in mir

war immer *Ehrlich*

u ha[be]

rechtschaffen

mich

ergeb[en]

Pflichttreuer Beamter

habe mit meinen Schwestern

understand[2] that I . . . with these

innocent

[vertically:]   [slip of paper]: only

look upon God's almighty

power

Translated from the original
German by Christine Granger

Notes

Note: Notes are arranged in sequential numerical order for each text. The English translator's notes are indicated by the abbreviation: e.t. (English translator). All other notes have been added by Han Israëls, who has explained his annotations in his introduction to the new texts. (eds.)

A.

1.   These four poems (A., B., D., and E.) and speech (C.) were written by Paul Schreber for his family on special occasions, as is often done in traditional families who consider their celebrations and milestones as especially important. It should not be assumed automatically that Schreber thought himself particularly gifted as a poet, but rather that he was fulfilling his duty as a caring member of the family who wanted to honor those for whom the celebrations were held.

In the four poems there is a rhyme scheme in the original German of ababcdcdefef, etc., which I have not tried to duplicate. The style even in the original is somewhat stiff and awkward in places, partly because of the writer's attempt to maintain rhyme and rhythm. The translation is as close as possible to the German meaning and tone, resulting in a style that is not the most free-flowing modern English. But it approximates the late nineteenth century poetic style of the author.

The line numbers of the translation match those of the German original much of the time, but some phrases have been moved a line or two ahead or back in the interest of comprehensible English. (e.t.)

2.   Anna Schreber (12/30/1840) married Carl Heinrich Ferdinand Jung (2/25/1839) on July 26, 1864.

3.   Friedrich Moritz Heinrich Jung (b. 4/15/1865, d. 1/28/1868).

4.   Friedrich Jung (b. 11/29/1801, d. 12/6/1884).

5.   Ann Margaretha nee Mengerssen (b. 11/3/1809, d. 11/27/1877).

6.   Pauline Schreber nee Haase (b. 6/29/1815, d. 5/14/1907).

nicht sprechen können

weil mir der [?]

sehe ein dass ich mit diesen

unschuldig

[vertikal :]   Zettel : nur
                                      Gottes Allmacht schauen

7.   Fritz Jung (Carl Friedrich Jung), born 3/23/1867.

8.   Helene Jung (Anna Pauline Helene Jung), born 12/22/1868, and Paula Jung (Anna Pauline Jung), born 4/10/1870.

9.   Wilhelm Jung (Carl Wilhelm Jung), born 2/15/1872.

10.   (Carl Woldemar) Felix Jung, born 5/5/1882.

B.

1.   *Scheldt* is the English name of the river whose source is in northern France (*Escaut* in French) and which then flows through Belgium and the Netherlands (*Schelde* in Flemish and Dutch). (e.t.)

2.   This refers to the Wagner opera *Lohengrin.*

3.   The Pleisse is a river that flows through Leipzig. (e.t.)

4.   This and following occurrences of *you* and *your* in this poem are familiar plural pronouns in German, and so refer to Fritz Jung's family. (e.t.)

5.   Certainly the wife of Fritz Jung, Käthe nee Metsch (10/10/1872).

C.

1.   This speech was written in prose, not poetry, and the original line contents and numbering have been retained as much as possible (e.t.)

2.   *Täufling* in German means the infant being baptized. It is translated in this poem as *godchild,* although she is not the godchild of all the addressees, of course. (e.t.)

3.   On September 30, 1904.

4.   Fritz and Käthe Jung.

5.   Carl-Heinz Jung (b. 12/5/1900) and Herbert (Friedrich) Jung (b. 8/11/1903).

6.   In German, *Vaterland* (the usual word for one's country) means *father country.* (e.t.)

D.

1. *Feuerkugel,* the name of the house in Leipzig, literally means *ball of fire.* (e.t.)

2. Napoleon.

3. On June 29, 1815.

4. *Hohmann's Hof* literally means Hohmann's Court, but in the sense of a country house or manor.

The second word of the name *Schwarzes Bret* means board or plank (it has a double *tt* in modern German), but it could also refer to a number of uses for a board, for example, in the construction of a house, for a table, seat, bench, bed or shelf. (e.t.)

5. Eduard (1812–1864); Therese (1817–1893); Gustav (1822–1871) and Fanny (1827–1895).

6. Wilhelm (Andreas) Haase (b. 1784), and Juliane (Emilia) Wenck (b. 1788).

7. Skat is a German card game. (e.t.)

8. Moritz Schreber, of course.

9. Wilhelm Andreas Haase died in 1837, according to the family tree of G. Friedrich.

10. Pauline Haase and Moritz Schreber were married to this church on October 22, 1838.

11. The pronouns *he* and *him* referring to the mother's deceased husband (Paul Schreber's father) are capitalized in German, which is somewhat out of the ordinary for third person pronouns. In English such capitalization would imply God or some other diety. Line 183, "when he still walked here below," sounds like it might refer to Jesus. In modern German, however, pronouns referring to God are not usually capitalized. But in letters, pronouns, mainly for second person *(you),* are capitalized to show respect, and this may be Schreber's intent here. (e.t.)

12. Honeymoon in the meaning of the first month or period of marriage, not the trip the couple takes after the wedding. The German word for this beginning period of marriage, *Flitterwochen,* means literally *sequin* (or *tinsel*) *weeks,* thus the discussion up to line 209. (e.t.)

13. (Daniel) Gustav was born on July 27, 1839.

14. Juliane Haase nee Wenck died in 1841.

15. Fanny Haase.

16. The boy is of course Daniel Gustav; the girl is Anna (b. 12/30/1840).

17. On July 25, 1842.

18. The fourth child was Sidonie (b. 9/4/1846).

19. The orthopedic clinic of Moritz Schreber.

20. Now called Karl-Liebknecht Strasse.

21. Klara (b. 1/25/1848).

22. A mysterious head ailment, that began in 1851 (not in 1858 or 1859, as is commonly thought).

23. Moritz Schreber died on November 10, 1861.

24. Gustav shot himself on May 7, 1877.

25. Carl Jung (1839–1912) who married Anna; Sabine Behr (1857–1912) who married Paul; Theodor Krause (d. 1906) who married Klara.

26. Anna's children (see Text A).

27. The Haase family owned a manor in both Beerendorf and Schenkenberg.

28. Two villages about thirty miles south of Leipzig. Kösen is a spa.

29. The Schrebers owned a building on this street. It was an important commercial thoroughfare in Leipzig, and was composed largely of Jewish fur trading businesses.

30. Two spots about seventy miles east of leipzig. Oybin is a spa.

31. Dresden.

32. Restaurant quite near the site of Paul Schreber's new house.

33. The new house of Paul Schreber, Angelikastrasse 15a.

34. Georg Jung, Carl's brother, owned a manor in Klitzschen, a village about twenty-five miles east of Leipzig. (*Friedrich*, 1933)

35. These four words, besides rhyming, are dialectal onomatopoeia (except for *Hitschen*) for splashing and slapping sounds. (e.t.)

36. The answer is *"Feuerkugel"* (Fireball).

37. The answer is *"Fürstenhaus"* (Princes' House).

E.

1. Paul's mother had died on May 14, 1907.

2. 1893–1902.

3. In Dresden, Angelikastrasse 15a.

4. Fridoline Schreber (d. 1981).

F.

1. Published in *Der Freund der Schreber-Vereine*, Vol. 3., (1907), pp. 292–93.

G.

1. [suffer] This is first person singular form of the verb, but without a pronoun. (e.t.)

2. [understand] This and all verbs in the twelve-line section are first person singular. (e.t.)

Fig. 1. Daniel Paul Schreber at Rosental Park, Leipzig (ca. 1906). Source: In the possession of the Schreber family, Leipzig.

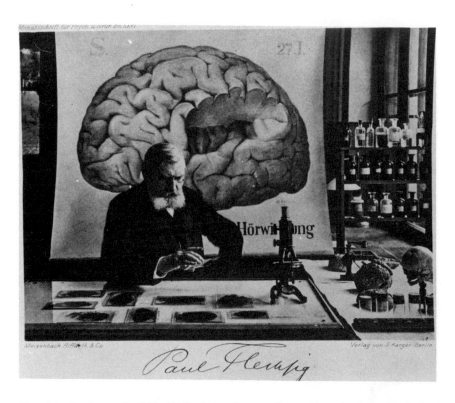

Fig. 1A. Professor Paul Emil Flechsig. Source: From *Festschrift für Paul Emil Flechsig* (1909).

Fig. 2. The Asylum at Sonnenstein. Source: *Deutsche Heil-und Pflegeangtalten für Psychischkranke,* Vol. 1, J. Brealer, ed. (Halle, 1910).

Fig. 3. Leipzig-Dösen Mental Hospital. Source: *Deutsche Heil-und Pflegeangtalten für Psychischkranke*, Vol. 1, J. Brealer, ed. (Halle, 1910).

Fig. 4. Daniel Gottlob Moritz Schreber. Source: Collection of Dr. Günther Friedrich.

Fig. 5. Schreber Family Portrait by August Richter. From Left to Right: Anna Schreber (1840–1944), Pauline Haase Schreber (1815–1907), Daniel Paul Schreber (1842–1911), Klara Schreber (1848–1917), Gustav Schreber (1839–1877), Daniel Gottlob Moritz Schreber (1808–1861), Sidonie Schreber (1846–1924). Source: Photo by Han Israëls.

Fig. 6. Schreber and Jung Family Photograph (ca. 1905). From Left to Right: Son of Helene Jung, Helene Jung (1868–?), Anna Jung (1840–1944), Sidonie Schreber (1846–1924), Klara Schreber Krause (1848–1917), Sabine Behr Schreber (1857–1912), Theodor Krause (d. 1906), Carl Jung (1839–1912). Source: Photo in possession of the Schreber Family descendants, Leipzig.

Fig. 7. Swans on the Estate of Mühlbach. Source: Photo in the possession of the Schreber family descendants, Leipzig.

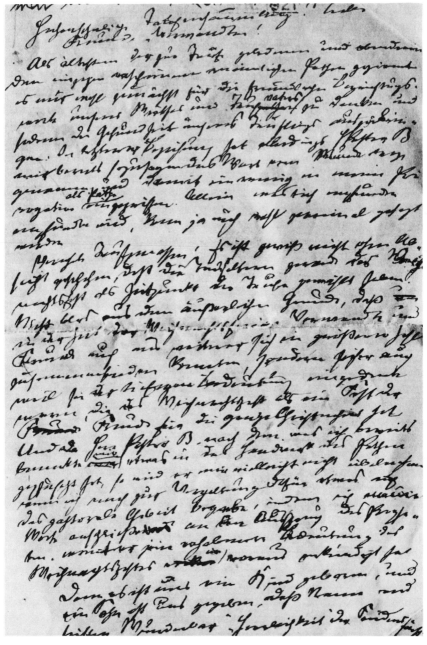

Fig. 8. Christening Speech Written by Paul Schreber (1904). Source: Photo by Han Israëls.

Fig. 9. Pauline Schreber (ca. 1860). Source: Collection of Dr. Günther Friedrich.

Fig. 10. The Garden at Zeitzer Strasse, 43 (ca. 1906). Source: In the possession of the Schreber family, Leipzig.

Fig. 11. The House at Zeitzer Strasse, 1863. Drawing by Klara Schreber. Source: Photo by Han Israëls.

Fig. 12. Sidonie Schreber (right) and a Daughter of Anna Jung with a Bust of Moritz Schreber (ca. 1906). Source: In possession of the Schreber family, Leipzig.

Fig. 14. Schreber's House at Angelikastrasse 15a, Dresden. Source:
Photo by Han Israëls.

Fig. 15. Melody from Wagner's *Siegried* carved in the lintel of Schreber's house at Angelikastrasse 15a, Dresden. Source: Photo by Han Israëls.

Fig. 16. Daniel Paul Schreber with his adopted daughter Fridoline (ca. 1905). Source: In the possession of the Schreber family, Leipzig.

Fig. 17. Daniel Paul Schreber with his adopted daughter Fridoline and a granddaughter of his sister Anna (ca. 1905). Source: In the possession of the Schreber family, Leipzig.

Fig. 18. Page from *Der Freund der Schreber-Vereine* (1913) depicting Moritz Schreber. Source: *Der Freund der Schreber-Vereine* (1913).

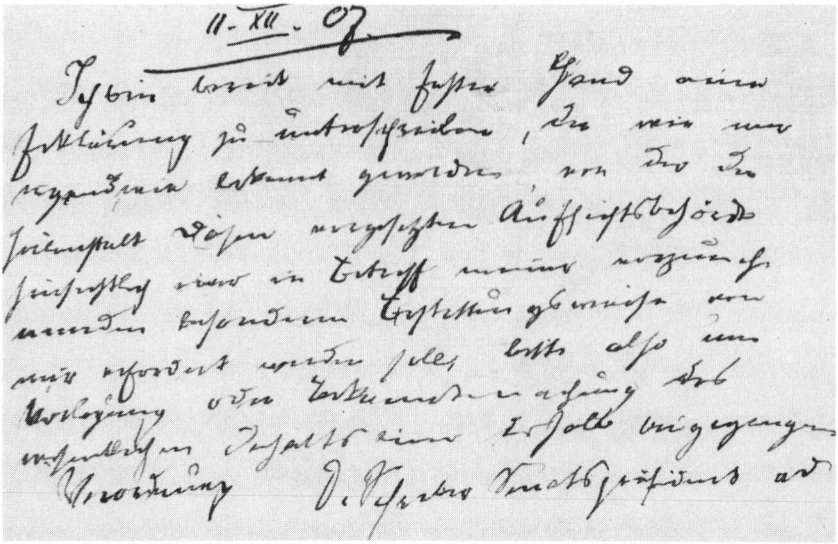

Credit: Courtesy of Han Israëls

Fig. 19. G (Manuscript I) Document written at the Leipzig-Dösen Mental Hospital by Daniel Paul Schreber (Dec. 11, 1907). Source: Photo by Han Israëls.

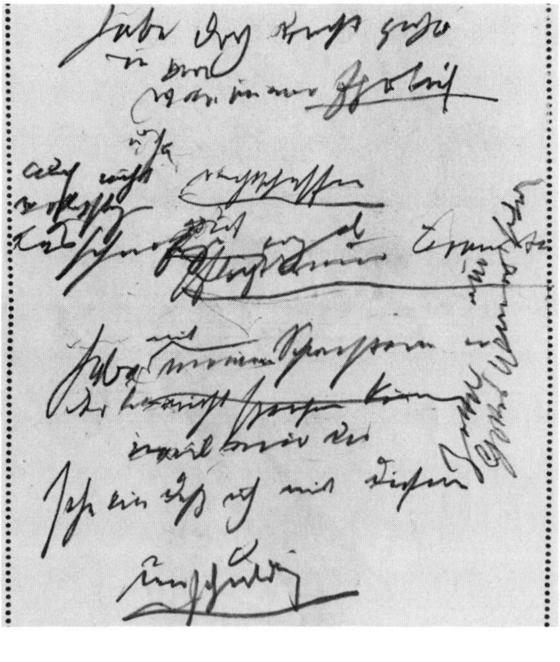

Fig. 20. G (Manuscript VIII). Document written by Daniel Paul Schreber at Leipzig-Dösen Mental Hospital (Undated). Source: Photo by Han Israëls.

Credit: Courtesy of Han Israëls

300

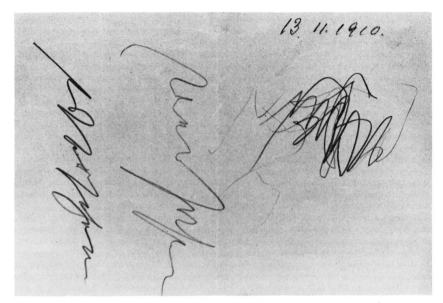

Fig. 21. G. (Manuscript VI) Document written by Daniel Paul Schreber at the Leipzig-Dösen Mental Hospital (Nov. 13, 1910). Source: Photo by Han Israëls.

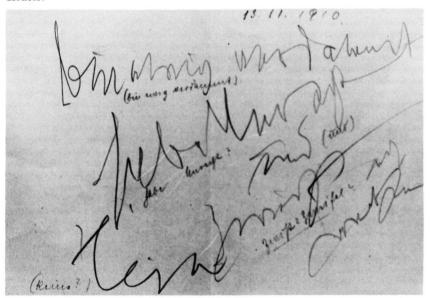

Fig. 22. G (Manuscript VII). Document written by Daniel Paul Schreber at the Leipzig-Dösen Mental Hospital (November 13, 1910). Source: Photo by Han Israëls.

Bibliography*

A(ckermann, W.) "Volksbelehrung als Grundlage der Volksgesundheit: Zum Gedächtniss von Daniel Gottlieb Moritz Schreber." *Die Gesundheits-Führung, Ziel und Weg: Monatsschrift des Hauptamtes für Volksgesundheit der NDSAP* (1943): 218.

Ackermann, W. "Daniel Gottlieb Moritz Schreber." *Der Landarzt* 24 (1943): 287–289.

"Acta der Frau Louise Henriette Pauline verw. Dr. Schreber geb. Haase: Heimathschein für's Ausland betr." Leipzig, 1863. Manuscript. Municipal Archives Leipzig.

Adelmann, Georg. *Ernst August Carus: Eine biographische Skizze.* Dorpat, 1854.

Alby, Jean M. "Concerning Sadomasochistic Fantasy." *Revue Française de Psychanalyse.* Vol. 35, #2–3, 1971. pp. 277–285.

Allgemeine deutsche Biographie. Vol. 32. Leipzig: Duncker & Humblot, 1891.

"Allgemeiner Verband der Schrebervereine Leipzig: Photo's, Postkarten, Zeitungsausschnitte, u.ä. um 1900." Library of the Museum der Geschichte der Stadt Leipzig.

Allgemeines Lexikon der bildenden Künstler von der Antike bis zum Gegenwart. Begründet von Ulrich Thieme und Felix Becker, herausgegeben von Hans Vollmer. Vol. 28. Leipzig: E. A. Seemann, 1934.

Arnemann-GroBschweidnitz. Review of *Denkwürdigkeiten eines Nervenkranken* by Daniel Paul Schreber. *Centralblatt für Nervenheilkunde und Psychiatrie* 14–26 (1903): 500.

Aschaffenburg. Review of *Denkwürdigkeiten eines Nervenkranken* by Daniel Paul Schreber. *Centralblatt für Nervenheilkunde und Psychiatrie* 14–26 (1903): 500.

---

*(The present bibliography is based on that compiled by Han Israëls for his *Schreber, vader en zoon*, Thesis, University of Amsterdam, 1980.)

B., H. "Schrebers Tochter wird hundert Jahre alt: Frau Anna Jung erlebte das Jahr 1848 als achtjähriges Mädchen." *Neue Leipziger Zeitung,* 30/12/1940.

B., K. See Bornstein, Karl.

Badcock, C. "*Freud on Schreber*—Chabot, C. B." *International Journal of Psychoanalysis.* Vol. 64, #2, 1983. pp. 243.

Baginsky, Adolf. *Handbuch der Schul-Hygiene.* 2d ed. Stuttgart: Enke, 1883.

Bakx, Hans. "Schreber, een klassiek psychiatrisch ziektegeval." *NRC-Handelsblad* (Holland), 12/3/1977, p. 12.

Bankhofer, Hademar. "Gepachtete Natur—wieder sehr gefragt" Wochenschau (Austria), 27/3/1977, p. 15.

Bateson, Gregory; Jackson, Don D.; Haley, Jay; and Weakland, John. "Toward a Theory of Schizophrenia." *Behavioral Science* 1 (1956): 251–264.

Bauer, Wilhelm. *Deutsche Kultur von 1830 bis 1870.* Handbuch der Kulturgeschichte, erste Abteilung, vol. 8. Potsdam: Akademische Verlagsgesellschaft Athenaion, 1937.

Baumeyer, Franz. "New Insights into the Life and Psychosis of Schreber." *International Journal of Psycho-Analysis* 33 (1952): 262.

Baumeyer, Franz. "Der Fall Schreber." *Psyche* 9 (1955): 513–536.

Baumeyer, Franz. "The Schreber Case." *International Journal of Psycho-Analysis* 37 (1956): 61–74.

Baumeyer, Franz. "Noch ein Nachtrag zu Freuds Arbeit über Schreber." *Zeitschrift für psychosomatische Medizin und Psychoanalyse,* 16 (1970): 243–245.

Baumeyer, Franz. "Nachträge zum 'Fall Schreber'." In *Bürgerliche Wahnwelt um Neunzehnhundert,* herausgegeben von Peter Heiligenthal und Reinhard Volk. Wiesbaden: Focus-Verlag, 1973.

Baumeyer, Franz. "Le cas Schreber." In *Le cas Schreber,* edited by Eduardo Prado de Oliveira. Paris: Presses Universitaires de France, 1979.

Bayerisches Ärzteblatt 16 (1961): 394–395. "Der Arzt der Kleingärten: Zu Dr. Schrebers 100. Todestag."

Bdt., E. "Zur Geschichte des Turnwesens in Leipzig." *Deutsche Turn-Zeitung* 4 (1859): 70–71.

(Beneke, F.) *Geschichte des Corps Saxonia zu Leipzig 1812 bis 1912.* Herausgegeben von der Genossenschaft "Corps Saxonia". Leipzig, 1912.

Benjamin, Walter. *Gesammelte Schriften.* Vol. 4. Frankfurt am Main: Suhrkamp, 1972.

Berliner Lehrerzeitung: Organ des Berliner Verbands der Lehrer und Erzieher in der Gewerkschaft Erziehung und Wissenschaft 8 (1954): 502. "Dr. med. D. G. H. Schreber (1808–1861): Ein Pionier für naturgebundene Erziehung."

Bernhardt, Walter. "G. M. Schreber und seine Bedeutung für die Entwicklung der Idee der Leibesübungen im 19. Jahrhundert." Staatsexamensarbeit, Institut für Leibesübumgen, Leipzig, 1929.

Biedermann, Karl. "Allgemeines Turnen." *Leipziger Tageblatt,* 7/12/1845, p. 3541–3542.

Biedermann, Karl. *Nein Leben und ein Stück Zeitgeschichte.* Vol. 1, 1812–1849. Breslau: G. Schottländer, 1886.

(Biedermann, Karl.) "Karl Biedermann, von ihm selbst." In *Nachrichten aus dem Allgemeinen Turnverein zu Leipzig für das Jubeljahr 1895.* Leipzig: Allgemeine Turnverein, 1896.

Bilz, Friedrich Eduard. *Lehr- und Nachschlagebuch der naturgemässen Heilweise und Gesundheitspflege: Das neue Naturheilverfahren.* 9th ed. Leipzig: F. E. Bilz, (1895).

Bilz, Friedrich Eduard. *Das neue Naturheilverfahren: Lehr- und Nachschlagebuch der naturgemässen Heilweise und Gesundheitspflege sowie aller verwandten Reformheilmethoden.* Neubearbeitung. Dresden-Radebeul & Leipzig: F. E. Bilz, 1927/1928.

Biographisches Lexikon der hervorragenden Ärzte aller Zeiten und Völker. See Hirsch, August.

Blum, Hans. *Lebenserinnerungen.* Vol. 1, 1841–1870. Berlin: Vossische Buchhandlung, 1907.

Böhmert, Wilhelm. *Die Verteilung des Einkommens in Preussen und Sachsen, mit besonderer Berücksichtigung der GroBstädte und des Landes.* Dresden: O. V. Böhmert, 1898.

Bormann, Friedrich Adolph. *Besprechung der Dr. Schreberschen Schrift: "Ein ärztlicher Blick in das Schulwesen" mit besonderer Berücksichtigung des Turnens in der Volksschule.* Döbeln, (1859).

B(ornstein), K(arl). "Dr. Daniel Gottlieb Moritz Schreber, Leipzig." *Blätter für Volksgesundheitspflege* 31 (1931): 161–162.

Bornstein, Karl. "Dr. Daniel Gottlieb Moritz Schreber, ein Kämpfer für Volkserziehung." *Zeitschrift für ärztliche Fortbildung* 28 (1931): 798.

Brauchle, Alfred. *Naturheilkunde in Lebensbildern.* Leipzig: Philipp Reclam Jun., 1937.

Brauchle, Alfred. *Grosse Naturärzte.* 2d rev. ed. of *Naturheilkunde in Lebensbildern.* Leipzig: Philipp Reclam Jun., 1944.

Brauchle, Alfred. *Zur Geschichte der Physiotherapie: Naturbeilkunde in ärztlichen Lebensbildern.* 4th ed. of *Naturheilkunde in Lebensbildern,* revised by Walter Groh. Heidelberg: Karl F. Haug, 1971.

Breger, L. "Schreber: From Male to Female." *Journal of the American Academy of Psychoanalysis.* Vol. 6, #2, 1978. pp. 123–156.

Bregman, Lucy. "Religion and Madness: Schreber's Memoirs as Personal Myth." *Journal of Religion and Health* 16 (1977): 119–135.

Brehme, Louis. "Dr. med. Carl Hermann Schildbach †." *Jahrbücher der deutschen Turnkunst* 35 (1889): 8–13.

Brocke Hiltrud. *Jugend- und Kindergruppenarbeit: Anregungen und Beispiele für unsere Gruppenleiter und -helfer.* Herausgegeben von der Deutschen Schreberjugend, Bundesverband. Krefeld, 1977.

Brown, Phil. "Review: Recent Anti-Psychiatry Books." *Rough Times,* April-May 1973, p. 19.

Buchheim, Karl. *Deutsche Kultur zwischen 1830 und 1870.* Handbuch der Kulturgeschichte, Abteilung 1 (vol. 9). Frankfurt am Main: Akademische Verlagsgesellschaft Athenaion, 1966.

Buchner, W. *Zur Schulbankfrage.* Berlin: Guttentag, 1869.

Calasso, Roberto. "Nota sui lettori di Schreber." In *Memorie di un malato di nervi* by Daniel Paul Schreber. Milano: Adelphi, 1974a.

Calasso, Roberto. *L'impuro folle.* Milano: Adelphi, 1974b.

Cancro, R. "*The Schreber Case:* Reply." *Psychiatric Annals.* Vol. 9, #8, 1979. pp. 387.

Canetti, Elias. *Macht und Überleben: Drei Essays.* Berlin: Literarisches Colloquium, 1972. English edition: *Crowds and Power* trans. Carol Stewart (New York, Ferrar, Straus, Giroux, 1984): pp. 434–462.

Canetti, Elias. *Die Provinz des Menschen: Aufzeichnungen 1942–1972.* Frankfurt am Main: Fischer Taschenbuch, 1976a.

Canetti, Elias. *Wat de mens betreft: Aantekeningen, 1942–1972.* Amsterdam: De Arbeiderspers, 1976b.

Carr, Arthur C. "Observations on Paranoia and their Relationship to the Schreber Case." In *The Schreber Case* by William G. Niederland. New York: Quadrangle/The New York Times Book Co., 1974.

Catalogus van de paedagogische bibliotheek van het Hederlandsch Onderwijzers-Genootschap. Amsterdam: 1891.

Chabot, C. Barry. *Freud on Schreber: Psychoanalytic Theory and the Critical Act.* (University of Massachusetts Press, 1982).

Chartier, Didier, A. "Freud et Haizmann: L'Artiste et l'Analyste." *Psychologie Medicale.* Vol. 14, #9, 1982. pp. 1363–1366.

Chasseguet-Smirgel, Janine. "A propos du délire transsexuel du président Schreber." *Revue française de psychanalyse* 60 (1966): 93–120.

Church, N. "The Schreber Memoirs: Myth or Personal Lamentation." *Journal of Religion and Health.* Vol. 18, #4, 1979. pp. 313–326.

Clare, Anthony. "Love or Hatred." *New Society* 27 (1974): 270–271.

Cohen, Alain A. "Proust and President Schreber: A Theory of Original 'Citation' or a Psychoanalytic Theory of Philosophic Desire." *Evolution Psychiatre.* Vol. 41, #2, 1976. pp. 437–450.

Cohen, David. "The Dr. Spock of the 1840s." *Times Educational Supplement,* 4/5/1973.

Colas, Dominique. "Le despotism pédagogique du docteur Schreber." *Critique: Revue générale des publications françaises et étrangères* 31 (1975): 78–91.

Croufer, Francis. "La vie du Président Schreber, une ordalie relative à la paternité?" *Les feuillets psychiatriques de Liège* 3 (1970): 214–251.

Daniels, George Eaton. Review of *The Schreber Case* by William G. Niederland. *Bulletin of the New York Academy of Medicine* 51 (1975): 1331–1343.

Deleuze, Gilles and Guattari, Félix. *L'anti-Oedipe.* Vol. 1 of *Capitalisme et schizophrénie* Paris: Les Éditions de Minuit, 1972.

deMause, Lloyd. "The Evolution of Childhood." In *The History of Childhood,* edited by Lloyd deMause. Reprint. New York, Hagerstown, San Francisco, London: Harper & Row, 1975.

Deutsche Schreberjugend, Herausgeber. "Arbeitshilfen für den Gruppenleiter." Mimeographed. n.p. n.d. (*c.* 1958).

Deutsche Schreberjugend, Herausgeber. "Over 100 Years of the German Schreberyouth Organization." Mimeographed. n.p. n.d. (1979 or a little earlier).

Deutsche Schreberjugend, Landesgruppe Berlin, Herausgeber. "Selbstdarstellung der Deutschen Schreberjugend." Mimeographed. (Berlin,) n.d.

Diem, Liselotte. "Aus Schrebers Kallipädie 1858: Das Kind in seinen Spielen." *Die Leibeserziehung* 7 (1958): 390–393.

Donadeo, John. Report of the talk on 29/9/1959 by William G. Niederland, "The 'Miracled-Up' World of Schreber's Childhood" and of the subsequent discussion. *Psychoanalytic Quarterly* 29 (1960): 301–304.

Dresdner Zeitung, 1944 no. 277 p. 3. "Die älteste Leipzigerin gestorben." (Source: Sächsische Landesbibliothek Dresden.)

Eagle, M. "*Freud on Schreber: Psychoanalytic Theory and the Critical Act*—Chabot, C. B." *Contemporary Psychology.* Vol. 28, #2, 1983. p. 149.

Edwards, A. "Schreber's Delusional Transference: Disorder of Self." *Journal of Analytic Psychology.* Vol. 23, #3, 1978. pp. 242–247.

Ehrenwald, Jan. "The Symbiotic Matrix of Paranoid Delusions and the Homosexual Alternative." *The American Journal of Psycho-Analysis* 20 (1960): 49–59.

Ehrenwald, Jan. *Neurosis in the Family and Patterns of Psychosocial Defence: A Study of Psychiatric Epidemiology.* New York: Hoeber, 1963.

Eickhoff, F.-W. Review of *Der Fall Schreber* by William G. Niederland. *Psyche* 33 (1979): 1058–1062.

Eigler, Gernot. "Die Wunder der Erziehung." Television play ZDF West Germany 21/9/1978, 22.05–23.15.

Elias, Norbert. *The Civilizing Process: The History of Manners.* Oxford: Blackwell, 1978.

Elliott-Smith, Monique. "La pédagogie Schreberienne." *Le coq-heron,* no. 37–38, June-July 1973, p. 4–8.

Engelsing, Rolf. *Analphabetentum und Lektüre: Zur Sozialgeschichte des Lesens in Deutschland zwischen feudaler und industrieller Gesellschaft.* Stuttgart: Metzler, 1973.

Enriquez, Micheline, *Aut carrefours de la haine: Paranoía, masochisme, apathie* (Paris, Descliede Brouwer, 1984).

Engelsing, Rolf. *Zur Sozialgeschichte deutscher Mittel- und Unterschichten.* Kritische Studien zur Geschichtswissenschaft vol. 4. 2d rev. ed. Göttingen: Vandenhoeck & Ruprecht, 1978.

Eschner, Max, Herausgeber. *Leipzigs Denkmäler: Denksteine und Gedenktafeln.* Leipzig: Otto Wigand, 1910.

Eulenberg, Hermann and Bach, Theodor. *Schulgesundheitslehre: Das Schulhaus und das Unterrichtswesen, vom hygienischen Standpunkte für Arzte, Lehrer, Verwaltungsbeamte und Architekten.* Berlin: J. J. Heines Verlag, 1891.

Euler, Carl, Herausgeber. *Encyklopädisches Handbuch des gesamten Turnwesens und der verwandten Gebiete.* Vol. 2. Wien, Leipzig: A. Pichler's Witwe & Sohn, 1895.

F., C. "Ein Vorkämpfer für das Jugendspiel: Zur Erinnerung an Dr. Daniel Gottlieb Moritz Schreber." *Gartenlaube* (1908): 891–892.

Fahrner. *Das Kind und der Schultisch: Die schlechte Haltung der Kinder beim Schreiben und ihre Folgen, sowie die Mittel, derselben in Schule und Haus abzuhelfen.* 2d ed. Zürich: Schulthess, 1865.

Fairbairn, R. D. "Considerations Arising Out of the Schreber Case." *British Journal of Medical Psychology.* Vol. 19, #2, 1956. pp. 113–127.

Festschrift für Paul Flechsig: Zur Feier seines 25, jührigen Jubiläums als ordentlicher Professor an der Universität Leipzig. Monatsschrift für Psychiatrie und Neurologie 26 (1909), Ergänzungsheft. Berlin: S. Karger, 1909.

Festschrift zur fünfzigjährigen Jubelfeier des allgemeinen Turnvereins zu Leipzig 1845–1895. Leipzig: Allgemeine Turnverein, 1895.

Finke, Wilko. "Leben und Wirken Dr. Daniel Gottlob Moritz Schrebers." Diplomarbeit, Deutsche Hochschule für Körperkultur, Leipzig, 1975.

Flechsig, Paul (Emil). *Meine myelogenetische Hirnlehre: Mit biographischer Einleitung.* Berlin: Julius Springer, 1927.

Foerster, O. G. "Moritz Schreber: Zur 125. Wiederkehr seines Geburtstages am 15. Oktober." *Allgemeine deutsche Lehrerzeitung* 62 (1933): 680–681.

Fortuin, Johanna. Review of *De ondergang van Daniel Paul Schreber* by Morton Schatzman and Sigmund Freud. *Jeugd en samenleving,* 6/2/1976, p. 143–144.

Freiheitskampf 1944 no. 311 p. 3. "Die älteste Leipzigerin gestorben." (Source: Sächsische Landesbibliothek Dresden.)

Freud, Sigmund. "Psychoanalytische Bemerkungen über einen autobiographisch beschriebenen Fall von Paranoia (Dementia paranoides)." *Jahrbuch für psychoanalytische und psychopathologische Forschungen* 3 1st half (1911): 9–68.

Freud, Sigmund. *The Case of Schreber, Papers on Technique and Other Works.* The Standard Edition of the Complete Psychological Works of Sigmund Freud, edited by James Strachey, vol. 12 (1911–1913). London: The Hogarth Press and the Institute of Psycho-Analysis, 1958.

Freud, Sigmund. *Werke aus den Jahren 1909–1913.* Gesammelte Werke, vol. 8. 4th ed. Frankfurt am Main: S. Fischer Verlag, 1964.

Freud, Sigmund. *Zwang, Paranoia und Perversion.* Studienausgabe, vol. 7. Frankfurt am Main: S. Fischer Verlag, 1973.

Freud, Sigmund and Jung, Carl Gustav. *Briefwechsel.* Frankfurt am Main: S. Fischer Verlag, 1974.

Freund der Schreber-Vereine 4 (1908): 210–212. "Dr. Daniel Gottlieb Moritz Schreber."

Friedreich's Blätter für gerichtliche Medicin und Sanitätspolizei 55 (1904): 239 and 392. Reviews of *Denkwürdigkeiten eines Nervenkranken* by Daniel Paul Schreber.

Friedrich, Edm. "Dr. Moritz Schreber †." *Neue Jahrbücher für die Turnkunst* 7 (1861): 321–322.

Friedrich, Günther. "Stammbaum der Familie Schreber." Manuscript. n.p.

Friedrich, Günther. "Ahnentafel der Familien Wenck und Haase." Manuscript. n.p. 1932/1933.

Friedrich, Günther. "Stammtafel der Familie Jung." Manuscript. n.p. 1933.

Friedrich, Günther. "Über den Ursprung der 'Schrebergärten'." *Schleswiger Hachrichten,* 25/4/1956. (Source: G. Friedrich.)

Fritzsche, Hugo. "Schreberverein oder Gartenverein?" *Der Freud der Schreber-Vereine* 3 (1907): 279–282.

Fritzsche, Hugo. "Dr. Daniel Gottlieb Moritz Schreber, ein Kämpfer für Volkserziehung: Zur 50. Wiederkehr seines Todestages († 11.Nov. 1861)." *Der Freund der Schrebervereine* 7 (1911): 179–181 and 195–198.

Fritzsche, Hugo. "Aus Dr. Moritz Schrebers Leben." *Garten und Kind: Zeitschrift der mitteldeutschen Schrebergärtner* 6 (1926): 12–14.

Fritzsche, Hugo and Brückner, G. A. *Dr. med. Schreber und die Leipziger Schreber-Vereine mit besonderer Berücksichtigung des Schrebervereins der Nordvorstadt: Denkschrift zur Deutschen Städteausstellung zu Dresden.* Herausgegeben vom Schreber-Verein der Nordvorstadt. Leipzig, 1903.

G., W. "Griff in die Geschichte." *Die geistige Welt,* 11/10/1958. (Source: G. Friedrich.)

Gasch, F. Rudolf. "Moritz Schreber." In *Nachrichten aus dem allgemeinen Turnverein zu Leipzig, für das Jubeljahr 1895.* Leipzig, Allgemeiner Turnverein, 1896.

Gasch, (F.) Rudolf, Herausgeber. *Handbuch des gesamten Turnwesens und der verwandten Leibesübungen.* Wien, Leipzig: A. Pichlers Witwe & Sohn, 1920.

Gasch, (F.) Rudolf, Herausgeber. *Handbuch des gesamten Turnwesens und der verwandten Leibesübungen.* Vol. 2. 2nd ed. Wien, Leipzig: A. Pichlers Witwe & Sohn, 1928.

Geahchan, Dominique J. "Metapsychological References for a Psychotherapy of Psychoses in an Institution." *Interpretation.* Vol. 4, #1–2, 1970. pp. 11–40.

Gesundheitswesen und Desinfektion 64 (1972): 160–161. "In Memoriam Dr. Schreber."

Gillie, Oliver. "Freud's Missing Link." *The Sunday Times,* 25/3/1973, p. 27.

Gmelin, W. "Horitz Schreber zum Gedenken." *Der Naturarzt: Zeitschrift für naturgemässe Lebens- und Heilweise* 83 (1961): 341.

Goudsblom, Johan. *Sociology in the Balance: A critical Essay.* New York: Columbia University Press, 1977.

Goudsblom, Johan. *Nihilism and Culture.* Oxford: Blackwell, 1980.

Gr., A. "Die Menschennatur als Ganzes auffassen: Moritz Schreber forderte die Einheit von verstandesgemässer Erziehung und praktischer Lebensertüchtigung." *Thüringische Landeszeitung,* 25/10/1958, n.p.

Graefe, Rudolf. "Vorwort zur sechsundzwanzigsten Auflage." In *Ärztliche Zimmergymnastik* by Daniel Gottlob Moritz Schreber. 28th ed. Leipzig: Friedrich Fleischer, 1902.

Green, André. "Transcription d'origine inconnue." *Nouvelle Revue de Psychanalyse,* no. 16 (1977): 27–63.

Greenleaf, Eric. "The Schreber Case: Remarks on Psychoanalytic Explanation." *Psychotherapy: Theory, Research and Practice.* Vol. 6, #1, 1969. pp. 16–20.

Groh, Walter. *Priessnitz, Grundlagen des klassischen Naturheilverfahrens.* Herausgegeben von Hans Haferkamp. Schriftenreihe des Zentralverbandes der Ärzte für Naturheilverfahren, vol. 3. Hamburg: Medizinisch-literarischer Verlag Dr. Blume & Co., 1960.

Grosse, Karl. *Geschichte der Stadt Leipzig von der ältesten bis auf die neueste Zeit.* Rev. ed. Vol. 1. Leipzig: Alwin Schmidt's Verlag, 1897.

Grosse, Karl. *Gesichte der Stadt Leipzig von der ältesten bis auf die neueste Zeit.* Rev. ed. Vol. 2. Leipzig: Alwin Schmidt's Verlag, 1898.

Grotstein, J. S. "The Schreber Case: A Reappraisal." *International Journal of Psychoanalytic Psychotherapy.* Vol. 10, 1984. pp. 321–375.

H., K. F. "Bock und Schreber—Gesundheitserzieher vor hundert Jahren." *Ärztliche Praxis: Die Wochenzeitschrift des praktischen Arztes* 11 (1959): 1078.

Haeckel, Ernst. *Natürliche Schöpfungsgeschichte: Gemeinverständliche wissenschaftliche Vorträge über die Entwickelungslehre im Allgemeinen und diejenige von Darwin, Goethe und Lamarck im Besonderen, über die Anwendung derselben auf der Ursprung des Menschen und andere damit zusammenhängende Grundfragen der Naturwissenschaft.* Berlin: Reimer, 1868.

Hänsch, Rudolf. "Moritz Schreber, Ernst Innocenz Hauschild und die Entstehung der Schrebervereine." *Leipzig* 2 (1925): pp. 288–291.

Hagen, Reinhard von dem. "Dr. Schreber und sein Werk: Zum allgremeinen sächsischen Schrebertag am 25. August." *Dresdner Anzeiger*, 23/8/1929a, p. 6.

Hagen, Reinhard von dem. "Dr. Schreber und sein Werk." *Dresdner Nachrichten*, 23/8/1929b. p. 6.

Harding, D. W. "Crazy Mixed-Up Kids." *New York Review of Books*, 14/6/1973, p. 24–27.

Hartmann, Ph. Karl. *Glückseligkeitslehre für das physische Leben des itenschen: Ein distetischer Führer durch das Leben.* Revised by (Daniel Gottlob) Moritz Schreber. 4th ed. Leipzig: Carl Geibel, 1861.

Hartung, D. "Trauerrede beim Begräbnis der Frau verw. Dr. Schreber." Mimeographed. Leipzig, 17/5/1907.

Hauschild, Ernst Innocenz. *Vierzig pädagogische Briefe aus der Schule an das Elternhaus.* Leipzig: Gustav Grädner, 1862.

Heijer, Jac. "Paul Gallis: Het decor is meer dan een plaatje." *NRC-Handelsblad* (Holland), 27/8/1976, p. CS3.

Heilbrun, Kurt. "Die Entwicklung der Kleingartenbewegung bis zum Jahre 1921 und ihr Einfluss auf die Volksernährung." Dissertation, Rostock, 1922.

Heiligenthal, Peter and Volk, Reinhard, Herausgeber. *Bürgerliche Wahnwelt um Neunzehnhundert: "Denkwürdigkeiten eines Nervenkranken" von Daniel Paul Schreber, mit Aufsätzen von Franz Baumeyer, einem Vorwort, einem Materialanhang und sechs Abbildungen. Der Fall Schreber, vol. 1.* Wiesbaden: Focus-Verlag, 1973.

Heilmann, Ernst. *Geschichte der Arbeiterbewegung in Chemnitz und dem Erzgebirge.* Chemnitz: Sozialdemokratischer Verein für den 16. sächsischen Reichstagswahlkreis Max Müller, (1911).

Heindl, Joh. Bapt., Herausgeber. *Galerie berühmter Pädagogen, verdienter Schulmänner, Jugend- und Volksschriftsteller und Componisten aus der Gegenwart in Biographien und biographischen Skizzen.* Vol. 2. München: Joseph Anton Finsterlin, 1859.

Hemelrijk, Jan. *Er is een weg naar de vrijheid: Zeven maanden concentratiekamp.* Hilversum, Antwerpen: W. de Haan and Standaard-Boekhandel, 1965.

Hennig, Carl. "Vorwort zur zweiten Auflage." In *Das Buch der Erziehung an Leib und Seele* by Daniel Gottlob Moritz Schreber. 2d rev. ed. of *Kallipädie.* Leipzig: Friedrich Fleischer, (1882).

Hirsch, August, Herausgeber. *Biographisches Lexikon der hervorragenden Ärzte aller Zeiten und Völker.* Vol. 5. Wien, Leipzig: Urban & Schwarzenberg, 1887.

(Hirschfeld, Adolf and Franke, August.) *Geschichte der Leipziger Burschenschaft Germania 1859–1879: Festgabe zum zwanzigsten Stiftungsfeste am 25., 26., 27. und 28. Juli 1879.* (Leipzig: Dr. v. G. G. Naumann, 1879.)

Hirth, Georg, Herausgeber. *Das gesammte Turnwesen: Ein Lesebuch für deutsche Turner, enthaltend gegen 100 abgeschlossene Muster-Darstellungen von den vorzüglichsten alteren und neueren Turnschriftstellern.* Leipzig: Ernst Keil, 1865.

Hoffmann. "Aus der Geschichte der Medizin: Daniel Gottlob Moritz Schreber, ein Gesundheitserzieher des deutschen Volkes im 19. Jahrhundert." *Der Landarzt* 21 (1940): 5–8.

Hoffmann, Carl Sam. *Historische Beschreibung der Stadt, des Amtes und der Dioces Oschatz in ältern und neuern Zeiten.* Vol. 1. Oschatz, 1815.

Hoffmann, Walther Gustav. *Das Wachstum der deutschen Wirtschaft seit der Mitte des 19. Jahrhunderts.* Enzyklopädie der Rechtsund Staatswissenschaft, Abteilung Staatswissenschaft. Berlin, Heidelberg, New York: Springer-Verlag, 1965.

Illustrirte Zeitung, 1/2/1862, p. 80–82. "Daniel Gottlob Moritz Schreber."

Infeld. Review of *Denwürdigkeiten eines Nervenkranken* by Daniel Paul Schreber. *Wiener Medizinische Presse* 46 (1905): 1660.

Israëls, Han. *Schreber, vader en zoon.* Thesis, University of Amsterdam, 1980. Republished as *Schreber: Father and Son* (Madison, Conn., International Universities Press, 1987).

J. "Nekrolog: Dr. med. Daniel Gottlob Moritz Schreber." *Leipziger Tageblatt,* 15/11/1851, p. 5813, 5814.

Jaccard, Roland. "Sciences humaines: Schreber père et fils." *Le Monde,* 6/4/1979, p. 23.

Jahn, Walter, "Vater der Laubenkolonie: Zum heutigen 75. Todestage des Arztes Schreber." *Berliner Lokal-Anzeiger,* 10/11/1936, 4. Beiblatt, p. 1.

Janssen, J. J. "Garden Club." *Sunday Times,* 1/4/1973, p. 13.

Jaynes, Julian. *The Origins of Consciousness and the Breakdown of the Bicameral Mind.* (Boston, Houghton Mifflin, 1976). pp. 414–416.

Juhnke, Klaus. "Darstellung und Einschätzung Dr. Daniel Gottlob Moritz Schrebers in der deutschsprachigen Sporthistorischen Literatur." Diplomarbeit, Deutsche Hochschule für Körperkultur, Leipzig, 1975.

Jung, Anna, geb. Schreber; Jung, Carl; Schreber, (Daniel) Paul; Schreber, Sidonie; and Krause, Klara, geb. Schreber. Letter "an das Polizeiamt zu Leipzig." Type-script. Leipzig and Dresden, Juni 1907. Municipal Archives Leipzig.

Jung, Carl. Letter beginning "Sehr geehrter Herr!" Leipzig, 26/3/1901. Manuscript collection Staatsbibliothek Preussischer Kulturbesitz.

Jung, Käte, geb. Metsch. "Erinnerungen an alt Leipzig und die Grossmama (Pauline) Schreber (geb. Haase)." 1907. Transcript, il.p. n.d.

Katan, Maurits. "Schreber's Hereafter: Its Building-Up (Aufbau) and Its Downfall." In *The Schreber Case* by William G. Hiederland. New York: Quadrangle/The New York Times Book Co., 1974.

Katan, Maurits. "Childhood Memories As Contents of Schizophrenic Hallucinations and Delusions." *The Psychoanalytic Study of the Child* 40 (1975): 387–394.

Katan, Maurits. "Schreber's Hallucinations About Little Men." *International Journal of Psychoanalysis*. Vol. 31, 1950. pp. 32–35.

Katan, Maurits. "Further Remarks About Schreber's Hallucinations." *International Journal of Psychoanalysis*. Vol. 33, 1952. pp. 429–432.

Katan, Maurits. "Schreber's Delusion of the End of the World." *Psychoanalytic Quarterly.* Vol. 18, 1949, pp. 60–66.

Katan, Maurits. "Schreber's Pre-psychotic Phase." *International Journal of Psychoanalysis*. Vol. 34, 1953. pp. 43–51.

Katan, Maurits. "The Importance of the Non-psychotic Part of the Personality in Schizophrenia." *International Journal of Psychoanalysis*. Vol. 35, 1954. pp. 119–128.

Katan, Maurits. "Childhood Memories as Contents of Schizophrenic Hallucinations and Delusions." *Psychoanalytic Study of the Child.* Vol. 30, 1975. pp. 357–374.

Katan, Maurits. "Schrebers Jenseits: sein Aufbau und Untergang." In *Der Fall Schreber* by William G. Niederland. Frankfurt am Main: Suhrkamp Verlag, 1978.

Katan, Maurits. "Schreber: l'au délà, sa construction (Aufbau) et sa chute." In *Le Cas Schreber,* edited by Eduardo Prado de Oliveira. Paris: Presses Universitaires de France, 1979.

K-d, E. M. "Der Arzt der Kleingärten: Zu Dr. Schrebers 76. Todestag am 10. November." *Wiener Medizinische Wochenschrift* 86 (1936): 1262–1263.

Keilman (Bernd Carson). "Die Idee des Dr. Schreber." Kleingärtner und Oho, instalment 6. *Die Leipziger Abendzeitung*, 24/12/1973, p. 4.

Kern, Stephen. *Anatomy and Destiny: A Cultural History of the Human Body.* Indianapolis, New York: The Bobbs-Merril Company, 1975.

Kilian, G. Werner (gwk). "Zum 150. Geburtstag von Moritz Schreber: Ein Leben 'dem Heile künftiger Geschlechter'." *Union* (Leipzig), 15/10/1958a, n.p.

Kilian, G. Werner. "Vorkämpfer des Gesundseins: Vor 150 Jahren am 15. Oktober wurde Dr. Moritz Schreber geboren." *Neue Zeit* (Deutschland-Ausgabe), 15/10/1958b, p. 8.

Kilian, G. Werner. "Ist Moritz Schreber noch gegenwartsnah?" *Beiträge zur Orthopädie und Traumatologie* 7 (1960): 416–421.

Kilian, (G.) Werner. "1. Die Anfänge der Orthopädie in Leipzig bis zur Gründung des Universitätsinstitutes." Type-script. (Leipzig, 1977.)

Kilian, G. Werner and Uibe, Peter. "Daniel Gottlob Moritz Schreber." *Forschungen und Fortschritte* 32 (1958): 335–340.

Kitay, P. M. "A Reinterpretation of the Schreber Case." *International Journal of Psychoanalysis.* Vol. 44, 1953. pp. 191–194.

Klein, Robert H. "The Lack of Differentiation Between Male and Female in Schreber's Autobiography." *Journal of Abnormal Psychology.* Vol. 83, #3, 1974. pp. 234–239.

Klein, Robert H. "A Computer Analysis of the Schreber Memoirs." *Journal of Nervous and Mental Disease.* Vol. 162, #6, 1976. pp. 373–384.

Klein, Robert H. "A Reply to Comments on 'A Computer Analysis of the Schreber Memoirs.'" *Journal of Nervous and Mental Illness.* Vol. 162, #6, 1976. pp. 394–400.

Kleine, Hugo Otto. *Ärzte kämpfen für Deutschland: Historische Bilder aus fünf Jahrhunderten deutschen Arztwirkens.* Stuttgart: Hippokrates-Verlag, 1942.

Kleine, Hugo Otto. *Ärzte in den Sturmen der Zeit: Medizinhistorische Miniaturen aus 5 Jahrhunderten.* Ulm/Donau: Haug, 1958.

Kliem, Manfred. *Friedrich Engels: Dokumente seines Lebens, 1820–1895.* Leipzig: Philipp Reclam Jun., 1977.

Kloss, M. "Dr. med. D. G. M. Schreber, geb. den 15. October 1808, † den 10. November 1861." *Neue Jahrbücher für die Turnkunst* 8 (1862): 10–16.

Knight, Robert P. "The Relationship of Latent Homosexuality to the Mechanism of Paranoid Delusions." *Bulletin of the Menninger Clinic* 4 (1940): 149–159.

Knorr. "Reisebericht über den Besuch gymnastischer Anstalten Nord- und Süddeutschlands." *Neue Jahrbücher für die Turnkunst* 4 (1858): 18–28.

Kochendorf, Richard. *Heilgymnastik gegen Nervosität nach dem von Daniel Gottlob Moritz Schreber entworfenen System.* Leipzig: Siegbert Schnurpfeil, 1907.

Kochendorf, Richard. *Lungen-Gymnastik ohne Geräte: Nach dem System von Dr. med. Daniel Gottlob Moritz Schreber.* Leipzig: Siegbert Schnurpfeil, 1907.

Koehler, K. G. "The Schreber Case and Affective Illness: A Research Diagnostic Reassessment." *Psychological Medicine.* Vol. 11, #4, 1981. pp. 689–696.

Koetschau, K. ".August Richter." *Wallraf-Richartz-Jahrbuch* 1 (1924): 151–157.

Kötzschke, Rudolf and Kretzschmar, Hellmut. *Sächsische Geschichte: Werden und Wandlungen eines deutschen Stammes und seiner Heimat im Rahmen der deutschen Geschichte.* 1935. Reprint. Frankfurt am Main: Weidlich, 1965.

Kohut, Heinz. *The Analysis of the Self: A Systematic Approach to the Psychoanalytic Treatment of Narcissistic Personality Disorders.* The Psychoanalytic Study of the Child, Monograph no. 4. New York: International Universities Press, 1971.

Kohut, Heinz. *The Search for the Self: Selected Writings, 1950–1978.* Edited by Paul H. Ornstein. 2 vols. New York: International Universities Press, 1978.

Krause, Klara, geb. Schreber. Passage from a letter to G. Richard Siegel. *Der Freund der Schreber-Vereine* 5 (1909): 75.

Krey, Bernh. "Schrebers Traum: Ein szenischer Prolog mit spiel und Reigen." *Der Freund der Schreber-Vereine* 9 (1913): 4–7.

Kron, H. Review of *Denkwürdigkeiten eines Nervenkranken* by Daniel Paul Schreber. *Deutsche Medizinal-Zeitung* 24 (1903): 918.

L., A. " 'Alt zu werden kann schön sein! Letzte Tochter. Dr. Schrebers wird 98 Jahre alt." *Leipziger Neueste Nachrichten,* 30/12/1938. (Source: G. Friedrich.)

L., A. "Eine hundertjährige Leipzigerin." *Leipziger Neueste Nachrichten,* 30/12/1940. (Source: descendants of Moritz Schreber.)

L., H. "Leipziger Stadttheater: 'Der ewige Jude'." *Leipziger Tageblatt*, 28/12/1845, p. 3806, 3807.

Lacan, Jacques. *De la psychose paranoiaque dans ses rapports avec la personnalité* (Paris, seuil; 1975).

Lacan, Jacques. *Écrits 2*. Paris: Éditions du Seuil, 1971.

Lacan, Jacques. *Séminaire III: Les psychoses* (Paris: Seuil, 1981).

Lange, P. "Die Kleingärtnerbewegung lebt heute noch: Dr. Schreber zum Gedächtniss." *Leipziger Neueste Nachrichten: Mitteldeutsche Rundschau, unabhängige Heimatzeitung für Sachsen, Thüringen, Provinz Sachsen und Anhalt*, May 1968, no. 9, p. 3.

Lange, Walter. "Durch Befreiung und Einigung zur modernen GroBstadt." In *Heimatgeschichte für Leipzig und den Leipziger Kreis*, herausgegeben von Karl Reumuth. Leipzig: Dürr'sche Buchhandlung, 1927.

Jean-Jacques Lecercle, *Philosophy Through the Looking-Glass: Language, Nonsense, Desire*. (LaSalle, Open Court, 1987); pp. 118–159.

Lehmann. "Sachsen: Städtische Anstalt Dösen." In *Deutsche Heil- und Pflegeanstalten für Psychischkranke*, herausgegeben von J. Bresler. Vol. 1. Halle: Carl Marhold Verlagsbuch-handlung, 1910.

Lehmann, Friedrich. "Lindenhof: Privatanstalt in Coswig bei Dresden." In *Deutsche Heil- und Pflegeanstalten für Psychischkranke*, herausgegeben von J. Bresler. Vol. 1. Halle: Carl Marhald Verlagsbuchhandlung, 1910.

Lehmann, O. "Ein halbes Jahrhundert echter Schrebervereinsarbeit." *Der Freund der Schreber-Vereine* 10 (1914): 158–185.

Leipzig: Ein Blick in das Wesen und Werden einer deutschen Stadt. (Leipzig: Poeschel & Tropte,) 1914.

Leipzig im Jahre 1904. Leipzig: J. J. Weber, (1904).

Leipziger Neueste Nachrichten, 10/11/1931, p. 9. "Dr. Moritz Schrebers 70. Todestag."

Leipziger Tageblatt, 26/8/1845, p. 2273. "Die Eröffnung des Turnplatzes zu Leipzig."

Leipziger Tageblatt, 17/5/1907a, erste Beilage, n.p. "Frau Dr. Pauline Schreber †."

Leipziger Tageblatt, 17/5/1907b, erste Beilage, n.p. Two mourning advertisements from Schreber Associations regarding Pauline Schreber.

Leipziger Tageblatt, 18/5/1907c, erste Beilage, n.p. Two mourning advertisements from Schreber Associations regarding Pauline Schreber.

Leonhardt, Hans, Zusammensteller. *Geschichte der Leipziger Burschenschaft Germania.* Leipzig: Selbstverlag der Burschenschaft, (1928).

Leucker, Peter. "Herzlichen Glückwunsch." *Wir: Informationen der Deutschen Schreberjugend aus Bund und Ländern,* March 1973, n.p.

Levy, Ghislain. "Miss Schreber or God's Prostitute: An Essay on Enjoyment." *Etudes Psychothérapiques.* #24, 1976. pp. 111–117.

Lewis, Dio. *The New Gymnastics for Men, Women, and Children: With a Translation of Prof. Kloss's Dump-bell Instructor and Prof. Schreber's Pangymnastikon.* Boston: Ticknor and Fields, 1862.

Lidz, Theodore. Review of *The Schreber Case* by William G. Niederland. *Psychoanalytic Quarterly* 44 (1975): 653–656.

Leibling, Friedrich. "Zum Geleit." In *Grosse Pädagogen* by Josef Rattner. München, Basel: E. Reinhardt, 1956.

Lion, J. C. Review of *Kallipädie* by Daniel Gottlob Moritz Schreber. *Deutsche Turnzeitung* 2 (1857): 111–112.

Lipsius. "Dr. Moritz Schreber: Zum hundertjährigen Geburtstage (15. Oktober 1808)." *Dresdener Anzeiger* 1908a, no. 286, p. 5.

Lipsius. "Dr. Moritz Schreber: Zum hundertjährigen Geburtstage (15. Oktober 1808)." *Sächsische Dorfzeitung und Elbgaupresse* 1908b, no. 241, p. 1–2.

Lipton, A. A. "Was the Nervous Illness of Schreber a Case of Affective-Disorder?" *American Journal of Psychotherapy.* Vol. 141, #10, 1984, pp. 1236–1239.

Listener, 17/5/1973, p. 652. "Out of the Air: Pollutions."

Loeffler, Friedrich, Herausgeber. *Festschrift zum 25—JahrFeier der orthopädischen Klinik der Karl-Marx-Universität Leipzig.* Berlin, VEB Verlag Volk und Gesundheit, 1955.

Lubach, D. and Coronel, S. Sr. *De opvoeding van den mensch van zijne kindsheid tot den volwassen leeftijd: Eene handleiding voor ouders en onderwijzers.* Haarlem: De Erven F. Pohn, 1870.

Lübbing, Hermann. "Die Familie Schreber-von Schreeb in Oldenburg und Hatten (1667–1845)." *Oldenburger Balkenschild,* no. 3–4, (1952), p. 15–22.

Lyons, J. "Schreber and Freud: The Colonizing of Taboo." *American Journal of Psychoanalysis.* Vol. 42, #4, 1982. pp. 335–347.

Macalpine, Ida and Hunter, Richard A. "Introduction." In *Memoirs of my Nervous Illness* by Daniel Paul Schreber. London: Wm. Dawson & Sons, 1955.

Macalpine, I., and Hunter, R. A. "The Schreber Case." *Psychoanalytic Quarterly.* Vol. 22, 1963. pp. 328–371.

Mangner, (K. F.) Eduard. "Dr. D. G. M. Schreber, ein Kämpfer für Volkserziehung." *Cornelia: Zeitschrift für häusliche Erziehung* 26 (1876): 129–141.

Mangner, (K. F.) Eduard. *Dr. D. G. M. Schreber, ein Kämpfer für Volkserziehung.* Leipzig: C. F. Winter'sche Verlagshandlung, 1877.

Mangner, (K. F.) Eduard. *Spielplätze und Erziehungsvereine: Praktische Winke zur Förderung harmonischer Jugenderziehung nach dem Vorbilde der Leipziger Schre.bervereine.* Leipzig: Friedrich Fleischer, 1884.

Mannoni, Maud. *Education impossible.* Paris: Éditions du Seuil, 1973.

Mannoni, Octave. "Président Schreber, Professeur Flechsig." *Temps modernes* 30 (1973): 624–641.

Mannoni, Octave. *Fictions freudiennes.* Paris: Éditions du Seuil, 1978.

Mannoni, Octave. "Le Cas Freud." *La quinzaine litteraire,* 15/5/1979, p. 21–22.

Masson, J. L. "Schreber and Freud: A review of *Soul Murder.*" Mimeographed. (University of Toronto,) 1973.

Mayrhofer, B. *Kurzes Wörterbuch zur Geschichte der Medizin.* Jena: Gustav Fischer, 1937.

McCawley, Austin. "Paranoia and Homosexuality: Schreber Reconsidered." *New York State Journal of Medicine* 71–12 (1971): 1506–1513.

Medical History, October 1974, p. 381. Review of *Soul Murder* by Morton Schatzman.

Meijer, Mia and Rijnders, Gerardjan. "Schreber: een stuk over de waanwereld van een 19e eeuwse rechter." Type-script. (Amsterdam, 1976.)

Meijer, Mia and Rijnders, Gerardjan. "President Schreber: gek, kunstobject, fascist." *Hollands Diep,* 12/3/1977, p. 22–25.

Melman, Charles. "De l'aventure paranoiaque." *Analytica: Cahiers de recherche du champ freudien* 18 (1980): 3–32.

Mencken, Franz Erich, Herausgeber. *Dein dich zärtlich liebender Sohn: Kinderbriefe aus 6 Jahrhunderten.* München: Heimeran, 1965.

Menninger, Karl Augustus and Menninger, J. L. *Love Against Hate.* New York: Harcourt, 1942.

Mette, Julius. "Daniel Gottlieb Moritz Schreber." *Der Naturarzt: Zeitschrift für naturgemässe Lebens- und Heilweise* 77 (1955): 135–136.

Milczewsky, Renate. Text for a radio programme on Litfass and Schreber. Type-script. Sender Freies Berlin, Nr. T-227 475. (Broadcast some time between 1960 and 1970.)

Mittenzwey, L. *Die Pflege des Bewegungsspieles insbesondere durch die Schrebervereine: Zugleich eine Darstellung der Entwickelung und Einrichtung, sowie der Ziele und Aufgaben dieser Vereine.* Leipzig: Eduard Strauch, (1896).

Möbius. Review of *Denkwürdigkeiten eines Nervenkranken* by Daniel Paul Schreber. *Schmidt's Jahrbücher der in- und ausländischen gesammten Medicin* 279 (1903): 105.

Monacovecchio, A. "The Schreber Case: Psychoanalytic Profile of a Paranoid Personality—W. G. Niederland." *Journal of Contemporary Psychotherapy.* Vol. 9, #1, 1977. pp. 120–121.

Moreau, Pierre F. "Une bonne éducation au XIXe siècle: Des principes et des méthodes à rendre fou." *Psychologie,* June 1974, p. 43–48.

Morning News, 29/3/1979, p. 18. "Unpeeling the Masks of Madness."

Müller, J. P. *Mein System: 15 Minuten tägliche Arbeit für die Gesundheit.* 5th ed. Leipzig: Tillge, 1906.

Nacht, S., and Racamier, P. C. "La théorie psychanalytique du délire." *Revue Française Pschanalyse.* 1958, #3. pp. 417–532.

Nagler, Georg Kaspar. *Neues allgemeines Künstler-Lexikon oder Nachrichten von dem Leben und den Werken der Maler, Bildhauer, Baumeister, Kupferstecher, Lithographen, Formschneider, Zeichner, Hedailleure, Elfenbeinarbeiter etc.* Vol. 14. Orig. pub. between 1841 and 1846. 3d ed. Leipzig: Schwarzenberg & Schumann, (1924).

Nemiah, John C. "Parsing Schreber: Reflections on Dr. Klein's 'Schreber Memoirs.' " *Journal of Nervous and Mental Disease.* Vol. 162, #6, 1976. pp. 391–392.

Neue Gartenlaube (1942): 505. "Wer war Herr Schreber?"

Neue Leipziger Tageszeitung, 21/11/1944, p. 3. "Die älteste Leipzigerin gestorben."

Neue Leipziger Zeitung, 13/3/1938, p. 26. "Wie die Schrebergärten zu ihren Namen kamen."

Neue Leipziger Zeitung, 30/12/1939, p. 3. "Stadtanzeiger: Besuch bei einer Neunundneunzigjährigen."

Neues Wiener Tagblatt, 23/11/1944, p. 3. "Wer war Dr. Schreber?"

Niederland, William G. "Three Notes on the Schreber Case." *Psychoanalytic Quarterly* 20 (1951): 579–591.

Niederland, William G. "Schreber: Father and Son." *Psychoanalytic Quarterly* 28 (1959a): 151–169.

Niederland, William G. "The 'Miracled-Up' World of Schreber's Childhood." *The Psychoanalytic Study of the Child* 14 (1959b): 383–413.

Niederland, William G. "Schreber's Father." *Journal of the American Psychoanalytic Association* 8 (1960): 492–499.

Niederland, William G. "Further Data and Memorabilia Pertaining to the Schreber Case." *International Journal of Psycho-Analysis* 44 (1963): 201–207.

Niederland, William G. "Schreber and Flechsig: A Further Contribution to the 'Kernel of Truth' in Schreber's Delusional System." *Journal of the American Psychoanalytic Association* 16 (1968): 740–748.

Niederland, William G. "The Schreber Case: Sixty Years Later." *International Journal of Psychiatry* 10 (1972): 79–84.

Niederland, William G. *The Schreber Case: Psychoanalytic Profile of a Paranoid Personality.* New York: Quadrangle/The New York Times Book Co., 1974.

Niederland, William G. *Der Fall Schreber: Das psychoanalytische Profil einer paranoiden Persönlichkeit.* Frankfurt am Main: Suhrkamp Verlag, 1978.

Niederland, W. G. *"The Schreber Case." Psychiatric Annals.* Vol. 9, #8, 1979. pp. 387.

Niemann, Edgar H. "Förderer der Jugenderziehung und des Volkssports: Zum 100. Todestag des hervorragenden Arztpädagoge und Orthopäde Dr. Schreber." *Sächsisches Tageblatt* (Leipzig), 9/11/1961, n.p.

Noordam, N. F. *Inleiding in de historische pedagogiek.* Groningen: Wolters-Noordhoff, 1968.

Nydes, J. "Schreber, Parricide and the paranoid mechanism." *International Journal of Psychoanalysis.* Vol. 44, 1963. pp. 208–212.

Ohayon, Stephen I. "In Search of Akhnaton." *American Imago.* Vol. 32, #2, 1982. pp. 165–179.

Ottmüller, Uta, " 'Mutterpflichten'—Die Wandlungen ihrer inhaltlichen Ausformung durch die akademische Medizin." Mimeographed. Max-Planck-Institut für Bildungsforschung. (Berlin, 1979.) *Gesellschaft: Beiträge zur Marx'schen Theorie,* in press.

Overall, John E. "Comments on 'A Computer Analysis of the Schreber Memoirs.' " *Journal of Nervous and Mental Disease.* Vol. 162, #6, 1976. pp. 393.

P., E. "Ein Atelier im Irrenhaus." *Gartenlaube* (1867): 14–16.

Pelman. Review of *Denkwürdigkeiten eines Nervenkranken* by Daniel Paul Schreber. *Allgemeine Zeitschrift für Psychiatric* 60 (1903): 657–659.

Pelman. Review of *Denkwürdigkeiten eines Nervenkranken* by Daniel Paul Schreber. *Deutsche medizinische Wochenschrift* 30 (1904): 563.

Periscoop, May 1975, p. 12. Review of *De ondergang van Daniel Paul Schreber* by Morton Schatzman and Sigmund Freud.

"Personalakte" about Daniel Paul Schreber of the Saxony "Justiz-Ministerium" 1864–1911. State Archives Dresden.

Pfeiffer, Kurt. *Daniel Gottlob Moritz Schreber und sein Wirken für die Volksgesundheit.* Dissertation, Medizinische Akademie Düsseldorf. Düsseldorf: Dissertations-Verlag G. H. Nolte, 1937.

Pfeiffer, R. Review of *Denkwürdigkeiten eines Nervenkranken* by Daniel Paul Schreber. *Deutsche Zeitschrift für Nervenheilkunde* 27 (1904): 352–353.

Pierer's Jahrbücher der Wissenschaften, Künste und Gewerbe: Ergänzungswerk zu sämmtlichen Auflagen des Universal-Lexikons. Vol. 3. Oberhausen: Spaarmann, 1873.

Politzer, L. M. "Nekrolog." *Jahrbuch für Kinderheilkunde und physische Erziehung* 5 (1862): Nekrologe 1–7.

"Polizeiamt der Stadt Leipzig 11." Municipal Archives Leipzig. "Polizeiamt der Stadt Leipzig 105." Fo. 119. Municipal Archives Leipzig.

"Polizeimeldebuch Chemnitz." Municipal Archives Karl-Marx-Stadt.

Prado de Oliveira, Eduardo. "Présentation." In *Le Cas Schreber,* edited by Eduardo Prado de Oliveira. Paris: Presses Universitaires de France, 1979a.

Prado de Oliveira, Eduardo, ed. *Le cas Schreber: Contributions psychanalytiques de M. Katan, W. G. Niederland, H. Nunberg, I. Macalpine, R. A. Hunter, F. Baumeyer, W. R. D. Fairbairn, R. B. White, Ph. M. Kitay, A. C. Carr, J. Nydes.* Sous l'orientation de Jean Laplanche. Paris: Presses Universitaires de France, 1979a.

Prado de Oliveira, Eduardo. "Trois études sur Schreber et la citation." *Psychanalyse à l'université* 4 (1979b): 245–282.

Prado de Oliveira, Eduardo. "Schreber, Ladies and Gentlemen." *Revue Française de Psychanalyse.* Vol. 46, #1, 1982. pp. 81–93.

Psychotherapy Review, Spring 1974. Review of *Soul Murder* by Morton Schatzman. (Source: M. Schatzman.)

R. Review of *Denkwürdigkeiten eines Mervenkranken* by Daniel Paul Schreber. *Wiener medizinische Wochenschrift* 55 (1905): 105.

Rabain, J. F. "The Schreber Case: Observations on the Reconstruction of the Past in the History of the Childhood Neurosis of Schreber and on the Fundamental Language." *Revue Française de Psychanalyse.* Vol. 44, #2, 1980. pp. 329–347.

Rabant, Claude, *Délire et théorie.* Paris: Aubier-Montaigne, 1978.

Racamier, P. C. and Chasseguet-Smirgel, Janine. "La révision du cas Schreber: revue." *Revue française de psychanalyse* 30 (1966): 3–26.

Randschau, Ilse. "Verrückt durch väterliche Zucht." *Stern,* 18/4/1974, p. 198, 199.

Rattner, Josef. *Grosse Pädagogen: Erasmus, Vives, Montaigne, Comenius, Locke, Rousseau, Kant, Salzmann, Pestalozzi, Jean Paul, Goethe, Herbart, Fröbel. Kerschensteiner, Aichhorn.* München, Basel: E. Reinhardt, 1956.

Reumuth, Karl. "Wesen und Aufgaben der Schreberjugendbewegung." *Schriften des Landesverbandes Sachsen der Schreber- und Gartenvereine,* no. 3. Leipzig: Landesverband Sachsen der Schreber- und Gartenvereine, 1926.

Reumuth, Karl, Herausgeber. *Heimatgeschichte für Leipzig und den Leipziger Kreis.* Leipzig: Durr'sche Buchhandlung, 1927.

Richter, Gerhard. "Ein erfüllter Traum." *Der Freund der Schreber-Vereine* 9 (1913): 39–41.

Richter, Gerhard. *Geschichte des Schrebervereins der Westvorstadt zu Leipzig: Festschrift zur Feier des 50-jährigen Stiftungsfestes am 13. und 14. Juni 1914.* (Leipzig, 1914a.)

Richter, Gerhard. "Aus Vergangenheit und Gegenwart des ersten Schrebervereins." *Der Freund der Schreber-Vereine* 10 (1914b): 106–113.

Richter, Gerhard. *Das Buch der Schreber-Jugendpflege.* Leipzig: Verlag des Kreisverbandes der Schreber- und Gartenvereine, 1925.

Richter, Gerhard. *Deutsche Schreberjugendpflege.* Schriften des Reichsverbands der Kleingartenvereine Deutschlands, vol. 19. Frankfurt am Main: Reichsverband der Kleingartenvereine Deutschlands, 1930.

Richter, Gerhard. Report of a visit to Anna Jung at 14/3/1935. Typescript. (Leipzig, 1935.)

Richter, Gerhard. "Wie die erste Schreberanlage der Welt entstand." *Der Kleingärtner und Kleinsiedler* 1 (1936a): 5–7.

Richter, Gerhard. Report of a visit to Anna Jung at 15/10/1936. Type-script. (Leipzig, 1936b.)

Richter, Gerhard. Report of a visit to Anna Jung at 9/5/1939. Type-script. (Leipzig, 1939a.)

Richter, Gerhard. *Geschichte des ältesten Schrebervereins, 1864–1939: Festschrift zum 75 jährigen Bestehen des Kleingärtnervereins Dr. Schreber.* (Leipzig, 1939b.)

Richter, Gerhard. "Leipzig, die Urzelle des Schrebergartenwesens: Ein Gedächtnissblatt für Dr. Schreber und Dr. Hauschild." *Leipziger Jahrbuch* 15 (1940): 48–51.

Richter, Gerhard and Dietze. "Denkschrift über die Schreberjugendpflege im Friestaat Sachsen zwecks Erlangung von Staatsmitteln." *Schriften des Landesverbandes Sachsen der Schreber- und Gartenvereine,* no. 7. Leipzig: Landesverband Sachsen der Schreber- und Gartenvereine, 1928.

Richter, Gerhard, and Wahl, Günter. "Dr. med. Daniel Gottlieb Moritz Schreber, der Kämpfer für wahre Volkserziehung, der Pionier der Jugendpflege." *Wir: Informationen der Deutschen Schreberjugend aus Bund und Ländern,* April 1973, n.p.

Richter, H. E. "Vom Gränzgebiet der erzieherischen und Heilgymnastik." *Neue Jahrbücher für die Turnkunst* 4 (1858): 1–6.

Richter, H. E. "Der Vater des Leipziger Turnwesens." *Gartenlaube* 11 (1863): 484–489.

Ringpfeil, K. "Was bieten wir unseren Schreberkindern an Leib und Seele?" *Schriften des Landesverbandes Sachsen der Schreber- und Gartenvereine,* no. 5. Leipzig: Landesverband Sachsen der Schreber- und Gartenvereine, 1927.

Rinsley, D. B. "Schreber's Illness: Dementia Paranoides or Affective Disorder." *International Journal of Psychoanalytic Psychotherapy.* Vol. 10, 1984. pp. 377–382.

Ritter, Alfons. *Schreber: Das Bildungssystem eines Arztes.* Dissertation, Erlangen, 1935. Erfurt: Verlag Ohlenroth, 1936a.

Ritter, Alfons. *Schreber: Künder und Streiter für wahre Volkserziehung.* Erfurt: Verlag Ohlenroth, 1936b.

Robertson, Priscilla. "Home As a Nest: Middle Class Childhood in Nineteenth-Century Europe." In *The History of Childhood,* edited by Lloyd deMause. Reprint. New York, Hagerstown, San Francisco, London: Harper & Row, 1975.

Rösler. Letter beginning "Sehr geehrter Herr College!" Leipzig, 13/4/1911. In "Krankengeschichte" on Daniel Paul Schreber. Archives Bezirkskrankenhaus für Psychiatrie Leipzig-Dösen.

Romein, Jan. *De biografie: Een inleiding.* Daad en droom, een reeks biografieën onder redactie van Annie Romein-Verschoor, vol. 1. Amsterdam, Uitgeverij Ploegsma, 1946.

Rondagh, Ferd. "Psychiater beschrijft hoe een strenge vader zijn zoon gek maakte." *Volkskrant,* 1/2/1975, p. 31.

Rosenkötter, Lutz. Review of *The Schreber Case* by William G. Niederland, *Die Angst vor dem Vater* by Morton Schatzman, and *Bürgerliche Wahnwelt um Neunzehnhundert,* herausgegeben von Peter Heiligenthal und Reinhard Volk. *Psyche* 29 (1975): 184–186.

Roughton, R. E. "*Freud on Schreber: Psychoanalytic Theory and the Critical Act—*

Chabot, C. B." *Psychoanalytic Quarterly.* Vol. 52, #4, 1983. pp. 637–641.

Rühl, Hugo. *Deutsche Turner in Wort und Bild.* Leipzig, Wien: A. Pichlers Witwe & Sohn, 1901.

Rutschky, Katharina, Herausgeberin. *Schwarze Pädagogik: Quellen zur Naturgeschichte der bürgerlichen Erziehung.* Frankfurt am Main, Berlin, Wien: Ullstein, 1977.

Saalfeld, Diedrich. "Einkommensverhältnisse und Lebenshaltungskosten städtischer Populationen in Deutschland in der Übergangsperiode zum Industriealter." In *Wirtschaftliche und Soziale Strukturen in saekularen Wandel.* Vol. 2, *Die vorindustrielle Zeit: Ausseragrarische Probleme.* Hannover: M. & H. Schaper, 1974.

Sächsische Kurier, 1933, no. 241. "Gedenkblatt für Dr. Schreber: Zum 125. Geburtstage am 15. Oktober."

"Sächsische Ordenskanzlei 61." State Archives Dresden.

Sächsische Vaterlandsblätter 3 (1843): 559. "Leipzig: Universität—Turnerei."

Sächsische Vaterlandsblätter 5 (1845): 833. "Leipzig: Die Wahlmänner der Stadtverordneten."

Sarro, Ramon. "L'idée de transformation de sexe dans le délire du président Schreber comme mécanisme de défense anti-hallucinatoire." *Evolution Psychiatrique.* Vol. 42, #2–3. pp. 835–842.

Schalmey, Peter. *Die Bewährung psychoanalytischer Hypothesen.* Wissenschaftstheorie und Grundlagenforschung, no. 7. Kronberg/Ts.: Scriptor Verlag, 1977.

Schatzman, Morton. "Paranoia or Persecution: The Case of Schreber." *Family Process* 10 (1971): 177–207.

Schatzman, Morton. *Soul Murder: Persecution in the Family.* London: Allen Lane, 1973a.

Schatzman, Morton. "Author's Reply to 'The Schreber Case, Sixty Years Later'." *International Journal of Psychiatry* 11 (1973b): 126–128.

Schatzman, Morton. *Die Angst vor dem Vater: Langzeitwirkungen einer Erziehungsmethode, eine Analyse am Fall Schreber.* Reinbek: Rowohlt Verlag, 1974a.

Schatzman, Morton. Review of *The Schreber Case* by William G. Niederland. *The History of Childhood Quarterly* 2 (1974b): 453–457.

Schatzman, Morton. *L'esprit assassiné.* Paris: Editions Stock, 1974c.

Schatzman, Morton. *Soul Murder: Persecution in the Family.* Middlesex, Penguin Books, 1976.

Schatzman, Morton. *El asesinato del alma: la persecucion del nino en la familia autoritaria.* Madrid: Siglo Veintiuno de Espana Editores, 1977.

Schatzman, Morton. *Die Angst vor dem Vater: Langzeitwirkungen einer Erziehungsmethode, eine Analyse am Fall Schreber.* Reinbek: Rowohlt Taschenbuch, 1978.

Schatzman, Morton and Freud, Sigmund. *De ondergang van Daniel Paul Schreber; Een klassiek geval van paranoia en schizofrenie; and Psychoanalytische aantekeningen over een autobiografisch beschreven geval van paranoia (dementia paranoides).* Amsterdam: Van Gennep, 1974.

Schefer, Jean-Louis. "Schreber: le dieu, le droit, la paranöia." in *Sexualité et politique.* Paris: Union Générale d'Editions, 1975.

Scheff, Thomas J., ed. *Labelling Madness.* Engelwood Cliffs, N.J.: Prentice-Hall, 1975.

Schildbach, Carl Hermann. *Bericht über die gymnastisch-orthopädische Heilanstalt der DD. Schreber und Schildbach zu Leipzig, Zeitzer Strasse 43.* Leipzig: J. C. Hinrichs'sche Buchhandlung, 1861.

Schildbach, (Carl Hermann). "Schreber." *Deutsche Turn-Zeitung* 7 (1862a): 4–6.

Schildbach, (Carl Hermann). "Nachtrag zu Schrebers Nekrolog." *Neue Jahrbücher für die Turnkunst*[8] (1862b): 16–18.

Schildbach, Carl Hermann. *Zweiter Bericht über die gymnastisch-orthopädische Heilanstalt zu Leipzig, nebst Mitthleilungen über die Grundsätze und Erfolge bei der Behandlung der Rückgratsverkrümmungen.* Leipzig: J. C. Hinrichs'sche Buchhandlung, 1864.

Schildbach, Carl Hermann. "Eine orthopädische Heilanstalt." *Cornelia* 7 (1867): 95–102.

Schildbach, Carl Hermann. *Die Skoliose: Anleitung zur Beurtheilung und Behandlung der Rückgratsverkrümmungen für praktische Arzte.* Leipzig: Veit & Co., 1877.

Schilling, Kurt. *Das Kleingartenwesen in Sachsen.* Dresden: Eigenverlag des Verfassers, 1924.

Schilling, Kurt. "Dr. Schreber und der Schrebergarten." *Kleingärtner-Jahrbuch* (1950): 33–39.

Schilling, Kurt. "Dr. Schreber." *Deutscher Kleingärtner* (1961): 218.

Schilling, Kurt. "Dr. D. G. M. Schreber und wir: Ein Leben für die Jugend und ein offenes Wort an alle." *Der Fachberater für das deutsche Kleingartenwesen,* June 1964, p. 1–23.

Schmidt, Carl. *Die Geschichte der Pädagogik von Pestalozzi bis zur Gegenwart.* Geschichte der Pädagogik, vol. 4. 2nd ed. Gothen: Schettler, 1867.

Schreber, Daniel Gottlieb Moritz. *Kinesiatrik oder die gymnastische Heilmethode: Für Ärzte und gebildete Nichtärzte nach eigenen Erfahrungen dargestellt.* Leipzig: Friedrich Fleischer, 1852.

Schreber, Daniel Gottlob Moritz, 1826, 1833a and 1833b. See: Schreber, Danielis Gottlobus Mauritius.

(Schreber, Daniel Gottlob) Moritz. Letter to his parents. Dresden, 30/9/1833c. Archives Kleingartensparte "Dr. Schreber" Leipzig.

Schreber, (Daniel Gottlob Moritz). Letter to his parents. Dresden, 25/9/1835. Archives Kleingartenspart "Dr. Schreber" Leipzig.

Schreber, (Daniel Gottlob) Moritz. *Das Buch der Gesundheit: Eine Orthobiotik nach den Gesetzen der Natur und dem Baue des menschlichen Organismus.* Leipzig: Friedrich Volckmar, 1839.

Schreber, Daniel Gottlob Moritz. *Die Normalgaben der Arztneimittel: Zum Gebrauche für praktische Arzte und Kliniker übersichtlich dargestellt.* Leipzig: Friedrich Volckmar, 1840.

Schreber, Daniel Gottlob Moritz. *Die Kaltwasser-Heilmethode in ihren Grenzen und ihrem wahren Werthe.* Leipzig: Bernh. Hermann, 1842.

Schreber, Daniel Gottlob Moritz. *Das Turnen vom ärztlichen Standpunkte aus, zugleich als eine Staatsangelegenheit dargestellt.* Leipzig: Mayer und Wigand, 1843.

Schreber, (Daniel Gottlob) Moritz. *Fyra gyllene reglor för barna-uppfostran.* Upsala: Torssell, 1845.

(Schreber, Daniel Gottlob Moritz.) Manuscript of a speech for the Leipziger Allgemeiner Turnverein. (Leipzig, 1849.) Archives Kleingartensparte "Dr. Schreber" Leipzig.

Schreber, Daniel Gottlob Moritz, 1852a. See: Schreber, Daniel Gottlieb Moritz.

Schreber, (Daniel Gottlob) Moritz. Letter to the police of Leipzig. Leipzig, 30/3/1852b. In "Polizeiamt der Stadt Leipzig 11." Municipal Archives Leipzig.

Schreber, Daniel Gottlob Moritz. *Die Eigenthümlichkeiten des kindlichen Organismus im gesunden und kranken Zustande: Eine Propädeutik der speciellen Kinderheilkunde.* Leipzig: Friedrich Fleischer, 1852c.

Schreber, Daniel Gottlob Moritz. *Die schädlichen Körperhaltungen und Gewohnheiten der Kinder nebst Angabe der Mittel dagegen: Für Altern und Erzieher.* Leipzig: Friedrich Fleischer, 1853a.

Schreber, Daniel Gottlob Moritz. *Nadeelige ligchaamshoudingen en kwade gewoonten der kinderen, benevens opgave der middelen daartegen, ten dienste van ouders en opvoeders.* Utrecht: W. F. Dannenfelser, 1853b.

Schreber, Daniel Gottlob Moritz. *Ärztliche Zimmergymnastik oder Derstellung und Anwendung der unmittelbaren—d.h. ohne Geräth und Beistand, mithin stets und überall ausführbaren—heilgymnastischen Bewegungen für jedes Alter und Geschlecht und für die verschiedenen speciellen Gebrauchszwecke als ein einfach natürliches System entworfen.* Leipzig: Friedrich Fleischer, 1855a.

Schreber, (Daniel Gottlob) Moritz. Letter beginning "An den Stadtrath zu Oschatz." Leipzig, 25/8/1855b.

Schreber, (Daniel Gottlob Moritz). "Vaterworte an meine liebe Anna bei ihrem Übergange aus den Kinderjahren in das Jungfrauenalter." Leipzig, Eastern 1856. *Der Freund der Schreber-Vereine* 5 (1909): 73–75.

Schreber, (Daniel Gottlob Moritz). "Macht nicht das Turnen grosse Hände?" *Neue Jahrbücher für die Turnkunst* 3 (1857a): 210–212.

Schreber, Daniel Gottlob Moritz. *Onze kinderen: Hunne kwade gewoonten en nadeelige ligchaamshoudingen, benevens opgave der middelen daartegen.* Utrecht: W. F. Dannenfelser, 1857b.

Schreber, Daniel Gottlob Moritz. *Aerztliche Zimmer-Gymnastik oder Darstellung und Anwendung der unmittelbaren heilgymnastischen Bewegungen für jedes Alter und Geschlecht.* 3rd rev. ed. Leipzig: Friedrich Fleischer, 1857c.

Schreber, Daniel Gottlob Moritz. *Kallipädie oder Erziehung zur Schönheit durch naturgetreue und gleichmässige Förderung normaler Körperbildung, lebenstüchtiger Gesundheit und geistiger Veredelung und insbesondere durch möglichste Benutzung specieller Erziehungsmittel: Für Altern, Erzieher und Lehrer.* Leipzig: Friedrich Fleischer, 1858a.

Schreber, (Daniel Gottlob) Moritz. "Über Anwendung der Sonnenbäder zu Heilzwecken, insbesondere gegen gewisse chronische Krankheiten des kindlichen Alters." *Jahrbuch für Kinderheilkunde und physische Erziehung* 1 (1858b): Original-Aufsätze 169–171.

Schreber, (Daniel Gottlob Moritz). Letter to Joh. Bapt. Heindl. Leipzig, 27/5/1858b. Manuscript. Bayerische Staatsbibliothek.

Schreber, (Daniel Gottlob Moritz). "Die Turnanstalt als Schule der Männlichkeit." *Neue Jahrbücher für die Turnkunst* 4 (1858d): 169–170.

Schreber, Daniel Gottlob Moritz. *Ein ärztlicher Blick in das Schulwesen in der Absicht: zu heilen, und nicht: zu verletzen.* Leipzig: Friedrich Fleischer, 1858e.

Schreber, Daniel Gottlob Moritz. *Anthropos: Der Wunderbau des menschlichen Organismus, sein Leben und seine Gesundheitsgesetze; ein allgemein fassliches Gesammtbild der menschlichen Natur für Lehrer, Schüler, sowie für Jedermann, der nach gründlicher Bildung und körperlich geistiger Gesundheit strebt.* Leipzig: Friedrich Fleischer, 1859a.

Schreber, Daniel Gottlob Moritz. *Die plannmässige Schärfung der Sinnesorgane als eine Grundlage und leicht zu erfüllende Aufgabe der Erziehung, besonders der Schulbildung.* Leipzig: Friedrich Fleischer, 1859b.

Schreber, (Daniel Gottlob Moritz). "Die Jugendspiele in ihrer gesundheitlichen und pädagogischen Bedeutung." *Gartenlaube* 8 (1860a): 414–416.

Schreber, (Daniel Gottlob Moritz). "Die Jugendspiele in ihrer gesundheitlichen und pädagogischen Bedeutung und die Nothwendigkeit ihrer Beachtung von Seite der Schulerziehung." *Jahrbuch für Kinderheilkunde und physische Erziehung* 3 (1860b): Original-Aufsätze 247–254.

Schreber, (Daniel Gottlob Moritz). *Die deutsche Turnkunst in der Gegenwart und Zukunft: Wesen, Bedeutung und Grundregeln bei Ausübung derselben.* Leipzig: Hermann Fries, 1860c.

Schreber, (Daniel Gottlob) Moritz. *Der Hausfreund als Erzieher und Führer zu Familienglück, Volksgesundheit und Menschenveredelung für Väter und Mütter des deutschen Volkes.* Leipzig: Friedrich Fleischer, 1861a.

Schreber, (Daniel Gottlob) Moritz. "An ein hohes Staatsministerium des Cultus und Erziehungswesens." Leipzig, 1861b. Hessische Landes-und Hochschulbibliothek Darmstadt.

Schreber, (Daniel Gottlob) Moritz. Letter to the king of Prussia. Leipzig, January 1861c. Manuscript. Staatsbibliothek Preussischer Kulturbesitz.

Schreber, (Daniel Gottlob Moritz). "Die Jugendspiele in ihrer gesundheitlichen und pädagogischen Bedeutung und die Nothwendigkeit ihrer Beachtung von Seiten der Schulerziehung." *Die Erziehung der Gegenwart: Beiträge zur Lösung ihrer Aufgabe mit Berücksichtigung von Friedrich Fröbels Grundsätzen* 1 (1861d): 137–140.

Schreber, Daniel Gottlob Moritz. *Das Buch der Gesundheit oder die Lebenskunst nach der Einrichtung und den Gesetzen der menschlichen Natur.* 2d rev. ed. Leipzig: Hermann Fries, 1861e.

Schreber, Daniel Gottlob Moritz. *Das Pangymnastikon oder das ganze Turnsystem an einem einzigen Geräthe ohne Raumerforderniss als einfachstes Mittel zur Entwickelung höchster und allseitiger Muskelkraft, Körperdurchbildung und Lebenstüchtigkeit: Für Schulanstalten, Haus-Turner und Turnvereine.* Leipzig: Friedrich Fleischer, 1862a.

Schreber, (Daniel Gottlob) Moritz. *Beknopte opvoedingsleer: Een boek voor vaders en moeders.* Vrij naar het hoogduitsch door Frans de Cort. Brussel, Zutphen: Ferdinand Claassen, P. B. Plantenga, 1862b.

Schreber, Daniel Gottlob Moritz. *Leerwijze om de ligchaamsbouw van kinderen te regelen, en hunne gezondheid te bevorderen.* Amsterdam: G. D. Funke, 1864.

Schreber, Daniel Gottlob Moritz. *Das Buch der Erziehung an Leib und Seele: Für Ältern, Erzieher und Lehrer.* 3d ed. Erweitert von Carl Hennig. Leipzig: Friedrich Fleischer, (1882).

Schreber, Daniel Gottlob Moritz. *Das Buch der Erziehung an Leib und Seele: Für Eltern, Erzieher und Lehrer.* 3d ed. Erweitert von Carl Hennig. Leipzig: R. Voigtlander, (1891).

Schreber, (Daniel Gottlob Moritz). Letter beginning "Leiber Freund!" n.p. n.d. University Library Leipzig.

Schreber, Daniel Gottlob Moritz and Neumann, A. C. *Streitfragen der deutschen und schwedischen Heilgymnastik: Erörtert in Form myologischer Briefe.* Leipzig: A. Förstner'sche Buchhandlung (Arthus Felix), 1858.

Schreber, (Daniel) Paul. Letter to the Saxony ministry of justice. Leipzig, 22/3/1865. In

"Personalakte" about Daniel Paul Schreber of the Saxony "Justiz-Ministerium". State Archives Dresden.

Schreber, (Daniel Paul. "Den 26. Juli 1889." Poem for the silver wedding of Anna and Carl Jung. Written down by a brother or sister of Paula Jung.

Schreber, Daniel Paul. Letter to the Saxony ministry of justice. Freiberg, 12/11/1892. In "Personalakte" about Daniel Paul Schreber of the Saxony "Justiz-Ministerium". State archives Dresden.

Schreber, Daniel Paul. *Denkwürdigkeiten eines Nervenkranken nebst Nachträgen und einem Anhang über die Frage: "Unter welchen Voraussetzungen darf eine für geisteskrank erachtete Person gegen ihren erklärten Willen in einer Heilanstalt festgehalten werden?"* Leipzig: Oswald Mutze, 1903.

(Schreber, Daniel Paul.) Speech. Manuscript. n.p. 26/12/1904.

(Schreber, Daniel Paul.) "Zum 29. Juni 1905." Poem for his mother's ninetieth birthday. Mimeographed. n.p. 1905.

(Schreber, Daniel) Paul. "Seinen lieben Sabchen zum neunzehnten Juni 1907 gewidmet." Poem for his wife's fiftieth birthday. Manuscript. (Dresden) 1907a.

Schreber, (Daniel) Paul. "Erklärung." *Der Freund der Schreber-Vereine* 3 (1907b): 292–293.

Schreber, Daniel Paul. *Memoirs of my Nervous Illness.* Edited by Ida Macalpine and Richard A. Hunter. London: W. Dawson & Sons, 1955.

Schreber, Daniel Paul. "Denkwürdigkeiten eines Nervenkranken nebst Nachträgen." In *Bürgerliche Wahnwelt um Neunzehnhundert,* herausgegeben von Peter Heiligenthal und Reinhard Volk. Wiesbaden: Focus-Verlag, 1973a.

Schreber, Daniel Paul. *Denkwürdigkeiten eines Nervenkranken.* Herausgegeben von Samuel M. Weber. Frankfurt am Main, Berlin, Wien: Ullstein, 1973b.

Schreber, Daniel Paul. *Memorie di un malato di nervi.* A cura di Roberto Calasso. Milano: Adelphi edizioni, 1974.

Schreber, Daniel Paul. *Mémoires d'un névropathe avec des compléments et un appendice sur la question "A quelles conditions une personne jugée aliénée peut-elle être maintenue dans un établissement hospitalier contre sa volonté évidente?"* Le champ freudien. Paris: Editions du Seuil, 1975.

(Schreber, Daniel Paul.) Poem, with explanatory note dating from 1937: "Vorstehende Zeilen schrieb mein Onkel Paul Schreber (†1911) als Grossmutter Schreber uns zwei Schwäne schenkte." Manuscript. n.p. n.d.

Schreber, Danielis Gottlobus Mauritius. Letter beginning "Rector Academiae Magnifice, Viri Summe Reverendi, Illustrissimi, Doctissimi, Honeratissimi." Manuscript. Lipsiae, 3/11/1826.

Schreber, Danielis Gottlobus Mauritius. *De tartari stibiati in inflammationibus organorum respirationis effectu atque usu.* Dissertation inauguralis medica. Lipsiae, 1833a.

Schreber, Danielis Gottlobus Mauritius. Curriculum vitae. In *Annotationes anatomicae et physiologicae,* Prol. XX by Ernestus Henricus Weber. (Leipzig, 1833b.)

Schreber, Johann Christian Daniel. *Novae species insectorum.* Lipsiae: Fritsch, 1760.

(Schreber, Johann Gotthilf Daniel.) "Stammbaum." Manuscript. Leipzig, 1812.

(Schreber, Johann Gotthilf Daniel.) Letter "an den Rathskämmerer Herrn Georg Friedrich Valz zu Oschatz." Transcript. Leipzig, 12/5/1829.

Schreber, Johann Gotthilf Daniel. "Kurze Geschichte meines Lebens." Manuscript. Leipzig, 1830.

(Schreber, Louise Henriette Pauline, geb. Haase.) Letter beginning "Liebe Käte!" n.p., 7/8/1899.

(Schreber, Louise Henriette Pauline, geb. Haase.) Poem for the christening of a grand-granddaughter at 26/12/1904. n.p., 1904.

Schreber, Moritz. See: Schreber, Daniel Gottlob Moritz.

Schreber, Ottilie Sabine, geb. Behr. Letter to the Saxony "Justiz-Ministerium". Dresden, 10/5/1911. In "Personalakte" about Daniel Paul Schreber of the Saxony "Justiz-Ministerium". State Archives Dresden.

Schreber, Paul. See: Schreber, Daniel Paul.

Schrebergärtner: Mitteilungsblatt des Schrebergarten-Vereins zu Stralsund, 16/6/1924, p. 33. "Sechzig Jahre Schrebertum."

Schreiber, Emil O. *Geschichte des Schrebervereins der West-vorstadt zu Leipzig: Festschrift zur Feier des 30-jährigen Stiftungsfestes.* (Leipzig, 1894.)

Schreiber, Emil O. "3. Die Schrebervereine zu Leipzig." *Jahrbuch für deutsche Jugend- und Volksspiele* 4 (1895): 122–128.

Schütze, Rudolf. "Moritz Schreber—der Leipziger Arzt und Pädagoge." *Deutsches Ärzteblatt* 36 (1936a): 1167.

Schütze, Rudolf. "Moritz Schreber und sein Werk: Aus Anlass der 75. Wiederkehr seines Todestages am 10. November." *Münchener medizinische Wochenschrift* 83 (1936b): 1888–1890.

Schütze, Rudolf. "Moritz Schreber—der geistige Vater der Schrebervereine: Zur 75. Wiederkehr seines Todestages am 10. November." *Politische Erziehung: Mitteilungsblatt des nationalsozialistischen Lehrebundes Gauverband Sachsen* (1936c): 527–528.

Schultz-Hencke, Harald. *Das Problem der Schizophrenie: Analytische Psychotherapie und Psychose.* Stuttgart: G. Thieme, 1952.

Schultze, (Ernst). Review of *Denkwürdigkeiten eines Nervenkranken* by Daniel Paul Schreber. *Arztliche Sachverständigen-Zeitung* 10 (1904): 298.

Schultze, Ernst. Review of *Denkwürdigkeiten eines Nervenkranken* by Daniel Paul Schreber. *Zeitschrift für Psychologie und Physiologie der Sinnesorgane* 37 (1905): 469.

Schwägrichen, (Christian) Frid(rich S.). Letter. Manuscript. Lipsiae, 14/2/1828.

Schwatlo, Hellmut. "Nie sah Herr Schreber Schrebergärten." *Neue Leipziger Zeitung,* 1938.

Schweighofer, Fritz. *Psychoanalyse und Graphologie, dargestellt an den Handschriften Sigmund Freuds und seiner Schüler.* Stuttgart: Hippokrates Verlag, 1976.

Searles, Harold F. *Collected Papers on Schizophrenia and Related Subjects.* The International Psycho-analytical Library, edited by John D. Sutherland, no. 63. London: The Hogarth Press and the Institute of Psycho-Analysis, 1965.

Ségur, Sophie de. *Comédies et proverbes.* 2d ed. Paris: Librairie de L. Hachette et Co., 1866.

Seidel, Peter. "Die Idee mit dem Spielplatz." Kinderfreude in kleinen Gärten, instalment 1, eine MNN-Serie über Dr. Schreber. *Mitteldeutsche Neueste Nachrichten: Bezirkszeitung der National-Demokratischen Partei Deutschlands,* 24/10/1974a, n.p.

Seidel, Peter. "Berühmt auch als Begründer der helfenden Heilgymnastik." Kinderfreude in kleinen Gärten, instalment 2, eine MNN-Serie über Dr. Schreber. *Mittel-*

deutsche Neueste Nachrichten: Bezirkszeitung der National-Demokratischen Partei Deutschlands, 30/10/1974b, n.p.

Seidel, Peter. "Nach der MNN-Serie über Dr. Schreber: Ein unerwarteter Fund." *Mitteldeutsche Neueste Nachrichten: Bezirkszeitung der National-Demokratischen Partei Deutschlands,* 15-16/10/1977, n.p.

Shengold, Leonhard. "Chekhov and Schreber." *International Journal of Psycho-Analysis* 42 (1961): 431-438.

Shengold, Leonard. "Soul Murder: A Review." *International Journal of Psychoanalytic Psychotherapy* 3 (1974): 366-373.

Shengold, Leonard. "An Attempt at Soul Murder: Rudyard Kipling's Early Life and Work." *The Psychoanalytic Study of the Child* 30 (1975): 683-724.

Shorter, Edward. *The Making of the Modern Family.* Glasgow: Fontana/Collins, 1977.

Shraberg, David. Review of *The Schreber Case* by William G. Niederland. *The Journal of the American Academy of Psychoanalysis* 3 (1976): 343-346.

Shulman, Bernard H. "An Adlerian View of the Schreber Case." *Journal of Individual Psychology* 15 (1959): 180-192.

Schweighofer, F. *"The Schreber Case." Psychotherapie Psychosomatik Medizinische Psychologie.* Vol. 32, #1, 1982. pp. 4-8.

Sieber, Alan L. "Freud and the Schreber Case: A Study of the Interaction Between Life and Work." *Dissertation Abstracts Annual.* Vol. 41, 1981.

Siegel, (G.) Richard. "Die Leipziger Schrebervereine, ihre Entstehung, ihr Wesen und Wirken." *Der Freund der Schreber-Vereine* 3 (1907a): 2-10.

Siegel, (G.) Richard. Speech. In "Trauerrede beim Begräbnis der Frau verw. Dr. Schreber" by D. Hartung. Leipzig, 1907b.

Siegel, G. Richard. "Frau Pauline verw. Dr. Schreber †." *Der Freund der Schreber-Vereine* 3 (1907c): 126-128.

Siegel, G. Richard. "Zur Abwehr." *Der Freund der Schreber-Vereine* 3 (1907d): 218.

Siegel, (G.) Richard. "Dr. Schreber und die Schrebervereine." *Der Freund der Schreber-Vereine* 3 (1907e): 251-255.

Siegel, G. Richard. "Die Wochenschrift 'Der Schrebergärtner' und die Leipziger Schre-bervereine." *Der Freund der Schreber-Vereine* 3 (1907f): 289–292.

Siegel, (G.) Richard. "Zur Geschichte des 'Verbandes Leipziger Schrebervereine' und des 'Allgemeinen Verbandes der Schrebervereine'." *Der Freund der Schreber-Vereine* 4 (1908a): 3–6.

S(iegel, G. Richard). "Direktor Dr. Karl Vogel über Dr. Schreber." *Der Freund der Schreber-Vereine* 4 (1908b): 25–26.

Siegel, (G.) Richard. "Zur einhundertjährigen Wiederkehr des Geburtstages Dr. Schre-bers und Dr. Hauschilds." *Der Freund der Schreber-Vereine* 4 (1908c): 205–210.

Siegel, G. Richard. "Gedenkfeier zur einhundertjährigen Wiederkehr des Geburtstages Dr. Schrebers und Dr. Hauschilds." *Der Freund der Schreber-Vereine* 4 (1908d): 220.

Siegel, (G.) Richard. Comments on Daniel Gottlob Moritz Schreber 1856. *Der Freund der Schreber-Vereine* 5 (1909a): 75.

Siegel, (G.) Richard. "Erinnerungen an Dr. Moritz Schreber: Nach Berichten von seinen Töchtern." *Der Freund der Schreber-Vereine* 5 (1909b): 205–209.

Siegel, G. Richard. "Schreber-Worte." *Der Freund der Schreber-Vereine* 10 (1914): 17–19.

Siemens, Hermann Werner. "Über unbekannte Ahnen von Werner Siemens." *Mit-teilungen der Arbeitsgemeinschaft für Familiengeschichte im Kulturkreis Siemens E.V.* (1966), no. 46, pp. 73 ff.

Skurnik, N., and Bourguignon, A. "Histoire, pedagogie et psychiatrie en Saxe au XIX siècle." *Annales Medico-Psychologiques.* Vol. 138, #1, 1980. pp. 1–17.

Slikker, Ria and Meijer, Quint. Review of *De ondergang van Daniel Paul Schreber* by Morton Schatzman and Sigmund Freud. *Pharetra,* 17/11/1975, p. 16.

S-r. "Über das Abhärten der Kinder, und dessen methodische Durchführung." *Jahrbuch für Kinderheilkunde und physische Erziehung* 6 (1863): Original-Aufsätze 247–256.

Starke, Werner. "Väter der Schrebergärten." In a Leipzig newspaper, 3–4/7/1976.

Stephani, Eberhard. "Die Laubenpieper." *Stern,* 8/5/1980, p. 40–58.

Stötzner, E. "Auf Leipzigs Schreberplätzen." *Gartenlaube* 31(1883): 368–373.

Stone, Irving. *The Passions of the Mind: A Biographical Novel of Sigmund Freud.* New York: Signet/The New American Library, 1972.

Storr, Anthony. "All in the Family." *Book World,* 4/2/1973, p. 4 and 10.

Striegler, B. "Leipzig als Turnerstadt." *Leipziger Kalender* (1904): 91–97.

(Tabouret-Keller, Andrée.) "Une étude: la remarquable famille Schreber." *Scilicet* (1973), no. 4, p. 287–321.

This, Bernhard. "La race Schreberienne." *Le coq-heron,* no. 37/38, June/July 1973a, p. 2–3; no. 40, November 1973b, p. 2–12; no. 41/42, December 1973/January 1974, p. 9–17.

Times Literary Supplement, 13/7/1973, p. 803. "The over-Spartan Schrebers."

Troitzsch, Rudolf. "Erinnerungen." Type-script. n.p. (written down between 1963 and 1968).

Troitzsch, Rudolf. Letter to Peter Heiligenthal and Reinhard Volk. Type-script. Hoxhohl, 14/1/1974.

Trouw, stadseditie, 6/3/1975, p. 12. Review of *De ondergang van Daniel Paul Schreber* by Morton Schatzman and Sigmund Freud.

Uibe, Peter. "Schreber als Orthopäde." *Hippokrates* 30 (1959): 216–218.

Union (Leipzig) 19 (1964) no. 135. "Entdecker der grossen Liebe zum kleinen Garten: Vor nunmehr 100 Jahren wurde in Leipzig der erste Schreber-Verein gegründet."

Ussel, Jozef Maria Willem van. *Geschiedenis van het seksuele probleem.* Meppel: J. A. Boom en Zoon, 1968.

Valentin, Bruno. *Geschichte der Orthopädie.* Stuttgart: Georg Thieme Verlag, 1961.

Vogel, (Karl). "Dr. D. G. M. Schreber, geb. 1808 + 1861: Eines bewährten Kinderfreundes letzter Rath und Wunsch." *Mittheilungen der allgemeinen Bürgerschule zu Leipzig an das Elternhaus ihrer Zöglinge,* 16/12/1861, p. 37–44.

Volhard, (J.) "Allgemeiner Familienabend im 'Sanssouci': Dienstag, den 22. Oktober 1912." *Der Freund der Schreber-Vereine* 8 (1912): 169–171.

Volgard, J. "50jährige Jubelfeier im Schreberverein der Westvorstadt." *Der Freund der Schreber-Vereine* 10 (1914): 115–118.

Vries, Leonard de. *Ha dokter Ho dokter: Knotsgekke geneeskunde uit grootvaders tijd.* 2d ed. Haarlem: De Haan, 1976.

W., G. "Zum hundertsten Geburtstag Dr. Moritz Schreber." *Leipziger Tageblatt,* 13/10/1908, p. 3.

Wahrig, Gerhard. *Deutsches Wörterbuch.* Gütersloh. Berlin, München, Wien: Bertelsmann Lexikon-Verlag, 1973.

Weber. Medical report for the "Oberlandesgericht" Dresden on Daniel Paul Schreber. (Pirna,) 21/11/1894. Transcript in "Personalakte" on Daniel Paul Schreber of the Saxony "Justizministerium". State Archives Dresden.

Weber. "Ärztliches Gutachten" on Daniel Paul Schreber. (Pirna,) 7/11/1895. In "Personalakte" on Daniel Paul Schreber of the Saxony "Justiz-Ministerium". State Archives Dresden.

Weber. "Anstaltsbezirkärztliches Gutachten." (Pirna,) 28/11/1900. In *Denkwürdigkeiten eines Nervenkranken* by Daniel Paul Schreber. Leipzig: Oswald Mutze, 1903.

Weber. "Die Heil-und Pflegeanstalt Sonnenstein bei Pirna." In *Deutsche Heil-und Pflegeanstalten für Psychischkranke,* herausgegeben von J. Bresler, Vol. 1. Halle: Carl Marhold Verlagsbuchhandlung, 1910.

Weber, Ernestus Henricus. *Annotationes anatomicae et physiologicae.* Prol. XX. Lipsiae, 1833.

Weber, Samuel M. "Die Parabel." In *Denkwürdigkeiten eines Nervenkranken* by Daniel Paul Schreber. Frankfurt am Main, Berlin, Wien: Ullstein, 1973b.

Wehlitz, H. "Schreber über körperliche Erziehung: Ein Auszug." *Deutsche Turn-Zeitung* (1927): 812.

Weinmeister, R. "Schreber, Hauschild und die Schrebervereins-Bewegung: Zum 75-jährigen Bestehen des Kleingärtnervereins Dr. Schreber in Leipzig." *Leipziger Beobachter,* 20/5/1939, p. 93–95.

Werner, Carl Edmund. Letter to the Saxony ministry of justice. Dresden, 26/11/1894. In "Personalakte" on Daniel Paul Schreber of the Saxony "Justiz-Ministerium". State Archives Dresden.

White, Robert B. "The Mother-Conflict in Schreber's Psychosis." *International Journal of Psycho-Analysis* 42 (1961); 55–73.

White, Robert B. "The Schreber Case Reconsidered in the Light of Psychosocial Concepts." *International Journal of Psycho-Analysis* 44 (1963): 213–221.

Wiener Neueste Nachrichten, 12/7/1943, p. 3. "Vom Schrebern zum Schrebergarten."

Wilden, Anthony. *System and Structure: Essays in Communication and Exchange.* London: Tavistock Publications, 1972.

Windscheid. Review of *Denkwürdigkeiten eines Nervenkranken* by Daniel Paul Schreber. *Monatsschrift für Psychiatrie und Neurologie* 15 (1904): 399.

Wulff, L. *Was können Schreber's Zimmergymnastik-Übungen, auch teils abgeändert, für Alte, Schwache und Kranke leisten?* Parchim: Kommissionsverlag H. Wehdemann's Buchhandlung, 1929.

Zielen, V. "The Case of Schreber: The Psychoanalytic Profile of a Paranoid Personality." *Analytische Psychologie.* Vol. 13, #1, 1982. pp. 68–69.

Zitz-Halein, Kathinka. *Dictionaire des gallicismes oder Taschenwörterbuch aller Ausdrücke der französischen Sprache, welche sich nicht wörtlich übersetzen lassen.* Revised by Christian Ferdinand Fliessbach. Leipzig: Ch. E. Kollmann, 1841.

Index